DATE DUE

STATES' GAINS, LABOR'S LOSSES

STATES' GAINS, LABOR'S LOSSES

China, France, and Mexico Choose
Global Liaisons, 1980–2000

Dorothy J. Solinger

CORNELL UNIVERSITY PRESS   ITHACA AND LONDON

First published 2009 by Cornell University Press
Printed in the United States of America

Library of Congress Cataloging-in-Publication Data
Solinger, Dorothy J.
  States' gains, labor's losses : China, France, and Mexico choose
global liaisons, 1980–2000 / Dorothy J. Solinger.
     p. cm.
  Includes bibliographical references and index.
  ISBN 978-0-8014-4777-8 (cloth : alk. paper)
  1. Labor policy—China. 2. Labor policy—France. 3. Labor policy—
Mexico. 4. China—Foreign economic relations. 5. France—Foreign
economic relations. 6. Mexico—Foreign economic relations. 7. Industrial
relations—China. 8. Industrial relations—France. 9. Industrial relations—
Mexico. I. Title.
  HD8736.5.S65   2009
  331.12'042—dc22   2009013041

Cornell University Press strives to use environmentally responsible suppliers and materials to the fullest extent possible in the publishing of its books. Such materials include vegetable-based, low-VOC inks and acid-free papers that are recycled, totally chlorine-free, or partly composed of nonwood fibers. For further information, visit our website at www.cornellpress.cornell.edu.

Cloth printing   10 9 8 7 6 5 4 3 2 1

I dedicate this book to the tens of millions of laid-off workers of China, sacrificed (certainly in part) on the altar of China's modernization and opening up. The exact causal links that led to their job losses are elusive; I celebrate their labor and their contributions nonetheless.

Contents

Figures and Tables

Preface

Three weighty entitles have engaged each other on the global stage in the nearly three decades since 1980: workers, states, and economically oriented supranational organizations (my name for international bodies comprised of several or a larger number of members, such as the North American Free Trade Association, the World Trade Organization, and the European Union). Many observers have concluded, for any number of reasons, that the supranationals should be the winners, hands down, with their larger presence, their economic clout, and their hegemonic hold on the rules of the game.

Although this book shies away from pronouncing any final judgment, it delves into the nature of the interrelationships among the three contenders, as they clashed over their respective roles in three unlikely cases. In each of the countries assessed here—China, France, and Mexico—the years under review saw foundational shifts in the place granted, the deference accorded, and the power wielded by each of the members of this set of players. My job was to unravel the threads of these changes.

The three states are an unlikely assemblage for an analyst to tackle in tandem: they sit in different world regions, have dissimilar economies, and had arrived, as of 1980, at quite unlike levels of development. Politically, each at that time represented a disparate form of regime, with varying numbers of political parties and conflicting approaches to the treatment of citizen groups outside the government. But I was intrigued by the broad similarities in the styles of linkage between workers and top state leaderships, and between states and the world economy in the prior thirty years. I also uncovered a relative sameness in the weakness of unions, paradoxically paired in each country with official concern for labor, in rather more than rhetoric, in accord with what were in all of them proud revolutionary traditions. Without spoiling the story, I can only say that the outcome is surprising as of late 2008, first of all in terms of the states' stances toward the supranationals and second in relation to the divergent fortunes of disgruntled workers in the three states.

I have four institutions to thank for the genesis and the realization of this book. First is the Smith Richardson Foundation, whose very generous grant enabled me to spend a year and a half reading widely in the early period of my work. Next comes the Center for the Study of Democracy at the University of California, Irvine, which, under the innovative leadership of Russell Dalton, provided a number of grants that allowed me to spend summers interviewing laid-off once-laborers in China. These conversations with the discarded gave me a serious appreciation of the wages of worklessness. Grants from the center also funded work by various graduate students (whom I name below) who collected data for me in France and Mexico, helped me organize and present my statistical data, and found some of the statistical information I needed to undergird my points.

The third institution, the Weatherhead East Asian Institute at Columbia University, is one whose name I cannot type now without feelings of fondness and gratitude—for the many, many years during which its administrators provided me a title, an office, access to the Columbia library, copying privileges, and the height of good scholarly comradeship, encouragement, and stimulation. Finally, as I sit at a desk in another East Asian Institute, this one at the National University of Singapore, putting the final touches on the manuscript, I thank Dali Yang for inviting me to come here as a visiting research professor for four months, during which time I have been able to carve out the undisturbed days to draw these pages to their end.

I acknowledge the journal *Eurasian Geography and Economics* for supplying me with permission to reprint in chapter 5 material from my article "Labor Discontent in China in Comparative Perspective," which appeared in *EGE* 48, 4 (2007), 413–38.

Thanking individuals is one of the chief pleasures of the final moments of writing a book. The students I alluded to above include Celine Jacquemin and Sharon Lean, who gathered data for me in France and Mexico, respectively; Willy Jou, who located the statistics I needed on worker disturbances; and Ting Jiang, who not only was always available to order my numerical data some years ago and to prepare my tables and figures several times over but also saved the book from total oblivion in 2003, when she presented me with all my notes and files on disk after a house fire burned up my computer, my laptop, and every piece of paper and diskette I had accumulated over six years of research.

I also acknowledge my debt to the following friends and colleagues who read one or more chapters and gave me insightful suggestions and reassurance: Salvatore

Babones, Tom Bernstein (as my husband, how could he not?), David Cameron, Ruth Collier, Alex George, Miriam Golden, Evelyne Huber, Robert Kaufman, Mark Kesselman, Helen Milner, Vicky Murillo, Liz Perry, Alberta Sbragia, and Vivien Schmidt. Another kind of thank-you goes to friends who spent time thoughtfully talking with me about elements of my argument. Aside from some of those already noted, they are Mark Frazier, Ken Pomeranz, Kellee Tsai, and Susan Woodward. I went to these people in recognition of their expertise, and yet if some errors remain, it is no fault of theirs. This project has been long in the doing, so I hope I have not forgotten the name of anyone who helped along the way.

The two anonymous readers were superb! I cannot thank them enough for pointing out to me all the infelicities of analysis in my early draft. I am aware that I have not exactly created the final product they may have had in mind, but this book could never have taken the shape it did without their invaluable criticism. I want to note here too, Kim Vivier's meticulous copyediting and Ange Romeo-Hall's masterly oversight of the entire process of producing the volume. I also wish to acknowledge Estela Mendez and S. James Press, who created some of the tables and figures.

I am very grateful, too, for the opportunity I had to present portions of the study at the following institutions, either on their campuses or at conferences they sponsored: the Centre d'Etudes et de Recherches Internationales, the British Association for Chinese Studies, the Hong Kong Polytechnic University, the Woodrow Wilson International Center for Scholars, the College of Social Sciences of the National Taiwan University, the Hoover Institution, the Center for Chinese Studies of the University of Michigan, the Patterson Center of the University of Kentucky, the Universities Services Centre at the Chinese University of Hong Kong, the Maureen and Mike Mansfield Center of the University of Montana, Beijing University, Furman University, the Institute for National Policy Research of the Executive Yuan of the Republic of China, Monash University, Murdoch University, the Copenhagen Business School, Nanjing University, the Asian Studies Centre of St. Antony's College at Oxford University, the Fondazione Giangiacomo Feltrinelli, St. Lawrence University, the Urban China Research Centre at Cardiff University, the East Asian Institute at Columbia University, the University of Washington's Chinese Studies Program, the École des Hautes Études en Sciences Sociales, the Center for Chinese Studies at the University of California–Berkeley, the University of British Columbia, the Center for Chinese Studies at Stanford University, the Asian Studies Center and the Global Studies Center at the University of Pittsburgh, Rutgers University, and the Columbia University Seminar on Globalization, Labor, and Popular Struggles. Feedback at all these venues, I am certain, made its way into the book before you now.

Two people must be acknowledged above all. The first is Roger Haydon, who waxed enthusiastic when we initially discussed my ideas in August 2005 and then kept me going for the next three years with his unfailingly sharp editorial eye and his constant support, advice, and advocacy behind the scenes. It is surely because of his sponsorship and drive for perfection that Cornell University Press has such distinction in the fields of political science and international political economy; that excellence is the reason I have aspired to publish a book with this press for many years.

The other person is Thomas P. Bernstein, who had to endure my ten years of immersion in this project—involving lots of time, a fair share of frustrations, and a large number of conversations, not to mention travel to places he did not always want to visit. Thanks much, Tom, for being my intellectual and personal best colleague and friend.

D. J. S.

Singapore

Abbreviations

AJCA	*Australian Journal of Chinese Affairs*
AS	*Asian Survey*
CF	*China Focus*
CH	*Current History*
CJ	*China Journal*
CLB	*China Labour Bulletin*
CND	*China News Digest*
CP	*Comparative Politics*
CQ	*China Quarterly*
CRF	*China Rights Forum*
FBIS	Foreign Broadcast Information Service
FEER	*Far Eastern Economic Review*
IO	*International Organization*
LAT	*Los Angeles Times*
LBT	*Laodong baozhang tongxun* [Labor Security Bulletin]
LDCY	*Lingdao canyue* [Leadership Consultations]
MC	*Modern China*
MP	*Ming Pao* [Bright Paper]
NBCY	*Neibu canyue* [Internal Consultations]
NYT	*New York Times*
RMRB	*Renmin ribao* [People's Daily]
SCMP	*South China Morning Post*
SWB	Summary of World Broadcasts
WP	*World Politics*
WSJ	*Wall Street Journal*
XH	Xinhua [New China News Agency]
ZGJY	*Zhongguo jiuye* [Chinese Employment]
ZGLD	*Zhongguo laodong* [Chinese Labor]

STATES' GAINS,
LABOR'S LOSSES

INTRODUCTION

States' Struggle between Workers
and the World Economy

In the spring of 1979 the maiden elections to the European Parliament were soon to be held. During the campaign in France, Premier Jacques Chirac—along with his fellow Gaullist, Michel Debré—both of them ever allegiant to Charles de Gaulle's tenacious devotion to French national sovereignty, orchestrated an assault from the right on President Valéry Giscard d'Estaing's pro-European position.[1] The charges broke out just as the president was sealing a deal on the European Monetary System (the EMS), one of the key institutions that was to pave the way for the European Union.

On the left, François Mitterrand himself favored the European Community. But he was forced to bow to the oppositional, anti-supranationality stance of the several worker-prone parties—the Communists, the left-wing Socialists, and the Parti Socialiste Unifié—in order to forge a winning coalition on the left. Public opinion overall went with the critics. Indeed, as Giscard's domestic political adviser later claimed, "the EMS was a huge political error that cost Giscard his reelection in 1981."[2]

In the same year, Mexican president López Portillo of the Partido Revolucionario Institucional (the Party of the Institutionalized Revolution, or PRI) was urged by multinationals to join the General Agreement on Tariffs and Trade (the GATT), and went so far as to complete the requisite negotiations. But Mexico had lately located huge oil deposits and was enjoying high rates of growth, so many people

---

1. Debré was then head of the Gaullist party, Rally for the Republic.
2. Quoted in Craig Parsons, *A Certain Idea of Europe* (Ithaca: Cornell University Press, 2003), 158–60, 147.

wondered, what was the point of scrounging for ways to attract foreign funds? Widespread negative political reaction emerged at home against the proposition, and in the end Portillo declined to go on with the bid. Membership would have entailed demolishing trade barriers, and many party politicians, intellectuals, and, significantly for our purposes here, labor officials joined domestic industrialists in lining up against it. As Nora Lustig has explained the choice, "At the time GATT membership was viewed as a sign of weakness; Mexico did not need or wish to subjugate its trade policy to a multilateral body dominated by the Western industrialized countries."[3]

Meanwhile, the year 1979 also witnessed some Chinese scruples about participation in the world economy. At the beginning of the year, cautious Communist Party elites used the forum of a Party work conference to inveigh vociferously against what they viewed as an overhasty, overambitious venture into the global marketplace. Suddenly and without warning, China froze a large number of contracts it had already initialed for plant imports and suspended all ongoing trade negotiations with Japan, in favor of a new policy of "readjusting, restructuring, consolidating, and improving" the national economy. A 1981 justification for these decisions included the curious phrase that "we should not indiscriminately import everything or regard everything 'foreign' as valuable and good. Our consistent policy is to give priority to self-reliance and regard foreign aid as supplementary."[4]

Each of these episodes evinces fidelity toward long-ensconced and profound nationalistic sentiments that had surrounded varying degrees of distance from the markets abroad for decades, feelings that were running particularly strongly at that juncture. Even though France had by that point been participating for several decades in the expanding effort to forge a unified Europe, the moves of some of its leaders in that direction had at every step of the way been matched by ambivalence or indifference—sometimes even negativity—among the populace at large, as well as among other political figures.[5]

True, China was just then surfacing from a longish stage of spurning the outside world. A major shift in trade which began with the initiation of détente with the United States in 1971 took off in full force after 1978, signaling such a transformation from what had gone before that one observer contrasted it with what he called "China's almost continuous isolation from the mainstream of the world economy

3. Daniel C. Levy and Kathleen Bruhn, with Emilio Zebadua, *Mexico: The Struggle for Democratic Development* (Berkeley: University of California Press, 2001), 162, 164; and Nora Lustig, *Mexico: The Remaking of an Economy,* 2d ed. (Washington, D.C.: Brookings Institution Press, 1998), 130–31.

4. Chae-Jin Lee, *China and Japan: New Economic Diplomacy* (Stanford, Calif.: Hoover Institution Press, 1984), 49–50; Ryosei Kokubun, "The Politics of Foreign Economic Policy-Making in China: The Case of Plant Cancellations with Japan," *CQ* 105 (1986), 30.

5. This theme runs throughout Parsons, *Certain Idea.*

and S & T [science and technology] system during the last three decades" (i.e., the thirty years before 1979).[6]

But the economic imbalances introduced by China's late-1970s purchasing spree so startled many of the top men in command that the more economically conservative among them were able to carry the day in the name of the "peoples' livelihood," and to do so for several years thereafter. Ryosei Kokubun has mused that the mood of the elite was very likely to have been affected by the contemporaneous appearance of Solidarity in Poland, especially given China's then current mounting social disorder, which included demonstrations by unemployed young people and strikes by workers. As master politician, soon to be China's paramount leader, Deng Xiaoping later explained, "We dared to cancel because of inflation and because a lot of complicated social problems might occur."[7]

As of 1979, prior to finding the petroleum, Mexico had only recently thrown off a spate of economic troubles: ongoing deficits in the current account, inflation, capital flight, deficit spending, and climbing debt had all blighted the second half of the 1970s there. For the argument of this book, it is notable that the state had gotten itself into this predicament in part by excessive spending and borrowing motivated by fear of disorder from the disadvantaged. Given that the late 1960s and early 1970s had already seen much unrest, including from labor, politicians believed that instability could have ensued had the government pressed for financial discipline. But the fiscal problems became severe enough that Portillo's predecessor, Luis Echeverria, had had to submit to an austerity program imposed by the International Monetary Fund in 1976. Just four years later, however, what turned out to be just a temporary relief provided by the oil find prodded Portillo suddenly to pronounce, sanguinely, that it was appropriate to "prepare ourselves to administer abundance" and to renounce external assistance.[8]

Nothing in these three nearly simultaneous events in a set of seemingly disparate nations would have disposed an onlooker to predict the denouement that followed these disavowals of the market-beyond-the-borders. Nonetheless, within a brief few years—from 1980 to 1983—every one of these long-time state-centric, import-substituting, fiercely independent, nationalistic, and, in their own perceptions, pro-labor revolutionary states was in the midst of gearing up for membership in a supranational organization, an accession that, for each, would spell the loss of

---

6. Dorothy J. Solinger, *From Lathes to Looms: China's Industrial Policy in Comparative Perspective* (Stanford, Calif.: Stanford University Press, 1991), 47; the quotation is from Denis Fred Simon, "The Evolving Role of Foreign Investment and Technology Transfer in China's Modernization Program," in *China Briefing 1987*, ed. John S. Major (Boulder, Colo.: Westview Press, 1987), 43.

7. Kokubun, "Politics," 29–30, 38.

8. Levy and Bruhn, *Mexico,* 161–64.

jobs for millions. Had the leaders forgotten about the laborers that their nations had once protected? And how did labor in each case respond to this switch?

Most significantly for our purposes, what did the common revolutionary backgrounds in all of their pasts mean at that moment for the struggle these states were about to join between their workers, on the one hand, and the world forces that were suddenly and synchronistically reshaping their political economies, on the other? This book is about how an enduring legacy of revolution in these apparently dissimilar places structured state-labor relations in a time of crisis. In all of them, revolutionary-era outcomes left their mark on the roles and functions of unions, vis-à-vis their own states and vis-à-vis their worker charges. In turn, these disparate relationships made for differing types and levels of response at the working-class grass roots to the states' moves after 1980; repercussions from workers then set the style for subsequent state welfare replies. This, then, is a book centered on distinct models of affiliation—what I call "terms of attachment"—between unions, states, and workers, and the forms of behavior to which these terms disposed actors as all three parties faced foreign markets in three postrevolutionary states after 1980. Its message, in short, is one of a causal chain: historical legacies of labor-state bonds produced variant forms of militancy when crisis struck; that militancy then led to variable levels of welfare response from the state involved.

To go on with the larger story: in China's case, the move to integrate externally was chiefly domestically generated, gingerly begun in 1979, and finally, after 1982, gathering force with time. A central impetus was to normalize the country and modernize its economy, in the interest of countering the recently deceased chairman of the Communist Party Mao Zedong's mobilizational upheavals. This was a play to the outside world, but it was also a step taken with an eye to the Chinese people: the new leaders intended thereby to win public legitimacy. In accord with these purposes, the political elite as early as 1980 began to associate with, and in 1986 chose to apply for entry into, the GATT.

True, China's negotiating partners did not grant it accession to the GATT's successor, the World Trade Organization (WTO), until 2001. Yet starting in the early 1980s, the country's leadership steadily undertook preparatory steps to hasten its acceptability to the organization's membership. And these steps amounted, implicitly, to what one might tag a "preemptive acquiescence" to the rules of the GATT. In the wake of the growing leniency to foreign investors, the increasing autonomy for enterprise managers, the tariff reductions, and the regime-sponsored redundancies and firm failures that unfolded one after the other between the early 1980s and late 1990s, tens of millions of workers lost their jobs.[9] Many of them reacted to this

---

9. The exact number of jobs destroyed will never be known. Dorothy J. Solinger, "Why We Cannot Count the Unemployed," *CQ*, 167 (2001), 671–88.

assault by openly and frequently protesting on the streets, egging the regime on to design national-scale welfare programs where none had obtained before. Though the old communist, state-labor alliance at first appeared to be wholly abandoned, public militancy reawakened the bond, if in starkly altered form.

In France an ominous currency crisis broke out in 1982 and threw into disarray then-Socialist Party president François Mitterrand's original plan to pump up the economy and, especially, to enhance benefits for the working class. The problem was that this course collided with contractionary measures then being carried out in the economies of France's European Community trading partners. Within a year and a half, Mitterrand had acted to remain within the confines of the EMS, a regimen that eight of the nine then-members of the Community had forged in 1979, with the aim of aligning the monetary regimes of these countries. The effort installed an Exchange Rate Mechanism that fixed the exchange rates of the participants within a relatively narrow band; to achieve this, the signatories made tight money and minimal inflation mandatory. As an outcome of Mitterrand's decision, France was forced to jettison its accustomed discretionary devaluations and disinflations which had previously recharged the economy, and which had thereby served as a boon to labor, ensuring steady high employment.

The French decision to sign the 1992 Maastricht Treaty, which created the European Union (the EU) a decade later, with its rules about keeping debts and deficits low, served to exacerbate the austerity program (termed "rigeur" in France) that President Mitterrand had installed in 1983 when he first coordinated French monetary policy with that of the EMS. Together these steps resulted in numerous firm bankruptcies and job losses: by 1997, the total losses over the years since 1970 had amounted to a stunning 41.6 percent of the original labor force.[10] Throughout the period, workers' rebuttal was relatively lame; in turn, the state did little.

And in Mexico an abrupt debt crisis erupted when oil prices plummeted at the same time as lending nations elevated their interest rates after 1980, leading the country to appeal again for outside assistance that once more came bound up in strings. Nevertheless, it was the officials in charge of the country, not outsiders, who set Mexico on a free-trade course as they deregulated, privatized, slashed trade barriers, and pledged themselves to follow the rules of the GATT in and after 1985. As in China, subsequent preparatory measures enabled the country later to seem suitable for entry into the North American Free Trade Association (NAFTA) by 1990, the year that talks toward the establishment of that body got under way.

---

10. Fritz W. Scharpf, "Economic Changes, Vulnerabilities, and Institutional Capabilities," in *Welfare and Work in the Open Economy: From Vulnerability to Competitiveness*, vol. 1, ed. Fritz W. Scharpf and Vivien A. Schmidt (Oxford: Oxford University Press, 2000), 108.

In the course of the structural adjustments Mexican politicians implemented, some millions of workers were severed from their posts, though the exact figures are difficult to gather. It is known, however, that by the end of 1994 the combined total of the unemployed plus those at work in the underground economy meant that at least 28 percent of the workforce was without steady employment;[11] additionally, the numbers of jobs in manufacturing declined continuously for 70 months between 1990 and 1996.[12] Another one to two million positions disappeared in the period between 1990 and 2000, over half of them in agriculture,[13] in a labor force of some 35 million. But workers were much more quiet than they had been in the past, and gained almost nothing in compensation.

This book examines this set of phenomena, which was prevalent across the planet in recent decades: once state-strong, inward-oriented, labor-respecting nations reversed course around 1980 in the face of forces their leaders felt were overpowering and inescapable, given the leaders' own instincts for the survival, the global inclusion, and the glory of their countries. Clearly, a contest was on, with such states caught between two powerful pressures vying for supremacy, what scholars would see as two "independent variables," each pulling as an opposing vector: the economic imperatives of the new world order, born of foreign exchange and petroleum crises, on the one side, and—especially in these postrevolutionary nations—timeworn state-labor partnerships, on the other, whose terms of attachment were nationally variable but in each case formerly crucial.

The book reviews this battle through an analysis of the actions of what could be viewed as these two competing independent variables. After presenting some roughly analogous background (along with some telling contrasts) to set the scene for the rest of the story, I go on to trace the effects of these variables. Following a chapter that sets out broad-brush political-sociological historical similarities among state-labor dyads in the three, I focus in the first section on the first of these variables, the forces of the global economy and their specific impact on

11. Lorenzo Meyer, "Mexico: Economic Liberalism in an Authoritarian Polity," in *Market Economics and Political Change: Comparing China and Mexico*, ed. Juan D. Lindau and Timothy Cheek (Lanham, Md.: Rowman & Littlefield, 1998), 144.

12. Jonathan Heath, "Original Goals and Current Outcomes of Economic Reform in Mexico," in *Mexico's Private Sector: Recent History, Future Challenges*, ed. Riordan Roett (Boulder, Colo.: Lynne Rienner, 1998), 54.

13. Orlandina de Oliveira and Brigida Garcia, "Socioeconomic Transformation and Labor Markets in Urban Mexico," in *Global Restructuring, Employment, and Social Inequality in Urban Latin America*, ed. Richard Tardanico and Rafael Menjivar Larin (Coral Gables, Fla.: North-South Center Press, 1997), 212. Roderic Ai Camp, *Politics in Mexico*, 2d ed. (New York: Oxford University Press, 1996), 219, estimates that one million jobs might have been lost at that time. John Audley, Sandra Polaski, Demetrios G. Papademetriou, and Scott Vaughan, *NAFTA's Promise and Reality: Lessons from Mexico for the Hemisphere* (Washington, D.C.: Carnegie Endowment for International Peace, 2004), 18.

the three particular places. I consider the consequences of these forces, both at the outset of the 1980s and again later, as promoted by what I take as their proxy, supranational economic organizations (SEOs), as these states complied with the rules of the organizations.

I proceed in the second part of the book to gauge the relative intensity of the blowback in each place, as workers in each country weighed the thrust of global forces (and their states' submission to them), as these forces affected themselves, and as states, in turn, reacted. For that second segment of the drama, the other independent variable is labor, and the respective role and effectiveness of its unions, as filtered by the state-assigned mission of unions, in each country. The book is about the nature of the interplay among these two competitors—global forces and workers—in their tug on the state over the tack to be taken by politicians. I seek to uncover differences among the three states in this struggle and to pin down the explanatory factor that accounts for the divergence. The answer, in this telling, is the variable terms dictating the nature of the ties between unions and their states and between unions and their workers.

Why These Three States?

At first glance the saga of these three states, straining under the double challenge of coping with the international debt, exchange, and oil crises of those times (at the *global* level) and of adapting their old promises to what had become a beleaguered labor force *at home* appear to be simply instances of a trajectory that many, if not most, states traversed after 1980. I have three justifications for choosing these three particular countries for this comparative exercise.

In the first place, two of them, China and Mexico, could be counted not just as longtime stubborn holdouts against the lure of the world economy in 1979, but also, soon afterward, as pacesetters. China was the first so-called socialist state in the particular "wave" of liberalization in which many such states began in 1980 to turn outward, leading, little by little, in its own case toward a total decimation of its command economy and onward to capitalism. Others followed, of course, but in most cases not for a decade.[14] As for Mexico, it was also a leader: in the words of Maria Victoria Murillo, "In the 1990s, Mexico triggered the debt crisis that spread

---

14. Mitchell A. Orenstein and Lisa E. Hale, "Corporatist Renaissance in Post-communist Central Europe," in *The Politics of Labor in a Global Age: Continuity and Change in Late-industrializing and Post-socialist Economies*, ed. Christopher Candland and Rudra Sil (Oxford: Oxford University Press, 2001), 258–82. For an earlier phase in which similar, but failed, efforts were undertaken, see Susan L. Woodward, *Socialist Unemployment: The Political Economy of Yugoslavia, 1945–1990* (Princeton, N.J.: Princeton University Press, 1995).

throughout Latin America, creating the conditions that provoked the political conversion of populism into neoliberalism."[15]

France was by no means a pacesetter in states of its sort, but it had distinction in a different way. Mitterrand's election as president at the head of the Socialist Party in 1981 delayed a process of acquiescence with the country's European confreres that would have matched that of the rest of the Community, had Giscard's 1981 election gone otherwise. So in each of these nations there unfolded a story that was special within that state's own particular category of countries. For this reason alone, they merit a joint and exacting examination.

Second, superficially speaking, each of these states experienced—or, perhaps better put, their leaders eventually chose to experience—the same train of events around the same time. That is, in or soon after 1980 the political elite in each aspired to solve the same generic problem, capital shortage, through joining the world. This was for all of them in one way or another a problem brought on by currents coursing across the globe. But significantly, these were currents whose jolts clashed with these states' particular and shared modi operandi. Each had long sustained a style of rule that had catered to at least an elite among labor, often in rhetoric but also in fact. Each decided (as did many other nations) to withstand the new global tides by preparing to enter supranational organizations. In each case, given the rules of the organizations to which they acceded (the European Union, the World Trade Organization, and the North American Free Trade Association, respectively), an offshoot of that move was to push workers from their posts.

And yet the sameness of this selected path, and of its critical effect for labor, went only so far, I contend. Because of the variant missions and vocations of the trade unions in each place (the "terms of attachment" of the unions to the polity and to their workers)—which, I show, fundamentally distinguished the behaviors of workers in one country from those in the others—the activism of the working class, and, as a result, I argue, the response of the state to workers, was markedly diverse in the three of them. I situate the origin of these differences in disparate revolutionary traditions in these three postrevolutionary states.

As for outcomes, where fragmented and competitive unions achieved little in representing French workers, unions allegiant to the state kept workers quiet in corporatist Mexico, and unions charged chiefly with sustaining productivity left angry workers largely to their own devices in China. Concretely, to give just one set of statistics, the number of strikes and lockouts in France over the years 1980 to 2001 peaked in 1982, the year before Mitterrand's U-turn toward the European Community's regimen, thereafter dropping to nearly half of that in many of the

---

15. Maria Victoria Murillo, *Labor Unions, Partisan Coalitions, and Market Reforms in Latin America* (Cambridge: Cambridge University Press, 2001), 92–93.

following years until 1999. In Mexico the contrasts between pre-1982 and there-after are sharper yet. Where in the first three years of the 1980s more than 1,000 strikes and lockouts broke out annually, reaching as many as 1,925 in 1982, imme-diately thereafter—just when the force of the debt crisis was felt the most—the numbers abruptly plummeted to around a mere 100 per year; by 1995 the counts had descended into the single digits. For China there are no overall numbers. But one scholar has noted as many as 9,559 incidents in just one province (the one hardest hit) between January 2000 and September 2002, an average of ten per day over nearly three years.[16] This equaled roughly two and half times the number of outbreaks in the city of Paris at about the same time.

In terms of welfare, chapter 6 points out that between 1990 and 2001 the French government's social expenditures rose from 26.61 percent to 28.45 percent of gross domestic product (GDP), an increase of just 1.84 percent, while Mexico's climbed from 3.84 to only 5.10 percent, an increase of 1.26 percent. In China, however, the central government hiked up its expenditures in this category as a percentage of GDP from under 2 percent in 1980 to about 8.3 percent in 2005, more than quadrupling its outlay, proportional to GDP. Certainly other factors can be called on to help make some sense of these discrepancies, such as the variable baselines in the respective sizes of the workforces or the disparate welfare starting points in each state, and I allude to these in the relevant chapters.[17] But the big sociopoliti-cal explanation I offer for the wide range in these reactions constitutes the chief empirical finding of this book. Studying three places whose leaders' past commit-ments to workers and whose later choices globally were similar but whose workers behaved rather differently, allows me to draw a conclusion about labor politics that would not have appeared so starkly otherwise. This is my second justification for considering these three places.

And third, these three countries would normally not be analyzed together. We have here a democracy with its multiparty system; a regime that was authoritarian with an overarching, dominant party during the time when the pivotal events unfolded, a regime that later became "semi-authoritarian" and finally democ-ratizing; and a post-totalitarian government yet ruled by a communist party.[18] Economically, a capitalist, a mixed, and a socialist economy obtained in them, respectively. Thus the enterprise of talking about them in tandem is ipso facto

---

16. Murray Scot Tanner, "China Rethinks Unrest," *Washington Quarterly* 27, 3 (2004), 140.

17. Thanks to one of my anonymous readers for this point.

18. Roderic Ai Camp, in *Politics in Mexico: The Democratic Transformation,* 4th ed. (New York: Oxford University Press, 2003), 10, refers to it as "semiauthoritarian" up to the year 2000. Totalitarian regimes are ones in which the regime attempts to control all activity, repress all antistate or otherwise autonomous behavior, and to indoctrinate the population with the values of the state. The term "post-totalitarian" refers to states that were once totalitarian but are no longer completely domineering and dominant.

novel. I hold that examining them together yields a set of surprising findings that disorient a number of prior understandings.

Putting it differently, I inquire, then: why did countries that elected to act similarly globally turn out to vary so strikingly internally, at the domestic level, when it came to resultant interactions between unions and the state? That the book focuses on three very dissimilar states serves to demonstrate the wide sweep of countries that, rather comparably, were compelled to confront the global economy in new ways at a critical historical moment. By picking pioneers and an outlier, it also deals with unlikely cases.

Thus, the book sets out to explain this concurrent asymmetry at different levels of analysis after 1980 in France, China, and Mexico, drawing on features of the domestic political economies of three countries that, counterintuitively—given all their apparent variation—had much in common at the outset but then diverged so much in the end. The first half of the book sets up the similarities, inspecting these states and exploring their predicaments and their leaders' choices in the late-twentieth-century world economy; the second half tackles the tale of these same states at home, as they encountered their own angry workers. In short, the work takes countries that began, as of 1979, by sharing traits, experiences, and inclinations, and then pits comparison of relative behavioral sameness (an unexpected sameness) at one level, the global one, against contrast at another level, the domestic one.

Previous Approaches

During the closing decades of the twentieth century, as global waves in their multiple guises washed across the map and states reacted to the meanderings of the currents, internal politics and their players in many states were altered, sometimes in abrupt and serious ways. The most obvious difference between this study and others about this phenomenon is that most other observers have addressed this large issue by considering countries that have much in common, rendering the findings relatively narrow and the variables the analyses settle on sometimes possibly spurious. Here it is not the type of regime, the kind of party system, the party in power, the nature of the labor movement, or the "depth of the economic crisis" faced—all factors that previous authors have relied on to drive their dependent variables—that accounts for the situations in the places under review.[19]

---

19. Juan J. Linz, "Totalitarian and Authoritarian Regimes," in *Handbook of Political Science, Volume 3: Macropolitical Theory,* ed. Fred I. Greenstein and Nelson W. Polsby (Reading, Mass.: Addison-Wesley, 1975), 175–411, and Juan J. Linz and Alfred Stepan, *Problems of Democratic Transition and Consolidation: Southern Europe, South America and Post-Communist Europe* (Baltimore: Johns Hopkins Uni-

These variables cannot explain the widespread commonality of the steps leaders in these countries (and in many others) took in inserting their so dissimilar nations more thoroughly into the world market, for the three states under review here differed in all these regards. Nor can they clarify why leaders in these three countries went on to differ in their replies to the variable militancy among their respective labor forces that followed that insertion—why it was, for instance, that, among the three, both the outcry and the compensatory outlay were the most pronounced in communist China.

In any event, earlier accounts ignore what I find to be key: the assigned mission and role of the labor unions in each state, which I connect with revolutionary histories. In two of the cases (China and Mexico) the functions of unions diverged somewhat from the jobs that unions are generally presumed to carry out, that is, representing and fighting for the workforce. Besides, the types of variables usually used to analyze labor politics—such as union density and union concentration—provide no guidance. Welfare rejoinders in these countries were also counterintuitive, as the nation among them usually thought to be least accountable, China, was also the one most responsive to its losers.

Not only were typically cited structural variables about states and unions not helpful in explaining the events under review; the quality of the economic crises that pushed the leaders in these countries onto new avenues varied substantially, even as their policy choices were essentially the same. Mexico's plight was the most desperate, as its economy was hanging on the brink of collapse in 1982; France's leaders' situation was dire, but by no means disastrous, as of that year. In China, to the contrary, the economy was poised to go on uninterruptedly, without change, as of 1980. But its efficiency and productivity were both judged to be unsatisfactorily low, at least in the eyes of the coterie of newly ensconced politicians who wished to validate their rule to their citizenry. And yet, despite this dissimilitude in the extent of catastrophe, the trajectory of their economic departures from the twentieth century was remarkably parallel for France, Mexico, and China. On the other hand, their respective workers' activism was not, and, in turn, neither were their states' reactions to workers.

Accepted theory relating to state policy on labor looks at the strength of labor unions and/or at the political parties to which unions are linked. But such approaches fail to make sense of the particular story here. First of all, consider the nature of what is known as the "labor regime": each of these countries could in

versity Press, 1996), 40–44. "Depth of economic crisis" is one of the variables suggested in Katrina Burgess and Steven Levitsky, "Explaining Populist Party Adaptation in Latin America: Environmental and Organizational Determinants of Party Change in Argentina, Mexico, Peru, and Venezuela," *Comparative Political Studies* 36, 8 (October 2003), 886–87 and 894–95.

some ways be categorized as the site of a "weak labor economy."[20] For labor was indeed "weak" in them all, in that in none of them was there a coherent or cogent labor movement operating expressly and autonomously to serve workers' interests and needs. Nor, as a result, could labor pose and be treated as an equal interlocutor in relation to the political regime in any of them. But categorization of these regimes as "weak labor economies" falls down in other ways: it was not the case in these countries that "powerful rightist political parties" "confronted much weaker labor movements" in these places as of 1980, which those who coined this label would expect. Nor were they arenas where, consequently, labor was often left to the mercy of unmitigated market forces, as the use of this term also suggests. Moreover, the polity in each one in some sense truly pursued labor's interests. So a study of these countries must put this oft-used label aside.

A second, similar feature of these polities counters another approach, one that explains variation of state policy toward labor in terms of party-union ties. Each of these states was under the governance of a *left*-leaning party (in China and France, indeed, parties that were named "communist" and "socialist," respectively; in Mexico, one called "revolutionary"), not a powerful rightist one, which that approach would have assumed, at the point when the anti-labor shift occurred. According to this theory, labor-based, socialist-styled parties are supposed to be partial to the working class, not to call for its displacement. So an argument that leftist parties will be kind to the working class and its unions also must fall by the wayside.

As noted above, when workers were dismissed and became disruptive, the three governments reacted with different forms and amounts of recompense, at least for some portion of the disaffected. The contrasts among them, however, are not explicated by the categories used in previous efforts to differentiate how states treat losers in the global economy. For the usual debate addresses only whether concerns over "compensation," or, alternatively, a drive for maximal "efficiency," determines the behavior that outwardly oriented nations adopt toward victims when the state intensifies the level of its foreign commerce. That hypothesis, too, figures that the choice is a function of the color of the party in power.

But I found that unions' appointed charge (in some ways a product of the revolutions out of which they each grew)—and their workers' corresponding conduct in each nation during the 1980s and 1990s—explains the greater restiveness displayed by the angered working people of the People's Republic, and also helps to make sense of the more thoroughgoing financial and social security responses adopted by that authoritarian polity, as compared with the states in France and

---

20. Geoffrey Garrett and Peter Lange, "Political Responses to Interdependence: What's 'Left' for the Left?" *IO* 45, 4 (1991), 547.

Mexico. The leanings of the parties in power as of 1983 were the same in all three countries—they were all leftist—but the outcomes varied.

From a different angle, researchers have inquired in general terms as to the degree to which international, as opposed to domestic, elements shape states' economic policies. Peter Gourevitch's seminal article in this field posed the question of the influence of international events and forces on domestic policymaking.[21] Since that article was published, other studies have grappled with the variety of ways in which outside factors might impinge on domestic politics and the channels through which this might occur. But the focus in many of these studies is on politics in—and only in—the advanced capitalist democracies; or, where the study includes a few nondemocratic countries, it makes the assumption that the politics of those other places will be governed by just the same rules as they are in states that are democratic.[22] Scholars tend to point, accordingly, to mechanisms that operate only in developed democracies—as, for instance, by normalizing the style of connections between interest groups and ruling elites in democratic regimes and then extrapolating their findings to regimes of quite different types.

One study, for instance, explained international economic policy transformations by hypothesizing that domestic groups affected by changes in relative prices will pressure their own governments to respond to such changes, with consequent policy repercussions.[23] That study credited the "policy preferences of actors with producing changes in domestic coalitions, policies and institutions." And yet, for instance, there is no evidence that in China (one of the cases in that study) the policy changes of 1980 had anything to do with the preferences of affected groupings, as opposed to being purely the product of leaders' choices.[24]

Thus, the focus on the advanced democracies inclines scholars to assume universality in the ability of well-placed social forces in democracies to influence their governments on their own behalf. But workers are not necessarily well placed; besides, we have here three cases in which all the states in the face of global change at least initially *ignored* the wishes of the workers, and in which powerful political executives took decisions without much if any social input at all. Indeed, what I am investigating is precisely how once favored social forces in fact *did* lose jobs or

---

21. Peter Gourevitch, "The Second Image Reversed: The International Sources of Domestic Politics," *IO* 32, 4 (1978), 881–911.

22. A major exception is Candland and Sil, *Politics of Labor,* though here states of a different sort are clumped together for analysis: late-industrializing and post-socialist ones.

23. Helen V. Milner and Robert O. Keohane, "Internationalization and Domestic Politics: A Conclusion," in *Internationalization and Domestic Politics,* ed. Keohane and Milner (Cambridge: Cambridge University Press, 1996), 243–258.

24. This claim appears in the introduction to ibid., 6. But in *From Lathes to Looms* I detail the impotence at the time of the country's turn outward of the industrial sectors that had been dominant until then.

benefits or both, not how such societal segments were able to stymie attempts to undercut their positions. For that is not the story in my cases.

Another version of this sort of study credits the electoral power of interest groups that had been the beneficiaries of the relevant programs. That angle may work to some extent to elucidate the situation for France as a democracy, and it goes part of the way toward explaining what happened in late-1980s Mexico. In addition to the problem that only one of my three nations had meaningful elections in the 1980s, looking to past recipients and their previous power cannot place the three countries within one explanatory framework, which is my objective here, as I look for answers that cross regime type. Neither is such a logic useful when only one party holds a hegemonic position, such that elections become largely empty exercises, as in both China and Mexico in the 1980s and still in China today. Nor does it work when the parties capable of capturing elections are largely in agreement about the thrust of policy, as in France after 1983. Neither is the argument valid when losers—at least at the moment of decision—have negligible if any channels of access to the deciders.

Other theories assert that alterations in state strategy are a function of changing power relations among domestic political forces, such as those within a governing party, those between that party and its coalition partners, or those between opposing parties.[25] But here, too, is a finding that would apply only to countries where competition between political parties is the stuff of politics. This would not have been the case where one party was perpetually dominant (as in Mexico between 1929 and, effectively, the end of the 1990s) or where the ruling party is the sole party on the scene, as in China right up to the present. One more claim attributes the way international forces are domestically processed to the workings of domestic institutions, as these institutions (allegedly) reflect citizens' preferences and as they structure the access to policymaking open to particular groups.[26] Again, such a formulation is suited just to democratic systems, for governmental institutions do not reflect citizens' preferences, nor do they provide formal entrée to the top, in all forms of state.

One more line of inquiry, referenced briefly above, studies specifically the impact of global economic forces on governmental welfare spending. It asks whether these effects are benign or deleterious for affected domestic groups. The chief question is whether governments are forced by competition in world markets to cut social

25. W. Rand Smith, *The Left's Dirty Job: The Politics of Industrial Restructuring in France and Spain* (Pittsburgh: University of Pittsburgh Press, 1998).

26. Peter J. Katzenstein, "Conclusion: Domestic Structures and Strategies of Foreign Economic Policy," in *Between Power and Plenty: Foreign Economic Policies of Advanced Industrial States,* ed. Katzenstein (Madison: University of Wisconsin Press, 1978), 295–336, and *Small States in World Markets: Industrial Policy in Europe* (Ithaca: Cornell University Press, 1985); Milner and Keohane, "Internationalization," 4.

spending at home in an effort to enhance efficiency or whether, instead, such competition compels state leaders to compensate domestic parties and groups that suffer from the inequalities and insecurities engendered by international trade, in the hope of forestalling unrest.[27] The initial study casting the issues in these terms judges that left-wing parties, especially if supported by strong labor movements, are apt to champion social welfare spending in times of externally induced adversity while parties on the right are not.[28] But its authors themselves admit that their research was unable to account for the fact that some governments, including Mitterrand's in France, "initially pursue partisan policies but subsequently turn dramatically away from them."[29]

The fact that what happened in France in the 1980s—and in Mexico and China after 1980, as well—cannot be addressed by the data in that work suggests that considering just the partisan color of the party in power (which one can do meaningfully only in democracies in any case, and not always even in them), and looking merely at domestic factors (whether they be domestic groups reacting to internationally driven changes, domestic governing coalitions and political parties, or domestic political institutions) is insufficient for seeking more general causal explanations for the heavy imprint of global economic power in recent decades on internal labor and welfare politics. Part of the problem, too, is that much of this form of research is quantitative and sometimes fails to explore the larger socioeconomic contexts, the pathways, or the political mechanisms involved when globalization promotes a heightened or a lessened welfare effort. I home in on just these circumstances and pathways for the three countries I investigate.

A major difficulty in all these analytical approaches is that none of them can systematically address situations in which—in the absence of any specific domestic pressures (whether because there are no channels for the transmission of the pressures or because the channels are temporarily discounted)—governments, in reaction to what their leaders see as sudden and threatening global provocations, switch their basic policy stance in ways that injure workers. The bias toward studying only democracies, with their special burden of explicit and overt accountability,

---

27. Geoffrey Garrett, "Globalization and Government Spending around the World," *Studies in Comparative International Development* 35, 4 (2001), 3–29, and "Global Markets and National Politics: Collision Course or Virtuous Circle?" *IO* 52 (1998): 787–824.

28. The initial study was Garrett and Lange, "Political Responses." Other prominent ones making similar arguments are John D. Stephens, Evelyne Huber, and Leonard Ray, "The Welfare State in Hard Times," in *Continuity and Change in Contemporary Capitalism*, ed. Herbert Kitschelt, Peter Lange, Gary Marks, and John D. Stephens (New York: Cambridge University Press, 1998), 164–93, and Evelyne Huber and John D. Stephens, *Development and Crisis of the Welfare State: Parties and Policies in Global Markets* (Chicago: University of Chicago Press, 2001). An excellent summary of approaches is in Brian Burgoon, "Globalization and Welfare Compensation: Disentangling the Ties that Bind," *IO* 55, 3 (Summer 2001), 509–551.

29. Garrett and Lange, "Political Responses," 563.

also inhibits analysts' ability to explain abrupt reversals and major alterations in states' customary coalitional stances which violate the interests of past domestic alliance partners. That bent may also miss the dynamism that develops when states are simultaneously battered by global shocks, on one side, and by their own workforces (and their former commitments to them), on the other.

That states of varying regime types behave similarly under like economic conditions—not only in respect to economic policy, but also in terms of leaders' choices about political allies and their initial disregard for losers—should direct the researcher to answers that go beyond the nature of domestic political institutions and democratic procedures. A critical point is that a review of the internal political institutions of states by no means always provides for adequate or accurate readings or predictions of state policy or behavior. That is very much the case in this book, where domestic institutions are fundamentally noncomparable, where a democratic multiparty state is to be considered alongside a single-party socialist state and a one-party-dominant authoritarian state, and where the nature of specific domestic groups' connections with, access to, and potency in regard to central power structures needs further exploration.

In short, none of these analyses are of much help in making sense of the variable downturns in the context of globalization of formerly employed people who were once endowed with satisfactory welfare benefits when those beneficiaries lack the backing of strong labor movements, where interest groups and support bases can be, and have been, abandoned at will by centralized, powerful states bent on greater productivity and competitiveness in global markets (such as France, Mexico, and China after 1980), and yet where the state has succored workers in the past and where an elite portion of the working class has long been privileged.[30] Under some conditions some of those workers can recapture some clout later on. The book seeks to search for those conditions.

Moreover, in some cases where the state concentrates enough power centrally that it is nearly autonomous from opposing viewpoints, it is the executive and not the parties or the social groups that define and can alter the status of various social elements.[31] In these cases, one can infer relative power resources only ex post facto

---

30. Robert Kaufman and Alex Segura-Ubiergo, "Globalization, Domestic Politics, and Social Spending in Latin America: A Time-Series Cross-Section Analysis, 1973–97," *World Politics* 53:553–87, suggest something related on 582.

31. Stephan Haggard and Robert R. Kaufman, "Introduction: Institutions and Economic Adjustment," in *The Politics of Economic Adjustment: International Constraints, Distributive Conflicts, and the State,* ed. Haggard and Kaufman (Princeton, N.J.: Princeton University Press, 1992), 8, emphasize the significance of "politicians' independence" in their ability to carry out adjustment. They do not note, however, that abandoned groups can still have some leverage. Jonah D. Levy, "France: Directing Adjustment?" in *Welfare and Work in the Open Economy: Diverse Responses to Common Challenges,* vol. 2, ed. Fritz W. Scharpf and Vivien A. Schmidt (Oxford: Oxford University Press, 2000), 326, points to the

by observing which groups have won or done not so badly in the end. But one cannot predict a future distribution of goods and benefits ex ante just by observing past state allocations—or even by simply ascertaining which groups seemed to be somehow in league with leaders in immediately prior periods.

Structure of the Study

The remainder of the book begins, in its first section, by pointing to *similarities* among the countries, first in terms of the political sociology of the recent past, in chapter 2. That second chapter sets out three broad similarities that the three countries to be treated here shared in generic terms in their state-labor relations over the years between the 1940s and 1980. Granted, these traits could describe a range of states. But it is rare to find so seemingly dissimilar states within this large set examined together in one study.

The *state-labor dyad*—which models the stance of labor as forged through enduring relationships—in each of them, my first major (or macro) independent variable, was characterized by three critical features. These were, first, *state protectionism* for both domestic firms and for the state-affiliated workers in them, an insulation tied to these states' import-substitution-oriented trading pattern; and second, *weakly organized labor unions* sheltered by, but also obligated to, the central government. A third feature particularly characterized these three nations, setting them apart from most others: a distant revolution waged at least in part on behalf of an underclass, plus a state constitution that enshrines the ideals of that revolution, resulting in specific state commitments and worker expectations. In line with that *revolutionary heritage*, each saw more recent rebellion that unnerved the leadership, rendering it notably risk-averse and therefore prone to accommodate workers. Significantly, however, the legacies of these revolutions were not the same, and this had implications later for the nature of the differing "state-labor dyads" (dyads that were connected by distinctive "terms of attachment") in the three. Those dyads lie at the core of the variable terms of attachment in the three states.

In chapters 3 and 4, *global forces* emerge as my second large (or macro) independent variable. These chapters use process tracing to uncover specific commonalities that were salient for these states around and just after 1980. Chapter 3 identifies like developmental patterns from the past, patterns connected to the three features in the labor-state dyad described in chapter 2. It then reviews particular commonalities among the political economies of the states that led up to the crises of the

---

"relative isolation of policymakers in France, given the fragmentation and inability to collaborate of the country's intermediary institutions.

1980s in these places. In brief, their prior Keynesian-style developmental modes culminated around 1980 in producing developmental cul-de-sacs and economic emergencies, *given the nature of the world economy at the time*. The chapter shows precisely how these states' respective domestic economic patterns caused predicaments as those patterns collided with conditions in the world economy in the late 1970s. The chapter also traces how leaders in each state ultimately handled those encounters by adopting comparable stances, especially by opting to join SEOs in the 1980s.

In chapter 4, SEOs enter the scene as a proxy for global forces, as key authorities in each of the three states steer their nation to enter one (or more) of them. Here I explain why the political elites in all three countries pursued membership in SEOs and, on obtaining it, subsequently ousted millions of workers from their jobs. I focus on the *rules of the SEOs* to underline the connections between turning outward and a concomitant loosening of an age-old commitment to labor in all three. Briefly, I argue, the rules of the supranational body each joined, and with which each country's top political elite agreed to comply (as its members assimilated the philosophy about growth and development that the rules embody), were either the immediate or at the very least the implicit spur for the shedding of labor in each of them. These rules had this effect not just because state officials strove to align their behavior with the rules once their states became members of the organizations. For Mexico and China, perhaps even more than after entry had been achieved, the rules possessed the power to coerce conformity during the period when these states were still struggling to qualify for entry.

After setting up these similarities in historical political sociology, in past developmental models that made for later susceptibility to global forces, and in the impact on the states of the SEOs they entered, I ask in the book's second section why the outcomes for both protest and welfare *differed* among the three places. I argue that the answer lay in the disparities among them in regard to the variable terms of attachment by which—or the dissimilar ways in which—unions were related both to the state and to their members in the three countries. This factor, in turn, I contend, can be traced back to diverse revolutionary legacies in the three. In chapters 5 and 6, I draw on the unions' resultant positions as the crucial variable that differentiated the state-labor dyad among these three countries, in order to account first for variant levels of protest and, second, given these states' high sensitivity to unrest, for welfare response in the three countries.

My simple answer is that unions had previously been *most ineffective* (in all ways) in China, as compared with those in France or Mexico. Thus, upon liberalization and economic reform, when unions became even more impotent there than ever, disgruntled workers were freed to engage in wildcat strikes without the involvement of the unions—without, that is, either enjoying the benefit (and sometimes the difficulty) of unions' coordination, as in France, or suffering the frustration of union bosses' forestallment, as in Mexico. The comparative upshot was that Chinese workers were both poised and released to resist much more vociferously than were those in either France or Mexico. Accordingly, I argue, their relatively more anxious rulers reciprocated with more of a welfare payback in that country. Chapter 7, the concluding chapter, weighs the relative contributions of my two large sets of factors—global forces-cum-SEOs versus workers (and state commitments to workers)—to the choices each of these states' politicians took as the past century began to come to a close.

Thus, within a matter of just a few years the political elites of all three of these countries abruptly left the track their predecessors had followed, seemingly abandoning the masses of their laboring followers, once a key part of their support base, as they did so. As, in so acting, they each turned to embrace a much more distant set of allies—that is, new associates in new global leagues—while the old domestic coalitions that had shored up (or, in the case of France, helped to shore up) their prior political economies at home came apart, and the millions of workers who had kept those economies in motion for decades were left without support.

Those thereby deposited outside the fold economically became for a time politically and socially excluded (though neither always nor everywhere with the same intensity or severity). National inclusion at the global or suprastate level, consequently, was for these countries to substitute for individual inclusion within the polity at the mass level, as the site of the tribunal imagined to judge the state's legitimacy was upgraded: where once the state in France, Mexico, and China had earned its right to rule as *provider*, via broad inclusiveness at home,[32] now these same states planned to gain that justification as *player*, by social closure at home and by incorporation abroad within an outside, august ensemble. But what was the upshot for labor politics?

Once France, Mexico, China entered—or prepared to enter—extranational economic organizations, these three countries were all constrained to shed their working-class supporters. Past economic policies and prior properties of states' ties with unions thereafter variably disposed workers to rally for their rights, regime type notwithstanding, my argument maintains. By looking simultaneously at the dynamics of global entry and labor loss, this book provides new insights into structurally comparable economic and political forces that, because of differing terms attaching unions to states and to workers, produced politically different outcomes in labor politics.

---

32. Vivienne Shue, "Legitimacy Crisis in China," in *State and Society in 21st-Century China: Crisis, Contention, and Legitimation,* ed. Peter Hays Gries and Stanley Rosen (New York: Routledge/Curzon, 2004), 24–49.

Part 1
SIMILARITIES

2

SIMILAR STARTING POINTS

The State for Labor, against the World

China, France, and Mexico began their outward journeys of the early 1980s from somewhat similar positions. In this chapter I focus on these states' connections with and commitments to their respective labor forces—or at least the elite portions thereof—from the 1940s to 1980. Three historical aspects of the state-labor dyad were roughly parallel in China, France, and Mexico.

The three patterns I employ to characterize these countries are these: pre-1980 *isolationist/protectionist* state policies, as opposed to strategies of economic openness; fundamental *political weakness of the working class,* as measured by the absence of workers' ability—through their unions—to find strong representation and promotion of their interests within the government, along with a lack of internal solidarity within the working class; and the existence of a distant, orienting *revolution,* combined with what were for the governments searing episodes of societal restiveness in the more recent past. Although my three cases do not fall at precisely the same spot along a continuum with regard to any of these measures, they would fit into the same boxes for these categories were this material to be presented as a typology.

These three historical features underwent a certain degree of alteration after 1980, but the older patterns nonetheless left their mark. As the states joined the global market, becoming progressively less and less protectionist toward labor in the 1980s and 1990s, workers and unions continued to display their respective customary forms of political weakness: through internal segmentation of the labor movement in France, because of monolithic party oversight in China, and through dependence and loyalty to the state in Mexico. At the same time, old revolutionary memories continued to render the states' leaders both fearful toward aroused workers and aware of their responsibility to labor. The "terms of attachment" between the state, labor, and unions in the three were thus alike in general outline, but they differed in accord with divergent revolutionary traditions. These divergences became critical in prompting different behaviors on the part of the members of these three respective sets of affiliations, as the countries accepted global market principles more and more.

In chapters 5 and 6, I come back to these findings, employing them to address the puzzle of why, in the wake of work post cutbacks and welfare withdrawal in the 1980s and thereafter it was the Chinese workforce that became the most combative of the three and, in turn, the Chinese state the most responsive. This finding is counterintuitive in that China's post-totalitarian polity would not be expected to present these results.

To turn to the issues at hand, each of these states fostered its economic growth in the decades from the 1940s to 1980 through variably *isolationist, protectionist, and import-substitution* (or functionally similar) programs of industrialization, all based politically on a form of *state/labor pact,* or implicit bargain, between the state and the workers (or at least the top-ranking, state-affiliated, formal portion of the working class). The extent of this isolationism-protectionism was high in China, medium in Mexico, and low but still a feature of the economic model in France.

Second, these were all polities where the institutions that distinguished the labor markets and the labor movements were relatively weak in the following ways: each had labor unions that were *either unable or not always willing to fight against the state on behalf of their memberships* and that were *low-density* (except for China, where nominal membership was high but labor was generally mute and powerless). But the situation was more complex than that, in comparable ways, in these countries: in each one the labor market, as fashioned by the state, was *dual* (as it frequently is in developing countries), with an upper tier variously tied to the state, the members of which secured significantly better official treatment than did the neglected lower echelon. Dualism, manufactured by the states themselves in all these cases, undercut solidarity among labor.

Notwithstanding their lack of direct determination over state policy—if for somewhat differing reasons in the separate cases—upper-tier workers had long received reliable protection and benefits from the regime as of 1980. A variation on this theme is that in Mexico the labor bosses who led unions tied to the ruling party (the Partido Revolucionario Institutional, the PRI) were actually accorded some policy input from time to time. But since these individuals' handling of their bond with the PRI could critically benefit or endanger their own careers, they often did not use their power either actively or solely in the interests of the workers.

While these first two features were widespread in the postwar period, a third factor uniting the three countries was not. This is that in each of them persisting reminiscences of a *long-ago revolution* took on mythic proportions over time—of commitments, promises, and supposed (but never fully realized) obligations on the part of the regime, along with expectations and a sense of entitlement among the workers. Those historical uprisings had in each place been executed at least in part on behalf of an underclass and had become enshrined accordingly, as their outcomes were formalized in rhetoric in state constitutions. At the same time, more recent episodes of mass antigovernment protest had burst out in the late 1960s and again in 1989 in China; in 1968 in France; and in the same year in Mexico (there in the form of a sudden student outburst but also in a wave of labor protest then plus more insurgency in the early part of the following decade).[1]

For the political elite, memories of these incidents later conjured up frightening visions of chaos and disorder. A critical legacy of these uprisings was that unease over adopting policies that might provoke confrontation from the populace had powerful effects on leadership behavior: in each country, if to variable degrees, the specter of an enraged proletarian mob could dispose politicians to improve wage levels and/or workers' welfare, at least in the past, when the grievances of labor were especially raw and serious disorder seemed a possibility. In more recent times these legacies also led the political elite in these states to attempt to pacify and placate workers after upheavals.[2] As we see later, a liberal revolution in France, a communist one in China, and an uprising that quickly resulted in a corporatist coalition between leading political forces and workers in Mexico all had their reverberations in later developments.

Historically, there was clearly variation in regime rejoinders to protest in these three countries, in accord with regime type. In France, a democracy in which contending political parties sometimes took opposed political stances, elections could make a difference: politicians up for office tended to cave in to worker demands when voting was in the offing, and thus the expression of public grievances could have a meaningful impact on welfare provision.[3] In Mexico, which at best could be labeled a semi-authoritarian regime with one party dominant into the 1990s, a connection existed between elections and protest, but it operated quite differently.

----

1. Ruth Berins Collier and David Collier, *Shaping the Political Arena: Critical Junctures, the Labor Movement, and Regime Dynamics in Latin America* (Princeton, N.J.: Princeton University Press, 1991), 601.

2. Mark Kesselman, conclusion to *The French Workers' Movement: Economic Crisis and Political Change*, ed. Kesselman with the assistance of Guy Groux (London: George Allen & Unwin, 1984), 312; Michelle Dion, "Mexico's Welfare Regime Before and After the Debt Crisis: Organized Labor and the Effects of Globalization," paper presented at the 2002 annual meeting of the Southern Political Science Association, Savannah, Ga., November 7–9, 7–10.

3. Anthony Daley, "The Steel Crisis and Labor Politics in France and the United States," in *Bargaining for Change: Union Politics in North America and Europe*, ed. Miriam Golden and Jonas Pontusson (Ithaca: Cornell University Press, 1992), 161.

There a principal role of the state-connected unions was to pacify their workforces, preventing or putting down disturbances at the time of the vote. Any subsequent state-sponsored disbursal of benefits for the workforce depended on the unions' success in that venture.[4] And in China, protests occurred on occasion, but their reception and disposal had no connection with any balloting. Strikes were rarely driven by the unions though sometimes had their support (as in 1957),[5] but could be readily repressed at the request of the state by its public security forces whenever the leadership deemed this necessary.

Regardless of these regime-based dissimilarities, as a group all these places experienced significant upheavals that engaged the state and engraved cogent recollections in the collective minds of both the perpetrators and politicians in each case. In short, to the extent that workers and/or unions had any clout within the polity in each of these cases, it was grounded in state leaders' pronounced apprehension of disorder and concern for social calm. It could be argued, too, that the substantial benefits the state in each place bestowed on the proletariat, if generally just on an upper tier among the workers, were an acknowledgment of the potency of labor for destabilizing protest.

Significantly, in each case that very generosity also became instrumental in pushing each of these states into the developmental cul-de-sac it encountered by 1980 (to be addressed in chapter 3), given the situation in the world economy at that time. I proceed to elaborate these points through a review of the three countries in accord with the three patterns just listed, which, for short, I label *protectionism-plus-pact; weak workers/divided labor markets;* and *revolutionary potential-cum-state commitments.*

China

Protectionism-plus-Pact

China's near-isolationism and protectionism were a hallmark of the Maoist strategy of development, which famously, if a bit falsely, proclaimed the country to be developing via "self-reliance." The label became nearer the truth after the country's 1960 break with its former benefactor of the 1950s, the Soviet Union. In fact, China's economy was never totally closed, but it embodied a variant of import substitution industrialization (ISI) up into the 1970s. After relying on the Soviet Union for investment credits and trading mainly with the East European socialist bloc states

---

4. Kevin J. Middlebrook, *The Paradox of Revolution: Labor, the State, and Authoritarianism in Mexico* (Baltimore: Johns Hopkins University Press, 1995), 30.

5. Elizabeth J. Perry, "Shanghai's Strike Wave of 1957," *CQ* 137 (1994), 1–27.

in the 1950s, China had only restricted economic intercourse abroad for most of the following two decades.

A moderate amount of exchange took place with a few West European nations, notably Britain and France, and with Japan through the 1960s and thereafter, while some transactions with the United States began to take off after the early 1970s (before China's major policy switch toward external openness).[6] That China was, however, substantially closed before 1979 is evident in these statistics: in 1977, following the rule of the practically omnipotent Mao Zedong, China ranked a mere number 30 in the list of trading countries; and as of 1980, when the country made its grand overture to the world market, foreign trade accounted for just 13 percent of gross domestic product (based on nominal figures), a rate referred to as a nation's trade dependency.[7] At the end of the 1970s, after the passing in 1976 of Mao, a revamped leadership was soon installed. Within just a couple of years these politicians undertook a nearly wholesale rejection of Mao's developmental tactics. Nevertheless, the new leaders hung onto his stance of alliance with the working class for quite some time.

Overall, protectiveness went well beyond the firms and the industrial sectors. The Chinese state's version of a custodial bond with its proletariat is captured in the words of Jackie Sheehan: "Security of employment offered some recompense for powerlessness and lack of voice in the workplace."[8] Or, in the terms of Andrew Walder, a kind of "organized dependence" kept the working force largely in line most of the time; alternatively, the relationship amounted to solicitude paired with surveillance, to draw on Janos Kornai.[9]

Weak Workers, Divided Labor Market

The place of labor within the Chinese polity was a paradoxical one: the workers in state-owned enterprises were weak as actors in their own right and in addition had no genuine union poised to go to battle on their behalf. Yet their hold on the state, which sheltered them, was tenacious nonetheless, for the Chinese Communist Party was founded in 1921 in the name of the proletariat, in true Leninist style. In response to orders coming from Moscow, it played primarily to a labor clientele

---

6. Peter Van Ness, "Three Lines in Chinese Foreign Relations, 1950–1983: The Development Imperative," in *Three Visions of Chinese Socialism*, ed. Dorothy J. Solinger (Boulder, Colo.: Westview Press, 1984), 113–42.

7. Thomas G. Moore, "China and Globalization," in *East Asia and Globalization*, ed. Samuel S. Kim (Lanham, Md.: Rowman & Littlefield, 2000), 107–8.

8. Jackie Sheehan, *Chinese Workers: A New History* (London: Routledge, 1998), 195.

9. Andrew G. Walder, *Communist Neo-traditionalism* (Berkeley: University of California Press, 1986); Janos Kornai, *The Socialist System: The Political Economy of Communism* (Princeton, N.J.: Princeton University Press, 1992), 315.

during most of the 1920s, as Party leaders incited strikes in the cities on behalf of the working class.[10]

Following the Party's 1949 takeover of the country, the social prestige of the working class was immense, as that sector of the population stood at the peak of the status hierarchy for decades.[11] Throughout the Mao years and indeed even throughout a lengthy stage of the post-1980 years of "economic reform," opening up, and marketization, the Party always styled itself as "the vanguard of the proletariat" and referred to the workers as "masters of the enterprise" and members of the "leading class."

In ennobling the working class, however, the Party had its own objectives. In order to ensure its control over the activities of the urban working-age population, as well as to keep this demographic group satisfied and loyal, from the 1950s into the early 1990s to the extent possible the Party assigned work posts to the great bulk of young people fit to labor, thereby doing away with the need for job searches for many, or indeed for any sort of free labor market. The Party also eliminated voluntary job mobility and determined all urban wages from the early 1950s until well into the reform years.[12] Even as late as the mid-1990s, managers of the largest state firms remained under great pressure to maximize employment, a mandate that led over the years to much overstaffing and consequent idleness on the shopfloor.[13]

But despite this push for full employment in the cities, when it came to welfare benefits, Chinese urban labor was decisively multilayered.[14] Only some of the workers, those employed in state-owned firms and in some of the large "collectively" owned ones, experienced all the perquisites that went with the special status granted in rhetoric to the working class.[15] Others—those recruited as "temporaries" or as contracted labor from the countryside, or those in the smaller, neighborhood- and lane-based collectives—lived a distinctly inferior existence.

---

10. Hans J. Van de Ven, *From Friend to Comrade: The Founding of the Chinese Communist Party, 1920–1927* (Berkeley: University of California Press, 1991); Benjamin I. Schwartz, *Chinese Communism and the Rise of Mao* (Cambridge, Mass.: Harvard University Press, 1966).

11. Shaoguang Wang, "The Social and Political Implications of China's WTO Membership," *Journal of Contemporary China* 9, 25 (2000), 373–405.

12. By 1957 every high school graduate was assigned to a workplace. Ming-kwan Lee, *Chinese Occupational Welfare in Market Transition* (New York: St. Martin's Press, 2000), 45–51; Xin Meng, *Labour Market Reform in China* (New York: Cambridge University Press, 2000), 3–10.

13. Edward S. Steinfeld, *Forging Reform in China: The Fate of State-Owned Industry* (Cambridge: Cambridge University Press, 1998), 120–22.

14. Andrew G. Walder, "The Remaking of the Chinese Working Class, 1949–1981," *MC* 10, 1 (1984), 3–48.

15. In the cities "collective" firms were factories that usually were managed and allegedly "owned" by neighborhood units and as a rule had somewhat less favored treatment as compared with state-owned ones. Gordon White, "The Changing Role of the Chinese State in Labour Allocation: Towards the Market?" *Journal of Communist Studies* 3, 2 (1987), 130.

Moreover, while all workers in the state-owned factories could count on lifetime tenure in their jobs, even among these firms much variation reigned in the levels of benefits and compensation accorded their workforces.[16]

Welfare was allocated directly by a worker's firm, as each enterprise served at once as a manufacturing outfit and a dispenser of social services.[17] Differential treatment was a function of the importance to the regime of the industrial sector in which a worker labored, the size of his/her unit, and the region of the country in which it was situated, as well as, very probably, the political connections of an enterprise's management.[18] One early study estimated that as of 1958, just under one-third of urban labor was receiving labor insurance; twenty years later, only 22 percent of the total workforce in the cities had this benefit.[19]

Thus higher-echelon workers enjoyed a superior level of privilege, while an immense number of lesser-status laboring people formed a lower stratum in a dualistic labor force.[20] A notable hardship in the workers' lot was that wages failed to rise over the period from the mid-1950s through the late 1970s.[21] This wage stagnation, though, may have seemed less oppressive to the labor force than one might imagine, since inflation was practically nonexistent during the pre-1980 years.

That there was scant agitation for fatter paychecks was no doubt also related to the supine character of the official trade union, the All China Federation of Trade Unions (ACFTU). This body, first established in 1925, expanded after 1949

---

16. There were brief periods of society-wide surges in unemployment before the reform era. But, not counting the time just after the Communist takeover in the early 1950s, those who lost their jobs at such times were either people from the countryside who had been holding urban positions only briefly or youths just returned to the cities from the countryside after the Cultural Revolution. Feng Lanrui and Zhao Lukuan, "Urban Unemployment in China," *Social Sciences in China* 3, 2 (March 1982), 123–42; Lei Guang, "Broadening the Debate on *Xiagang*: Ideological Change, Policy Innovation and Practices in History," in *China's Shattered Rice Bowl: Laid-off Workers in a Workers' State*, ed. Thomas B. Gold (New York: Palgrave McMillan, 2009), 15–37.

17. Nelson W. S. Chow, *The Administration and Financing of Social Security in China* (Hong Kong: Centre of Asian Studies, 1988), 31–33; Elisabeth J. Croll, "Social Welfare Reform: Trends and Tensions," *CQ* 159 (September 1999), 684–99; Linda Wong, *Marginalization and Social Welfare in China* (London: Routledge, 1998).

18. Andrew G. Walder, "Property Rights and Stratification in Socialist Redistributive Economies," *American Sociological Review* 57 (August 1992), 524–39.

19. The figure given for 1958 is about 14 million of 45 million, in Charles Hoffman, *Work Incentive Practices and Policies in the People's Republic of China, 1953–1965* (Albany: State University of New York Press, 1967), 35. Thanks to Elizabeth Perry for this information. The percentage of the workforce receiving full benefits declined over time because the 17 million young people sent to the countryside who returned to the cities were placed in collective firms with few if any welfare perquisites. Also, new smaller firms were created over time that did not offer benefits.

20. Louis Putterman, "Dualism and Reform in China," *Economic Development and Cultural Change* 40 (1992), 467–93, describes the pre-reform Chinese economy as "dual" in a different sense, referring to the distinction between the capital-intensive industrial sector in the cities and the labor-intensive agricultural one in the countryside.

21. Meng, *Labour Market Reform*, 8.

with its monopolistic absorption of all other existing labor associations at that point.[22] The working class that it served more or less relinquished its ability to put forward demands on its own behalf most of the time before the late 1980s, while being forced to entrust its welfare to the federation's leadership.[23] The union's chief charge, as set out in the 1950 Trade Union Law, was simply to serve as a liaison between the workers and the Party, which principally entailed ensuring that Party objectives were well internalized by labor.

Union density (often alluded to as an important measure in work on democratic countries) was remarkably high as compared with the rate in the advanced industrial democracies; as much as 64 percent of the workforce belonged to the trade unions, as of the early 1980s, according to one account.[24] But this fact meant little, as the workers themselves were largely impotent in pre-reform days. The union too had its mouth clamped shut decisively at an early juncture, when several of its leaders dared to criticize the Party in the 1957 Hundred Flowers Movement.[25] Later the Party leadership went so far as to close down the union entirely in the name of "anti-bureaucratism" during the 1966–76 Cultural Revolution. Even before that happened, its daily responsibilities remained simply administering and apportioning welfare, stimulating production, nurturing "model workers," and encouraging worker performance.[26] Thus what I designate the "terms of attachment" between the state and the union dictated that its local branches and firm-level units cooperate with management to control and mobilize the workers, not to agitate as their deputy.

Revolutionary Heritage-cum-State Commitments

Historically, it was the Communist Party itself that had championed and churned up the proletariat in the Party's own infant days, especially in the 1920s.[27] Before giving up on the possibility of staging revolution just on the basis of China's then tiny working class, party cadres strove to organize especially the more highly skilled among urban laborers, in the cadre's interest of establishing a Marxist-style

---

22. Jude Howell, "Organising around Women and Labour in China: Uneasy Shadows, Uncomfortable Alliances," *Communist and Post-Communist Studies* 33 (2000), 363.

23. Gordon White, Jude Howell, and Shang Xiaoyuan, *In Search of Civil Society: Market Reform and Social Change in Contemporary China* (Oxford: Clarendon Press, 1996), 40.

24. Richard Morris, "Trade Unions in Contemporary China," *AJCA* 13 (1985), 51. The figure was low as compared with other socialist countries, where the entire workforce belonged to the union. Calvin Chen and Rudra Sil, "Communist Legacies, Postcommunist Transformations, and the Fate of Organized Labor in Russia and China," *Studies in Comparative International Development* 41 (Summer 2006), 62–87.

25. Perry, "Shanghai's Strike Wave," 16–18, 21.

26. Morris, "Trade Unions," 51–54.

27. Elizabeth J. Perry, *Shanghai on Strike* (Stanford, Calif.: Stanford University Press, 1993).

foundation for their later rule. In the end, however, Mao Zedong judged that the peasants were more ripe for rebellion, and workers had much less of a role. As noted above, with victory, the array of unions that had existed in revolutionary times became subsumed under the Communist Party and were forced to be totally answerable to its changing objectives—with encouraging productivity and ensuring peace in the factories always present as central goals. Unions, thus, had no independent power, and their pairing with the Party was always predominant over any promotion of the cause of the proletariat. Over the years after 1949, the Party—perhaps cognizant of labor's potential for learned insurgency—took to watching the workers with a guarded eye, as the two became less partners in a shared revolution than potential combatants over the control of calm in the cities. Indeed, a critical drawback restricting the working class was the pervasive silence under which its members were compelled to toil, at least in normal times.

True, some strikes and unrest occurred on rare occasions during the Mao period, most notably in 1957 and then again at junctures during the ten years of the Cultural Revolution.[28] But the rarity of such disturbances marked them as the exceptions that proved the rule, and their result was repression by the police in pre-reform days, not assistance or even any relief from the union. So even as memories of a revolution waged in the name of the working class of the past—plus benefits that bolstered these memories—bestowed a sense of entitlement on its heirs, later protests staged by the workers acting independently were quite unwelcome, striking dread into the hearts of the Party politicians who had to deal with them. All told, the state-labor dyad in China on the eve of the country's outward turn was one in which the state—through its public security—clearly held the strong arm, even as its ongoing and dependable succor, dispensed by the unions, served to keep the workers-as-potential-wolves at bay.

France

Protectionism-plus-Pact

After following its historically based mercantilist tradition earlier in the century, France after World War II appeared at first to be inclined to continue in a protectionist mold.[29] But its membership in the European Coal and Steel Community

---

28. On periods of upheaval, such as the 1966–77 Cultural Revolution, see Elizabeth J. Perry and Li Xun, *Proletarian Power: Shanghai in the Cultural Revolution* (Boulder, Colo.: Westview Press, 1997), as well as Perry, "Shanghai's Strike Wave."

29. Philip H. Gordon and Sophie Meunier, *The French Challenge: Adapting to Globalization* (Washington, D.C.: Brookings Institution Press, 2001), 4. According to Andrea Boltho, "Has France Converged on Germany? Policies and Institutions since 1958," in *Regional Diversity and Global Capitalism,*

beginning in April 1951 reduced the possibility for enacting a full-fledged version of that approach.[30] Still, the government was able to use high tariffs to guard domestic producers in a number of sectors while also regulating labor markets in order to protect workers directly.[31] In fact, imports and exports combined amounted to just 13 percent of gross domestic product (GDP) in 1953 (the same trade dependency existing in China as late as 1980). Even after nearly a decade of growing closer to Europe in the 1950s, by 1960 only a few sectors were participating in the global marketplace.[32] Twenty years later, when France's customary practice of substituting devaluations (to boost its exports) for outright protectionism was no longer permitted by its European Community partners,[33] its trade as a proportion of GDP had climbed, but just to 23 percent.[34]

France progressively admitted more imports. But it was not until the late 1960s that the country began significantly enhancing its foreign trade participation.[35] Illustrative of the low base from which they took off, French exports and imports rose in value by 637 percent while its GDP only tripled in the three decades after the formation of the European Economic Community in 1959, according to William James Adams.[36] So, somewhat similarly to China, the French economy grew under a certain degree of isolation in the first decades after 1950, certainly relative to its Community partners. And in France a tacit contract undergirded the state's bond with labor, somewhat as one also did in China. But the terms were different: if the bargain struck in China was silence in the factory for security, in France the deal that was forged for workers entailed a rise in wages and social

---

ed. Suzanne Berger and Ronald Dore (Ithaca: Cornell University Press, 1996), 101, French trade policy was protectionist in the 1950s but became less so with integration into the Common Market.

30. Sonia Mazey, "European Integration: Unfinished Journey or Journey without End?" in *European Union: Power and Policy-Making*, 2d ed., ed. Jeremy Richardson (London: Routledge, 2001), 35; Daley, "Steel Crisis," 151.

31. Mark Kesselman et al., *European Politics in Transition*, 4th ed. (New York: Houghton Mifflin, 2002), 256.

32. William James Adams, "France and Global Competition," in *Remaking the Hexagon: The New France in the New Europe*, ed. Gregory Flynn (Boulder, Colo.: Westview Press, 1995), 91. Kesselman et al., *European Politics*, 256, note that French policymakers before 1983 had installed stiff tariffs to shelter French producers.

33. Robert Boyer, "Wage Labor, Capital Accumulation, and the Crisis, 1968–82," in Kesselman, *French Workers' Movement*, 24–25.

34. Howard Machin and Vincent Wright, "Economic Policy under the Mitterrand Presidency, 1981–1984: An Introduction," in *Economic Policy and Policy-Making under the Mitterrand Presidency, 1981–1984*, ed. Machin and Wright (London: Frances Pinter, 1985), 4.

35. Adams, "France and Global Competition," 104; Boyer, "Wage Labor," 25.

36. Adams, "France and Global Competition," 93. David Cameron notes that by the early 1990s, French exports and imports each constituted 20 to 25 percent of GDP, about twice what they had been in the early 1960s; at that point French economic dependence on the Community had increased more than threefold since the early 1960s. David Ross Cameron, "From Barre to Balladur: Economic Policy in the Era of the EMS," in Flynn, *Remaking the Hexagon*, 120–21.

transfers with expansion of the economy over the years, in the absence of institutionalized political participation.[37] For both of these reasons—trade barriers and material benefits—French workers would have had reason to be grateful to their state.

Weak Workers, Divided Labor Market

Throughout the postwar years, the French state continued its habitual regulation of labor markets with the goal of protecting workers. Paradoxically, these moves were made always under the rule of the right. Thus it has been surmised that probably protections were extended largely in the interest of maintaining a peaceable workplace.[38] As in China, burned by the past and cautious into the present, the state placed a high value on an orderly shopfloor; also like China, if for quite different reasons, the French state's bond with its workforce is not one that can be easily summarized.

Compared with elsewhere in Western Europe, where labor tended to be tied into corporatist arrangements with political parties, French labor unions were traditionally further to the left, so much so that during the extended, multidecade rule of right-wing parties up through the 1970s, unions generally preferred to absent themselves from party politics altogether, sustaining an old radical strain in the workers' movement of the late 1800s.[39] This was an option not available to coerced Chinese workers, who, through the ACFTU as a tool of the Communist Party, were inextricably linked to that one party, especially those employed for life in China's urban state-owned sector.

But in France, labor—reflecting the laissez-faire stance of the democratic French government toward worker organization—was divided into as many as five competing federations, the rancor between which could be considerable at times.[40] Moreover, further eviscerating a French workers' "movement," and unlike the case in much of the rest of Western Europe, density was never high, with unions

---

37. *Mark* Kesselman, "Introduction: The French Workers' Movement," in Kesselman, *French Workers' Movement*, 2; see also Boyer, "Wage Labor," 23.

38. Kesselman et al., *European Politics*, 256; personal communication from Chris Howell, July 30, 2005.

39. On the late 1800s, see Helen Harden Chenut, *Fabric of Gender: Working-Class Culture in Third Republic France* (University Park, Pa.: Pennsylvania State University Press, 2005).

40. The five are the Confédération Générale du Travail, tied to the Communist Party; the Confédération Française et Démocratique du Travail, at times close to the Socialist Party; the more moderate Force Ouvrière; the lesser Confédération Française des Cadres. Peter Morris, *French Politics Today* (Manchester, U.K.: Manchester University Press, 1994), 159.

encompassing at best only one-quarter of the workforce at an immediate postwar peak and catering to perhaps as little as 15 percent by the mid-1980s.[41]

Given the fragmentation of labor and the low participation rate in unions, particularly in comparison with elsewhere in Western Europe, the French labor movement is characteristically described in the literature as quite "weak." Some have attributed the alleged impotence of the unions to the country's late and gradual industrialization. As was also true of Mexico and China, in the early part of the last century only a minority of the French working-age population was employed in industry, and urbanization was still proceeding at only a gradual pace into the 1950s.[42]

Another aspect of labor's purported powerlessness was that unions were without legal protection within the workplace until after workers had joined in the massive public strikes of 1968;[43] it has even been judged that it was not until the promulgation of the Auroux Laws of 1982 that substantial protection was won.[44] Not only did the labor movement long operate without recourse to the law, but even had they wished for it, the unions were effectively excluded from participation in policymaking, which was primarily the province of the state and employers.[45] Indeed, a so-called tripartite *économie concertée* enshrined in France's late 1940s–early 1950s Monnet Plan, which had been aimed at reviving and modernizing the French economy, was initially designed to involve cooperation among business, the bureaucracy, and unions. But the union leadership, feeling excluded at the outset, quickly absented itself in a pique and thereafter never participated in

---

41. Mark Kesselman, "The New Shape of French Labour and Industrial Relations: Ce n'est plus la même chose," in *Policy-Making in France: From de Gaulle to Mitterrand*, ed. Paul Godt (London: Pinter, 1989), 170; Kesselman, "Introduction," 1; Daley, "Steel Crisis," 158–59. The percentage dropped below 10 in the 1990s.

42. In both France and China, artisans and peasants predominated over laborers until well into the twentieth century. On France, D. S. Bell and Byron Criddle, *The French Socialist Party: The Emergence of a Party of Government*, 2d ed. (Oxford: Clarendon Press, 1988), 12, state that not until 1946 was there an urban majority in the country. On China, see Gail Hershatter, *The Workers of Tianjin, 1900–1949* (Stanford, Calif.: Stanford University Press, 1986), and Kam Wing Chan, *Cities with Invisible Walls: Reinterpreting Urbanization in Post-1949 China* (Hong Kong: Oxford University Press, 1994). On Mexico, see Ruth Berins Collier, *The Contradictory Alliance: State-Labor Relations and Regime Change in Mexico* (Berkeley: International and Area Studies, University of California, 1992), 26, and Bryan R. Roberts, "The Dynamics of Informal Employment in Mexico," in *Work without Protections: Case Studies of the Informal Sector in Developing Countries*, ed. Gregory K. Schoepfle (Washington, D.C.: U.S. Department of Labor, Bureau of International Labor Affairs, 1993), 105 (which states that between 1940 and 1980, the proportion of the population engaged in agriculture dropped by 35.7 percent).

43. Chris Howell, *Regulating Labor: The State and Industrial Relations Reform in Postwar France* (Princeton, N.J.: Princeton University Press, 1992), 209.

44. Kesselman, "Introduction," 2, and "Does the French Labor Movement Have a Future?" in *Chirac's Challenge: Liberalization, Europeanization, and Malaise in France*, ed. John T. S. Keeler and Martin A. Schain (New York: St. Martin's Press, 1996), 146.

45. Daley, "Steel Crisis," 153, 158; Stephen Cohen, *Modern Capitalist Planning: The French Model* (Berkeley: University of California Press, 1977), 130, 195–98.

policy councils.[46] Moreover, employers generally eschewed collective bargaining with workers.[47]

Regardless of workers' abstention from politics and their inability to bargain, they made their presence felt in their strike activity. As a liberal democracy, the French state permitted strikes, which throughout much of the twentieth century were frequent and disruptive, especially in the period before the 1980s. This energetic activism served to counter somewhat the fact of unions' low density.[48] Mark Kesselman notes that in the decade after the first oil crisis of 1973, 230,000 days were lost to strikes on average each month, a figure that declined rapidly in the 1980s.[49] Hence the terms of attachment here were different from those in China, even, one might say, completely opposite: unions were entirely free to agitate and organize as they wished; they were, however, quite unattached from the sources of power in the polity.

Some observers have remarked that strikes, though brief, could sometimes bring gains for the workers, even to the extent that French labor has been labeled a "veto group."[50] An important instance occurred when, in response to the broadly based upheavals of May 1968, accords in Grenelle produced a 33 percent increase in the minimum wage; also, in the aftermath of these disturbances benefits improved in the 1970s as well.[51] Another feature of working-class politics that acted to reduce the salience of modest union density was that during major strikes many non-unionized workers would join in with the unionized.[52]

Even where unions could often be sadly inconsequential, workers in France were nevertheless blessed by having the state as their benefactor of last resort.[53] Two particularly significant state regulations underwrote the welfare of the working class in a way that went beyond firm-specific, collectively negotiated bargains. The first was a ruling set down as early as 1947 which decreed a compulsory minimum wage. And the other was the Labor Law of 1950, which proclaimed that

---

46. Cohen, *Modern Capitalist Planning;* Stephen Cohen, Serge Halimi, and John Zysman, "Institutions, Politics and Industrial Policy in France," in *The Politics of Industrial Policy,* ed. Claude E. Barfield and William A. Schambra (Washington, D.C.: American Economic Institute, 1986), 106–27.

47. George Ross, "The CGT, Economic Crisis, and Political Change," in Kesselman, *French Workers' Movement,* 52.

48. Kesselman, "Introduction," 1.

49. Kesselman, "New Shape," 169, states that by 1985 the monthly average had gone down to just 60,000, still an arresting sum.

50. Kesselman, "French Labor Movement," 158, 169; and Daley, "Steel Crisis," 162. This analysis is similar to that of Mari Miura and Bruno Palier, "Veto Players and Welfare Reform: The Paradox of the French and Japanese Unions," paper presented at the annual meeting of the American Political Science Association, Philadelphia, August 27–31, 2003.

51. Boyer, "Wage Labor," 24; Howell, *Regulating Labor,* 110.

52. Kesselman, "French Labor Movement," 149.

53. Kesselman, "Introduction," 2; Daley, "Steel Crisis," 153–54 and 159; Howell, *Regulating Labor,* 69.

agreements reached within one firm could be "extended" to an entire industry or even regionwide.[54] The enforcement of this right was only made easier with subsequent revisions, enabling benefits won in one negotiation to apply much more broadly, including to sectors of the economy where unions might be either too feeble to win benefits on their own or even nonexistent.

Another proclivity of the state that countered French labor's organizational fragility or assessments of it as anemic was the state's strong stand against layoffs up into the 1980s. On this point the French state took a position rather like that of the Chinese government. This behavior was especially notable in the critical downturn in the steel industry in the 1970s, when the state drew on the National Employment Fund to underwrite schemes geared to assisting the potentially jobless; in some instances state loans and subsidies even enabled firms in trouble to avoid redundancies altogether.[55] In 1974 the government forced through an agreement that called for laid-off workers to receive 90 percent of their salaries and demanded that companies obtain administrative authorization if firing more than ten workers for economic cause.[56]

Politically, the story is double-edged as well. While, as noted, labor often attempted to steer clear of politics, if it became involved at all its support was for the parties of the left. But this meant that from the late 1940s up through the 1970s, when these parties were out of power, the workers' intermediaries were sidelined as well. Sometimes the unions flatly rejected offers to enter; more often they were simply shut out. Still, this withholding accorded labor and its agents one advantage as the economy ground down: since the left was not governing when economic slowdown and stagnation appeared in the 1970s, the path was open for a Socialist Party victory in the presidential election of 1981, thus finally presenting a chance for labor to be affiliated with the governing party, which did occur, at least briefly.[57]

Revolutionary Heritage-cum-State Commitments

It could be argued that the Revolution of 1789, with its ideals of citizenship and equality, bestowed on future generations a sense that state leaders supported a commitment to the well-being of the individual, even the underprivileged individual. Indeed, some have linked the popular explosion of 1968 to memories of the Revolution. In the same vein, both the Communist Party and the Socialists, each

---

54. Howell, *Regulating Labor*, 42, 59, 98, 109; Boyer, "Wage Labor," 22.

55. Daley, "Steel Crisis," 161–62. The fund made possible interplant transfers, retraining, and early retirement packages between the late 1960s and the mid-1980s. See also Howell, *Regulating Labor* 69; Boyer, "Wage Labor," 27.

56. Howell, *Regulating Labor*, 69.

57. Kesselman, "Introduction," 3–4; Frank Wilson, "Trade Unions and Economic Policy," in Machin and Wright, *Economic Policy and Policy-Making*, 255.

of which was historically close to one of the two chief unions, trace their goals and values to the Jacobin revolutionary tradition.[58] According to William Sewell, the notion of "association" and the freedom to engage in it was the form of liberty that mattered to workers and their conglomerations, and they explicitly located this right in the 1789 Revolution. Another union inheritance from the revolutionary ethic was the concept of "fraternity."[59]

But ultimately, two dimensions of the Revolution mattered for the late twentieth century and the state-labor dyad in France by then. First was the liberal Revolution's recognition of the "rights of man," which included not only association but also freedoms of conscience, speech, belief, and the press. Though French unions had to suffer nearly a hundred years of outlaw status as tainted "intermediate organizations" that could disrupt the Revolution's ideal of a tight tie between the individual and the state, when they were finally legalized in 1886 they were able to emerge in numbers and were relatively free of state control, if not always of its monitoring.[60] And second, any reverberations of the revolutionary tradition immediately unsettled the political elite. Chris Howell, for example, maintains that popular demonstrations after 1968 were seen by all governments of any political cast as potential echoes of the past, and notes that the state therefore "sought to respond to them as if they amounted again to the same threat posed by the events of 1968."[61]

Somewhat as in China, then, the bond between a reasonably caring but a strongly interventionist state and a relatively protected, if organizationally weak (but perceived by state leaders as possibly dangerous) working class managed to keep at least a segment of labor covered by benefits and more or less in line much of the time. But France's democratic form of regime meant that benefits could be actively wrung from the state on occasion, both because workers were free to demonstrate disruptively (and did so often) and because politicians wanted their ballots at the polls.

Mexico

Protectionism-plus-Pact

Up to the 1980s the Mexican market was "one of the most protected in the world," thanks to active and explicit governmental promotion of import substitution industrialization (ISI), which took off in the late 1930s and continued into the

---

58. Samuel H. Beer et al., *Patterns of Government: The Major Political Systems of Europe,* 3d ed. (New York: Random House, 1973), 97, 395, 406.

59. William H. Sewell Jr., *Work and Revolution in France* (New York: Cambridge University Press, 1980), 201–2, 205–6.

60. Chenut, *Fabric of Gender.*

61. Howell, *Regulating Labor,* 209.

1970s.[62] This program was a natural outgrowth of a nationalistic pride stirred to life in the 1930s by then-president Lázaro Cárdenas. The government was able to carry off this effort, even as it also welcomed some investment, technology, and loans from abroad.[63] As of 1980, the country's trade dependency rate was only a bit above China's at that time, at 16 percent, and much less than France's.[64]

Accordingly, Mexico's level of protectionism was much more thoroughgoing than France's, as its policymakers—as was widely the case throughout Latin America—drew on every possible means to keep native industry sheltered. As elsewhere in Latin America, in Mexico ISI meant that the state put a wide range of protective measures into play for business, in the hope of ensuring that domestic industry would have the maximum opportunity to develop. In addition to high tariffs, the government imposed quotas on and required licenses for most imports, limited procurement of other goods to government agencies and state firms, devised product exclusionary standards, placed controls on the use of foreign exchange, and demanded domestic sourcing for inputs, while failing to safeguard foreign-owned patents or copyrights.[65] Even exports were limited at first, such that their proportion of GDP dropped from 15 percent in the 1940s to under 4 percent by 1975. But beginning in the 1970s, as balance-of-trade problems began to crop up, the government started to promote exports.[66]

The state's high level of investment, along with its substantial expenditures of many sorts (including various kinds of subsidies for workers), was made possible principally by profits that accrued to the state from its involvement in sectors protected by import substitution. Using the proceeds from sales of its own petroleum to subsidize the process, for example, the country sacrificed the foreign exchange that oil exports would have yielded in the interest of fostering the

---

62. As late as 1973, new, restrictive Foreign Investment Laws and Limits were announced. James F. Rochlin, *Redefining Mexican "Security"* (Boulder, Colo.: Lynne Rienner, 1997). The quotation is from Meyer, "Mexico," 143.

63. Gustavo V. del Castillo, "NAFTA and the Struggle for Neoliberalism: Mexico's Elusive Quest for First World Status," in *Neoliberalism Revisited: Economic Restructuring and Mexico's Political Future*, ed. Gerardo Otero (Boulder, Colo.: Westview Press, 1996), 28; Middlebrook, *Paradox of Revolution*, 209; Daniel C. Levy and Kathleen Bruhn, with Emilio Zebadua, *Mexico: The Struggle for Democratic Development* (Berkeley: University of California Press, 2001), 151–52, 162.

64. According to Economist Intelligence Unit, EIU dataservices, http://wwwa2.secure.alacra.com/cgi-bin/euisite.exe, in 1980 Mexico's real GDP (in US$ at 1996 prices) was 244.17 billion; in the same year its total exports fob (free on board) plus total imports cif (cost insurance and freight) amounted to US$39.12 million.

65. Peter Morici, "Grasping the Benefits of NAFTA," *CH* 2 (1993), 50.

66. Nora Lustig, *Mexico: The Remaking of an Economy*, 2d ed. (Washington, D.C.: Brookings Institution Press, 1998). Also see Barbara Stallings and Wilson Peres, *Growth, Employment, and Equity: The Impact of the Economic Reforms in Latin America and the Caribbean* (Washington, D.C.: Brookings Institution Press, 2000), 36–37.

manufacture of homemade products. An overvalued peso was employed to render the capital goods that were imported cheaper than they would otherwise have been. Under this strategy, foreign investment was also heavily restricted, falling from the 45 percent of gross fixed investment it had occupied in the early years of the century to just 3 percent by 1960.[67]

Indeed, in the postwar period, until the strategic reversal of the early 1980s, tariffs as well as nontariff barriers together successfully fended off much foreign competition. By 1970, 68 percent of the value of imports required permits to enter the country, a figure that shot up to 100 percent during the height of the debt crisis of 1982. Even as late as 1985, on the eve of the large-scale liberalization of the Mexican economy, over 90 percent of domestic production fell under a system of import licenses, with the highest tariff still reaching 100 percent.[68]

An exception to this protective regime got under way in the mid-1960s, but just in one particular portion of the country: the government began to nurture the formation of export-processing firms (*maquiladores*) along its northern border, with the double objective of absorbing idle labor and boosting exports. There foreign ownership was permitted, and the required inputs and equipment were allowed to enter the country duty-free.[69] Workers toiling in these plants were decidedly members of the lower, informal tier in the labor market, as opposed to those treated preferentially in enterprises owned by the state or closely controlled by PRI-favored unions.

Protection of business and industry spelled protection for the favored segments of the working class as well. As throughout Latin America, the large role of the Mexican state in the economy, plus steady economic growth in and after the 1940s, enabled political leaders to provide much secure and legally regulated public sector employment.[70] Under that regimen, the more privileged workers of the country had opportunities for skill training and improved living standards. The supply of these benefits, here as elsewhere in the region (and, similarly, in China and France), was enforced in an unspoken agreement in the interest of achieving the political support of the working class, as well as ensuring its composure at the

67. Levy and Bruhn, *Mexico*, 151–62.

68. Lustig, *Mexico*, 114–15, 117.

69. Gary Gereffi, "Mexico's 'Old' and 'New' Maquiladora Industries: Contrasting Approaches to North American Integration," in *Neoliberalism Revisited: Economic Restructuring and Mexico's Political Future*, edited by Gerardo Otero, 85–105. Boulder, Colo.: Westview Press, 85; Levy and Bruhn, *Mexico*, 165; Leslie Sklair, *Assembling for Development: The Maquila Industry in Mexico and the United States* (London: Unwin Hyman, 1989).

70. Stallings and Peres, *Growth, Employment, and Equity*, 36–37; Susan Fleck and Constance Sorrentino, "Employment and Unemployment in Mexico's Labor Force," *Monthly Labor Review* 117, 11 (1994), 3.

work post.[71] As one analyst characterized this deal, it was an exchange of "perks for peace and votes."[72]

Weak Workers, Divided Labor Market

At the same time that it offered protection, the Mexican state maintained a firm grip on the activities of the labor force, in part through restrictive legislation, in part through the iron fists of labor boss union leaders bound to, and rewarded for good behavior by, the PRI. The state also managed to hobble even the privileged among the workers by rendering them deeply dependent on the PRI.[73] The chief mechanism employed by the party-state was to dispense patronage to workers (through their unions) in favored sectors, a classic dual labor market strategy.[74]

In Mexico, as also in China and France, the state—first through the Confederation of Mexican Workers (Confederación de Trabajadores Méxicanos, or CTM, formed in 1936 by President Cárdenas) and even more so after 1966 with the creation of an umbrella Labor Congress (the Congreso del Trabajo, or CT) for the PRI's affiliates[75]—found it quite convenient to manage the proletariat in a top-down fashion.[76] This arrangement resembled China's ACFTU, a classic "transmission belt" mass association, which also monitored and serviced the workers. An important difference, however, is that in China the unions were not in charge of repressing workers as they were in Mexico but were instead tasked with mediating for them with management when necessary. Ruth Berins Collier and David Collier also emphasize the ability of unions in Mexico truly to represent the workers, a function not really applicable in communist China. As the Colliers explain, in

71. Richard Tardanico, "From Crisis to Restructuring: Latin American Transformations and Urban Employment in World Perspective," in *Global Restructuring, Employment, and Social Inequality in Urban Latin America,* ed. Richard Tardanico and Rafael Menjivar Larin (Coral Gables, Fla.: North-South Center Press, 1997), 6; and Richard Tardanico and Rafael Menjivar Larin, "Restructuring, Employment, and Social Inequality: Comparative Urban Latin American Patterns," in Tardanico and Larin, *Global Restructuring,* 233.

72. Rochlin, *Redefining Mexican "Security,"* 28.

73. Middlebrook, *Paradox of Revolution,* 73; Collier and Collier, *Shaping the Political Arena,* 198.

74. Robert Kaufman, "Economic Orthodoxy and Political Change in Mexico: The Stabilization and the Adjustment Policies of the de la Madrid Administration," in *Debt and Democracy in Latin America,* ed. Barbara Stallings and Robert Kaufman (Boulder, Colo.: Westview Press), 109.

75. Rochlin, *Redefining Mexican "Security,"* 29.

76. Other important confederations connected to the PRI that appeared later were the Confederación Regional de Obreros (Regional Confederation of Mexican Workers) and the Confederación Revolucionaria de Obreros y Campesinos (the Revolutionary Confederation of Mexican Workers and Peasants).

Mexico "a key aspect of the functioning of the regime was…the capacity of union leaders to represent their constituencies as well as to discipline them."[77]

The Mexican state relied on a process of incorporation of labor—but only of its preferred segments—into the governing alliance. A predecessor of the post-revolutionary dominant party, the PRI, initially took this step in the interest of being better able to manipulate the labor movement, at the same time obtaining a reliable partner, in the very midst of the 1911–17 Revolution. Maria Victoria Murillo details how in the battles of those times revolutionary elites joined with labor leaders, organizing six Red Battalions to combat the Constitutionalist army (whose members were mainly middle-class urbanites and liberals), for which they were granted a set of labor rights in the Constitution of 1917. This deal set a foundation for a later pattern of concessions in exchange for support.[78]

Here, too (as in Mexico's early debt crisis and early entry into the global market), Mexico was a leader: much of the rest of Latin America followed its model by adopting the same basic pattern two decades later. When President Cárdenas reshaped the party in the 1930s, he went so far as to institutionalize the participation of workers—along with the peasantry and the middle class—as special sectors within the governmental party.[79] In this Mexico stood out from other Latin American countries: in the solidity and longevity of its compact with the workers, it took its close tie to the proletariat further than other states in the region, such as Argentina and Brazil.[80]

But unlike in China, where there are no political parties besides the ruling communist one (and so where voting played no role), and France, where the unions were linked only to opposition parties that had no hope of election from the late 1940s to 1981 and where unions largely stayed aloof from normal politics, what happened at polling time in Mexico was critical to the governing party, and it lay at the core of the PRI's bargain with workers.[81] So long as those workers tied to the party gave their votes to it and remained quiet in the days surrounding elections, the payoffs poured in. In the event of any worker unrest, the party would show its muscle, something for which there was no parallel in France.

The rewards for votes and decorum included a range of subsidies and welfare benefits, plus wages that rose with productivity for ordinary workers (at least for those in the official unions). For union leaders in several PRI client unions,

---

77. Collier and Collier, *Shaping the Political Arena*, 584–86.

78. Maria Victoria Murillo, *Labor Unions, Partisan Coalitions, and Market Reforms in Latin America* (Cambridge: Cambridge University Press, 2001), 28, 41.

79. Collier and Collier, *Shaping the Political Arena*, 100, 196–97; and Collier, *Contradictory Alliance*, 11–14, 32.

80. Ian Roxborough, "Organized Labor: A Major Victim of the Debt Crisis," in Stallings and Kaufman, *Debt and Democracy in Latin America*, 198, 91.

81. Middlebrook, *Paradox of Revolution*, 30.

including most prominently the CTM, but also the Mexican Regional Confederation (Confederación Regional Obrera Mexicana, or CROM) and the Revolutionary Confederation of Peasants and Workers (Confederación Revolucionaria de Obreros y Campesinos, or CROC), the payoffs were even better: official posts could be expected where loyalty was displayed.[82] These posts were delivered formally when the PRI nominated these bosses for elective positions in ballotings that the PRI's candidates invariably won.

Despite the many similarities among the three countries in the fundamentally subordinate position—rhetoric notwithstanding—in which workers were placed, there were certainly variations in the details. If as capitalists in a capitalist nation French business (represented through 1981 by the ruling parties of the right) and the state formed a political alliance that excluded the workers (and from which workers also withheld their allegiance), and if China, as a socialist state, celebrated the workers in status but subjugated them in practice, in the mixed, state-capitalist, Mexican economy, labor (or at least the portion of it within the officially sponsored unions) could sometimes serve as a genuine partner—or at least a prominent sector within the ruling party. In that capacity labor leaders sometimes had an opportunity to insert their views into policy that was, nonetheless, mostly written by the central government, with the consent of private business.

Thus, Mexican labor may on occasion have had at least an indirect voice in decision making, if a small one, in contrast to the case in France (where workers were not attached to a governing voice until 1981) and China (where all policy formation was in the hands of the Communist Party).[83] Yet it must be underlined that this was at best an indirect influence, as union leaders could only convey their ideas under the aegis of their membership in the official party. One should not forget, either, that their own careers, perquisites, and chances for corruption were always at stake as they did so.[84] In all these cases, then, workers themselves—regardless of the protection for them that the resultant policy often produced—were sidelined from the forum where policy was hammered out, and for practical purposes had scant (in Mexico) or no (in China and arguably France) access to it.

This paradox of protection joined with powerlessness applied for the most part just to those in state firms. Like those in China and France, Mexican state firms

---

82. Kenneth M. Coleman and Charles L. Davis, "Preemptive Reform and the Mexican Working Class," *Latin American Research Review* 18, 1 (1983), 5; Collier and Collier, *Shaping the Political Arena,* 197; Middlebrook, *Paradox of Revolution,* 76–77, 100. As Marcus J. Kurtz, "Understanding the Third World Welfare State after Neoliberalism," *CP* 34, 3 (2002), 307, points out, the PRI had no other powerful, autonomous, organized opposition (though there were other parties in Mexico) up into the 1980s. See also Roxborough, "Organized Labor," 102.

83. According to Collier and Collier, *Shaping the Political Arena,* 582, unions could not initiate policy through their membership in the PRI, only influence policy and alter decisions.

84. Camp, *Politics in Mexico,* 2d ed., 140; and Middlebrook, *Paradox of Revolution,* 154.

clearly stood in the upper echelon of the dual labor market, paid higher salaries and supplied superior benefits, compared with those in other sorts of enterprises.[85] In Mexico, workers in state firms linked to the PRI and the CTM were privileged over three other types of labor: those in other, less conciliatory unions;[86] those in the private sector;[87] and non-unionized workers in the informal sector.[88] All these other sets of workers were disadvantaged in regard to pay and perquisites and either neglected or repressed.[89]

In all three countries devices of differing sorts kept the unions from directly serving their own charges. In China after 1957, state domination over labor was achieved via the trade unions, at least for those workers subject to their purview (which meant at a minimum everyone laboring in a state-run or collectively operated urban firm), as the unions acted strictly on behalf of the Party. Still, it is worth noting that enterprise unions fulfilled this charge not through outright repression of workers but by controlling and disbursing their benefits and by mobilizing their activism on behalf of the Party's objectives and campaigns.

French unions, on the other hand, were autonomous from the state, but this also meant isolation from power. In Mexico the bond between the elite elements of the working class and the ruling party was one worth having, but it operated as a different kind of limitation: by the late 1940s, unionized labor, especially that in the CTM and its affiliates, was locked to the regime in a classic case of corporatism. In unwritten terms of attachment, the CTM, as the primary support base of the regime, had an official imprimatur to represent the Mexican working class, and it received a monopoly on this privilege. But its leaders alone—and never any ordinary workers—had access to those holding the reins of power. In return, the ruling party had the power to choose union leaders and to compel them to work on behalf of party goals, no matter what the impact on the workers themselves,

85. Levy, "France: Directing Adjustment," in Scharpf and Schmidt, *Welfare and Work;* James G. Samstad, "The Unanticipated Persistence of Labor Power in Mexico: The Transition to a More Democratic Corporatism," paper presented at the annual meeting of the American Political Science Association, Boston, August 28–September 1, 2002, 5; Judith A. Teichman, *Privatization and Political Change in Mexico* (Pittsburgh: University of Pittsburgh Press, 1995), 50; Camp, *Politics in Mexico,* 2d ed., 139; Middlebrook, *Paradox of Revolution,* 30. Subsidies covered scarce consumer goods and housing.

86. Middlebrook, *Paradox of Revolution,* 71, 73, 77–79, 95, 98, 101, 153; Collier, *Contradictory Alliance,* 14, 27–28.

87. In state-owned firms, the unionization rates were as high as 97 percent, as against just 26 percent across the board as of 1975. Teichman, *Privatization and Political Change,* 48, notes that in the most strategic sectors the state was especially attentive to the workers since it was most dependent on their cooperation. Camp, *Politics in Mexico,* 2d ed., 141, wrote in the mid-1990s that government employees amounted to over a third of all organized workers. See also Samstad, "Unanticipated Persistence."

88. Roberts, "Dynamics of Informal Employment," 107; Levy and Bruhn, *Mexico,* 74–76.

89. Robert R. Kaufman and Alex Segura-Ubiergo, "Globalization, Domestic Politics, and Social Spending in Latin America: A Time-Series Cross-Section Analysis, 1973–97," *WP* 53 (2001), 558; Middlebrook, *Paradox of Revolution,* 18.

a power that became critical in the downturn of the 1980s.[90] Again, when necessary, repression did come into play, particularly for those not within the party's preferred union.

Those with the most privileged status in the labor community in Mexico were the notoriously corrupt union chiefs in the CTM, called *charros,* who were provided with sufficient resources to bribe and, on occasion, to coerce the working class, and who frequently ruled—in accord with regime policy—through patron-client pressures, authorized to weed out any potential opposition.[91] Sometimes union leaders performed as genuine intermediaries, bargaining and negotiating on behalf of their charges, though it was always possible for the oligarchs at the top of the union hierarchy to ignore the demands of their worker constituents in the interest of anchoring securely their own personal liaisons with the PRI and, by extension, the state.[92] In turn, workers had to buckle under the sometimes authoritarian actions and demands of many of these individuals.[93]

Another area of comparability had to do with labor's rights in the three countries. On paper, at any rate, the Mexican working class would appear to have had more legal rights than did those in the other two countries before 1980. In China, of the four state constitutions after 1949, only the very short-lived 1975 one, written in the midst of the 1966–76 Cultural Revolution and superseded by a new document just three years later, decreed that workers held a right to go on strike, among other powers. Later constitutions remained silent on the strike, but a fearsome 1989 Law on Assemblies, Marches, and Demonstrations made any street activity contingent on prior submission of a petition that had to be—and virtually never was—approved by the police.[94] And French unions, as noted above, were without any legal protections at all until 1968.

But in Mexico, Article 123 of the 1917 constitution granted workers an official sanction to hold strikes, form unions, take part in collective bargaining, and enjoy a variety of other social and participatory rights, although the 1931 Labor Law watered these prerogatives down somewhat.[95] In practice, however, the Mexican state arrogated to itself the authority to determine just which unions were permitted to register and also to require that unions seek permission before going

---

90. Stephan Haggard and Robert R. Kaufman, "The Political Economy of Inflation and Stabilization in Middle-Income Countries," in Haggard and Kaufman, *Politics of Economic Adjustment,* 284; Middlebrook, *Paradox of Revolution,* 95; Roxborough, "Organized Labor," 102.

91. Rochlin, *Redefining Mexican "Security,"* 35; Teichman, *Privatization and Political Change,* 29.

92. Roxborough, "Organized Labor," 102; Haggard and Kaufman, "Political Economy," 283.

93. Collier, *Contradictory Alliance,* 34; Middlebrook, *Paradox of Revolution,* 32.

94. The law appeared in *RMRB,* November 1, 1989.

95. Collier, *Contradictory Alliance,* 21–22; and Middlebrook, *Paradox of Revolution,* 41–42, 62–66, 96.

out on strike.[96] In this way, curiously, the government maintained a system for labor in which only a few select unions were at liberty to follow the law.

In the state's relation to labor in the three countries under review, despite variable authoritarian, corporatist, or exclusionary approaches to the working class, there was also a concomitant effort to provide services. And all three governments saw to it up to 1981 that employment rates stayed high. In both China and Mexico, the effort to avoid unemployment in the cities went so far as widespread overstaffing.[97] In welfare policy, again, in all three a reasonable array of benefits existed for a significant, if limited, proportion of the economically active population at the start of the 1980s.[98]

The situation was by far the best in France, and next of all for China's pre-reform state-employed workers, especially if they were on the payroll of a large-scale firm in a critical sector. In Mexico, provision for social security got under way in 1940, a gesture not unrelated to the creation of a new competing, if never power-holding, opposition party at the time: labor raised a demand for welfare just before the 1940 presidential election, during the closing days of the pro-worker rule of President Cárdenas. Bargaining led to legislation that provided welfare insurance to some of the workforce in 1943.

Two decades later, coverage was granted to all federal government employees, again contemporaneously with a presidential election.[99] But generally speaking, up through most of the 1960s, welfare was often sacrificed in the name of economic growth. It was only when the economy had taken off in the late 1960s that the government began to provide more steady investment in social spending.[100] Otherwise, when workers had a specific demand they typically approached their local union bosses in the hope of obtaining patronage, a product of the corporatist model through which the state addressed its workers. It was not until 1977 that the CTM even obtained a budget of its own.[101]

Revolutionary Heritage-cum-State Commitments

Like France and China, Mexico had a heritage of revolutionary promises for the workforce; like them too, its history imparted to the political elite unsettling recollections of unrest and disorder. A famous copper strike that broke out in

---

96. Levy and Bruhn, *Mexico,* 77.

97. Samstad, "Unanticipated Persistence," 5.

98. Kaufman and Segura-Ubiergo, "Globalization, Domestic Politics," 560, state that the proportion provided with benefits by the 1980s was in the range of 50 percent in Mexico.

99. Dion, "Mexico's Welfare Regime," 7–8.

100. Middlebrook, *Paradox of Revolution,* 211, 220.

101. Peter M. Ward, "Social Welfare Policy and Political Opening in Mexico," *Journal of Latin American Studies,* 25, 3 (1993), 623–24.

1905 has been heralded as the initial blow of the 1910 Revolution; it has also been claimed that suppression of workers then under the dictator Porfirio Díaz, whose reign came to a crashing halt with the outbreak of the Revolution, was one of the causes of that famous convulsion.[102] And both the ideals of the Revolution, which included economic redistribution and social justice, and the Constitution that concluded it—with its associational rights for labor—laid down a set of myths that later surrounded the regime and its ruling party and that seemed to augur well for the subordinate classes.[103]

An alliance between worker organs and various political camps began in the revolutionary era from 1910 and 1917 and went on until a coalition was consolidated in 1946. Indeed, the unions exchanged mobilized political support for various political parties over the years in return for some degree of power and perquisites. This persistent feature of Mexican politics amounted to an arrangement that Ruth Berins Collier and David Collier have called "controlled mobilization from above."[104] This ever-tighter mutual reliance came to color the way unions and the PRI interacted in the 1980s and 1990s, as we see later.

But at the same time, a notion that revolution might always crop up again one day intimidated the ruling elite.[105] Indeed, two observers have termed the "most profound historical legacy of the Revolution" to be a "fear of disorder."[106] It was only following the outburst of unprecedented student disruptions in 1968—accompanied by some labor insurgency then and in the following half dozen years—that new reform initiatives for workers got under way in the succeeding decade.[107] One can easily surmise that it was the ferocity of that 1968 confrontation that prompted these later reforms, as it suggested the caution that would be required to keep labor at bay (as in France in the wake of its own spring 1968 disturbances). So here, too, the memory of frightening urban unrest alerted the leadership to a need for significant pro-labor changes in Mexico, and served for another fourteen years to forestall state moves that might anger the workforce.

102. Collier, *Contradictory Alliance,* 78; Collier and Collier, *Shaping the Political Arena,* 77–79, 118.

103. Rochlin, *Redefining Mexican "Security,"* 12; Teichman, *Privatization and Political Change,* 48; Middlebrook, *Paradox of Revolution,* 15; Dietrich Rueschemeyer, Evelyne Huber Stephens, and John D. Stephens, *Capitalist Development and Democracy* (Cambridge: Polity Press, 1992), 199; and Collier, *Contradictory Alliance,* 11, 20.

104. Collier and Collier, *Shaping the Political Arena,* 123, 197.

105. Middlebrook, *Paradox of Revolution,* 154.

106. Coleman and Davis, "Preemptive Reform," 5–6.

107. Haggard and Kaufman, "Political Economy," 284.

Conclusion

I have used broad, overarching concepts to illustrate the ways in which each of the three states operated to contain, and also to coddle, their working classes, at least the upper tiers of these classes, in the years between the 1940s and the early 1980s, in similar versions of a relationship I have labeled the state-labor dyad. All three, I have argued, shared histories marked, first, by protectionism toward domestic industry, which correlatively involved unspoken understandings of exchange with labor; and, second, by weakly organized and/or low-density trade unions operating within state-molded dual labor markets.

Third, and most distinctive, the dyad was distinguished by a distant revolution that both inspired and sometimes invigorated workers, while also lending them a sense of their just deserts, and that at the same time kept the leadership on its guard. I explain variation in the style of the dyad in terms of the differing legacies of the respective revolutions: a liberal revolution allowed a panoply of unions to compete in France; Mexico's corporatist arrangements tethered its chief unions to the ruling party, sometimes in coercive ways; and in China, as in communist states elsewhere, the monopoly of the Party was matched by the single union, a largely impotent body whose job it was to keep the machinery moving and the workers peaceful.

The sketches outlined above suggest that the respective state-labor dyads in the three countries historically fell along a continuum in the degree to which workers were left out of influence. This outcome occurred as they were either linked dependently to the ruling party (whether chiefly through corporatism and co-optation in Mexico, or by controls coupled with privileges in China) or simply excluded, as in France. The major point of dissimilarity grew out of unlike revolutionary legacies. In the late twentieth century that discrepancy expressed itself in the terms according to which unions were intended (or permitted) to engage with the state and with workers: in China, unions were meant to enforce Party policy in such a way as to create an obedient and loyal set of laborers; in France, unions were at liberty to organize as they chose but had no bond with the ruling leadership before 1981; and in Mexico, union chiefs, with their access to the dominant party, could become deputies for workers but might repress them in the interests of that party as well.

I pose this question: If these countries share a largely congruent historical dyad that set up an analogous (though by no means identical) dynamic in the interactions between the three states and their proletariats, and if comparable clashes with the global economy led the countries to pursue decisions that eliminated many of these workers' jobs, how can we best account for the variable levels of protest and welfare provision that emerged in each of them, respectively, by the 1990s? Regime and economic system type accounted for some of the variance. Ultimately more important, however, was a particular disparity in the way unions related to the state and also to the workers for which they were variously responsible. That is, what counted were the terms that the respective states specified (whether implicitly or explicitly) according to which unions were to be attached both to labor and to the government. And, I argue, that set of terms related back to hallowed uprisings decades or even centuries in the past.

3

THE CUL-DE-SAC IN THE ROAD OF THE PAST

Global Forces versus States and Workers

According to the picture drawn in chapter 2, prior to 1980 the state-labor dyad in France, China, and Mexico operated such that the political leadership in them all had harbored labor; the two stood together, more or less against the world, in a sheltered home market. This chapter embellishes that story of parallelisms by pointing to the ways in which the operative terms of attachment in these places positioned the states to undergo similar economic experiences after 1980.

Around that year, once the world economy had shifted fundamentally, critical leadership switches came about in each of the three nations, with more technocratically inclined politicians rising to the surface in response to emergent crises—which really amounted to clashes with new currents propelling the global economy. In France there was a currency crisis, which could also be dubbed a *devaluation* crisis, and in Mexico, a severe *debt* crisis. In China the leadership experienced an insistent sense of predicament over the flaws in the planned economy, which within another fifteen years indeed became an objectively existing crisis, one of mounting state-enterprise *deficits*. The extent to which each was pushed into a corner differed, with Mexico the most confined and China and France arguably having greater degrees of freedom. Among the three, it was only in Mexico and (if to a lesser extent) in France that the difficulties of the 1970s culminated in a specific moment of sheer urgency in the years 1981 and 1982. In the early 1980s, in the face of these crises, the developmental path that top politicians in each place had been traveling for some three decades or even longer appeared to the newly inducted leaders to be no longer appropriate in the environment presented by an altered world economy. So what once had been perceived consensually at home as a passage forward was summarily closed off, and came to be seen as a cul-de-sac. Instead of their long-accustomed inward orientation, these states, now under different leadership, turned outward rather precipitously, and, chronologically, almost all as one. And concomitantly, in each of them it soon became clear that no section of the working class was anymore to be the pet of the polity.

The changes took place just at the historical moment when the Keynesian assumptions and similar, related prescriptions on which these (and many other) countries had relied for decades clashed jarringly and inescapably with the newly changed workings of the international economy. All three of these states had run their economies on the assumption that a domestic manipulation of economic relationships could invigorate the economy and solve employment problems. For Western Europe, this approach was embodied in Keynesian demand management; in Latin America, in import substitution industrialization (ISI). But Keynesian principles—and ISI—had both been conceived originally in terms of a more relatively closed economy, such as the ones in France and Mexico. These two countries had been typical of the regions in which they were located in this regard, in the words of Katrina Burgess, "In Western Europe [labor-backed parties] tended to pursue Keynesian demand management in the context of a mixed-economy welfare state. In Latin America [parties of this type] tended to adopt a demand-driven model of import-substitution industrialization.... Both strategies involved extensive state intervention in the economy."[1]

According to the Keynesian model, governmental demand stimulation could be counted on to produce employment, and so it did in the early postwar decades;[2] ISI had like effects. In both France and Mexico, for example, officials relied on these formulas, using expansionary policies to placate the disgruntled protesters of the late 1960s and hoping to forestall the spread or repetition of such challenges.[3] But beginning in the 1970s, pump-priming programs, which had once seemed a remedy for popular discontents and the threat of job loss, eventuated not in domestic recovery from the shocks but in even worse domestic crises instead as the decade came to a close.

For China the situation was rather different, even if, arguably, it could be modeled as an exaggerated version of what went on in the other two countries. Here the planned economy envisioned and implemented a much more thoroughgoing statist direction than either Keynesianism or ISI prescribed. But some of the most

---

1. Katrina Burgess, "Loyalty Dilemmas and Market Reform: Party-Union Alliances under Stress in Mexico, Spain, and Venezuela," *WP* 52, 1 (October 1999), 109.

2. Michael Ellman, "Eurosclerosis?" in *Unemployment: International Perspectives*, ed. Morley Gunderson, Noah M. Meltz, and Sylvia Ostry (Toronto: University of Toronto Press, 1987), 55–56; Peter Sinclair, *Unemployment: Economic Theory and Evidence* (Oxford: Basil Blackwell, 1987), 9–17.

3. For Mexico, see Kenneth M. Coleman and Charles L. Davis, "Preemptive Reform and the Mexican Working Class," *Latin American Research Review* 18, 1 (1983), 3, 7.

decisive symptoms—economic distress and leadership disenchantment with developmental strategies deployed up to that point—were the same. And at the same historical point, mainly for domestic political reasons of their own, China's leaders elected a course that in functional terms resembled the steps these other two countries were following.

The framework I develop here could be extended beyond my three cases. For in a number of respects each of these cases could serve as a model for the typical state in one of three different regions—Mexico for the corporatist Latin American state, China for the East Asian one (as well as for the standard, actually existing socialist one), and France for the continental, democratic Western European state.

France, for instance, was a case of the generous democratic welfare state model that prevailed in Western Europe in the wake of the Second World War; Mexico represented the classic pre-1990 authoritarian political systems of Latin America, where one party and one strong president often dominated the government and where state capitalism marked the economy; and China, in some ways like South Korea and Taiwan up to the mid-1980s, in others more like the Soviet Union and its satellites, was governed by a one-party state that was politically repressive, where labor was silenced and state-owned economic institutions ran programs of state-led development. By concentrating on states so outwardly different, all of which fell victim to the same dynamic, I am able to underline more emphatically the coming of a course that crossed regime type, party system, economic model, and developmental level, all factors often employed in other studies as independent variables capable of explaining these events.

In this chapter I demonstrate consistencies in how all three abandoned former growth paths at the same point in time. In doing so, I underline the connections between this turning outward and a concomitant loosening of commitments to labor in all three. The chapter emphasizes how for all these countries the modified operation of the global economy by the late 1970s—the drastic reshaping of the world of capital and finance, the rearrangements in monetary conventions and in the handling of currencies and exchange rates, and the shocks in prices, raw material availability, and interest rate levels—jolted congruent old political-economy approaches, causing crises and altering these states' approaches in equivalent ways.

Thus a shared context drove the predicaments of the three, and also confronted these countries with a new set of conditions with which to grapple, once they turned outward, in similar efforts to navigate their problems. I use process tracing to review that pattern and the impasse it produced as the global economy shifted, for its contributions to a shared dependent variable, that is, the macroeconomic choice made by each state's leaders at or soon after the year 1980: to *engage* more deeply at the level of the global market and, at home, to *disengage* workers from the domestic labor market. Stated a bit differently, the politico-economic crisis (or perceived crisis) that each faced had a double root, one part domestic and the other foreign: *internally*, the economic design in place in each for the previous three decades had become incompatible with—and vulnerable to—what had become a changed economy *externally*.[4]

Though the resulting shifts were most explicit and thoroughgoing in China and Mexico, France's new journey was to depart from the past as well, if less sharply. Politically, there were fine points of divergence too in the degree of switch entailed in moving away from long-standing governmental stances sympathetic to labor. Still, as a common pattern, all these governments formed a new political alliance at home (or bolstered an older one), one that undervalued workers while elevating their employers. That move amounted to a change that was the most radical in China, where capitalists had been eliminated (or, better put, "transformed") more than twenty years before; in the other two countries, capitalists had always been courted, but never so exclusively as they would thenceforth be.

Schematically, the big decision to push outward represented a foundational reorientation of these states' positions in two ways: first of all, newly installed state leaders in each country decided to privilege the global market over workers at home. This move overturned decades of relative isolation from external trade and meant abrogating much of the protections for native workers that went with that confinement. And second, leaders opted to favor business (both domestic capitalists and foreign ones) over labor far more than they had in the past in France and Mexico, and for the first time in the post-1949 People's Republic. In what follows I expand this story by explaining how it unfolded in each of these three seemingly such diverse countries.

Mexico

Past Economic Development Pattern: A Strong, Central, Interventionist State

Mexico, like both China and France, was in some significant ways very similar to its regional neighbors, even as it exaggerated some of their traits. Throughout Latin America in the early twentieth century, countries followed an economic model that led to high growth rates but also domestic inequalities.[5] In this area, development

---

4. On the vulnerability of Mexico, see Kaufman, "Economic Orthodoxy and Political Change," 114. For France, see Machin and Wright, "Economic Policy under the Mitterrand Presidency," 4, 8.

5. Rueschemeyer et al., *Capitalist Development and Democracy*, 203.

was state-led and, after the 1930s, grounded in ISI.[6] With other nations in Latin America into the 1980s, Mexican leaders shared an explicit and pronounced historical antagonism toward the philosophy of economic liberalism.[7] And like other nations in its region—if more enthusiastically and in greater amounts—Mexico too turned to borrowing abroad beginning in the 1960s, which resulted in disastrous consequences two decades later.[8]

Under the presidency of Lázaro Cárdenas in the 1930s, the state began its long and largely successful at least until 1982—launch into state-directed and subsidized development.[9] Roderic Ai Camp has termed the role of the state in Mexican economic growth to have been a "decisive, sometimes overpowering" one[10]; the same could have been written of the Chinese or the French state of those years. Stephan Haggard and Robert Kaufman have emphasized the stable, sustained quality of the growth that was fostered in Mexico, which reached an average of at least 6 percent per annum for nearly thirty years. The state was responsible here too, as it was in China and France, for price controls and a consequent long-lasting absence of inflation.[11] And as in China, the state effected a high rate of investment.[12]

But the economy, unlike the Chinese one, was by no means entirely state-owned. Instead, though the state dominated, private capital had a definite role to play in Mexico's mixed private-public economy. Still, Mexico stood out in Latin America in the first half of the 1970s in the percentage of total fixed gross domestic investment undertaken by the state: in public investment in 1973, its 56.8 percent far

---

6. For more on this model, see Atol Kohli, *State-Directed Development: Political Power and Industrialization in the Global Periphery* (New York: Cambridge University Press, 2004).

7. Robert A. Packenham, "Market-Oriented Reforms and National Development in Latin America," in *Market Economics and Political Change: Comparing China and Mexico,* ed. Juan D. Lindau and Timothy Cheek (Lanham, Md.: Rowman & Littlefield, 1998), 59.

8. Rudiger Dornbusch, "The Latin American Debt Problem: Anatomy and Solutions," in *Debt and Democracy in Latin America,* ed. Barbara Stallings and Robert Kaufman (Boulder, Colo.: Westview Press, 1989), 7–8. Murillo, *Labor Unions,* 92–93, notes that Mexico was the earliest among them to fall into serious debt.

9. Meyer, "Mexico," in Lindau and Cheek, *Market Economics,* 4.

10. Camp, *Politics in Mexico,* 2d ed., 59.

11. Stephan Haggard and Robert R. Kaufman, *The Political Economy of Democratic Transitions* (Princeton, N.J.: Princeton University Press, 1995), 283; Heath, "Original Goals," 151; Rochlin, *Redefining Mexican "Security,"* 21; Coleman and Davis, "Preemptive Reform," 6; Castillo, "NAFTA," 28; Fleck and Sorrentino, "Employment and Unemployment," 3; Levy and Bruhn, *Mexico,* 153; and Stallings and Peres, *Growth, Employment, and Equity,* 37. The thirty years spanned the period 1950 to 1980. Haggard and Kaufman point to the years between the mid-1950s and the early 1970s as ones of stabilizing development.

12. According to Kaufman, "Economic Orthodoxy," 112, the state's share of fixed capital investment climbed from just one-third to over half by the early 1980s. See also Rochlin, *Redefining Mexican "Security,"* 21; Coleman and Davis, "Preemptive Reform," 5. Levy and Bruhn, *Mexico,* 151–52, write that the public sector injected more than half of total capital formation in the early years of industrialization and about 40 percent from 1940 to 1970.

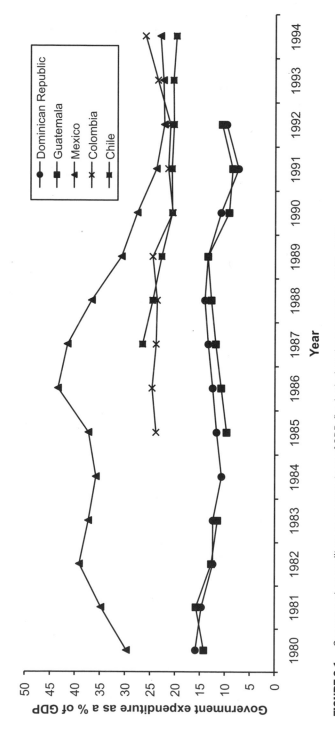

FIGURE 3.1. Government expenditure as a percentage of GDP, five Latin American countries, 1980–1994.

Source: http://www.columbia.edu/cgi-bin/cul/resolve?APQ5915/, Economic Intelligence Unit.

Table 3.1. Public investment for nineteen Latin American countries as a percentage of total fixed gross domestic investment at current prices, selected years, 1960–1977

	1960	1970	1973	1974	1975	1976	1977
Argentina	25.1	37.0	38.6	36.5	40.2	—	—
Bolivia	44.6	55.9	38.1	34.0	42.0	—	—
Brazil	36.4	41.8	46.4	45.1	—	—	—
Colombia	18.6	29.2	31.2	27.9	29.9	25.9	—
Costa Rica	21.2	22.8	28.2	27.5	31.6	35.7	36.5
Chile	41.2	56.9	—	—	—	—	—
Ecuador	47.4	34.2	38.5	42.9	38.2	13.8	38.0
El Salvador	23.4	23.4	27.8	29.2	34.6	30.9	34.3
Guatemala	27.6	18.9	24.5	19.9	20.7	23.4	24.0
Haiti	24.6	21.1	26.9	34.8	57.0	—	—
Honduras	23.6	34.4	27.9	33.0	33.5	34.3	39.2
Mexico	38.2	37.9	56.8	65.9	—	—	—
Nicaragua	23.1	25.3	30.7	29.1	30.8	36.6	42.1
Panama	23.2	26.4	26.6	33.9	49.5	51.7	69.2
Paraguay	24.6	27.1	24.6	17.3	24.4	40.4	31.9
Peru	9.4	23.8	29.3	42.6	35.6	33.2	30.9
Dominican Republic	54.4	30.9	34.4	34.9	42.7	35.7	—
Uruguay	17.6	25.6	25.8	32.2	37.7	—	—
Venezuela	35.2	27.0	35.3	32.4	40.9	40.1	—
Total	30.5	36.8	43.9	45.6	—	—	—

Source: Statistical Yearbook for Latin America (United Nations, 1981), 156.

outdid any other country in Latin America, as did its 65.9 percent in the next year. At each of four junctures for which data are available, its percentage was well above the mean (see Figure 3.1 and Table 3.1).[13]

By the 1980s and into the 1990s, Mexico's degree of what could be termed "statism"—defined loosely as intensive state involvement in the economy, as measured by its investment, expenditure, and revenue—was more outstanding than in other countries in the region: compared with four other nations for which data are available (and whose percentages ranged both above and below Mexico's earlier), Mexico's government expenditure and revenue as a percentage of GDP was high.[14] For instance, in 1987 Chile's expenditure and revenue were 26.7 and 26.6 percent of GDP, respectively; Colombia's were 22.5 and 23.9 percent, and Guatemala's 10.6 and 11.9 percent, while Mexico's stood at 28.1 and 41.5 percent, respectively (see Table 3.2).

---

13. Comisión Económica para América Latina, *Statistical Yearbook for Latin America* ([New York]: United National Publication, 1981), 156. The averages for these years among the twenty countries listed was 30.5 percent in 1960, 43.9 percent in 1973, and 45.6 percent in 1974. See Table 3.1.

14. From http://www.columbia.edu/cgi-bin/cul/resolve?APQ5915/, Economic Intelligence Unit.

Table 3.2. Government revenue and expenditure as a percentage of GDP, five Latin American countries, 1980–1995

		1980	1981	1982	1983	1984	1985	1986	1987	1988	1989	1990	1991	1992	1993	1994	1995
Dominican Republic	R	13.4	12.7	9.5	10.0	10.1	10.4	13.2	13.1	13.9	13.8	11.5	8.2	12.4	—	—	—
	E	15.9	14.7	12.4	12.4	10.7	11.7	12.5	13.4	14.1	13.5	10.9	7.4	9.8	—	—	—
Guatemala	R	9.6	8.7	8.6	8.2	—	7.6	9.2	10.6	11.2	10.1	8.1	9.1	10.3	—	—	—
	E	14.2	15.8	12.7	11.5	—	9.7	10.8	11.9	12.8	13.5	9.3	8.6	10.7	—	—	—
Chile	R	—	—	—	—	—	—	—	26.7	26.6	27.0	23.1	22.5	22.5	22.0	21.4	21.8
	E	—	—	—	—	—	—	—	26.6	24.6	22.8	20.7	20.8	20.4	20.5	19.9	18.7
Colombia	R	—	—	—	—	—	21.0	23.5	22.5	21.8	22.7	20.0	21.7	22.7	23.8	26.2	—
	E	—	—	—	—	—	23.9	24.7	23.9	23.7	24.6	20.6	21.5	21.1	23.6	26.1	—
Mexico	R	24.4	23.6	25.8	30.3	29.7	30.6	30.4	28.1	28.0	26.0	25.4	26.7	26.4	23.1	23.1	—
	E	29.7	34.8	39.1	37.3	35.8	37.7	43.4	41.5	36.7	30.8	27.7	23.9	22.3	22.5	23.1	—

Source: http://www.columbia.edu/cgi-bin/cul/resolve?APQ5915/, Economic Intelligence Unit.

Note: R = revenue; E = expenditure.

Overall, the state was able to act as a sort of fulcrum, balancing the interests of business and labor over time as it saw fit and as differing administrations took disparate stances. For instance, as distinct from the practice in France, Mexican taxes were kept low, a result of the state's conceding to pressure from private business.[15] Although in general, Mexican business approved of the government's strategies, sometimes the two sides disagreed or were in tension and sometimes the state needed actively to court the private sector; the two parties did not act as a coalition engaged in constant joint policy formulation, as was the case in France. Often, however, private capital in Mexico saw its interests served, for the state, intent on fueling the Mexican domestic economy, built up the necessary infrastructure and subsidized the electricity, transport, steel, and cement industries, as well as providing inputs essential to the success of Mexican enterprise.[16]

The Predicament of the Early 1980s

Of the three countries, it was Mexico whose plight as of the early 1980s was most obviously drastic. Two highly detrimental events hit the economy at once: first, national income receipts which in the late 1970s had hinged on international purchases of high-priced Mexican oil—suddenly encountered a precipitous drop in petroleum costs on the world market after 1981. And second, at nearly the same time the United States, battling rampant inflation and needing to attract capital to underwrite its own deficits, abruptly raised its prime rate on loans to 20 percent, indirectly penalizing Mexico, for the main part of Mexico's loans had been tied to this rate.[17]

These two developments wholly deprived the government of the financial wherewithal to run the country. The disaster launched Mexico on a trip into the world beyond for remedies, as the ruling party, the PRI, feared for its own survival.[18] Seen in this light, the regime was confronted with a crisis that was at once both

---

15. Kaufman, "Economic Orthodoxy," 112, 122.

16. Levy and Bruhn, Mexico, 152; Roderic Ai Camp, Politics in Mexico: The Decline of Authoritarianism, 3d ed. (Oxford: Oxford University Press, 1999), 138–40; and Rochlin, Redefining Mexican "Security," 21.

17. Enrique Dussel Peters, "From Export-Oriented to Import-Oriented Industrialization: Changes in Mexico's Manufacturing Sector, 1988–1994," in Neoliberalism Revisited: Economic Restructuring and Mexico's Political Future, ed. Gerardo Otero (Boulder, Colo.: Westview Press, 1996), 64; Heath, "Original Goals," 40. The following paragraphs draw on Kaufman, "Economic Orthodoxy," 114–23; Levy and Bruhn, Mexico, 150–96; and other material as cited.

18. Luis Rubio, "Economic Reform and Political Change in Mexico," in Political and Economic Liberalization in Mexico: At a Critical Juncture? ed. Riordan Roett (Boulder, Colo.: Lynne Reinner, 1993), 36.

economic and political, and that foretold the state's choice to enter SEOs.[19] Maxwell Cameron and Brian Tomlin judge, "The journey toward the North American Free Trade Association (NAFTA) began for Mexico in the punishing recession of 1981–82."[20]

Mexico's 1982 crisis was not entirely as sudden as it appeared superficially to be: the difficulties had begun gradually, as the Mexican version of the import-substitution model ran down and its several-decades-old strategy of "stabilizing development" slowly faltered. The country's achievements under that model were plainly fortuitous for the proletariat, then the most favored sector of the PRI's alliance: while yielding a respectable degree of industrialization and substantial profits, and even attracting considerable—but still constrained—foreign investment, the model also included relatively high-wage, widespread, and stable employment.[21] Indeed, the state was partnered much more with domestic labor than it was with any foreign entity.

But the program of ISI, unfortunately, became increasingly costly with time, for state protectionism of native industry and its workers called for subsidies, ever more state infrastructural investment, and repeated low-cost loans, while producing only scant foreign exchange. With the growing sophistication of the economy, moreover, what foreign exchange did flow into the country was eventually exhausted by mounting demands for foreign technology and materials.

It is possible to trace Mexico's early 1980s troubles not just to structural defects in its economic framework rooted in the ISI model—though those there surely were[22]—but also specifically to a special case of stepped-up state spending in the 1970s. This was the result of outlays in the aftermath of the outpouring of

19. Mexico first entered the General Agreement on Tariffs and Trade (GATT) in 1986. On the general point, see Collier, *Contradictory Alliance*, 80; and Clark W. Reynolds, "Power, Value, and Distribution in the NAFTA," in Roett, *Political and Economic Liberalization*, 73. Luis Rubio judges that by that point economic growth had become for the PRI "a matter of political survival." Rubio, "Economic Reform," 36.

20. Maxwell A. Cameron and Brian W. Tomlin, *The Making of NAFTA: How the Deal Was Done* (Ithaca: Cornell University Press, 2000), 56.

21. A range of scholars have termed the pre-1976 Mexican development path a success, in terms of achieving growth and keeping inflation low. For instance, see Levy and Bruhn, *Mexico*, 154; Meyer, "Mexico," 132, 142; Heath, "Original Goals," 38; Castillo, "NAFTA," 28; Robert R. Kaufman, "Democratic and Authoritarian Responses to the Debt Issue: Argentina, Brazil, Mexico," in *The Politics of International Debt*, ed. Miles Kahler (Ithaca: Cornell University Press, 1986), 197; Lustig, *Mexico*, 17; and Fleck and Sorrentino, "Employment and Unemployment," 4.

22. Teichman, *Privatization and Political Change*, 79, points to, among other things, a chronic balance of payments deficit in the current account—a result of poor export performance due to the economy's fundamental lack of competitiveness in manufacturing and its dependence on imports of many sorts—and a public sector deficit as the state increased its investment in and paid out subsidies to private firms. Each of these flaws can be related to the import substitution developmental strategy that had helped out labor in addition to serving the country well in the preceding decades.

student grievances in the 1968 rebellion.[23] The government's ruthless crushing of that movement provoked an acute downswing in the state's popular acceptance, as well as worries among the political elite that workers could be the next to rise up. Recognition of how that episode had squandered regime legitimacy led Presidents Luis Echeverría Álvarez and José López Portillo (1970 to 1982) to engage in even more extreme programs of expansionary state investment than leaders had committed in the past, in a play to win over disgruntled elements of the public, as well as to shore up support within the laboring class.[24]

Danger unfolded as deficit spending was underwritten at first by ever greater amounts of foreign borrowing, already reaching some $20 billion by 1976. Mounting liabilities finally forced a devaluation of what had become a disastrously shaky peso. The debt also compelled a desperate call on the International Monetary Fund (IMF) for assistance, a request that was answered but with a demand that the Mexicans enforce austerity.[25] What was most vital from the point of view of my story is that the Mexican economy had reached an impasse at which its troubles could no longer be addressed—as they had been in the past—by fiscal stimulation at home, as the funds for pursuing that course were now lacking to the Mexican government. And so the alliance with the proletariat was already shifting, as it became clear that the commands of international organizations were coming to take priority over the pocketbook preferences of the Mexican working class.

Soon thereafter, newly discovered oil reserves—on the basis of which even larger loans were taken out—seemed to Mexican leaders to be capable of absorbing the country's myriad costs during the second half of the 1970s.[26] That solution, however, turned out to be short-lived. Not only were petroleum reserves less plentiful than policymakers had hoped and expected. In addition, the formation of the Organization of Petroleum Exporting Countries and its abrupt hike in oil prices after the 1973 Yom Kippur War plunged the developed world into recession, putting a serious damper on the ability of the industrialized countries to continue importing petroleum on the scale of the past. The outcome was to rob Mexico of a significant portion of its revenue.

---

23. Coleman and Davis, "Preemptive Reform," 3–8.

24. Ibid., 9. By the 1980s, the state was accounting for more than 50 percent of all fixed capital formation. See also Kaufman, "Economic Orthodoxy," 112, and "Democratic and Authoritarian Responses," 199. Echeverria's strategy is also analyzed in Kaufman, "Economic Orthodoxy," 112–14. See also Haggard and Kaufman, Political Economy, 284; Lustig, Mexico, 18; Coleman and Davis, "Preemptive Reform," 3–8. Heath, "Original Goals," 38, notes that by 1971 "concerns about income maldistribution and poverty" convinced the government to become more deeply involved in the economy.

25. Castillo, "NAFTA," 28–29.

26. Haggard and Kaufman, Political Economy, 285, refer to 1978–81 as the years of an "oil boom."

Meanwhile, the resultant inflation in the developed countries drove up the prices of the machinery and other goods that Mexico (and other developing countries) needed to import. As the industrialized part of the world stopped buying its customary quantities of petroleum, a subsequent rapid plunge in the cost of oil threw the Mexican economy entirely off balance. And like the rest of the region, Mexico was struck powerless when—confronting a current account deficit of over US$16 billion and a foreign debt of $100 billion[27]—private foreign lending was cut off, making Mexico wholly unable to finance its outstanding loans.[28]

Mexico was a representative instance—if a precocious one—of the assaults on the Keynesian/ISI model that were suffered throughout the region after 1982. In Mexico, and later elsewhere in Latin America, overvalued exchange rates, used to fight inflation, only spurred trade deficits. Countries in these circumstances all initially attempted to finance their shortfalls by borrowing. But that effort soon became prohibitively costly with the rise in interest rates worldwide in the early 1980s. The same sequence played itself out across the area, climaxing in a punishing regional debt crisis, first to break out in Mexico, followed by an abrupt termination of loans.[29] Thereafter, just as Mexico was a leader in the lending crunch, so it soon stood out for the rapidity and extent of its privatization program in a part of the world where a few years later such schemes became commonplace in the race toward presumed competitiveness and efficiency.[30]

Costs mounted over time for another reason, too. As the peso, pegged to the U.S. dollar for twenty-four years, became steadily more and more overvalued, the country's ability to export was damaged,[31] especially since a decades-long protectionist dearth of intercourse with the outside world had kept Mexican industry less efficient and competitive than it might otherwise have become. As Mexican scholar Lorenzo Meyer sums up the situation, "Trade deficits became unsustainable, and by the second half of the 1970s [neither was] economic development based on a relatively small internal market...viable." For foreign trade deficits had overwhelmed Mexico's monetary system, at once producing inflation and a greatly overvalued currency.[32] Hence, as of the end of the 1970s, Mexico was for a number of reasons both poised to fall victim to a serious national financial disaster and vulnerable to any unexpected jolts from abroad.[33]

---

27. Lustig, *Mexico*, 24. Susan Kaufman Purcell, "Mexico's New Economic Vitality," *CH* 2 (1992), 54, states that the foreign debt stood at $100 billion in the early 1980s.

28. Tardanico, "From Crisis to Restructuring," 15.

29. Dornbusch, "Latin American Debt Problem," 7–9.

30. Teichman, *Privatization and Political Change*, 208.

31. Samstad, "Unanticipated Persistence," 7–9; Meyer, "Mexico," 142; Levy and Bruhn, *Mexico*, 158.

32. Meyer, "Mexico," 132, 142.

33. Lustig, *Mexico*, 14; Haggard and Kaufman, *Political Economy*, 285.

Here we see a perfect conjunction between two paired developments: a domestically engendered economic trauma—produced over time by the grinding to a halt of a once workable growth pattern—coinciding with exogenous shocks. These two parallel developments, though analytically separate, were in practice tightly interconnected, as first and second world nations' ability to thrive industrially had rested on cheap oil, while lenders in these states had bet their dollars on loans to petroleum-rich but capital-poor underdeveloped countries, such as Mexico.

And Mexico, in turn, had staked its final years of high-level state investment on that self-same resource, oil, and on foreign loans. From another angle, Mexico's historical, inward-looking program of development had relied on domestic, Keynesian-style demand stimulation by the state. The demand produced could be more or less satisfied before the late 1970s by native products purchased by domestic consumers who more or less ignored the global market and its players. But after 1980 that formula ceased to apply, given the monumental shifts in the global economy by that point.[34]

Prolongation of the Crisis and the Turn Outward

In 1982 the Mexican government announced its inability to meet the payments on its foreign debts. At that point, Mexico had to cut public spending drastically in order to receive help from the IMF, which, as it had in 1976, again imposed strict budgeting targets. Miguel de la Madrid Hurtado, who ascended to the presidency just as this crisis was breaking, immediately felt compelled to lay off over a fifth of the state workforce within his first few years in office and oversaw the shutting down or selling off of large numbers of money-losing state firms. Thus, quite quickly it became apparent that the state was now turning its face abroad and showing its back to its workers.

Though Mexico's trade balance improved, the situation became tense once again in 1985 when, in time for an election at home, de la Madrid relaxed the tight policies the IMF had instituted, just as another collapse in oil prices occurred.[35] Though the IMF at first halted its loans in response, rendering the country unable to meet its payments, in the next year one more IMF loan was granted, imposing yet further austerity.[36] But even with the state—in response to IMF requests—stepping

---

34. Levy and Bruhn, *Mexico,* 156.

35. Fleck and Sorrentino, "Employment and Unemployment," 5, note that in late 1985 the average price Mexico took for oil dropped by over half. This resulted in a loss of $330 million in foreign exchange in early 1985. Teichman, *Privatization and Political Change,* 83.

36. The orders were for reducing the public deficit, increasing the interest rate, stimulating exports, allowing more flexibility in the exchange rate, and cutting back on tariffs and licenses. See Teichman, *Privatization and Political Change,* 80.

further and further back from its customary stimulation of the economy, it rapidly became evident that yet more funds were going to be necessary.

It was at this moment in the mid-1980s that the government of de la Madrid, in the wake of the refusal of domestic business to accept higher taxes, saw no alternative but to seek foreign exchange in two new ways: through enhanced foreign investment and by increases in export earnings. These dire straits form the context in which Mexico rounded a turning point:[37] its leaders embarked on a major effort at economic restructuring, entailing now not only austerity at home but also transformative trade liberalization and deregulation targeted abroad, in the hope of attracting increased foreign capital.[38] At the same time, Mexico prepared to join the General Agreement on Tariffs and Trade (GATT), which it did in 1986, in the expectation that this would provide entry for its exports into the world market.

At this point the state reoriented its stance in a double sense—in favor of the institutions of the global market for the first time since the Revolution, and for business over labor at home—positions from which it has yet to move in any significant fashion more than two decades later. Here, then, in skeletal form, is the sequence of events that drove Mexico from an import substitution model that relied on an interdependent and mutually relatively trusting alliance between the PRI and its favored segments of the workforce to a fundamentally different program that radically discounted labor.

One other factor played a pivotal role in this saga, one more political and, arguably, volitional. When the economic crisis first surfaced in 1982, the governing elite was divided.[39] The older, traditional section of the PRI, standing for the working class and in league with a set of bureaucracies (such as commerce, industrial development, and others tied to the prior growth strategy), plus businesses whose fate had been linked to policies of import substitution, preferred not to waver from the party's habitual stance of relying on state funds and injections of investment capital to solve economic difficulties. But by the middle of the decade, as the floundering Mexican economy became more and more entangled with the now volatile world market—and as it became apparent that earlier politicians had inadvertently steered the country into a cul-de-sac—the scene was set for a rise in power of politicians who had training, connections, and outlooks geared to the international

37. Ibid., 87, 95; Collier, *Contradictory Alliance*, 78; Cameron and Tomlin, *Making of NAFTA*, 59.

38. See Collier, *Contradictory Alliance*, 88–104. Collier points out that in 1987 tariffs were lowered to about 20 percent on most goods; the percentage of imports that required a license dropped from 75 to 38; subsidies for domestic producers were substantially cut; and price controls were removed on many products.

39. Lustig, *Mexico*, 25–27, and Teichman, *Privatization and Political Change*, 70–89. Also see Judith A. Teichman, *The Politics of Freeing Markets in Latin America: Chile, Argentina and Mexico* (Chapel Hill: University of North Carolina Press, 2001); Sylvia Maxfield, *Governing Capital: International Finance and Mexican Politics* (Ithaca: Cornell University Press, 1990).

economy. These were men who were dedicated to adjustment, restructuring, and free market strategies, and here is where pure political choice came in.

These men were by background more like representatives of international organizations than examples of traditional Mexican politicians. Technically educated, often abroad, they dominated the Ministry of Finance and the central bank, and, in line with the education they had received, prized halting inflation and erasing deficits as their primary goals. The sorry state of the economy provided these specialists with an entrée, and with their new, heightened leverage they insisted on particular policies, supported first by President de la Madrid and then by his successor, Carlos Salinas de Gortari. Their remedies amounted to acceding to that set of rules that foreign banks, investors, and monetary institutions determined could solve Mexico's problems. Their demands for further, severe alterations in the way the domestic economy was to be operated—fashioned in the course of negotiations with the GATT, the IMF, the World Bank, and foreign governments willing to provide loans—meant further hardship for the working class.[40] Here, in the ascendancy of these men, is the lever that pushed the state toward the business end of the old balance between labor and capital.

In the years that followed Mexico's entry into the GATT, the fruits of the early and mid-1980s' efforts at capital acquisition remained insufficient. Wages stagnated and even fell,[41] and servicing the domestic financial deficit still required more foreign exchange than Mexico was able to muster, given its policies at the time. Moreover, foreign debt and inflation were far from being conquered. Nor were a series of corporatist stabilization pacts beginning in 1987—billed as bringing business, the government, and the official unions together (but in reality favoring business much more than labor)—the final answer.[42] While these agreements succeeded in fighting back inflation, the country remained in dire need of foreign exchange. And neither was debt rescheduling, also essential to further recovery, sufficient in itself. For though rescheduling was achieved in 1989 through financial assistance from the IMF and the World Bank—with aid that was tied once more to further restructuring and trade liberalization—difficulties persisted.[43]

Though the de la Madrid presidency attempted to resolve these issues, the root of the problem continued to be the lack of the two kinds of funds that were yet mostly out of reach for the Mexican economy as it neared the end of the decade: direct foreign investment was the first and a receptive market for its exports would

---

40. Teichman, *Privatization and Political Change,* 84–87.

41. According to Kaufman, "Economic Orthodoxy," 117, real wages dropped by about 40 percent during the 1980s.

42. Reynolds, "Power, Value, and Distribution," 79–84; Dussel Peters, "From Export-Oriented," 64ff.; Collier, *Contradictory Alliance,* 264; Sidney Weintraub, "The Economy on the Eve of Free Trade," *CH* 2 (1993), 67–68.

43. Jorge G. Castañeda, "The Clouding Political Horizon," *CH* 2 (1992), 60–61.

be the source of the second.[44] At home, President Salinas began to tackle these issues very explicitly soon after taking office in 1989, initially by extending massively the privatization of state enterprises begun under de la Madrid; then by loosening the 1930s Cárdenas-era limitations on foreign investment, permitting external investors to finance over 49 percent of any venture; and last by opening almost the entire economy to outside capital.[45]

Yet before putting down their money, investors from abroad still required some sign that could bolster their confidence that the Mexican economy was a safe, dependable place for that money, and that it would continue to be so. Relinquishing state ownership in what had been public firms helped, even as that move often also meant implicit and sudden abdication of state protection of labor, thereby sweetening the package for the purchasers, as workers' jobs, wages, and benefits fell by the wayside.[46] Indeed, it was as if the new pact with global business pushed the proletariat out of sight.

As for creating openness for Mexican exports, the second way the leadership hoped to amass some funding, Mexico was looking for a way to drive a chink into the protected American market, at which the bulk of its exports was directed.[47] For throughout the 1980s, as Mexican leaders attempted to reorient their economy, they had persistently found a frustrating obstruction in the stringent application of Section 301 of the U.S. trade law, which often charged Mexico with unfair trade practices.[48] Though Mexico did sign a "Framework of Understanding on Trade and Investment" with the United States in 1987, it did little more than point to areas in which negotiations were needed.[49]

The North American Free Trade Agreement with the United States and Canada was, for Mexico, to be the jackpot that eliminated all these issues. For it was geared at resolving this very set of twin dilemmas, one about exports and the other about foreign investment.[50] As Peter Morici, writing on the eve of the inauguration of NAFTA, explains, Salinas sought free trade primarily to curb unilateral trade actions by the United States—such as quotas on clothing, duties for dumping steel, and the discriminatory use of quality standards for fruits and vegetables—as well as to calm the nerves of foreign investors.[51]

---

44. Purcell, "Mexico's New Economic Vitality," 54.
45. Lustig, *Mexico,* 116; Meyer, "Mexico," 131, 143; Dussel Peters, "From Export-Oriented," 67–69; Teichman, *Privatization and Political Change,* 92.
46. Collier, *Contradictory Alliance,* 256; Camp, *Politics in Mexico,* 3d ed., 231, states that as of the late 1980s state-owned firms employed 79 percent of all workers.
47. Morici, "Grasping the Benefits," 50; Weintraub, "Economy on the Eve," 71–72.
48. Castillo, "NAFTA," 30–36.
49. Cameron and Tomlin, *Making of NAFTA,* 59.
50. Ibid., 226.
51. Morici, "Grasping the Benefits," 50.

Additionally, Salinas hoped to upgrade the country's industry through competition and to push for the efficiency in domestic industry that he was convinced
would ensue only with trade liberalization.[52] To this end, he signed onto a body of
rules aimed at a reciprocal opening of markets throughout the North American
region. It was clear that the assent of the United States to a free-trade agreement
with Mexico was an arrangement that could never have come about without all
the prior outward strides de la Madrid and Salinas had taken—joining the GATT,
restructuring the economy through privatizing and deregulating, and cutting away
impediments to trade and investment.[53] So according to this—perhaps rather
roundabout—logic, letting workers go was linked to joining SEOs and following
their rules, as chapter 4 will detail.

France

Past Economic Development Pattern

As noted above, in certain ways the political economy of postwar France reflected
that prevalent in Western Europe generally. Like the other "advanced capitalist
industrialized democracies," France saw a golden age of speedy growth in the early
postwar decades—in France's case this growth was in the range of 5.5 percent
per annum, on average, over the years 1958 through 1973.[54] In other ways, too,
as in the case of France's social policy, the country's approach to governance was
cut out of the same piece of cloth as its neighbors. The government established
an institutionalized welfare system,[55] in a pattern for the most part powered by
a continental-cum-British style of catering to Keynesian principles of demand
management.[56] As China also did, France experienced full employment or at least

---

52. Heath, "Original Goals," 51.

53. Weintraub, "Economy on the Eve," 71.

54. Gordon and Meunier, *French Challenge*, 16; David Cameron, "Unemployment, Job Creation,
and Economic and Monetary Union," in *Unemployment in the New Europe*, ed. Nancy Bermeo (New
York: Cambridge University Press, 2001), 7, notes that throughout Western Europe in the 1960s and
early 1970s the rates of unemployment remained at the level of 2 to 3 percent of the workforce or
even lower.

55. What China had did not constitute a formal, nationwide welfare system. But for the upper crust
of the urban workforce it amounted to the functional equivalent.

56. Herbert Kitschelt et al., introduction to *Continuity and Change in Contemporary Capitalism*,
ed. Kitschelt et al. (New York: Cambridge University Press, 1998), 1–3; Richard Jackman, "The Impact
of the European Union on Unemployment and Unemployment Policy," in *Beyond the Market: The
EU and National Social Policy*, ed. David Hine and Hussein Kassim (London: Routledge, 1998), 60;
Ivor Roberts and Beverly Springer, *Social Policy in the European Union: Between Harmonization and
National Autonomy* (Boulder, Colo.: Lynne Rienner, 2001), 27; Howell, *Regulating Labor*, 59; Cameron,
"Unemployment," 7.

low unemployment paired with low inflation most of the time from the 1950s through the 1970s. But unlike China, France was a democracy whose leaders had to court votes, and so French wages rose for the first two postwar decades, in part a function of politicians' plays to the voters.

In a few critical regards, though, France deviated from the Western Europe prototypical model, rendering it rather more like Mexico and China. For one thing, its welfare provision was much more centralized and state-led than that in any other Continental country. And overall, as one scholar characterized the country, France appeared as an "outlier" in Western Europe in the extent of its *dirigiste* (or state interventionist) approach to growth and modernization. This management style meant that the government not only set macroeconomic policy but became involved in microeconomic management as well, through a strategy of indirect or "indicative" planning—a form of state guidance that catered to the private sector by rewarding firms with subsidies, credit, favorable tax policy, and the like if they agreed to produce items on the state's list of preferred outputs. Certainly up to the time of its major policy switch in 1983, the government monitored the economy meticulously.[57] Even through the end of the century, the French continued to maintain one of the largest state sectors in Western Europe, and as of 1980—unlike the case in Mexico—its overall tax imposition (at about 40 percent) was one of Europe's highest.[58]

An important comparative quantitative indicator of the dominance of the state in France is its general government current receipts as a percentage of nominal GDP. France's figures for 1970 (38.5 percent), 1979 (45.0 percent), 1982 (50.4 percent), 1984 (52.0 percent), 1989 (49.5 percent), and 1990 (50.4 percent) placed it far above the average for Organization for Economic Cooperation and Development (OECD) countries (which stood at 32.3, 37.4, 41.5, 41.2, 40.0, and 40.7 percent, respectively, in the same years). France's figures were even above the average for European members of the OECD in every one of those years except for 1979 (where the average was 36.9, 45.3, 49.3, 49.6, 47.6, and 48.6 percent, respectively; see Table 3.3).[59]

---

57. Mark Kesselman et al., *European Politics in Transition*, 256.

58. The information in the last two paragraphs comes from Cohen, *Modern Capitalist Planning;* Vivien A. Schmidt, "Values and Discourse in the Politics of Adjustment," in *Welfare and Work in the Open Economy: From Vulnerability to Competitiveness*, vol. 1, ed. Fritz W. Scharpf and Vivien A. Schmidt (Oxford: Oxford University Press, 2000), 269–70, 293; Jonah D. Levy, "France: Directing Adjustment"; Vivien A. Schmidt, *From State to Market? The Transformation of French Business and Government* (New York: Cambridge University Press, 1996), 193; and Gordon and Meunier, *French Challenge*, 8–9, 16.

59. Howard Oxley and John P. Martin, "Controlling Government Spending and Deficits: Trends for the 1980s and Prospects for the 1990s," *OECD Economic Studies* 27 (Autumn 1991), 186.

Table 3.3.   General government outlays[1] as a percentage of GDP, Western OECD countries, 1970–1990 selected years

	1970	1979	1982	1984	1989	1990
Austria[2]	39.2	48.9	50.9	50.8	49.6	48.6
Belgium	42.2	58.1	64.2	62.8	55.5	54.7
Denmark	40.2	53.2	61.2	60.3	58.7	57.5
Finland	30.5	36.7	39.1	39.8	38.2	40.8
France	38.5	45.0	50.4	52.0	49.5	50.4
Germany	38.6	47.7	49.7	48.1	45.4	46.0
Greece	22.4	29.7	37.0	40.2	47.7	50.4
Iceland	30.7	32.8	34.2	32.1	39.8	—
Ireland	39.6	46.8	55.8	54.0	46.6	44.5
Italy	34.2	45.5	47.4	49.3	51.7	53.2
Luxembourg	33.1	52.5	55.8	51.8	—	—
Netherlands	43.9	55.8	61.6	61.0	56.0	56.3
Norway	41.0	50.4	48.3	46.3	54.6	55.1
Portugal	21.6	36.2	43.0	44.4	41.7	—
Spain	22.3	30.5	37.6	39.4	41.8	41.9
Sweden	43.3	60.7	66.3	63.5	60.1	61.5
Switzerland[3]	21.3	29.9	30.1	31.4	29.9	—
United Kingdom	38.8	42.5	46.0	47.2	40.9	42.9
United States	31.7	31.7	36.5	35.8	36.1	37.0
OECD Europe	36.9	45.3	49.3	49.0	47.0	48.0
OECD	32.3	37.4	41.5	41.2	40.0	40.7

Source: OECD National Accounts and OECD Economic Outlook 49. See Table 2 for method, in Howard Oxley and John P. Martin, "Controlling Government Spending and Deficits: Trends for the 1980s and Prospects for the 1990s," *OECD Economic Studies 17* (Autumn 1991): 186.

Note 1: Total outlays consist mainly of current disbursements plus gross capital formation.

Note 2: Fiscal year beginning 1 July.

Note 3: Current disbursements only.

But again differing significantly from the case in China, although the state was deeply involved in the direction that economic growth took in France (and in Mexico), the private sector was by no means eliminated or replaced here (or in Mexico), as it was in China. So the extent of state interference in economic affairs, while considerable in all three, differed among them in the forms it took. In line with the generalized duality of the French economy[60]—a feature it shared with Mexico and China—the state's intervention was in a number of ways discriminatory. In the French case it was often a matter of the government's privileging some sectors over others, furthering its favored *grands projets* of the 1960s or offering special assistance in times of crisis for lagging firms and sectors. At such moments the state utilized the tools it controlled to benefit preferred clients, exempting them from price controls and corporate taxes or extending to them below-market-rate

---

60. Howell, *Regulating Labor*, 109.

credits extracted from its national economic and social development fund, the
Fonds de Développement Économique et Social.[61]

The disbursal of French welfare, too, installed after the war as part of a generalized drive for what was viewed as a "modern" state, was differentiated in degree by
the status of the recipients, favoring the upper classes. Paradoxically, though, despite
the rank-consciousness the system embodied (and, one could surmise, also in reference to the ideals of the French Revolution), Charles de Gaulle, as the first president
of the Fifth Republic, expanded unemployment insurance. Moreover, in what seems
to have been another nod in the direction of revolutionary principles, he based his
welfare program on "universal rights" and the "obligations" of the state.

The Predicament of the Early 1980s

The chief crisis in France after 1980 was not one of indebtedness (as it was in
Mexico) but of being forced to devalue its currency repeatedly—in 1981, 1982,
and 1983—as a result of its membership in the European Monetary System.[62] By
the late 1970s, France, like Mexico, suffered difficulties that were emblematic of, if
worse than, those of the countries in its own region. In France's case, the reference
group was the countries belonging to the Organization for Economic Cooperation
and Development, particularly those in Western Europe.[63]

The commonality was that, for all these industrialized countries, the decade
of the 1970s was a time of dire upsets and new adjustments, as noted above. The
1970s got under way with the United States' abandonment of the Bretton Woods
regime of fixed exchange rates, throwing unexpected havoc into the world of currencies; not long afterward France and its European neighbors fell victim to first
one and then a second sudden oil price hike.[64] But like Mexico, France was not only
typical but distinctive in its region. One clear piece of evidence is that, of eighteen
OECD countries examined in a 1980s study, France had by far the steepest decline
in industrial employment.[65] Moreover, after the mid-1980s unemployment stayed

---

61. On the former, see Suzanne Berger, "Lame Ducks and National Champions: French Industrial Policy in the Fifth Republic," in *The Fifth Republic at Twenty*, ed. William Andrews and Stanley
Hoffmann (Albany: SUNY Press, 1981); for the latter, see Daley, "Steel Crisis," 170–71, 146–80, especially 151–52.

62. Anton Hemerijck and Martin Schludi, "Sequences of Policy Failure and Effective Policy
Responses," in Scharpf and Schmidt, *Welfare and Work*, 1:167, refer to the emergency as a "currency
crisis."

63. Cameron, "Unemployment," 8, 13; Smith, *Left's Dirty Job*, 5.

64. The first bout of serious unemployment hit with the first oil shock in 1974 and the international recession that followed it. Kesselman, "New Shape of French Labour," 168. The second one, in
1979, caused factor prices to shoot upward, cutting the sales of traditional French exports. See Daley,
"Steel Crisis," 170–71; also Cameron, "Unemployment," 7, 11–12.

65. Hemerijck and Schludi, "Sequences of Policy Failure," 168.

high in France while it fell elsewhere within the European Community.[66] These sorts of outcomes suggest a somewhat differential pattern of growth in the past, with a higher measure of state involvement (in welfare and in policies that coddled certain sectors and workers), as compared with others in its region.

France's differences with its Community neighbors grew yet more significant with political shifts. At the start of the 1980s, after his presidential victory in 1981, François Mitterrand briefly attempted to run an economy out of sync with the economic policies of the nation's allies (and major trading partners). As a result, the country quickly found itself confronting difficulties structurally similar—if different in provenance—from those simultaneously being experienced in Mexico. These problems included severe imbalances in foreign trade (for each, the result of purchasing imports for which there was no comparable outflow of marketable exports); a desperate need for foreign exchange (chiefly, here, to acquire the raw materials, especially petroleum, on which the French economy was grounded);[67] firm indebtedness; and double-digit inflation.[68]

As noted earlier, in both France and Mexico, an expansionary period in the 1970s had preceded the crash, in both cases in part an effort to play to the proletariat, and for both governments a bid to stave off further havoc. For in both countries this pandering of the early 1970s occurred in the hope of ameliorating angers stoked by governmental harshness against the 1968 protests.[69] Thus, right up to the onset of economic crisis in France and Mexico, these two states still saw their survival as tied to the support of and partnership with their working classes.

Yet one more important similarity was that in both these countries a turn to politicians with a technocratic bent became central to addressing the difficulties. Though virtually all important politicians in France had attended the National School of Administration (or École Nationale d'Administration, the ENA) before holding office, Chris Howell labels Laurent Fabius in particular, Mitterrand's premier from 1984 to 1986, a "technocrat."[70] In both cases as well, leaders at the time of the crisis had gambled on what were rapidly revealed to be faulty conceptions. In the Mexican case this misunderstanding lay in false hopes for the continuation of high oil prices and for the presence of more petroleum reserves than the country turned out actually to possess. In France the misperception was a view

---

66. Schmidt, *From State to Market?* 141.

67. Smith, *Left's Dirty Job*, 32; Kesselman et al., *European Politics*, 254. Schmidt, *From State to Market?* 95, also mentions the shortage of funds to underwrite social programs and industrial projects, and Machin and Wright, "Economic Policy," 8, speak of "a lack of capital for industry."

68. W. Rand Smith, "International Economy and State Strategies—Recent Work in Comparative Political Economy," *CP* 25, 3 (April 1993), 362.

69. See Kesselman, conclusion to *French Workers' Movement*, 312; and Levy, "France: Directing Adjustment."

70. Howell, *Regulating Labor*, 190.

that it remained possible to power its national economy purely through domestic demand stimulation, along the lines of Keynesian principles. But this was a judgment rooted in the government's failure to grasp the extent to which the French economy had already become interconnected with the world market.[71]

And in both cases a political party with ties to labor, the PRI in Mexico (where labor was the predominant "sector") and the Socialists in France (dependent on the votes of workers) was governing when the crisis broke. Thus in each state at least a portion of the ruling elite maintained a proclivity for the proletariat. Given the presence of such people among the top politicians, in each instance the party stalled at first, split on how to handle the crisis.

For France, as for Mexico, it was an external shock—the 1973 oil price crisis—that first set in train a lengthy series of politicized moves. The first reaction in France was that of President Giscard's premier, Jacques Chirac, who attempted to bring the economy out of its slump through traditional expansionism in 1975.[72] The inflation, mounting unemployment, and trade deficits that resulted prompted Giscard to turn in the next year to the more technocratically minded Raymond Barre, whose tight money policies, higher taxes, cutbacks on subsidies to firms in trouble, and relaxation of trade barriers—harsh though they seemed at the time— were taken even further with the second oil shock, three years later.[73]

The French people generally and the political left in particular, however, had yet to be convinced that such an approach was truly warranted. The Socialist Party under Mitterrand was able to ride into office with the Communists in 1981 on a platform that was to return the nation to more customary state interventionism and redistribution, and—with a bow to the beneficiaries who had helped put them into power, the proletariat—a priority was placed on reducing

---

71. Pierre-Alain Muet, "Economic Management and the International Environment, 1981–1983," in *Economic Policy and Policy-Making under the Mitterrand Presidency, 1981–1984,* edited by Howard Machin and Vincent Wright (London: Frances Pinter, 1985), 94, notes that from 1945 to 1974, economic growth had been highly dependent on strong demand stimulation. On 70 he says that the "about-turn [in economic policy] was partly an outcome of an underestimation of the external constraints within which the French economy has to operate." In the same volume, Machin and Wright, "Economic Policy," 4, state that by 1983 foreign trade dependence was 23 percent of gross domestic product, as compared with just 13 percent three decades earlier, though the figures in Gordon and Meunier, *French Challenge,* 19, are, inexplicably, quite different: they record that the rise was from under 25 percent in the late 1950s to almost 45 percent in 1983. Levy, "France: Directing Adjustment," explains that up until the European Monetary System came into being in 1979, French growth policy was inflationary, dependent on the use of slack monetary and fiscal measures to stimulate the economy, moderated by occasional devaluations for the sake of international competitiveness. See also Boyer, "Wage Labor," 22.

72. Boyer, "Wage Labor," 22–27; Gordon and Meunier, *French Challenge,* 17.

73. Boltho, "Has France Converged on Germany?" 997–98. On Giscard's push for stable prices, see Lloyd Gruber, *Ruling the World: Power Politics and the Rise of Supranational Institutions* (Princeton, N.J.: Princeton, 2000), 177–78.

unemployment.[74] According to David Cameron, this program was stymied from the outset, however, by the numerous problems that the external shocks of the 1970s, along with the coping policies of the Barre team, had bequeathed to the country: inflation, unemployment, recession, trade deficits, and foreign debt.[75] One glaring outcome of this set of strains was that, as of the end of the year 1981, some two million people had already been thrown out of work.[76]

Persevering on his initial path, during the first two years of his presidency Mitterrand kept the thrust of policy pointed toward overcoming the legacy of his predecessors and toward reigniting fast-paced growth, in the habitual French manner.[77] This approach involved return to a package of expansionary measures, including a sudden boost in the level of state direction (*dirigsme*), enhanced welfare benefits (though with a rollback in what employers had to contribute), a higher minimum wage, and nationalizations, which managed to achieve new job creation.[78] The idea behind these procedures—all costly for both the government and employers was to stimulate the flagging economy by resort once more to older tactics of Keynesian-style demand management. This was plainly a bid to those who were at that time still Mitterrand's chief constituencies, labor and the left. The underlying objective remained, as traditional Keynesian philosophy had long dictated, to engineer growth by means of activating domestic demand.[79]

But here familiar strategy ran headlong into a changed external environment.[80] Given France's steadily deepening involvement with European Community trade,[81] Mitterrand's initiative rapidly ran up against a sharp incompatibility with the forces of foreign demand that his country was facing. For where the president was presenting his populace with remuneration and relief, elsewhere in the European

---

74. Gordon and Meunier, *French Challenge,* 17–19; Gruber, *Ruling the World,* 177–78; Bell and Criddle, *French Socialist Party,* 153.

75. Cameron, "From Barre to Balladur," 124–25. See also Machin and Wright, "Economic Policy," 1–2.

76. Boyer, "Wage Labor," 29.

77. Kesselman, conclusion to *French Workers' Movement,* 317; Schmidt, *From State to Market?* 94ff.

78. Kesselman et al. *European Politics,* 254; Scharpf, "Economic Changes," 66; Bell and Criddle, *French Socialist Party,* 154–63; Cameron, "From Barre to Balladur," 129ff.; Machin and Wright, "Economic Policy," 2; Muet, "Economic Management," 71–79; Hemerijck and Schludi, "Sequences of Policy Failure," 167. According to W. Rand Smith, "Unemployment and the Left Coalition in France and Spain," in Bermeo, *Unemployment in the New Europe,* 16, government spending shot up 27 percent in just the one year between 1981 and 1982. See also Schmidt, *From State to Market?* 107–8.

79. Bell and Criddle, *French Socialist Party,* 154–55.

80. K. G. Knight, *Unemployment: An Economic Analysis* (London: Croom Helm, 1987), 361. Cameron, "From Barre to Balladur," offers a superb analysis of how the economic logic behind French choices played themselves out in this period.

81. Cameron, "From Barre to Balladur," 121, states that France's economic dependence on the Community increased more than threefold over the three decades from 1962 to 1992.

Community inflation had already been targeted as the number one enemy. Other countries, accordingly, were cutting real wages, thereby diminishing demand among consumers, even for their own domestic products, not to mention those turned out in France.[82]

And as France's trade partners were individually adopting policies of austerity incompatible with Mitterrand's methods, the rules of membership in the recently created European Monetary System (EMS)—drawn up in 1979 in response to the 1971 collapse of the fixed-exchange-rate Bretton Woods agreement[83]—also worked against what France was attempting. EMS participation permitted a currency to fluctuate only within narrow bands and called for high interest rates to maintain currency stability.[84] The agreement also clearly signaled the subservience of the future exchange rate policy of the remaining members to the conservative German Bundesbank, because of the preeminence of Germany within the Exchange Rate Mechanism. That acquiescence did not bode well for labor, as both the EMS and its ERM required the maintenance of high interest rates within the member countries.[85] One observer, writing in the mid-1990s, proclaimed the ERM the "major constraint on French economic policy."[86] At the same time, the United States initiated a strong dollar policy, which had the effect of keeping interest rates high around the developed world[87]—a tactic that, as we have seen, adversely affected Mexico.

82. Bell and Criddle, *French Socialist Party,* 160.

83. Jacques E. Le Cacheux explains that the EMS was "presented as the first step toward full monetary union." Le Cacheux, "The Franc Fort Strategy and the EMU," in *Remaking the Hexagon: The New France in the New Europe,* ed. Gregory Flynn (Boulder, Colo.: Westview Press, 1995), 70. See also Cameron, "From Barre to Balladur," 117–57; Jackman, "Impact of the European Union," 60–78; Gordon and Meunier, *French Challenge,* 32; and Eric Helleiner, "Sovereignty, Territoriality, and the Globalization of Finance," in *States and Sovereignty in the Global Economy,* ed. David A. Smith, Dorothy J. Solinger, and Steven C. Topik (London: Routledge, 1999), 146.

84. The band was set at ± 2.25 percent for the stronger currencies and ± 6 percent for the weaker ones, and the rates were allowed to float with regard to currencies outside the partnership. See Valerio Lintner, "European Monetary Union: Developments, implications and prospects," in *European Union: Power and Policy-Making,* 2d ed., ed. Jeremy Richardson (London: Routledge, 2001), 326; Philippe C. Schmitter, "The Emerging Europolity and Its Impact upon National Systems of Production," in *Contemporary Capitalism: The Embeddedness of Institutions,* ed. J. Rogers Hollingsworth and Robert Boyer (New York: Cambridge University Press, 1997), 400–402; and Paul Hirst and Grahame Thompson, "Globalization in Question: International Economic Relations and Forms of Public Governance," in Hollingsworth and Boyer, *Contemporary Capitalism,* 343, 349.

85. Germany's economic success, with its pre-1990 low inflation, helped it to serve as the norm-setter within the system. See Smith, *Left's Dirty Job,* 65; Matthias Kaelberer, "Review Article: Ideas, Interests, and Institutions—The Domestic Policies of European Monetary Cooperation," *CP* 35 (October 2002), 105–23 [review of Kathleen R. McNamara, *The Currency of Ideas: Monetary Politics in the European Union* (Ithaca: Cornell University Press, 1998), 109].

86. Le Cacheux, "Franc Fort Strategy," 82.

87. Scharpf, "Economic Changes," 66; Boyer, "Wage Labor," 33; and Cameron, "From Barre to Balladur," 126. Writing of this period, Andrea Boltho puts it this way, "Throughout, the constraints of the

So these external changes meant that as Mitterrand boosted his own economy, raising wages and handing out benefits in the hope of achieving a heightened output, the result was inflation, a widening of the trade gap, and a budget deficit.[88] French products—manufactured in an inflationary environment[89] with an appreciating currency—became too expensive for what were their relevant markets, which were situated now not just in France but also abroad. Making matters even worse, all this took place just as French consumers made use of their newly higher wages to purchase more and more relatively cheap foreign goods.[90] The result was a flood of imports to which—given the macroenvironment with its inhospitable foreign market—French producers were unable to respond through adequate amounts of exports of their own.[91]

The ensuing balance of payments deficit forced successive devaluations along with a June 1982 wage and price freeze that presaged further austerity to come.[92] The process reached its denouement at last—after much indecision and intra-left disagreement[93]—in March 1983. At that juncture, Mitterrand was pressed to decide between complying with the rules of the EMS, which required that France obtain the acquiescence of its other members (especially Germany) were it to revalue its currency, or bailing out of the European project altogether.[94] At that point Germany laid down the condition that France introduce a contractionary policy, to be initiated by a third devaluation. Mitterrand's submission stabilized and strengthened the franc at last, in exchange for which Germany and the other Community members gave France permission to devalue.[95]

Common Market, the EMS and the EMU [European Monetary Union] were essential ingredients in this retreat." Boltho, "Has France Converged on Germany?" 102.

88. Gordon and Meunier, *French Challenge* 18–19. On 19 they state that the budget deficit rose from 0.4 percent of gross domestic product in 1981 to 3 percent in just one year.

89. French inflation during the years 1981–82 shot up to 14 percent as rates dropped in the economies with which France was now paired in the EMS. See Bell and Criddle, *French Socialist Party,* 160.

90. Boyer, "Wage Labor," 33; Machin and Wright, "Economic Policy," 74–83.

91. Cameron, "From Barre to Balladur," 131.

92. Kesselman, conclusion to *French Workers' Movement,* 318; Cameron, "From Barre to Balladur," 132.

93. Smith, "Industrial Crisis and the Left," 18–19, and *Left's Dirty Job,* chap. 3, elaborates on the polarization this decision occasioned, especially within Mitterrand's Socialist Party; see also Wayne Sandholtz and John Zysman, "1992: Recasting the European Bargain," *WP* 42 (October 1989), 111; Cameron, "From Barre to Balladur," 133; Machin and Wright, "Economic Policy," 24–26; and Schmidt, *From State to Market?* 110–11.

94. Sandholtz and Zysman, "1992," 112, make the point that the rules of the EMS demanded that a country withdraw if it were to pursue independent expansionary policies. See also Levy, "France: Directing Adjustment"; Schmidt, *From State to Market?;* and Cameron, "From Barre to Balladur," 128ff.

95. The details of what France carried out at Germany's behest are in Cameron, "From Barre to Balladur," 133–34.

Subsequently, as in Mexico, the official solution in France after the early 1980s entailed, above all, working to enhance national competitiveness and fighting inflation (both of which goals were already in place in the rest of the Community), which replaced high employment as paramount state policy objectives.[96] And the drive for global competitiveness became inexorably connected in the minds of French policymakers, as it also was in Mexico, to attracting capital from abroad.[97] When Mitterrand's original out-of-sync policies failed to jibe with those of his major trading partners and therefore wreaked havoc within the French economy, his choice to reaffirm France's relation to the Community in 1983 amounted to a foundational shift in the country's customary economic policy instruments. France's decades-old planning and industrial policies (both of which had already been weakened considerably by uncertainties in the petroleum market and by new competitors abroad after the mid-1970s) were greatly diminished or in some cases even discarded.[98] Additionally, nearly all the priorities that had been the mainstays of the government's economic work (especially high employment and economic growth) were shunted aside in favor of new Community goals and the rules written to reach them.

These new goals found their expression in France in brand-new domestic economic guidelines, ensconced within an overall austerity program, popularly labeled "rigeur." This program emerged to structure the changed shape of French economic policy and, more specifically, to accord with Community rules. Low inflation (necessary to meet the demands of the ERM, and to realize the hope of beating out France's competitors in the world market by the use of steadier and lower prices)—along with the tight money (i.e., high interest rates) needed to attain it—took on transcendent importance, through a policy that came to be dubbed "competitive disinflation."[99]

Moreover, as Mexican president de la Madrid was to do a few years later, Mitterrand at this stage also encouraged the entry of foreign money into his economy.[100] Here, then, was the turning point, where the needs of the workers were demoted and those of international actors and agencies elevated, as France finally threw off its outlier status within the Community. Thus, the agreement with Germany and France's other Community partners launched Mitterrand and his policy team on a program that resembled the austerity agenda that Mexican president de la Madrid had instated in his country just a year before. The planks in the platform involved

96. Boyer, "Wage Labor," 28–29; Schmidt, *From State to Market?* 133–34; Machin and Wright, "Economic Policy," 3, 26; Kaelberer, "Review Article," 110.

97. Scharpf, "Economic Changes," 108.

98. Boltho, "Has France Converged on Germany?" 102.

99. Schmidt, *From State to Market?* 175–76; Cameron, "From Barre to Balladur," 138, 145; Smith, *Left's Dirty Job,* 66.

100. Machin and Wright, "Economic Policy," 3.

an immediate and drastic cutback on spending. Of necessity, this meant as a corollary quickly displacing some hundreds of thousands of workers from their posts, sending a clear message about the regime's new stance toward labor.[101]

Job loss ballooned not only directly, with the new limits put on spending in the public sector, but also indirectly, with the slower growth that contractionary monetary and fiscal policy were to bring about.[102] And in an approach echoed later on in China, the government's measures to spur productivity and profits called for restructuring at the industrial sector and firm levels, a process that was, along yet another avenue, to entail the discharge of massive numbers of workers.[103] Enforcement of deregulatory policies started at this time as well, deepening the government's 1969 within-Community termination of tariffs—import barriers that once had protected French firms (and, of course, the workers in them).[104] The same steps became the practice in Mexico by 1985 and in China within another few years.

So in France, as in Mexico, the old, more autarchic approach of statism and worker-friendly policies, which had pushed their economies into a cul-de-sac, collided with a new, open ended, liberalized, and more competitive program that was coming to characterize the world economy in the early 1980s. Though France, unlike Mexico, had already inserted its economy into that world through its membership in the European Community, new challenges after 1980 forced French leaders to rethink that participation. When they elected to affirm their membership, the rules to which they had to succumb decisively undercut their proletariat. As Richard Jackman characterized the outcome in 1998: "In 1983, France embarked on the franc fort policy and its unemployment rate has been climbing ever since."[105]

China

Past Economic Development Pattern: A Strong, Central, Interventionist State

China, as a Communist Party–led, self-proclaimed "socialist" state, has usually been compared just with other such states. But it is also reasonable to take a regional approach, pointing to some features it shared with two of its nonsocialist

---

101. Kesselman et al., *European Politics,* 253; Cameron, "From Barre to Balladur," 130–32. Elsewhere Kesselman states that the rate of unemployment nearly doubled in the decade from 1980 to 1990. Additionally, from the early 1980s until the mid- 1990s, one-quarter of industrial jobs disappeared, especially in sunset industries such as metalworking, mining, steel, and printing, which had been mainstays of the French economy. Kesselman, "French Labor Movement," 143, 154.

102. Cameron, "From Barre to Balladur," 144–45, 150.

103. Smith, *Left's Dirty Job,* 213.

104. Kesselman et al., *European Politics,* 256–67.

105. Jackman, "Impact of the European Union," 69.

East Asian neighbors, South Korea and Taiwan, in the period from the 1950s into the 1980s. In all of them, labor activism was suppressed and the state intervened heavily in the economy, in part through its ownership of key assets.[106] Yet China, as an avowed socialist country ruled by a communist party, developed these features to a much more extreme degree than did the other two, and, of course, much more than France or Mexico.

After its victory in the Chinese civil war of the late 1940s, the Communist Party, as the sole political force controlling the country from that time onward—like Taiwan up to 1986 but unlike France, Mexico, or South Korea—never permitted any opposing political groups or parties even to become established. In the absence of rivals, the state, through that Party, was able unflinchingly to rule each separate section of the populace, each geographical district, each work unit, and each agricultural division through a party core group and "mass associations" (women's, youth, or trade union groups), at least through the early 1980s and, for several of these collectivities, into the 1990s, too.

Under Party-state leadership, China's war-torn, disintegrated economy was rapidly resurrected within just three years of takeover in 1949, with most sectors reaching prewar (1937) output levels again by 1952. Then, soon after the revival of healthy growth and the taming of inflation in 1952, a multiple-year series of sometimes violent, always upheaving campaigns was set into motion. In these movements state cadres confiscated whatever land, machinery, materials, and indeed property of any sort that had belonged to private owners, in order to convert it

---

106. For China, see Mark W. Frazier, *The Making of the Chinese Industrial Workplace: State, Revolution, and Labor Management* (New York: Cambridge University Press, 2002); Sheehan, *Chinese Workers;* Walder, *Communist Neo-traditionalism;* and Elizabeth J. Perry, "Labor's Battle for Political Space," in *Urban Spaces in Contemporary China,* ed. Deborah Davis et al., 302–25 (New York: Cambridge University Press, 1995). On Korean labor, see Hagen Koo, *Korean Workers: The Culture and Politics of Class Formation* (Ithaca: Cornell University Press, 2001). Gordon Fairclough and Kim Jung Min, "Labour: The Dangers of Militancy," *FEER* (November 27, 2003), 20, note that in Korea, "until the authoritarian rule of military leaders began to give way to electoral democracy in the late 1980s, employers generally didn't bother to bargain with labour, instead relying on the government and police to use force to break strikes. And since most union activity was illegal, labour was forced to fight for its rights in the streets." Labor's treatment in Taiwan is discussed in Thomas B. Gold, *State and Society in the Taiwan Miracle* (Armonk, N.Y.: M. E. Sharpe, 1986). Good accounts of Korea and Taiwan's economic development can be found in various chapters of *The Political Economy of the New Asian Industrialism,* ed. Fred C. Deyo (Ithaca: Cornell University Press, 1987). See also Alice Amsden, *Asia's Next Giant: South Korea and Late Industrialization* (Oxford: Oxford University Press, 1989); Gold, *State and Society;* Robert C. Wade, *Governing the Economy* (Princeton, N.J.: Princeton University Press, 1990); and Leroy Jones and I. Sakong, *Government, Business and Entrepreneurship in Economic Development: The Korean Case* (Cambridge, Mass.: Harvard University Press, 1980). On China's economic development, see Alexander Eckstein, *China's Economic Revolution* (New York: Cambridge University Press, 1977); Carl Riskin, *China's Political Economy: The Quest for Development since 1949* (Oxford: Oxford University Press, 1987); and Barry Naughton, *Growing Out of the Plan: Chinese Economic Reform, 1978–1993* (New York: Cambridge University Press, 1995).

into state property, thereby bringing the entire economy under the Party's own control and management. This revolution in ownership and in the organization of production also served the purpose of undercutting potential leadership by any persons of means, simultaneously permitting the government single-handedly to determine the disposal of productive assets and the distribution of all profits, goods, and factors of livelihood. In the decades that followed, into the twenty-first century, state-owned firms continued to receive preferential treatment in bank loans, material supply, taxation, investment, wages, and labor benefits.[107]

By the mid-1950s, the state was embarked on a model of rapid industrial growth, averaging just under 10 percent per annum for more than twenty years.[108] The strategy featured a hybrid style of state-led, state-dominated planning that was interspersed repeatedly with campaign-style development. Given the frequent interruptions mandated by the fantastic visions of the impulsive Mao Zedong, the effort was marked by fits and starts, and thus was all too often charged more with energy and purpose than shepherded by careful analysis or stock-taking. By and large, the emphasis was on the fostering of heavy industry—metals, chemicals, petroleum, machinery, and transport infrastructure—while the production of consumer goods, along with light industry in general, was shortchanged in Mao's time.

The Predicament of the Early 1980s

The domestic root of China's economic crisis of 1980 was its socialist planned economy, but in particular it was the wearing down of that economic framework's efficacy after three decades in use. By the late 1970s, this style of development had produced soft budgets for the state firms, thoroughgoing administrative interference at all levels of the system, imbalances among industrial sectors, gross shortages of consumer products, an overemphasis on speed and quantity of output with a concomitant neglect of quality, and as an offshoot of all the other problems, declining productivity.[109]

But despite all these malfunctions, much of the working class benefited from this form of governance. Under socialism, motives of power and ideology interacted

---

107. Preferential treatment for state enterprisees is discussed in Gary H. Jefferson and Thomas G. Rawski, "Unemployment, Underemployment and Employment Policy in China's cities," *MC* 18, 1 (1992): 42–71. See also Walder, "Property Rights and Stratification." A recent treatment is Margaret M. Pearson, "The Business of Governing Business in China: Institutions and Norms of the Emerging Regulation State," *WP* 57 (2005): 296–322.

108. Riskin, *China's Political Economy*, 133–36 and 257–58; and Naughton, *Growing Out of the Plan*, 52.

109. Chinese economic analysts of the time themselves made these criticisms. See Solinger, *From Lathes to Looms*, 51ff.

to keep the ranks of the workforce huge. The planned economy permitted factory managers to plea for (and usually receive) extra investment if they had large numbers of workers on their books; their firms also could rise in status as their payrolls—and, consequently, their level of output—expanded.[110] Having additional hands on call made possible speedy responses to superiors' demands for schedule acceleration or abrupt increases in output quotas. At local levels, state-owned enterprises that soaked up labor were boons to local officials, who were less likely to have to contend with jobless idlers or demonstrators on their streets. In any event, ideologically, one of the chief justifications for socialist Party rule hinged on the regime's ability to keep the maximum possible number of able-bodied adults in jobs in the cities. These factors had left China with a vast surplus of underemployed or "hidden unemployed" people on its payrolls by 1980.

Regime-fashioned demography produced a backlash that compounded the economic troubles. China's enormous working-age population was one more contributor to the dead-end alley into which socialist-era leaders, especially Mao—with his green light for multiple births in the 1950s—had steered the nation, insofar as employment was concerned.[111] The massive numbers of work-seekers who came of age under Mao's aegis only added to problems of job scarcity by the late 1970s. Neither France nor Mexico had to contend with populations of anything near China's proportions: for instance, whereas at the end of the 1990s China was adding about ten million new working-age adults to the labor market per year, in Mexico just one million new jobs were needed per annum.[112]

Once Mao had passed from the scene in September 1976, stock-taking and skillful politicking permitted leaders who had been pushed off the stage in the previous decade to regain it at the end of the 1970s. Their decision was to reassess and reorient the economy, although the degree and the speed of this redirection

---

110. Jefferson and Rawski, "Unemployment, Underemployment," 48. For some figures on the costs of holding surplus workers on the payroll, see Hong Yung Lee, "Xiagang, the Chinese Style of Laying Off Workers," *AS* 40, 6 (2000), 918.

111. Susan Greenhalgh and Edwin A. Winckler, *Governing China's Population: From Leninist to Neoliberal Biopolitics* (Palo Alto, Calif.: Stanford University Press, 2006); Susan Greenhalgh, *Just One Child: Science and Policy in Deng's China* (Berkeley: University of California Press, 2008).

112. For China, see Richard Jackson and Neil Howe, *The Graying of the Middle Kingdom: The Demographics and Economics of Retirement Policy in China* (Washington, D.C.: Center for Strategic and International Studies and the Prudential Foundation, 2004), 9; for Mexico, see John Audley et al., *NAFTA's Promise and Reality: Lessons from Mexico for the Hemisphere* (Washington, D.C.: Carnegie Endowment for International Peace, 2004), 14. Earlier analyses for China are in Lin Lean Lim and Gyorgy Sziraczki, "Employment, Social Security, and Enterprise Reforms in China," in *Changes in China's Labor Market: Implications for the Future*, ed. Gregory K. Schoepfle (Washington, D.C.: U.S. Department of Labor, Bureau of International Labor Affairs, 1996), 46–48; Barry Naughton, "China's Emergence and Prospects as a Trading Nation," *Brookings Papers on Economic Activity* 2 (1996), 281–83; and United Nations Development Program, *China Human Development Report—1999: Transition and the State* (New York: United Nations, 1999), 104.

was a matter of internal dispute within the political elite throughout the 1980s.[113] But all more or less agreed to activate the market and stimulate productivity in response to the ossification and consumer-blindness of the command economy, and this was where the opening to the outside world became important and was intensified.[114]

In China, as in France and Mexico, leadership deliberations brought about the victory of the less ideological, indeed, the less socialist, wing of the ruling party. In Mexico and France that meant the immediate ascendancy of technocratically trained and oriented elites; for China such politicians did not at once emerge at the very top, though criteria for leadership recruitment, placement, and advancement at all administrative levels shifted fundamentally from political to technical ones in the early 1980s.[115]

Prolongation of the Problems

The switch from commands to markets was a prolonged one, begun in 1979. While planning receded progressively, protection for the working class was more resistant to change. Indeed, a grant of genuine autonomy to enterprise managers over the hiring and firing of their workforces was especially slow in coming; in the early 1980s only trials and quite limited powers were authorized (but remained mainly just on paper).[116] Despite several rulings and a new Labor Law in 1995, there was no explicit prodding from the state to throw workers out of overstaffed and inefficient plants until the mid-1990s.[117] Indeed, it was quite the contrary: for years there was instead a directive to retain them no matter what.

A new program of decentralization after 1980 also served to encourage employment. In order to promote profitability, policymakers granted authority over funds, profits, and price-setting to enterprises and lower administrative echelons. This initiative led local leaders to collaborate with firm managers in their districts in constructing projects that could serve local fiscal needs while employing their

---

113. Joseph Fewsmith, *Dilemmas of Reform in China: Political Conflict and Economic Debate* (Armonk, N.Y.: M. E. Sharpe, 1994).

114. The locus classicus for the background and development of the reform is Naughton, *Growing Out of the Plan*, which informs the discussion in the next several paragraphs.

115. Cheng Li, *China's Leaders: The New Generation* (Lanham, Md.: Rowman & Littlefield, 2001); Hong Yong Lee, *From Revolutionary Cadres to Party Technocrats in Socialist China* (Berkeley: University of California Press, 1991).

116. Pat Howard, "Rice Bowls and Job Security: The Urban Contract Labour System," *AJCA* 25 (January 1991), 97–99.

117. Up into the early 1990s, employment in the public sector was in fact still expanding. See Hiroshi Imai, "Special Report: China's Growing Unemployment Problem," *Pacific Business and Industries RIM* (Tokyo) II, 6 (2002), 25.

area's populace.[118] In the process, politicians at the grass roots put people to work whose labor was no more necessary than the often excess output their duplicated projects created. So both time-tested tactics from the days of the plan, along with tricks devised in the course of economic relaxation, led to overstaffed rosters. Thus reforms at first actually added to the workforce.

Nevertheless, marketization gradually undermined the old proletariat. With the liberalization of the economy, rural collectively owned enterprises arose along the coast, in tandem with privately owned firms. Combined with the growing presence of foreign factories, nonstate alternatives emerged to the state-owned enterprises whose operation had run the national economy into a dead end. The bulk of such ventures—operated on a foundation of minimal or no welfare benefits and low-cost labor—outcompeted many state firms, which had been built decades earlier on the principles of planning and a welfare-rich socialism. These new, responsibility-free ventures easily drove many of the state firms into the red.[119] Corruption, made more prevalent by the multiple opportunities for illicit moneymaking that came with closing down the planned economy and the elaboration of market practices, forcefully emerged in that transitional environment. Graft led to the collapse of some untold number of plants, as managers milked them for personal profit.[120] Combined with the pitfalls delivered from the weaknesses of the past economy, all these innovations eventually led to mounting enterprise deficits.[121]

By 1996, a sharp increase had occurred in the number of state-owned firms throughout the country that were losing money,[122] and state industry for the first

---

118. Andrew Wedeman, *From Mao to Market: Rent Seeking, Local Protectionism, and Marketization in China* (New York: Cambridge University Press, 2003); Sheehan, *Chinese Workers,* details the advances in greater managerial authority, especially on 199–224. "Overbuilding" and the "undisciplined investment boom" of the 1980s and early 1990s are described in Thomas G. Rawski, *China: Prospects for Full Employment,* Employment and Training Papers 47 (Geneva: International Labour Office, Employment and Training Department, 1999), 10.

119. Barry Naughton, "Implications of the State Monopoly over Industry and Its Relaxation," *MC* 18, 1 (1992): 14–41.

120. Feng Chen, "Subsistence Crises, Managerial Corruption and Labour Protests in China," *CJ* 44 (July 2000), 41–63; Yan Sun, *Corruption and Market in Contemporary China* (Ithaca: Cornell University Press, 2004); X. L. Ding, "The Informal Asset Stripping of Chinese State Firms," *CJ* 43 (January 2000), 1–28.

121. Jie Chen, *Popular Political Support in Urban China* (Palo Alto, Calif.: Stanford University Press, 2004), 39–40; Wedeman, *From Mao to Market,* 244. Yuk-shing Cheng and Dic Lo, "Research Report: Explaining the Financial Performance of China's Industrial Enterprises; Beyond the Competition-Ownership Controversy," *CQ* 170 (June 2002): 413, state that "almost one quarter of all enterprises suffered from losses by 1997," compared with a mere one-eighth of them seventeen years earlier.

122. Loraine A. West, "The Changing Effects of Economic Reform on Rural and Urban Employment," draft of paper presented at the conference "Unintended Social Consequences of Chinese Economic Reform," Harvard School of Public Health and the Fairbank Center for East Asian Studies, Harvard University, May 23–24, 1997, 6.

time experienced an overall loss.[123] In the succeeding year, more than half of all state enterprises were struggling in the red;[124] these widespread losses became a major impetus behind a state-sponsored retrenching of workers.[125] Not only were the firms themselves in trouble. Even more crucially, since state enterprise taxes were the engine that fueled the finances of the entire central government, there was a serious deterioration in the level of returns that truly worried the leadership. The synchronicity of China's further push into the world market in the late 1990s—accompanied by an intensified promotion of profit-seeking at home—and this crisis of firm-level deficits seems more than coincidental. What appears to have happened is that a lack of capital (and a fear of an even more severe future dearth) motivated a new, much deeper reorientation of the national economy than had taken place before.

The clinching factor appears to have been the Asian financial crisis that erupted in 1997, prodding the Chinese leadership to make a final and wholehearted push for entering the WTO. For with that crisis, Chinese products encountered unfriendly Asian markets, a situation particularly ominous at a time when domestic firms were failing in droves or, at a minimum, piling up deficits. Shedding labor in China was thus a by-product of elites' discernment of impending doom more than it was an immediate crisis. It was a consequence of the same mix that proved critical in France and Mexico: the adoption of globally current business behaviors and beliefs in a place whose prior social-political-economic patterns no longer suited the world market.

Comparisons

Insights from the study of France and Mexico reinforce this reasoning about the contemporaneity of China's dual decisions after 1996, one about labor and the other about finally joining a supranational economic organization. A set of like problems existed in each of these nations in 1980: all three were struggling with firms filled with obsolescent technology, a result of varying levels of import substitution, lack of external competition, and failures to upgrade, all outcomes of prior developmental strategies that had run down. For all, too, the unemployment

---

123. Thomas G. Rawski, "Reforming China's Economy: What Have We Learned?" *CJ* 41 (January 1999), 144.

124. Meng, *Labour Market Reform,* 131. See also Cheng and Lo, "Explaining the Financial Performance," 413.

125. Meng, *Labour Market Reform,* 189, says that in the first half of that year, state industry for the first time experienced an overall loss and, on 131, that in the succeeding year more than half the state enterprises were struggling in the red. Also see Rawski, "Reforming China's Economy," 144.

that surfaced can be attributed to inadequately trained workforces incapable of meeting the kind of demand that had come to exist in the world economy. That undertraining, in turn, was a product of management strategies and state protectionism that had held sway for decades under the previous labor regime in each place, where both of which programs were later viewed as dysfunctional.

On the face of it, China's most decisive leap into the global economy, effectively sealed in its November 1999 bilateral agreement with the United States on entering the WTO[126]—and the almost concomitant dismissal of tens of millions of workers in and after 1997—would seem to be markedly different from the situations in Mexico and France, in at least four ways. In the first place, unlike the other two, in China the leaders quite *voluntarily* elected to join the world market, initially as early as the first years of the 1970s, predating the major moves outward of the others.[127] As Harold Jacobson and Michel Oksenberg have noted, "China's overtures [to the key international economic organizations] followed rather than preceded its basic decision to reorient and restructure its economy."[128]

In France and Mexico, however, the renunciation of the past economic model and the turn to the world market and to supranational organizations were much more *pressed on them from without,* with France delaying because of loyalty to a certain view of the state's charge to labor, and Mexico predating its neighbors because of the more dire situation of its debt—a debt that partly grew as the state spent to please the proletariat. For France, it was the European Economic Community, especially Germany, that applied the pressure; in Mexico, it was international financiers. In China's case, the death of the radical socialist leader Mao Zedong and the rise of the capable and flexible Deng Xiaoping and his cohort—a rise itself made possible by a consensual acknowledgment within top policy councils that economic troubles were legion—*enabled* the shift to come about via internal choices.[129]

---

126. Margaret M. Pearson, "The Case of China's Accession to GATT/WTO," in *The Making of Chinese Foreign and Security Policy in the Era of Reform, 1978–2000,* ed. David M. Lampton (Stanford, Calif.: Stanford University Press, 2001), 337–70.

127. My introductory chapter has referred to the preliminary thrust into the world market after 1971. See Harold K. Jacobson and Michel Oksenberg, *China's Participation in the IMF, the World Bank, and GATT: Toward a Global Economic Order* (Ann Arbor: University of Michigan Press, 1990), which states, "In the 1970s, the path of development [to increase China's level of involvement in the global economy] was largely self-determined" (55).

128. Ibid., 105.

129. The scholar-politician Yu Guangyuan recounts how in 1975, while acting as a senior member of the Political Research Office under the State Council, directed by Deng Xiaoping, he drafted a policy leading to the big shift to economic reform. After August 1977, when Deng was reinstituted after his second purge, Yu served as one of three senior members of the Political Research Office, as a deputy president of the Chinese Academy of Social Sciences, and as a deputy director of the Science and Technology Commission of the State Council. Yu Guangyuan, *Deng Xiaoping Shakes the World,* ed. Ezra F. Vogel and Steven I. Levine (Norwalk, Conn.: EastBridge, 2004), xiv, xvii.

Granted, in China the political elite was subjected to a certain measure of foreign pressure after 1986 when it first applied to join the GATT. And true, that pressure escalated over the fifteen-year period of negotiations, shaping the country's changing policy stance and its macro modus operandi, until China was finally formally admitted into the WTO at the end of 2001. But the persuasion-cum-coercion that started after the application of 1986 occurred a full half dozen years after the Chinese leadership first chose, of its own accord, to move outward decisively; indeed, China first signaled its interest in joining the GATT as early as 1980. Consequently, it is clear that for China external pressure over the management of its own economy had a far lesser part to play in the country's step into the global economy than it did in France and Mexico.[130] China, in other words, had the power to pick its own policy toward the world market relatively free of exterior compulsion, unlike the situation in the other two countries.

Second, the discharges of Chinese working people occurred in a period of rapid, sometimes double-digit growth, not in a time of slowing down or recession, as was the case in France and Mexico.[131] A third difference lay in the style used in cutting the old bond between the state and its working class: neither of the other countries curtailed the security, benefits, and privileges it had afforded its state workers as suddenly or as radically as China did.[132]

And a fourth difference is that in China's case, it is difficult to disentangle that other giant metamorphosis that the country's leaders introduced at the same time as their commercial step abroad. This change was the edging of their economy—if gradually—away from the planning that had ordered its production and business for some three decades and toward the forces and the regimens of the market, writ large. While both France and Mexico had experienced high degrees of governmental management of their economies, and variable but evident amounts of protection for their industries and workers, both had been capitalist, market economies all along. And neither, in the course of its own global intensification, underwent such a total shift of economic developmental model as China did.[133]

But still, these disparities—in the impetus for external deepening, in economic health, in the rapidity and extent of the switch in the nature of the state's link to workers, and in the coexisting marketization of the domestic economy—were

130. On this pressure in the case of China's effort to join the GATT, see Margaret M. Pearson, "China's Integration into the International Trade and Investment Regime," in *China Joins the World: Progress and Prospects*, ed. Elizabeth Economy and Michel Oksenberg (New York: Council on Foreign Relations, 1999), 161–205.

131. United Nations Conference on Trade and Development, *Trade and Development Report, 2002* (New York: United Nations, 2002), 142–43.

132. United Nations Development Program, *China Human Development Report*, 3.

133. On China's economy being largely insulated from the global one before the 1980s, see Pearson, "China's Integration," 168.

paired with several macrolevel likenesses. These structural similarities in prior developmental pattern, in the role of the state in the economy, and in the cul-de-sacs those policies produced around the same time amounted to similar dead ends. And in each case, the leaders then paradoxically turned to the very world economy whose shifts had rendered the old developmental pathways obsolete. And all of them selected supranational economic organizations to guide their agendas in lieu of old and once steadfast liaisons with and loyalties to their workers.

In both France and Mexico, an abrupt and desperate need for capital to rectify serious economic disorder at home—occasioned in their cases by the concurrence of domestic meltdowns and international shocks—left foreign investment and export trading the most viable ways to secure the needed funds. These connections, between cash shortage and the plunges abroad, direct attention to the two key junctures in China's decisions to engage ever more decisively in the world market. One of these moments was in 1979, when the initial enthusiastic turn outward took place, and the second one was twenty years later, when China's chief leaders determined once and for all to enter the WTO.

In the first of these episodes, at the start of 1979, domestic petroleum output peaked just as a serious foreign trade deficit became apparent. These coeval misfortunes only compounded the growing sense among the post-Mao elite that their economy was in danger and required a drastic overhaul. The country's plight then, and its leadership's interpretation of that plight, was the background against which China's new foreign economic policy was initially set.[134] In fact, that early 1979 shift brought to fruition and clinched irreversibly a choice made as early as 1971 by then-premier Zhou Enlai and then–party chairman Mao Zedong: to instigate a major move into the world market.[135]

In the years between 1971 and 1979, especially in the first year or two following Mao's demise in 1976, his immediate successor sponsored a mammoth shopping jaunt abroad for entire foreign plants, coupled with enormous capital construction expenditures.[136] As the funds and resources for financing these schemes rapidly ran down, and as economic problems accordingly intensified, it became necessary— and also possible, given Mao's passing—in the eyes of the new mainstream political elite to promote significant macroeconomic restructuring and an outwardly oriented commercial policy. These events suggest that China's landmark thrust outward into the world market after 1978 was, like France's and Mexico's, driven by domestic financial shortages.

---

134. Jude Howell, *China Opens Its Doors: The Politics of Economic Transition* (Hemel Hempstead, U.K.: Harvester Wheatsheaf, 1993), 50; Lee, *China and Japan.*

135. Jacobson and Oksenberg, *China's Participation,* 50ff.

136. At the end of 1978, Party leader and economic specialist Chen Yun noted that the years 1977–78 had been marked by serious errors. Solinger, *From Lathes to Looms,* 80–82.

This advance abroad was also coupled in China, as it was in France and Mexico, with a sudden introduction of a program of austerity, in which inflation had to be tamed and the state's funds carefully husbanded.[137] And austerity and the new priority placed on fighting inflation (instead of generating employment) was in all three places the first signal that workers and their jobs would stand to lose. These coincidences of timing highlight how turning outward was the outcome of a decision taken in the face of funding crises for all three countries.

The second pivotal point at which China escalated its involvement in the world market was in 1999, when the most powerful actors in the top political elite consensually and unequivocally determined to join the World Trade Organization, again in a period of economic foreboding. The key actors at this point were Communist Party chief and regime president Jiang Zemin and his premier, Zhu Rongji.[138] The backdrop this time was the 1997–99 financial crisis that centered on a number of countries in East and Southeast Asia. Though China itself was not yet fully enough engaged in the world market to sustain substantial losses, foreign investment flattened out and fell (as much of it had come from neighboring affected nations), exports dropped alarmingly (as the purchasers for a great portion of China's goods were in Southeast Asia), and foreign loans became unavailable.[139] Combined with the alarming level of losses in the state firms after the middle of the decade, these setbacks in China's business abroad were sufficient to shift the leadership's outlook.

The Chinese political elite had placed the nation on a course of increasingly substantial linkage with the world economy as early as 1979 and had begun a relationship with, and then formally requested to join, the GATT in 1986. But the course of the application turned out to be tortuous, with the acquiescence of the member states another fifteen years in the making.[140] Inside China's own leadership, too, uncertainties and reversals were evident, especially after 1994, when—largely

---

137. Dorothy J. Solinger, "The 1980 Inflation and the Politics of Price Control in the PRC," in *Policy Implementation in Post-Mao China,* ed. David M. Lampton (Berkeley: University of California Press, 1987), 81–118.

138. On this period, see Joseph Fewsmith, *The Impact of the Kosovo Conflict on China's Political Leaders and Prospects for WTO Accession* (Seattle: National Bureau of Asian Research, 1999), and *China and the WTO: The Politics behind the Agreement* (Seattle: National Bureau of Asian Research, 1999).

139. Nicholas R. Lardy, *Integrating China into the Global Economy* (Washington, D.C.: Brookings Institution Press, 2002), 16, 20; Barry Naughton, "The Chinese Economy through 2005: Domestic Developments and Their Implications for US Interests," in *China's Future: Implications for US Interests; Conference Report,* ed. Library of Congress (Washington, D.C.: Library of Congress, 1999), 54–55. Xiao-Ming Li, "China's Macroeconomic Stabilization Policies Following the Asian Financial Crisis: Success or Failure?" *AS* 40, 6 (2000), 944, notes a sharp decline in foreign demand for Chinese goods and services with this crisis in Asia, manifested in a precipitous drop in net export growth from nearly 23 percent in 1997 to just 8 percent the following year.

140. See three works by Margaret M. Pearson: "China's Integration," 161–205; "China's Accession to GATT/WTO," 337–370; and "The Major Multilateral Economic Institutions Engage China," in

because of Western nations' ongoing disenchantment with China in the wake of the 1989 Tiananmen Square violence—it became clear that China was not going to be admitted to the GATT.

In response, China dropped its eagerness of earlier years and began slow-pedaling in its campaign for admission.[141] But a few years later, as the shocks of the Asian crisis dealt a distinctive downturn in the Chinese economy, the political faction that was in favor of aligning with the global economy beyond East Asia was able to win the day.[142] As Nicholas Lardy has explained, "It seems that the top leadership in the wake of the Asian crisis saw that there was no viable alternative to the globalization of production and that, indeed, China through WTO membership would benefit from greater participation in the trend."[143]

The Chinese data, in turn, help us understand the other two countries better. They point to the potential of economic crises for begetting new leadership with the managerial strengths to diagnose and deal with these dilemmas, regardless of the type of regime, other things being equal.[144] In China's case, Deng Xiaoping after 1980 relied on the reports of study delegations he sent to Eastern European countries, where economic reforms had been pioneered.[145] As soon after his 1977 comeback as was politically possible, he was also quick to reshape the qualifications for political office at all levels, rewarding only those who were educated and prepared for foundational change.[146]

It was not just Mao Zedong's successors who came to the fore perceiving that circumstances dictated a change in course and pushing successfully for it. This same sequence of events took place in France, too, with the 1984 turnover in prime ministers from Pierre Mauroy, an old-line social democrat concerned for

---

Engaging China: The Management of an Emerging Power, ed. Alastair Iain Johnston and Robert S. Ross (London: Routledge, 1999), 207–34.

141. Pearson, "China's Integration."

142. See David M. Lampton, *Same Bed, Different Dreams: Managing U.S.-China Relations, 1999–2000* (Berkeley: University of California Press, 2001), 193–94. Lampton writes, in reference to the drop in foreign investment once the Asian financial crisis started: "Such a loss of investment, of course, would make it only more difficult to keep growth, employment, and the pace of SOE [state-owned enterprise] reform on track. Not all these concerns fully materialized, but they clearly drove Chinese policy…eventually it was this need to keep FDI [foreign direct investment] flowing into the PRC that tipped Beijing in the direction of reaching agreement with Washington on terms of accession to WTO in late 1999, despite the pain of the necessary concessions." See also Lardy, *Integrating China,* 17–20.

143. Lardy, *Integrating China,* 20. Moore, "China and Globalization," 110, observes that some had linked China's bid to enter the WTO with the leaders' concern about then-recent weak growth in foreign investment and exports when they chose to push for admittance.

144. Pearson, "China's Integration," 175, makes much of the nature and inclinations of the pro-reform leadership in place at the time in accounting for China's shifts.

145. Yu, *Deng Xiaoping Shakes the World,* 55–56; Michal Korzec, "Contract Labor, the 'Right to Work' and New Labor Laws in the People's Republic of China," *Comparative Economic Studies* 30, 2 (1988), 140.

146. Lee, *Revolutionary Cadres.*

the working class, to Laurent Fabius, a technocratic modernizer, a man prepared to lead France into the world of "flexibilization" and programs of austerity, even though the president of the country remained the same.[147] Similarly, in Mexico, in the face of crushing economic setbacks in 1981, the "dinosaur" segment of the PRI, comprised of men tied to the proletariat and to programs of protectionism, were made to give way to technically educated politicians who had studied Western economics abroad. Thus, in the 1982 election the PRI put forward for president Miguel de la Madrid, a leader boasting a close connection to the finance bureaucracy and strongly biased toward market reforms.[148]

What is remarkable here is that in all three countries under consideration it was moments of alarm over problems in the domestic economy—essentially problems growing out of the blind alleys into which former developmental patterns and past politicians had led the respective domestic economies—plus in each case capital shortages that were the culmination of those policies, that triggered decisions to join or commit more thoroughly to supranational organizations. Loss of jobs was in each of them a closely paired corollary.

Conclusion

This chapter has shown how old, broad, sociopolitical samenesses in the state-labor dyad were challenged, as politicians in each of the three states—France with its trade-cum-currency devaluation crisis,[149] Mexico with its debt crisis,[150] and China with its frayed and (suddenly then viewed as) fallacious command economy—all nearly concurrently determined that unanticipated capital shortage meant that their only recourse lay in heightened trade and funding from abroad. For each, what presented themselves as defects in their economies in 1980 could instead be characterized more as anachronisms, given the nature of the global economy then, rather than as flaws in an absolute sense. A similar political-economic response in each unfolded, as new leaders in these states determined that their countries' sole way out of their crisis involved reaching beyond their own borders for foreign exchange to fix their home economies.[151] This in turn necessitated rerouting the roads their own markets had followed for decades to connect with exterior ones,

---

147. Chris Howell, *Regulating Labor*, 190.

148. Haggard and Kaufman, *Political Economy*, 287.

149. Levy, "France: Directing Adjustment," refers to a currency crisis sparking the decision to terminate strong-armed state involvement in the economy.

150. Collier, *Contradictory Alliance*, 73, termed the debt crisis beginning in 1982 "the most proximate cause for regime change."

151. Purcell, "Mexico's New Economic Vitality," 54; Castañeda, "Clouding Political Horizon," 61.

through more trade and investment, the more securely and dependably the better.

In each case, too, the political product of these states' economic decisions was consonant one with the next: the state's customary tie to labor was traded in for new or refashioned liaisons within two different relationships. In one of these, bonds with organizations in the global market edged out workers; in the other, business at home came to matter much more to the state than it had done in the past. Thus all three once left-leaning governments after 1980 chose to become players in larger games, leaving behind prior domestic partners for vaster arenas featuring multiple contestants. For each of them, the incentive was the hope of expanding the narrow confines of an economy that had catered largely to domestic demand. The hugeness of the world market beyond seemed to offer that very promise. I go on to explore the outcome of each country's membership in supranational economic organizations.

4

ENTERING SUPRANATIONAL ECONOMIC ORGANIZATIONS
States and Global Forces against Workers

Having looked at the structural factors that produced similar predicaments in China, France, and Mexico—through a clash between new global forces and a tried development pattern—I now carry the story forward. Here I examine the processes involved for each set of politicians as, in a bid to resolve these predicaments, each of them elected to enter supranational economic organizations (SEOs). The three SEOs I consider, the World Trade Organization (the WTO; and its forerunner, the General Agreement on Tariffs and Trade [GATT]); the European Union (EU; and its predecessor, the European Economic Community [EEC]); and the North American Free Trade Association (NAFTA), are bodies of different sorts. Most obviously, the number of members in each varies widely; besides that, the EU entails much more than trade whereas the WTO and NAFTA are principally about commercial behavior. Still, entering each of these bodies imposed regulations written beyond the borders of the new members; moreover, in each case the regulations in force were in the same spirit.

Again, my focus is on similarities. Here, however, I point especially to the common *volitional element* entailed in determining to embark on those processes, the element of deliberate choice. I underline that in picking SEOs and their participants as their principal partners, politicians consciously and for the first time—if with varying degrees of reluctance—acted to jettison the old proletariat. In deciding to line up with SEOs, each set of leaders was committing their country to the constraint of rules whose content was more or less congruent, I argue.

Put precisely, choice was present in two analytically separable senses. First of all, in the face of economic crisis (or perceived economic crisis), leaders in these countries opted to turn outward, and bolstered their initial decision to do so by choosing to join supranational economic organizations. And second, in committing to join, these officials ipso facto agreed to act in accord with statutes devised outside their own borders, regulations whose fallout would mean the fundamental refashioning not just of their states' usual economic practices and institutions, but also of each state's former domestic political alliances. These regulations (along with the philosophy about growth and development that they embody)—and the reactions they set into motion—I contend, were the immediate spur for the shedding of labor in each country. Thus, it was not just analogous past developmental patterns and their eventual disharmony with the world market that drove parallel outcomes; the explicit embrace of similar types of regulations contributed to like consequences as well.

I explore too the ways in which *preparing to enter* these entities—not just adhering to the demands that entry imposed—affected workers' jobs prior to entry, especially in Mexico and China. Indeed, perhaps even more than after entry had been achieved, for Mexico and China the rules possessed the power to coerce conformity as these states struggled to qualify for entry. When new leaders arose, ready and able to undertake fundamental change independently of affected domestic social groups' demands and desires, space was opened for the rules of the SEOs they strove to join to determine the shape of their policy shifts.[1]

In Mexico, the behavior in question was only in part the result of "conditionality," defined by Miles Kahler as "the bargains struck between outside agencies—private creditors, national governments, international financial institutions and national governments";[2] thus he notes that the bargains were not imposed on the country but mediated by technocratic elites in league with international financial institutions.[3] This writing of state economic policy in accord with global expectations occurred as Mexico contrived to connect with the United States in a free trade agreement at the end of the decade, the North American Free Trade Association (NAFTA), just as it had earlier reshaped policy to enter the GATT.

France's predicament being less severe than Mexico's, the 1983 choice to abide by the EMS rules was less the result of what politicians in power perceived as inescapable external pressure than it was a belief among those close to the president

---

1. J. Rogers Hollingsworth and Robert Boyer, "Coordination of Economic Actors and Social Systems of Production," in *Contemporary Capitalism: The Embeddedness of Institutions*, ed. Hollingsworth and Boyer (New York: Cambridge University Press, 1997), 5, 32.

2. Miles Kahler, "External Influence, Conditionality, and the Politics of Adjustment," in *The Politics of Economic Adjustment: International Constraints, Distributive Conflicts, and the State*, ed. Stephan Haggard and Robert R. Kaufman (Princeton, N.J.: Princeton University Press, 1992), 89; Manuel Pastor, *The International Monetary Fund and Latin America* (Boulder, Colo.: Westview Press, 1987), 88–89. Barbara Stallings, "International Influence on Economic Policy: Debt, Stabilization, and Structural Reform," in Haggard and Kaufman, *Politics of Economic Adjustment*, 65–66, refers to this process as "leverage." She sets out the conditions for the effectiveness of leverage on 76–77.

3. Kahler, "External Influence," 126–30. See also Stallings, "International Influence."

that France's best hope for international economic strength, power, and economic success was through the medium of European integration.[4] In China, submission to the rules of first the GATT and then the WTO in advance of being invited to join—but in the hope of and preparation for that membership—is best explained by the notion put forth by Lloyd Gruber of "go-it-alone-power." His meaning was that a country may acquiesce to terms that are not necessarily all in its best interest in order to avoid the risk of being left behind in the global race.[5] Indeed, in the minds of China's leaders, being a part of the WTO was to assist substantially in the fulfillment of their dream of world-class stature for the country.[6]

One might picture the three countries as standing at differing points along a continuum of compulsion: for Mexico, compliance appeared essential to the ongoing economic functioning of the country. In France, following a pattern out of sync with its trading partners threatened continuing economic descent, while conformity seemed to promise heightened clout and vigor. And for China's elite, membership spelled the solution to the nation's century-plus drive for international inclusion and prominence, a venture that, if successful, was sure to boost the regime's legitimacy at home. Nonetheless, despite this variation in degree of the urgency of action, this chapter adds one more plank to my assertion that the three disparate countries underwent generically like processes at contemporaneous points. It also dissects the prompt that SEOs provided to pushing workers out of their posts in each case.

Mexico

Beginning around the middle of the 1980s—as happened a bit later throughout much of Latin America—Mexico profoundly altered its developmental strategy, initiating a program of radical structural adjustment. Compared with most of the other states in the region, though, on the whole Mexico's shift was less the outcome of direct pressure applied by international banks and financial organizations than it was the result of the rise of technically trained, economically liberal leaders and bureaucrats within the country who themselves favored the same approaches as did the lending agencies. True, Mexico acceded to some demands from the International Monetary Fund (IMF) and the World Bank—such as to

---

4. Kitschelt et al., introduction to *Continuity and Change,* 6.

5. Gruber, *Ruling the World,* 47.

6. Moore, "China and Globalization," 113, 127; Naughton, "Chinese Economy through 2005," 60; Pearson, "Major Multilateral Economic Institutions," 226; Joseph Fewsmith, *China since Tiananmen: The Politics of Transition* (New York: Cambridge University Press, 2001), 205.

cut public spending. But its authorities also managed to negotiate down on other orders from outside.[7]

A story can be told that both directly and indirectly draws a chain from Mexico's 1985–86 turning point in trade policy to three separate spates of unemployment that followed in the wake of that decision. The first of these spells was associated with new policies selected and implemented in response to the same mid-decade crisis that pushed Mexican leaders to apply to join the GATT; the next came with measures executed specifically to accord with GATT rules—and with an intensifying drive to prepare to sign a free trade agreement with the United States in the early 1990s. And the third instance appeared in the aftermath of the 1994–95 peso crisis. This crisis itself was connected to Mexico's prior pro-trade liberalization activity, as well as the country's leaders' hopes of pleasing the United States and its businesspeople on the eve of NAFTA. In each of these episodes of sudden unemployment, Mexico's trade behavior was chosen domestically; nonetheless, the pertinent policy was clearly attuned to the rules of trade liberalization being promoted by external bodies, echoing the ethos that lay behind those rules.

Granted, besides Mexico's macroeconomic choices, there were other causes for the loss of jobs in Mexico: for one thing, the numbers of people in the labor force spurted upward from 32.3 million in the early 1990s just before NAFTA was concluded to 40.2 million in 2002;[8] for another, technological progress led to layoffs or reduced job creation during the 1990s.[9] These factors certainly contributed to the substantial plunge in the numbers of manufacturing jobs per applicant that took place between 1988 and 1992, as compared with 1970–81. In the earlier period, the average annual growth rate of jobs had been 3.6 percent, a rate thirteen times higher than that in the later years. Also, while employment grew at a rate of 4.9 percent per year between 1970 and 1981, that rate was more than cut in half during the period 1988–96, when it fell to a mere 2 percent.[10] Another way of delineating this decline is to say that there was a fall in the percentage of the total workforce employed in manufacturing between 1980 and 1989, from 46 down to just 37 percent. Jobs in the state sector also dropped between 1988 and 1993, from 23.3 percent of all jobs down to only 10.8 percent.[11] Between 1988

---

7. In 1986, Mexico received a $1 billion World Bank loan to assist it in increasing its exports and to facilitate its entry into the GATT; the following year the government accepted an aid package from the IMF, the Bank, and fifteen creditor governments that required further privatization. Teichman, *Privatization and Political Change*, 80–86. In its 1986 debt rescheduling with the IMF, Mexico agreed to continue pursuing policies of liberalization on which it was already embarked. Collier, *Contradictory Alliance*, 90–91.

8. John Audley et al., *NAFTA's Promise and Reality*, 14.

9. Stallings and Peres, *Growth, Employment, and Equity*, 197.

10. Dussel Peters, "From Export-Oriented," 80, and *Polarizing Mexico: The Impact of Liberalization Strategy* (Boulder, Colo.: Lynne Rienner, 2000), 162.

11. Oliveira and Garcia, "Socioeconomic Transformation," 213, 214.

and 1992, although one million new jobs were needed per year, 583,000 were created.[12]

Thus not all the fallout can be laid at the feet of the new technological elite and its choices. But the changing nature of the labor market was surely in part a function of the massive transformations that unfolded in the wake of the country's debt crisis of the early 1980s and the new decision makers' mode of dealing with it. The period directly leading up to Mexico's entry into NAFTA, 1990–92, saw just 28 percent of the economically active population finding work in a formal sector job.[13] This was also a period when 100,000 jobs were lost, as some 10 percent of the country's small and medium businesses shut down as a result of President Salinas's aggressive reduction in tariffs, even before NAFTA required that he make these cuts.[14]

But immediately following Mexico's accession to NAFTA in early 1994, the picture for labor became even more grim. During 1994 and 1995, the severe deterioration of the labor market could be blamed mainly on the building peso crisis that erupted at the close of 1994. By the end of 1994, the country had already become home to 2.3 million unemployed in a labor force of 35 million, with another 7 to 8 million estimated to inhabit the underground economy.[15] These two groups, added together, amounted to a startling 26 percent of the labor force that was without any steady employment.

These problems, however, were not solely the result of the peso crisis; they were also the continuation of ongoing trends. According to Jonathan Heath, the number of jobs in manufacturing declined continuously for 70 months between 1990 and 1996, not all at once after 1994.[16] Nonetheless, it has been shown that in 1995 alone, as many as 800,000 positions disappeared.[17] And where officially recorded open unemployment had stood at just 2.6 percent in 1988, it had risen to 3.7 percent by 1994, and then more than doubled, to 7.6 percent, in 1995.[18] In what follows I trace the decisions that contributed to the three consecutive spates of Mexican job loss from 1982 to 1995 (the period during which consecutive Mexican presidents determined to enter and did enter first the GATT and then NAFTA), and I point to how the resultant choices made this contribution.

---

12. Castañeda, "Clouding Political Horizon," 65.

13. Dussel Peters, "From Export-Oriented," 79.

14. Morici, "Grasping the Benefits," 52. Manuel Pastor and Carol Wise, however, state that just 43,000 jobs were lost from 1988 to 1993. Manuel Pastor and Carol Wise, "State Policy, Distribution and Neoliberal Reform in Mexico," *Journal of Latin American Studies* 29, 2 (May 1997), 432.

15. Meyer, "Mexico," 144.

16. Heath, "Original Goals," 54.

17. Oliveira and Garcia, "Socio-Economic Transformation," 212. Camp, *Politics in Mexico,* 2d ed., 219, estimates that as many as one million jobs might have been lost at that time.

18. Dussel Peters, *Polarizing Mexico,* 162.

Mid-decade, the GATT, and the Late 1980s

Mexico's 1986 bid to join the GATT was its second such effort. As I noted in the introductory chapter, the first time around was in 1979, when large stocks of petroleum had recently been uncovered in the country and the price of oil remained high. Overconfidence in the country's ability to subsist on that income alone, plus opposition from some politicians and intellectuals, killed that project.[19]

But in 1985, following the country's second debt crisis in just three years, the scene looked quite different. Oil prices had dipped dangerously to half what they had been; a punishing earthquake had deeply shaken the nation and its economy; the public deficit was threatening to become unmanageable, at more than 15 percent of GDP; high inflation was running amok; lenders were refusing to grant new loans; and Mexico found itself once again unable to pay back what it already had been given.[20] The conjuncture of so many negative phenomena served to rally elite opinion behind a move toward multinational trade collaboration this time around.

Thus the recognition by Mexico's then-current leaders that it would no longer be prudent to rely on petroleum alone for revenue prodded them to turn anew to the GATT. They managed to win admission in mid-1986, an achievement that was characterized as a great turning point for the country. This step by itself constituted a definite signal that protectionism had come to an end for Mexico,[21] as the chief price of entry into GATT was Mexico's promise to slice away trade barriers.[22] The de la Madrid administration's initial step on entry was to intensify its recent drive to substitute tariffs for direct controls (such as quotas and licensing restrictions).[23] The government even surpassed the demands of the GATT, slashing tariff rates down to an average of 10 percent: the maximum tariff as of 1989 was just 20 percent, where GATT rules had simply required that it be below 50 percent.[24]

Over the following years, an era capped by President Carlos Salinas's signing of the NAFTA accord, Mexico pursued a largely one-sided pattern of what could be labeled "preemptive liberalization." Nora Lustig describes the stance of these politicians:

---

19. Lustig, *Mexico,* 130–31; Cameron and Tomlin, *Making of NAFTA,* 58.

20. Teichman, *Privatization and Political Change,* 81; Levy and Bruhn, *Mexico;* and Dussel Peters, "From Export-Oriented," 64, 167.

21. Stallings, "International Influence," 80; Heath, "Original Goals," 44.

22. Levy and Bruhn, *Mexico,* 169, 250. By that time GATT had gone through seven rounds of negotiations, all emphasizing tariff cuts; in 1979, in the Tokyo Round, nontariff trade barriers were also eliminated.

23. Jaime Ros, "Free Trade Area or Common Capital Market? Mexico-U.S. Economic Integration and NAFTA Negotiations," in *Assessments of the North American Free Trade Agreement,* ed. Ambler H. Moss Jr. (Coral Gables, Fla.: North-South Center Press, 1993), 55–56.

24. Teichman, *Privatization and Political Change,* 86–87; Collier, *Contradictory Alliance,* 91; Levy and Bruhn, *Mexico,* 103, 131; Lustig, *Mexico,* 103, 131, 117–18.

"By 1985 [i.e., even before applying for membership in the GATT], Mexico's policy strategy was compatible with the liberalizing principles prevalent in the GATT." The several planks in the two presidents' program were not themselves called for by the GATT, whose rulings centered simply on the elimination of protection in trade. But as de la Madrid and Salinas resolved to reshape the country's total developmental pattern, it was generally understood that the effort was geared to impress its new national partners within the GATT, and especially their businesspeople.[25]

In 1987, the last year of de la Madrid's term, liberalization went forward with a new urgency, once more to the extent of overfulfilling external requirements. This effort entailed removing most trade permits, along with shaving away the average tariff, which had dropped by as much as 14 percent, such that by 1989 the average tariff was a mere 6.2 percent. That year a full 96 percent of Mexico's imports were permitted to enter the country free of quotas altogether, as export promotion schemes were also arranged.[26]

Thus in a number of ways the government undertook unilateral reforms even in the absence of any explicit orders to do so or any reciprocated moves by its trade partners. Mexican leaders' pressing desire to stimulate trade and to have their country be considered an active and respected member within the global trade regime prodded their proactivity.[27] Welcome as Mexico's moves were to its new-found international business allies, the refurbished trade regime, along with the ancillary measures that made up this project—an agenda first of overqualifying for the GATT and later of laying the groundwork for closer commercial collaboration with the United States—augured clear hardship for labor.

Probably the most powerful spur to cutting jobs was the challenge from the imports that flowed in after tariffs were slashed; severe competition for multitudes of domestic firms ensued. Only the most efficient and profitable among them could bear up under the lower pricing occasioned by the changed trade regime.[28] The drive to free up trade only mounted in intensity as Mexico neared its entry date into NAFTA.[29] Combined with a liberalization of credit domestically and an overvalued real exchange rate,[30] tariff reduction pulled in over US$20 billion worth

25. John Gledhill, *Neoliberalism, Transnationalization and Rural Poverty: A Case Study of Michoacan, Mexico* (Boulder, Colo.: Westview Press, 1995), 2; Heath, "Original Goals," 44. Lustig, *Mexico,* 131, notes that Mexico's liberalization far surpassed what was called for in the GATT agreement.

26. Heath, "Original Goals," 44, 52.

27. Gruber, *Ruling the World,* and Cameron and Tomlin, *Making of NAFTA.*

28. Dussel Peters, "From Export-Oriented," 64–65; Middlebrook, *Paradox of Revolution,* 286, 297.

29. By 1989 Mexico's tariffs already averaged 6.2 percent, and a full 96 percent of its imports came into the country free of quotas. Cameron and Tomlin, *Making of NAFTA,* 59.

30. Manuel Pastor and Carol Wise, "NAFTA and the WTO in the Transformation of Mexico's Economic System," in *Mexico's Politics and Society in Transition,* ed. Joseph S. Tulchin and Andrew D. Selee (Boulder, Colo.: Lynne Rienner, 2003), explain that the rate became overvalued as the peso remained pegged to the U.S. dollar while Mexico's inflation climbed above that of the United States.

of goods from the late 1980s to the early 1990s, decimating the native domestic toy and electronic industries, among others, in the process.[31] As the average annual growth rate of imports mounted to 21.3 percent for the years 1988–92, up- and downstream industries were affected as well; naturally, troubles for these sectors affected the jobs of the workers in them.[32]

The resulting current account deficit only served as a strong incentive for the government to find a way to attract even more foreign capital.[33] This effort, in turn, set into motion processes that would eventually mean further danger for the native workforce. Export restrictions were also terminated, along with direct export subsidies, moves that, while facilitating selling abroad, amounted to harsher production conditions for manufacturers. Thousands of smaller firms—where most workers had found employment—were squeezed out, while larger ones combined, profiting from the new situation.[34]

Besides these programs, throughout the 1980s under the rule first of de la Madrid, and then even more fiercely under Salinas into the 1990s, privatization of state firms went forward with a vengeance. By the time Salinas came to power in 1988, the original set of 1,155 publicly owned enterprises was down to just 420. In another four years, Salinas disposed of nearly US$24 billion more of state assets. A mere 150 concerns remained in the hands of the state at the end of the 1990s.[35] As public enterprises were put on the auction block, a decline of state jobs ensued; often working conditions worsened under new management as well.[36]

Another example of revamping the economy that hurt labor was the late 1987 Pact of Economic Solidarity, the first in a string of a dozen such compacts to follow.[37] This pledge, taken by the government in cooperation with Mexican business and pro-government unions, aimed at curbing inflation through commitments to freeze wages and prices. Braking inflation would cut the prices of Mexico's exports, but it would also require high interest rates, which were to result in bankruptcies and dismissals. This arrangement and those like it that came later amounted to granting the government enhanced strength in its mission of more rapid reform.[38] Yet more liberalization of import controls followed, along with the pegging of the peso to the dollar and a further cutback of subsidies, all of which were to decimate

---

31. Rubio, "Economic Reform," 37.

32. Stallings and Peres, *Growth, Employment, and Equity,* 200. Dussel Peters, "From Export-Oriented," 69, gives a rate of 21.3 percent, but on 79 he says it was 22.4 percent. Ros, "Free Trade Area," 61, offers a figure of "over 30 percent" for the period 1987–88.

33. Castañeda, "Clouding Political Horizon," 61–63; Levy and Bruhn, *Mexico,* 172.

34. Gledhill, *Neoliberalism,* 2.

35. Levy and Bruhn, *Mexico,* 167; Pastor and Wise, "State Policy," 428.

36. Dussel Peters, "From Export-Oriented," 64–65; Middlebrook, *Paradox of Revolution,* 286, 297.

37. Ros, "Free Trade Area," 56ff.; Haggard and Kaufman, *Political Economy of Democratic Transitions,* 288–90; Dussel Peters, *Polarizing Mexico,* 65; Pastor and Wise, "NAFTA."

38. Middlebrook, *Paradox of Revolution,* 264.

the labor market in the years just ahead.[39] Another critical element in the shock to the labor market developed with Salinas's pre-NAFTA discontinuation of price supports to agriculture in 1990. Combined with that, his reduction of the tariffs on American agricultural products resulted in the disappearance of much work in farming even before the pact was concluded. As a consequence, a sizable stream of peasants flowed from the small farms, swelling the already expanding urban informal sector, again even prior to NAFTA's coming into existence. The process only accelerated after 1994.[40]

Cutting the deficit, yet one more measure mandated by the larger liberalization project, was in line with the anti-price-support principle of the GATT (whose Article XVI restricts governmental subsidies on products to be traded), as it meant a pullback on government subsidies and other assistance to producers and consumers in need. And simplifying regulations for foreign investment entailed the deterioration of working conditions, as Salinas put to rest the country's highly protectionist foreign trade law of 1973.[41]

In 1989, in a new investment law, the old, once sacred, upper limit of 49 percent for foreign investors was abolished in most sectors, while some industries previously off-limits to foreigners suddenly became eligible for their funding or shareholding.[42] On top of this gesture, the financial liberalization that attended GATT membership for Mexico erased the main checks on capital and foreign exchange trade. The upshot was that capital could move in and out of the country much more smoothly than before, with disastrous consequences soon to follow.[43]

Thus this period from Mexico's signing of the GATT in 1986 to the initialing of the NAFTA accord in 1993 played a double role in Mexico's ongoing process of opening up and liberalizing. On the one hand, the country's leaders were able to impress the outside world with the steadiness and boldness of their liberalization and with their determination to become an active player in the new global economy—and, eventually, an appropriate ally in a future North American pact for free trade. As one analyst expressed this on the eve of Mexico's joining NAFTA, "In key sectors such as petrochemicals, Mexicans have unilaterally implemented NAFTA provisions to catch the attention (and dollars) of investors and to emphasize their enthusiasm for trade liberalization."[44] But on the other hand, the measures these officials adopted had two negative outcomes which they could not have consciously chosen but which flowed from their choices nonetheless: first was

---

39. Lustig, *Mexico*, 155.

40. Pastor and Wise, "State Policy," 441, 444.

41. Meyer, "Mexico," 143.

42. Teichman, *Privatization and Political Change*, 92; Cameron and Tomlin, *Making of NAFTA*, 59.

43. Audley et al., "NAFTA's Promise," 18.

44. George W. Grayson, *The North American Free Trade Agreement*, Headline Series 299 (New York: Foreign Policy Association, 1993), 47.

a peso crisis at the close of President Salinas's term, and second was the resultant huge shock of unemployment just a year after NAFTA was put into effect.

The Early 1990s and the Lead-Up to NAFTA

For NAFTA, even more than for the GATT, Mexico's compliance arrived in advance, presaging—and facilitating—what was to come. Indeed, according to Sidney Weintraub, "the initiative for free trade with the United States would not have been possible had the restructuring of the Mexican economy not taken place" ahead of it.[45] Cameron and Tomlin put it a different way, suggesting that in the forging of the NAFTA agreement Mexican leaders "[gave] away the bargaining chips before entering negotiations."[46] In the several years before the idea of broaching the free trade agreement matured, Mexico entered into several bilateral liberalization accords with the United States, in one of which, in 1985—even before Mexico's accession to the GATT—it agreed to terminate direct export subsidies. In 1987 the two countries signed a "Framework of Understanding on Trade and Investment," setting forth agendas for discussions on grain, steel, textiles, intellectual property rights, and investment. Two years later another sweeping accord between the two appeared, the "Regulations of the Law to Promote Mexican Investment and Regulate Foreign Investment," one of several to materialize that predated the formation of NAFTA.[47]

The concept of a cooperative trade region in North America first took root in the United States in the late 1970s, when Mexico seemed blessed with large, lucrative oil reserves. Into the 1980s, as the EEC coalesced ever more tightly and, later, turned its investment energies to Eastern Europe; and—as characterized by a Mexican scholar—Presidents Reagan and Bush strove to ensure the hegemony of the United States' economic power and the supremacy of its neoliberal ideology throughout its home region, the plan gained further acceptance in Washington.[48] Still, it was President Salinas and not the Americans who proposed the notion of a free-trade bond in early 1990. This was a scheme that President George H. Bush readily seized on as a means of expanding U.S. exports to Mexico.[49] The next year, after the U.S. Congress approved fast-track negotiations, Canada, along with Mexico and the United States, opened formal talks. With the conclusion of the

---

45. Weintraub, "Economy on the Eve," 71.

46. Cameron and Tomlin, *Making of NAFTA*, 60.

47. Lustig, *Mexico*, 117, 132; Kaufman, "Economic Orthodoxy," 116; Pastor and Wise, "NAFTA"; Cameron and Tomlin, *Making of NAFTA*, 59; Ros, "Free Trade Area," 58.

48. Castillo, "NAFTA," 32–35.

49. Cameron and Tomlin, *Making of NAFTA*, 63.

discussions at the end of 1993, the three nations' legislatures ratified the accord, which became effective on January 1, 1994.[50]

So while the United States, as the great power among the three, harbored its own motives for partaking in this partnership, Mexico's dire need of capital,[51] both for modernizing industry and for servicing its external debt, led its leaders to seize what seemed a great opportunity. Salinas and his advisers saw regional commercial integration as a means of providing assurance to potential foreign investors that exports from the country had free passage into the massive U.S. market, while also demonstrating that Mexico's decade of domestic economic stabilization reforms and its more recent trade liberalization were cemented into place. And through the binding mechanism the agreement installed, Salinas also aspired to stave off any remaining resistance at home to his reforms, for the present and into the future.

For this president, the move into NAFTA appeared as a means of fulfilling a "myth" of entry into the First World, a "scramble for inclusion."[52] As described by outside observers, the treaty represented the "peak" or "culmination" of the Mexican reform process, a consolidation and institutionalization of the reforms the country had undertaken to date. At once it both illustrated where Mexico's developmental model had brought the country as of the start of the last decade of the twentieth century and locked the nation into that place securely.[53] An ironic sidelight in view of the unemployment soon to erupt is that one of the publicity tactics Salinas employed to get the deal supported and passed at home was to promise that it would produce new jobs.[54]

Salinas was able almost immediately to capitalize on his decision to combine with his regional partners. The very announcement of the intention to collaborate—leaked just a month after Presidents Salinas and Bush pledged to negotiate—served a critical function: it alerted possible investors, both at home and abroad, that the country's investment climate was about to undergo a fundamental metamorphosis with the immensely greater access that Mexico was to receive to the American market. This implicit promise created a clear impression of reduced risk and led,

---

50. Enrique de la Garza Toledo, "Free Trade and Labor Relations in Mexico," paper presented at the International Labor Standards Conference, Stanford Law School, Stanford, California, May 19–21, 2002, 1.

51. Pastor and Wise, "NAFTA," 5; Cameron and Tomlin, *Making of NAFTA*, 15; Stallings, "International Influence," 82; Dussel Peters, *Polarizing Mexico*, 75.

52. Rochlin, *Redefining Mexican "Security,"* 24 and Gruber, *Ruling the World*, 123, respectively. Cameron and Tomlin, *Making of NAFTA*, 209, make the same points.

53. Toledo, "Free Trade and Labor Relations," 1; Heath, "Original Goals," 58; Collier, *Contradictory Alliance*, 135; Gruber, *Ruling the World*, 124; Lustig, *Mexico*, 1.

54. Rubio, "Economic Reform," 44; Weintraub, "Economy on the Eve," 71; Levy and Bruhn, *Mexico*, 250; Lustig, *Mexico*, 2, 116–17; Cameron and Tomlin, *Making of NAFTA*, 1, 226; Stallings, "International Influence," 82; Jorge G. Castañeda, "NAFTA at 10: A Plus or a Minus?" *CH* 2 (February 2004), 51; Purcell, "Mexico's New Economic Vitality," 58.

as hoped, to an influx of foreign and returning financial capital.[55] By 1994, the year
the accord took effect, a total of more than $90 billion in foreign investment had
made its way into the country just in the years since 1989, the time when the two
presidents accelerated the pace of their talks.[56] This feverish excitement over the
supposed fertility of the Mexican investment environment, however, set the stage
for a collapse that was quick in coming.

The investment that, to use Jorge Castañeda's term, "gushed" into the country[57]
carried with it a string of ominous consequences. These were externalities that
issued inexorably from politicians' preemptive overeagerness to take advantage
of—and to enhance and secure the benefits of—their new engagement overseas.
Mexico's recent financial liberalization, plus the high interest rates on offer for
invested funds, made investing in the country especially easy and alluring for speculative financiers.[58] Some 70 percent of the monies that poured into the country
in the first years of the 1990s were indeed speculative, portfolio, or "hot" money
(bonds, stocks, equities) that could be withdrawn instantly in the event of perceived instability.[59] Much of the capital, too, was the returning "flight" capital of
Mexico's own investors, attracted back home by the privatization of the banks and
the phone company in mid-1990. Neither of these types of funds constituted the
kind of direct investment that could contribute to productive growth.

Simultaneously, Salinas's sense that devaluing the peso would scare away investors and create perceptions that the Mexican market had become unstable led him
to sustain an overvalued peso throughout his presidency when he should not have
done so.[60] He had supported a fixed exchange rate (whereby the nominal exchange
rate for the peso was pegged to the U.S. dollar) between December 1987 and January 1989. But thereafter Salinas chose to depreciate the currency—but just at a
rate of one peso per day. This paltry amount of downgrading was insufficient to
compensate for the gap between internal and external relative prices, and the result
was a highly overvalued exchange rate.

In January 1994, immediately after the NAFTA agreement was implemented,
a series of untoward political events exploded in Mexico, putting a harsh light on
the serious vulnerability of the country's investment climate. Armed rebellion in

55. Reynolds, "Power, Value, and Distribution," 85; Lustig, Mexico, 155.

56. Pastor and Wise, "State Policy," 428; Meyer, "Mexico," 143; Cameron and Tomlin, Making of
NAFTA, 60.

57. Castañeda, "Clouding Political Horizon," 64.

58. Interest rates were raised in the early 1990s in a bid for foreign capital, as well as being part of
the effort to overcome inflation. Rogelio Ramirez de la O., "The Mexican Peso Crisis and Recession of
1994–1995: Preventable Then, Avoidable in the Future?" in The Mexican Peso Crisis: International Perspectives, ed. Riordan Roett (Boulder, Colo.: Lynne Rienner, 1996), 12; Haggard and Kaufman, Political
Economy, 304.

59. Castañeda, "Clouding Political Horizon," 64; Pastor and Wise, "NAFTA," 7–8.

60. Gledhill, Neoliberalism, 5; Cameron and Tomlin, Making of NAFTA, 209.

the poverty-stricken state of Chiapas in January (in part itself a reply to the liberalization policies Salinas was pursuing); the assassination of the PRI's presidential candidate, Luis Donaldo Colosio, in March; and the murder of the PRI's secretary-general, José Francisco Ruiz Massieu, in September were just the sort of shocks that frightened new investors away and induced current ones precipitously to withdraw their capital.[61] These outcomes paved the way for the seemingly sudden peso crisis that cracked the economy apart at the end of 1994, with disastrous repercussions for jobs into 1995.[62]

By the time NAFTA had safely passed the U.S. Congress, the peso had already become obviously and seriously depreciated, with the exchange rate overvalued by as much as 30 percent. That discrepancy, combined with the several political shocks of the year and the ease with which investors could now slide money in and out of the country, produced an extraction of funds that ran into the billions.[63] This denouement appeared to suggest that Salinas and his advisers had tried too hard to draw in capital, damaging their frail economy in the process. The negative implications for employment appeared immediately.

Inauguration of NAFTA and Its Rules

NAFTA was created in order to expand market access for trade and investment among all three of the negotiating parties within the North American market. With this objective, the principals devised an inclusive body of regulations aimed at eliminating barriers to trade of all sorts, at the same time erecting a dispute settlement mechanism to handle any controversies among the partners, plus rules about financial services and intellectual property. On trade, the accord began by demanding the conversion of all nontariff barriers to tariffs and then went on to call for a gradual, mutual reduction of 99 percent of outstanding tariffs over a ten-year period, with the rest to disappear five years later.[64] Meanwhile, import quota amounts were raised and licensing requirements for imports were erased.[65] These were the very sorts of measures that Mexico had been instituting in the years before signing the pact, in the interest of appearing worthy of membership.

---

61. Cameron and Tomlin, *Making of NAFTA*, 211. Manuel Pastor, "Globalization, Sovereignty and Policy Choice: Lessons from the Mexican Peso Crisis," in *States and Sovereignty in the Global Economy*, ed. David A. Smith, Dorothy J. Solinger, and Steven C. Topik (New York: Routledge, 1999), 210–28.

62. Castañeda, "NAFTA at 10," 53; Pastor, "Globalization."

63. Lustig, *Mexico*, 155–56; Dussel Peters, "From Export-Oriented," 68–69. Gledhill, *Nationalism*, 5, estimates that $11 billion exited the country just in the first six months of 1994. See also Castañeda, "NAFTA at 10," 53.

64. Morici, "Grasping the Benefits," 50, lists the types of nontariff barriers that were widely employed in Mexico historically to defend against imports from the United States.

65. Audley et al., *NAFTA's Promise*, 14.

Affected items included agricultural and livestock products and all manufactured goods. Product standards and testing procedures were to be harmonized among the three states, and specific percentages of North American content were required for duty-free importation of car parts. Both price supports and government subsidies (for production as well as for export) were lowered or eliminated, but more so in Mexico than in the United States. For investment, a "national treatment" rule—already honored in the GATT—dictated that each member state treat foreign investors according to the same terms as domestic ones.[66]

Obstacles to free trade in agricultural products had been a source of grievance for American farmers, but the removal of the obstructions was ominous for the two million indigent Mexican producers of fruits and vegetables. In response to Mexican fears, tariffs on corn and beans, particularly sensitive crops in Mexico, were given an extra five-year phase-out adjustment period. Still, overall, within a mere five years of the pact's coming into force, Mexican tariffs on American goods—which had averaged 10 percent on its eve—dropped to a mere 2 percent.[67] Petrochemical production, previously sacrosanct to Mexicans, opened to outside investment, and cars and their parts from the United States, in the past virtually banned in Mexico, could now be shipped there.

Not surprisingly, an immediate effect of the treaty was a new spate of unemployment in Mexico, even before the peso crisis. Heightened competition washed out smaller firms, which, in turn, meant the liquidation of the jobs they had supplied.[68] Enhanced trading brought in foreign technology, leading to technical progress that caused layoffs in labor-intensive plants. Other firms, under pressure to upgrade, tended to substitute imported for national inputs, thereby undermining primary products and parts made at home. Commercial agriculture and manufacturers in the formal sector invested in modern equipment, forcing the disappearance of manual labor.[69] So via a number of different avenues, workers in many separate sectors found themselves suddenly out of work.

NAFTA stipulated that each country was to specialize in the crops in which it had a competitive advantage. Soon, however, Mexico registered a growing trade deficit in agricultural products with the United States. Since the United States continued subsidizing the products it shipped to Mexico, some commodities that were critical to the Mexican economy—such as corn, grain, and oilseeds—saw their prices drop off at home. This downslide continued over time, such that by

---

66. Morici, "Grasping the Benefits," 50–52; Heath, "Original Goals," 52; Dussel Peters, "From Export-Oriented," 68; Gruber, *Ruling the World*, 146–48, 152; Cameron and Tomlin, *Making of NAFTA*, 34–50; Grayson, *North American Free Trade Agreement*.

67. Levy and Bruhn, *Mexico*, 251, 253.

68. Pastor and Wise, "NAFTA."

69. Stallings and Peres, *Growth, Employment*, 197–201.

2003 Mexico had carried a net deficit in agricultural goods with the United States every year except for the peso crisis year of 1995, when American goods were too expensive for Mexican buyers. Farmers in droves were forced to give up their land and their occupation.[70]

Unlike in agriculture and much of manufacturing, jobs in the low-skill, low-pay, insecure maquiladora sector did increase with NAFTA. By the end of the 1990s, about a million workers, or one-quarter of the workforce, were employed in these export-assembly operations, which put together car parts, electrical and electronic products, and garments.[71] Some caveats must be noted, however: first, over the course of the 1990s, about 30 percent of the new jobs in that sector were later wiped away.[72] And second, those who were able to remain in these jobs, much like those who took up spots on the sidewalks, became participants in the ballooning informal sector, where salaries are substandard, working conditions often hazardous, tenure unstable, and benefits nonexistent. In the words of Dussel Peters, "liberalization" led to "the vast exclusion of the population from…the formal economy." Put otherwise, tiny microenterprises and second-rate jobs along the border became the main providers of new employment.[73] According to one study, informal employment accounted for almost half of all jobs held as of the 1995 peso crisis and during the ensuing economic austerity program designed to alleviate that crisis.[74]

True, the full effects on employment of the first decade of NAFTA's operation cannot really be assessed independently of the fallout of the 1994–95 peso crisis. At the same time, it is difficult to disentangle that crisis entirely from the move to join NAFTA, especially from the period immediately preceding Mexico's entry. For the peso crisis was in large part a function of the rapid inflow and subsequent outflow of capital in the early 1990s—a set of surges induced by Mexico's financial liberalization, by state-set elevated interest rates (at a time when world rates were low), and, of course, by the promise of NAFTA. The crisis was by no means directly caused by NAFTA. Nonetheless, its occurrence cannot be understood in isolation from the behaviors encouraged by NAFTA's imminent enactment or from the

70. Sandra Polaski, "Jobs, Wages, and Household Income," in Audley et al., NAFTA's Promise, 17.

71. The apparel trade was initially stimulated by NAFTA's tariff cuts, but with the phasing out of the special tariff and tax advantages enjoyed by this sector, the gains began to slip away by the end of the 1990s. Plants in this trade added about 800,000 jobs between January 1, 1994, and the sector's peak year of 2001, but they then lost about 250,000 jobs within another two years. Thus, as of mid-2003, about 550,000 more people were employed in that sector than before NAFTA was put into place. But by then China had entered the WTO and became a formidable competitor in apparel manufacturing. Polaski, "Jobs, Wages, and Household Income," 15.

72. Stallings and Peres, Growth, Employment, 197; Toledo, "Free Trade and Labor Relations," 12; Pastor and Wise, "State Policy," 433; Castañeda, "NAFTA at 10," 53; Pastor and Wise, "NAFTA."

73. Stallings and Peres, Growth, Employment, 197–201; Dussel Peters, Polarizing Mexico, 166.

74. Audley et al., NAFTA's Promise, 24.

actions that Mexico's political elite adopted in anticipation of the realization of the accord. The sudden bankruptcy of thousands of firms—along with the layoffs of their workers—resulted from the peso's collapse and the IMF-decreed economic contraction pursuant to it.[75] It seems that the story is all of a piece.

Thus, from the debt crisis of 1981–82 to the peso crisis of 1994–95, Mexico's spates of trade liberalization—first leading up to joining the GATT and then oriented toward entering NAFTA, as well as in the immediate aftermath of both accessions—were either directly or indirectly linked to Mexican workers' loss of jobs. In particular, these losses were connected to liberalization by the leadership's choice to observe SEO regulations. For in both instances Mexican politicians were either made to or chose to sign on to policies whose attendant rules bore negative implications for manual labor.

France

Unlike the case in either Mexico or China, France's sudden spurts of unemployment, in the early 1980s and again in the early and mid-1990s, initially appeared with President Mitterrand's surrender, if a hesitating and somewhat reluctant one, to externally imposed rules, and not because of any preemptive play on his part. Despite his initial lack of enthusiasm, however, by the time the decision was taken, Mitterrand and his advisers had concluded that their choice for Europe was in France's best national interest.[76] Once the move was made to reconfirm policies in line with the evolving EEC, France thus elected to submit its major economic decisions to this ongoing integration.[77] And the regulations to which the nation had to adhere grew gradually stiffer with time, in accord with a series of increasingly stricter Community decrees. Analysts' general consensus is that—though other factors also played a role[78]—affirming and intensifying its commitment to

---

75. Heath, "Original Goals," 55; Castañeda, "NAFTA at 10," 53; Pastor and Wise, "State Policy," 425; Audley et al., *NAFTA's Promise*, 18. On the austerity program, see Cameron and Tomlin, *Making of NAFTA*, 218, 220.

76. Le Cacheux, "Franc Fort Strategy," 69; Smith, *Left's Dirty Job*, 217; Mark Kesselman et al., *European Politics in Transition*, 255. Smith, "Industrial Crisis and the Left," 18, maintains that ever since the late 1950s French leaders had considered the country's economic and security interests to rest in solidarity with the European Community.

77. France had affirmed its participation in the European Monetary System with Giscard's vote in 1979, as noted in my introductory chapter. But from 1981 to 1983 Mitterrand struggled mightily over whether to continue to pursue this commitment.

78. Other causes included structural change, resulting in a disjuncture between the skills on supply and the nature of demand; "Eurosclerosis," meaning that generous wages and benefits had created inflexible labor markets; and deepening economic internationalization, entailing competition and profit-seeking by mobile capital. See Valerie Symes, *Unemployment in Europe: Problems and Policies*

Community requirements was the proximate root of France's exploding unemployment in the 1980s and 1990s.[79]

Just as Mexico's plight reverberated throughout much of Latin America in the mid and late 1980s, France's situation reflected that of much of Western Europe at the time. Across the twenty-four states that were members of the Organization for Economic Cooperation and Development then, those counted as out of work jumped from just 5.5 percent of the labor force at the end of the 1970s to 10 percent in just four years, with the numbers growing from 18 million to 32 million. And after 1990, when Western Europe stood poised on the brink of yet another multistate economic downturn, an average unemployment level of 8 percent surged up to 11.5 percent over the following four years. In some countries the rate even continued to rise thereafter.[80]

Throughout the region high unemployment was both an effect of the shocks of the 1970s and, with time, the price of the demand restraint imposed throughout the Community after 1980 in an ongoing battle to keep inflation at bay.[81] David Cameron points to "processes and changes in the international economic and geopolitical environments" as the source of the three recessions in Western Europe between the mid-1970s and the early 1990s, all of which were the precipitating cause of high unemployment throughout most of the region. Tellingly, he also notes that joblessness within the European Union in the 1990s cannot be understood apart from the rules of the European Monetary System, which clearly aggravated it immensely.[82]

Yet even among countries where job creation was a prominent source of trouble, France's position was, again, that of an outlier: a study of twelve Western European nations during the 1980s and 1990s found that France experienced "by far the sharpest drop in industrial employment."[83] There the figure surpassed 12 percent by 1994, and it remained as high as 12.5 percent at the end of 1996, affecting more than three million workers. The rate stuck at around 12 percent for some

---

(London: Routledge, 1995), 18; Michael Ellman, "Eurosclerosis?" in *Unemployment: International Perspectives,* ed. Morley Gunderson et al. (Toronto: University of Toronto Press, 1987), 58; and Scharpf, "Economic Changes," 108.

79. Cameron, "Unemployment," 13.

80. James Tobin, "Macroeconomic Diagnosis and Prescription," in Gunderson et al., *Unemployment,* 12; Cameron, "Unemployment," 11.

81. Ellman, "Eurosclerosis," 55; Jackman, "Impact of the European Union," 60, 67; Jens Bastian, "Putting the Cart Before the Horse? Labour Market Challenges Ahead of Monetary Union in Europe," in *Beyond the Market: The EU and National Social Policy,* ed. David Hine and Hussein Kassim (London: Routledge, 1998), 91; Smith, "Unemployment"; Symes, *Unemployment in Europe,* 10.

82. Cameron, "Unemployment," 11–12; Gruber, *Ruling the World,* 174, 177–78.

83. Hemerijck and Schludi, "Sequences of Policy Failure," 168.

time thereafter.[84] Cameron has written that France's international economic and political context and policy choice were set by the exchange rate policy in Europe; he goes on to state that "above all French macroeconomic policy was constrained by its European Community membership."[85] The notion that job loss was linked to Community rules seems vindicated by the much more serious level of unemployment within the Community nations than in other, nonmember, major industrialized nations in Western Europe, from the late 1970s onward.[86]

Left to its own devices, France—according to its traditional practices—would probably have continued to shelter surplus labor rather than to push for layoffs: when, for instance, the country experienced a crisis in the steel industry in the second half of the 1970s, even under the rule of a party on the right, dismissals were avoided for the most part by resort to early retirements and transfers.[87] Soon thereafter, though, with Giscard's 1979 signing of the EMS accord, France was subject to the first external rule-dictating decree to affect workers' situations, setting in motion a process that, as chapter 3 spelled out, led inexorably to Mitterrand's U-turn and the job cuts that ensued. In fact, as W. Rand Smith discovered, "after 1983 state officials in France encouraged and even ordered targeted firms to cut their losses" and to take other moves that led to large numbers of job reductions in five industries.[88]

Thus, as we have seen in Mexico (and will see again in China), overt official orders—the result of more or less voluntary governmental choices—exacerbated the damage done by purely economic forces. During the years just before and spanning the U-turn, the numbers discharged went from about two million in early 1982, or 7.3 percent of the workforce, to 2.48 million, or more than 10 percent, within a mere two years.[89] Further increases led to a high of 13.4 percent without jobs on a seasonally adjusted basis during 1984.[90] Throughout the rest of the decade the rate continued to hover around and above 10 percent, mitigated a bit by early retirements. By 1997, the total losses over the years since 1970 had amounted to a stunning 41.6 percent of the original labor force.[91]

Propping up the interest rate to strengthen the franc—another feature of the closer connection with the Community—continued through the 1980s and into

---

84. Cameron, "Unemployment," 16, shows an average figure of 11.3 percent for the period 1991–96; Schmidt, *From State to Market?* 187.

85. Cameron, "From Barre to Balladur," 119; see also ibid., 134. Boltho agrees in "Has France Converged on Germany?" 102.

86. Jackman, "Impact of the European Union," 60.

87. Daley, "Steel Crisis," 146–80.

88. Smith, *Left's Dirty Job,* 213.

89. Bell and Criddle, *French Socialist Party,* 187.

90. Machin and Wright, "Economic Policy," 28.

91. Scharpf, "Economic Changes," 108.

the early 1990s. With the right wing commanding the daily workings of the government from 1986 to 1988 under Jacques Chirac's premiership, interest rates rose as high as 12.75 percent, then the very steepest throughout the West.[92] Even under subsequent Socialist prime ministers, rates remained elevated, causing growth to slacken and firms to fold as the heightened price of borrowing added its strain to a new cutoff in state aid for troubled enterprises. A French recession was the long-term outcome, and employment fell accordingly.[93] The imprint of France's partners' preferences had grown sharp and deep.

Other prominent features of France's tighter pairing with its partners (its policy of "rigeur") involved cuts in public expenditures, budget deficit reduction, and a call to lower workers' wages. All this was accompanied by demands for a rise in firm profitability, to be achieved through economic modernization and cuts in excess capacity, including reductions in surplus labor, particularly for firms and sectors already in decline[94]—and heightened productivity. Along with that went a focus on open markets and efforts to achieve a favorable balance of payments in external trade.[95] Above all, the lofty objective of maintaining a strong currency, the *franc fort*, to which all of these policies were meant to contribute, was adopted by politicians of all hues thenceforth, not just for enhancing the competitiveness of French trade but, significantly, for satisfying the orders of the Community and its ERM.[96] Like the contemporaneous policies in force in Mexico, every one of these emphases spelled slower growth and a corresponding cutback in the numbers of people formally at work.[97]

Two other prominent features of this program of austerity were not specifically mandated by the Community or the EMS, but they appeared necessary to French politicians intent on enforcing a strict economy. Both of them, privatization and deregulation, were unusual in France, given two special features of the country: first was its stronger and lengthier tradition of bureaucratic regulation as compared with elsewhere in Western Europe; the other was its more substantial degree

---

92. Bell and Criddle, *French Socialist Party,* 188.

93. Schmidt, *From State to Market?* 112, 141, 184, 187.

94. In part this was undertaken in response to rationalization measures promulgated by the European Community. After 1984, 30,000 jobs were dropped as a component of a European program to cut back capacity deemed unnecessary. Daley, "Steel Crisis," 175–76. See also Smith, *Left's Dirty Job,* 14.

95. Kesselman, "French Labor Movement," 156; Schmidt, *From State to Market?* 95, 111–12; Smith, *Left's Dirty Job,* 14; Symes, *Unemployment in Europe,* 21; and Cameron, "From Barre to Balladur," 117–18, 132.

96. Schmidt, *From State to Market?* 163; Cameron, "From Barre to Balladur," 118, 150; Jackman, "Impact of the European Union," 69; Le Cacheux, "Franc Fort," 69. Jospin, who became prime minister in 1997, worked for job creation and the termination of unemployment, but the large objectives remained during his term. See Smith, "Unemployment," 118.

97. Ellman, "Eurosclerosis," 55; Cameron, "From Barre to Balladur," 145, 149.

of state ownership in the time before 1983.[98] Part of these efforts entailed welcoming foreign buyouts and demanding that firms showing deficits slim down their payrolls and undertake restructuring of other kinds.[99] The final step in the process of cleaning up balance sheets was to cancel Mitterrand's project of nationalization altogether and to sanction privatization on a massive scale, just as the Mexicans had done in the 1980s, in many cases by denationalizing firms that had just lately been claimed by the state.[100] A number of the industries that had been under state ownership shed excess labor as they were sold.[101] Sacking workers was seen as conducive to saving, striving to become profitable, and surviving without subsidies, all aims of the post-1983 state and of the EEC as well.

Deregulation also involved several measures contributory to unemployment. One of these was, for French firms, a novel encouragement to use labor "flexibly," with less state oversight and a loosening of state dictates. In practice, this meant more resort to jobs with irregular working schedules, fewer or no benefits, and more insecure tenure.[102] In 1986 the government put to rest the prior requirement that employers dismissing more than ten workers for an economic cause first receive permission from an inspector from the Ministry of Industry.[103] Another example of retiring older national regulations was the abandonment of price controls that had benefited cost-heavy sectors, thereby increasing the competition such industries had to face. Eliminating tariffs and quotas, meanwhile—along with cutting back on technical standards for imports and removing other forms of state-organized protection—also exacerbated the impact of foreign competition.[104] All this occurred in tandem with France's plunge much more decisively than in the past into the sea of global trade.[105]

---

98. Kesselman et al., *European Politics*, 256.

99. Machin and Wright, "Economic Policy," 3.

100. Kesselman et al., *European Politics*, 255.

101. Schmidt, *From State to Market?* 127–28; Hemerijck and Schludi, "Sequences and Policy Failure," 168; Scharpf, "Economic Changes, Vulnerabilities," 67.

102. Howell, *Regulating Labor*, 187–91.

103. Levy, "France: Directing Adjustment," 325; Howell, *Regulating Labor*, 203.

104. Kesselman et al., *European Politics*, 257. The notion of enhancing competitiveness was not new to France, but the means of attaining it were: instead of depending on government-assisted "industrial policies" and devaluations of the currency—both of which were radically limited by the EMS—France relied on market-based methods after 1983. Boltho, "Has France Converged on Germany?" 91, 102. Not just the state, but the international environment as well, placed heavy pressure on French industry as a whole to find ways to increase its productivity in order to survive. Smith, *Left's Dirty Job*, 14. Also see Gordon and Meunier, *French Challenge*, 30.

105. According to Adams, "France and Global Competition," 88, in 1990 exports and imports each amounted to about 23 percent of production and consumption, respectively. Adams also holds that from the time of the formation of the European Economic Community, in 1959, France's GDP tripled but its exports increased a startling 637 percent (ibid., 96). Machin and Wright, "Economic Policy," 4, write that by 1983 the value of imports and exports combined amounted to 23 percent of GDP, as compared with the 13 percent of 1953, while Cameron, "From Barre to Balladur," 120, states

The combination of all these changes, many of which put serious strains on the French economy, did their part to drag France into yet one more recession after 1990 (following one in the mid-1970s and another surrounding Mitterrand's U-turn in the early 1980s). But this particular downturn was fueled not just by the *rigeur* resulting from Mitterrand's choice to conform with his EEC partners more than half a dozen years earlier. At this juncture, France's prior decision to go along with the Community meant that higher German interest rates (in turn spurred by heavy German spending and consequent budget deficits and inflation connected to its 1989 unification) ricocheted back on France and Germany's other partners in the EMS. At any rate, boosting interest rates was the direct result of the exchange rate policy to which Community members had agreed in 1979.[106]

France's signing on to the Maastricht Accord in autumn 1992 subjected the country's economy to a much more strenuous set of rules, regulations that came with correspondingly serious side effects for labor. Indeed, within a few years, it was even possible to conclude that unemployment was no longer the result of fighting inflation (as it had been in the previous decade), for the problem of price control had been nearly totally overcome. Instead, the unemployment that so doggedly hung on through the 1990s and beyond derived nearly entirely from France's compliance with the terms of the 1992 accord.[107] The Community set forth specific and stringent standards of economic behavior that participating countries had to meet by 1999 in order to share in the usage of a common currency that was to come into force in 2001. The aim of the new European Union created by the accord was nothing less than the full convergence of macroeconomic performance among these nations within one market, to be monitored and controlled by a European Central Bank.[108]

Most prominently, these standards ruled that member states limit their domestic budget deficits to under 3 percent of GDP and that government debts be kept

---

that by the early 1990s exports and imports *each* accounted for somewhere between 20 and 25 percent, about twice as much as thirty years before. If the Cameron and the Machin/Wright figures are comparable, this would be quite a jump in just one decade. According to Gordon and Meunier, *French Challenge*, 4, trade's share of GDP only continued upward as the 1990s progressed, moving from just under 25 percent in 1962 to nearly half (49.4 percent) by 1997. By the end of the century, the eleven other members of the European Union accounted for half of France's foreign trade (ibid., 33).

106. Cameron, "Unemployment," 12; Le Cacheux, "Franc Fort," 77–82; Jackman, "Impact of the European Union," 67–68; Lintner, "European Monetary Union," 329–30.

107. Paul Krugman, "First, Do No Harm," in "Responses to Kapstein: Workers and Economists; The Global Economy Has Left Keynes in Its Train," *Foreign Affairs* 75,4 (July–August 1996), 169; Scharpf, "Economic Changes, Vulnerabilities," 107; Jackman, "Impact of the European Union," 69; Symes, *Unemployment in Europe*, 174; Schmidt, *From State to Market?* 195; Nancy Bermeo, "Conclusion: Unemployment, the New Europe, and the Old Inequalities," in Bermeo, *Unemployment in the New Europe*, 342; Lintner, "European Monetary Union," 322–23, 328.

108. Schmitter, "Emerging Europolity," 401.

below 60 percent of GDP. In 1997 the 1992 agreement was solidified with a Stability and Growth Pact that laid down procedures for ensuring that the criteria for membership be met, along with new regulations to sanction states that broke the rules.[109] With the inauguration of the European Central Bank in 1998, designed in accord with the operational principles of the German Bundesbank, the additional objective of sustaining inflation rates below 2 percent added yet one more restrictive prescription for the member states of the EU.[110]

Paradoxically enough, as in Mexico, this very set of arrangements that was instrumental in the disappearance of so many jobs was initially fashioned—or at least fostered—on the assumption, or perhaps the hope, that it would work to create jobs, at least in time. Alternatively and less optimistically, there was the minimal expectation that these regulations would allow for a lessening of unemployment as price levels stabilized.[111] But instead, within the nearly three decades since the EMS was first installed, that was not to be.

All these offshoots of meeting membership obligations must have turned out quite differently from what French president Valéry Giscard d'Estaing—a man who had governed in an age when workers' jobs were to be preserved or rescued—had had in mind when he approved the EMS in 1979.[112] These rules came in waves: first there was the 1979 Exchange Rate Mechanism, next Maastricht in 1992, after that the 1997 Stability and Growth Pact, and last the dicta of the European Central Bank and the common currency it governed from 1999 onward. Perhaps, given the changes in the global economy and the shocks of the 1970s, large numbers of laboring people would have been out of a job after 1980 even without this relentless appearance of pronouncements. But it seems more than likely that the figures would not have been quite so high or the layoffs quite so sudden.

China

Unlike France—and even less like Mexico—China did not reach outward from the throes of a clear-cut, desperate, and immediately urgent economic predicament.[113] To the contrary, as economist Barry Naughton has aptly characterized the

---

109. Cameron, "Unemployment," 36; Lintner, "European Monetary Union," 329.

110. Bermeo, "Conclusion," 342; Kaelberer, "Review Article," 111. See also Kesselman et al., *European Politics,* 257. Kathleen R. McNamara, *The Currency of Ideas: Monetary Politics in the European Union* (Ithaca: Cornell University Press, 1998), is a study of the Bank.

111. William Walters, *Unemployment and Government: Genealogies of the Social* (New York: Cambridge University Press, 2000), 116; Le Cacheux, "Franc Fort," 77.

112. Gruber, *Ruling the World,* 174–78.

113. United States Trade Representative, *2002 Report to Congress on China's WTO Compliance* (Washington, D.C., 2002), 142.

situation, the Chinese economy as of the late 1970s was still "muddling through and growing steadily."[114] But as noted in chapter 3, an altered group of leaders after Mao was open to a range of new possibilities, including consulting the experiences of Eastern European reformers, looking at their own East Asian neighbors, and even investigating the lessons of the Western, capitalist, industrialized world.[115] It was not long before they settled on the notion of opening to the global market as their primary course for curing the many economic ills they diagnosed at home. This decision ipso facto drove them into the realm of the same liberal trade and investment regime designed and run by the Western capitalist powers that also enticed Mexico and, in a sense, entrapped France.[116] Margaret Pearson has made a strong case for the subsequent, if gradual, impact of the norms of that regime on the governors of the Chinese economy.[117]

Acceptance of the entire package of free trade tenets was by no means either complete or pervasive throughout Chinese officialdom in the 1980s—or even into the 1990s, for that matter. Thus indecision and internal disagreements within the decision-making elite characterized politics in China as it did in France and Mexico at the same juncture. But those who were generally inclined to experiment with external trade were in a sufficiently forceful political position to engineer a rudimentary shift in the national policy climate as early as 1979, and to hold that course for the more than two decades it took to attain entry into the WTO, and, of course, beyond.

The altered consciousness of this political elite included a previously unheard-of acknowledgment of profit-seeking in the PRC,[118] a radical departure from the days of Mao. Along with that went other such essential reversals of Maoism as beliefs that commerce was an admissible good,[119] that unemployment was requisite to boosting productivity,[120] that competitive pressure was a positive stimulus and not a wayward evil, that comparative advantage was an acceptable and universal precept, and, undergirding all these values, a view that it was justified to resort to market forces in setting wages and even in recruiting and dismissing labor.[121] By the 1990s, not just marketization, which by then was increasingly dominating the economy at home, but "globalization" as well had become the widely recognized

114. Naughton, *Growing Out of the Plan*, 54–55.

115. Nina Halpern, "Economic Specialists and the Making of Chinese Economic Policy, 1955–1983" (Ph.D. dissertation, University of Michigan, 1985).

116. Pearson, "China's Integration," 165.

117. Pearson, "Case of China's Accession," 338, 353–56, 358–59.

118. Jefferson and Rawski, "Unemployment, Underemployment," 44.

119. Dorothy J. Solinger, *Chinese Business under Socialism* (Berkeley: University of California Press, 1984).

120. Korzec, "Contract Labor," 139.

121. Thomas G. Rawski, "Recent Developments in China's Labor Economy," unpublished manuscript, 9; Pearson, "Case of China's Accession," 354.

framework among the elite for thinking about how to enhance China's material strength.[122]

As the leadership voluntarily ingested capitalist modes of reasoning about economics and imbibed the materialistic mores that were internationally au courant, the country's linkage with the global market tightened, over a span of some twenty years, a period capped by China's accession to the WTO in December 2001. Along the way, the central government pursued in parallel two related processes that pertain to my subject. The first, really a function of the larger, contemporaneous program of enterprise reform, was a slowly escalating official propaganda crusade aimed at transforming customary popular notions about employment, accompanied by steadily more explicit and intentional moves to bring about the dismissal of workers from their posts. I call this campaign "engineering unemployment." The second process was an intensifying offensive to make China a member first of the GATT and, after 1995, of the WTO. This second drive, one that began as early as 1980, was eventually to entail a total revamping of the Chinese foreign trade sector and all its activities.[123]

The two processes did not just occur simultaneously by chance; they were interconnected, and both were informed by economic norms and aspirations that were by then orthodox globally. Thus, had China's political elite not decided to thrust its economy into international bodies as a means of rapidly developing and modernizing its economic structures and behaviors, it would not have revamped the country's labor regime. And planning to join supranational economic bodies, similarly, meant readying the Chinese economy for compliance with the rules of these bodies, most of which either directly or indirectly entailed the downsizing of the workforce. But in contrast to the case of France, and even more unlike the situation in Mexico, neither of these two pushes was strictly speaking economically essential; both were at bottom fully politically fashioned and purposefully pursued.[124]

Engineering Unemployment

New ideas and official decisions about handling labor were not the only reasons for the massive discharge of workers that began in the mid-1990s. The employment problem had several roots. Decades of emphasis on full urban employment (or a practicable approximation thereof) had led to a vast amount of surplus urban labor, a phenomenon referred to in China in the 1990s as "hidden unemployment."

122. Moore, "China and Globalization," 106.

123. Naughton, *Growing Out of the Plan*, and Lardy, *Integrating China*, 16, 20.

124. H. Lyman Miller, "Institutions in Chinese Politics: Trends and Prospects," in *China's Future: Implications for US Interests; Conference Report*, ed. Library of Congress (Washington, D.C., September 1999), 37.

Already in the late 1980s and continuing into the 2000s, the government pronounced the excess labor in the cities as being about one-third of that on the job.[125] Other difficulties arose in the labor market as China began to modernize in earnest from the 1980s, with its industry becoming progressively more capital-intensive and labor-saving technology replacing workers.[126]

At the same time, the mismatch between the low-skill, undereducated workforce that a range of Maoist policies had fostered (not least the anti-intellectualism of the 1966–76 Cultural Revolution), on the one hand, and the state-of-the-art aspirations of the regime, on the other, brought about an inexorable process of structural unemployment.[127] For example, as Chinese policy analyst Hu Angang points out, some 80 percent of the job loss that had taken place as of late 2001 was in mining, quarrying, manufacturing, and construction. This would appear to constitute prima facie evidence that sunset industries were falling in significance, just as they were elsewhere.[128]

With these extra-political forces working to crowd out human labor, the employment elasticity of economic growth steadily declined. By the late 1990s, this rate had become a mere third of what it had been in the 1980s.[129] And while the second half of the 1980s had seen a 1 percent increase in the growth rate of GDP, spawning 1.51 million jobs, in the following half-decade (between 1991 and 1995) the yield was only 840,000 jobs.[130] Yet another statistic makes these points even more dramatically: in the 1980s the rate of employment growth was as high as

---

125. Michel Bonnin, "Perspectives on Social Stability after the Fifteenth Congress," in *China under Jiang Zemin*, ed. Hung-mao Tien and Yun-han Chu (Boulder, Colo.: Lynne Rienner, 2000), 154; Pat Howard, "Rice Bowls and Job Security: The Urban Contract Labour System," *AJCA* 25 (January 1991), 102; Imai, "China's Growing Unemployment Problem," 30; Albert Park and Fang Cai, "How Has Economic Restructuring Affected China's Urban Workers?" unpublished manuscript, October 2003, 2.

126. A. S. Bhalla and Shufang Qiu, *The Employment Impact of China's WTO Accession* (London: RoutledgeCurzon, 2004), 104.

127. Rawski, "Recent Developments," 7.

128. Bhalla and Qiu, *Employment Impact*, 104; Hu Angang, *Employment and Development: China's Employment Problem and Employment Strategy*, National Conditions Report (Beijing: National Conditions Analysis and Study Group of the Chinese Academy of Sciences, April 30, 1998), 5, 15–16; United Nations Development Program, *China Human Development Report*, 61.

129. In the 1990s, the elasticity coefficient of employment growth was just 0.106, meaning that for each percentage point of economic growth there was only 0.106 of a percentage point of employment growth, a decrease of two-thirds since the 1980s, when a percentage point of growth in GDP pushed up job numbers by about one-third of a percentage point. Hu Angang, "Shishi jiuye youxian zhanlue, wei renmin tigong gengduode gongzuo gangwei" [Realize employment preference strategy, for the people supply more jobs], Chinese Academy of Science and Tsinghua University National Conditions Research Center, Speech outline delivered at Specialists' Forum directed by State Planning Commission Vice Chairman Wang Chunzheng, September 29, 2000, 3; Hu Angang, *Employment and Development*, 6.

130. Dai Lushui and Li Yan, "Qiantan jiaru WTO dui jiuye xingshi de yingxiang yu duice" [Superficially talking about the influence of entering the WTO on the situation of employment and how to handle that], *ZGLD* 9 (2001), 12.

9 percent annually. But by the second half of the 1990s it had fallen to an average of just 0.9 percent per year.[131] One more, particularly critical new force attacking the workforce in state firms in the 1990s was the growing competition noted in chapter 3. But all these demand-side factors just amounted to one element in the total picture. Official efforts to remake the labor regime—by way of pilot programs, pronouncements, temporary rulings, regulations, and laws—were critical as they channeled and sped up the influence of these economic forces.

The first experiments pertaining to the labor system took place almost immediately after the Party's official switch in late 1978 away from class politics and revolutionary mobilization to a focus on rapid modernization and, soon, outward opening. As early as 1980—at the same time the country first demonstrated an informal interest in the GATT—trial schemes in term-limited labor contracting were undertaken in a few limited localities, an early threat to the lifetime tenure that had characterized employment up to that time.[132] Three years later the Ministry of Labor announced a set of temporary regulations for the contracting system. But years of debate and indecision followed,[133] and throughout the 1980s unemployment remained unlegitimized, much less officially encouraged.

Still, the initiation of industrial and enterprise reforms early in the decade—with their encouragement of money-making and high productivity, and with their granting of new financial and decisional powers to managers—rendered workers' security less certain.[134] Little by little, plant managers took advantage of their powers and heightened autonomy to transfer workers, and occasionally to let them go. This power was further enhanced when enterprise directors were allowed after 1986 to lease the firms that they had been running.[135] Also in 1986, just as China submitted its application for membership in the GATT, a set of labor-related regulations appeared, including one officially instituting labor contracting which built on the early 1980s trial runs.[136] These new rulings put the concept of unemployment squarely on the table, and by the last half of the decade more and more layoffs were taking place.[137]

---

131. Hu Angang, "China's Present Economic Situation and Its Macro-Economic Policies," paper presented at the RAND-China Reform Forum Conference, Santa Monica, Calif., November 29–30, 2001, 10.

132. Howard, "Rice Bowls," 97.

133. White, "Changing Role of the Chinese State."

134. Sheehan, *Chinese Workers*.

135. Ibid.; and Meng, *Labour Market Reform*, 82, 83, 113.

136. But as of 1995, just over a third of the new entrants to state firms were being placed under the system. Meng, *Labour Market Reform*, 82.

137. Andrew G. Walder, "Wage Reform and the Web of Factory Interests," *CQ* 109 (1987), 22, 40, and "Workers, Managers and the State: The Reform Era and the Political Crisis of 1989," *CQ* 127 (1991), 473, 478–79.

In 1992, a critical turning point, then-preeminent leader Deng Xiaoping made an abrupt reentry onto the decision-making scene following the 1989 Tiananmen demonstrations, instigating a sudden thrust forward for market reform. Probably relatedly, it was also in that year that the country took its first step in what was to become an accelerating movement of cutting back its tariffs, as its leadership began to press actively for entry into the GATT. According to Pearson's interviews, "those negotiating China's entry to GATT felt that they were given a strong positive signal to proceed with negotiations" at that point.[138] Several critical labor market decisions appeared in 1992 too, including one specifically permitting managers to dismiss labor.[139]

In the following year, the pivotal Third Plenum of the 14th Central Committee convened in November and announced the landmark "Decision on Issues Concerning the Establishment of a Socialist Market Economic Structure." Henceforth the goal was to create a full-scale market economy, albeit one quaintly still billed as "socialist."[140] Soon thereafter, in 1994, China's Labor Law was rewritten, the first one in the PRC to sanction firing,[141] and in 1995 the old system of lifelong employment was officially terminated.[142] In these years, with these new pronouncements, those who comprised the "hidden unemployed," whose disposal had been undecided for a decade, started to confront the real danger of being discharged.[143] It was around this time as well that then president Jiang Zemin openly acknowledged that the country's ongoing tariff cuts amounted to a "down payment" on China's bid to enter the GATT.[144]

Two regime-decreed austerity programs, one from 1988 to 1990 and the second from 1993 to 1995, also constituted politically induced circumstances that affected the fate of labor. In both instances the contractions were undertaken to control the inflation that had exploded in the wake of overvigorous growth spurts in the respective previous year or two. During those two periods, most firms were

---

138. Margaret Pearson, "The Institutional, Political, and Global Foundations of China's Trade Liberalization," in *Japan and China in the World Political Economy,* ed. Kellee S. Tsai and Saadia M. Pekkanen (London: Routledge, 2005), 98.

139. Deborah S. Davis, "Self-employment in Shanghai: A Research Note," *CQ* 157 (1999): 28–29; Feng Chen, "Subsistence Crises, Managerial Corruption and Labour Protests in China," *CJ* 44 (July 2000), 46.

140. Miller, "Institutions in Chinese Politics," 45; Yi-min Lin and Tian Zhu, "Ownership Restructuring in Chinese State Industry: An Analysis of Evidence on Initial Organizational Changes," *CQ* 166 (June 2001), 305, 329–30.

141. Ching Kwan Lee, "From Organized Dependence to Disorganized Despotism: Changing Labour Regimes in Chinese Factories," *CQ* 155 (1999), 55.

142. Chen, "Subsistence Crises," 46.

143. Hu, "Employment and Development," 1; United Nations Development Program, "China Human Development Report"; Rawski, "Recent Developments," 4, 6.

144. Communication from Nicholas Lardy, November 11, 2005.

denied governmental loans,[145] and the forced budget-trimming and plant failures that resulted drove out labor.[146] After the second one ended, in early 1996, a decision was announced to "grasp the large [firms] and let go of the smaller ones"—through sales, leasings, and mergers (*zhuada fangxiao*).[147] This slogan became the rallying cry that authorized the first massive labor dismissals; concurrently, tariffs were carved away on nearly five thousand items, with the average rate dropping down to 23 percent.[148]

Soon thereafter, the September 1997 meeting of the 15th National Party Congress took two steps that were to have a precipitous impact on the fate of the state-sector workforce: one was its invigoration of an earlier drive to remodel state firms into share and limited-liability companies; the other was its explicit mandate for an enormous wave of worker dismissals under the slogan "cut the workforce and raise efficiency" (*jianyuan zengxiao*).[149] Although these dismissals were related to economic forces, the retrenchments were also the outcome of specific political pressure placed on the firms.[150] The best evidence of this pressure was the quota system devised around this time to force factories to dispose of set percentages of their workforces. The fulfillment of these target figures became one basis for evaluating leading cadres' work.[151] At the same time, with another 4,874 tariff reductions, the average rate slid to 17 percent.[152] As on several other

---

145. Lardy, *Integrating China*, 17–18; Miller, "Institutions and Chinese Politics," 45; Xiao-Ming Li, "China's Macroeconomic Stabilization Policies Following the Asian Financial Crisis: Success or Failure?" *AS* 40: 6 (2000), 942–45. See also Yang Yiyong et al., *Shiye chongji bo* [The shock wave of unemployment] (Beijing: Jinri zhongguo chubanshe [China Today Publishing], 1997), 217–18.

146. Barry Naughton, "China's Emergence and Prospects," 294. Rawski records an "abrupt decline in the demand for labor" beginning in 1995. Rawski, *China*, 19.

147. Miller, "Institutions and Chinese Politics," 45; Hang-Sheng Cheng, "A Mid-Course Assessment of China's Economic Reform," in *China's Economic Future: Challenges to U.S. Policy*, ed. Joint Economic Committee, Congress of the United States (Armonk, N.Y.: M. E. Sharpe, 1997), 29; Joseph Fewsmith, "China in 1998: Tacking to Stay the Course," *AS* 32, 1 (1999), 100.

148. Lardy, *Integrating China*, 35.

149. Party general secretary Jiang Zemin put forward two critical chores at the 1997 congress: first, to "adjust and improve the ownership structure," and second, to "accelerate the reform of state-owned enterprises." Also at that congress, in a policy already enunciated at a smaller meeting in January that year (a State Council National Work Conference on State Enterprise Staff and Workers' Reemployment), attendees were asked "to cut the workforce and raise efficiency" and were told that solving their firms' difficulties depended on enterprise reform, system transformation, cutting staff, normalizing bankruptcies, and encouraging mergers. Yang et al., *Shiye chongji bo*, 220. For Jiang's report to the congress, see Summary of World Broadcasts FE/3023 (September 13, 1997), S1/1–S1/10.

150. Naughton, "Chinese Economy," 52. Lardy, *Integrating China*, 23, states that over 36 million state workers lost their jobs between 1998 and 2001.

151. Tian Bingnan and Yuan Jianmin, "Shanghai xiagang renyuan de diaocha yanjiu" [Investigation research on Shanghai laid-off personnel], *Shehuixue* [Sociology] 2, 1997, 11; Feng Tongqing, "Social Transition and Positive Adjustments in the State Enterprise-Worker Relationship," *Chinese Sociology and Anthropology* (Summer 2005), 35–36.

152. Lardy, *Integrating China*, 35.

occasions in these years, measures to scale down the labor force accompanied tariff cuts.

Making sense of Chinese unemployment statistics is notoriously difficult.[153] But even the officially admitted numbers "laid off" and those newly "unemployed" from the mid-1990s onward is impressively large: between the end of 1992 and the end of 1998—even before the discharge drive escalated, but in the time when China was preparing for entry into the GATT and later the WTO—state and urban collective firms combined let go some 37 million workers, according to government figures; put otherwise, the "public sector" firms combined cut one-third of their workforce. Later, a State Council "White Paper" acknowledged that between 1998 and 2001 another 25.5 million persons had been laid off from state enterprises alone.[154] Hu Angang's estimate of the total of state and urban collective firms' workers who had lost their jobs had shot up to a staggering figure of 60 million by late 2004,[155] a statistic already published internally in mid-2001 as the sum of the "laid-off" and the "unemployed" combined.[156]

A late 1990s study conducted by China's official trade union found that 48.7 percent of the "reemployed" laid-off people it counted were self-employed, while of the other 51.3 percent who had been rehired, well over half (59 percent) were engaged in informal work that was only temporary.[157] This development the turn to the informal sector—was unfolding at the same time in France and Mexico, as their own workforces underwent a similar transformation, if on a far smaller scale.

---

153. Solinger, "Why We Cannot Count the Unemployed." The term "unemployed" was used in official records to refer only to once-workers whose firms had disappeared, who had registered their joblessness, and who hailed just from enterprises that had been owned by the state and had paid into the unemployment insurance fund set up after 1986. The figure counting such people omits those people said to have been "laid off" (*xiagang*), a status devised to refer to people who had also lost their jobs but who, in theory, were still connected to their firms (which still existed) and who were receiving a "basic livelihood allowance" from them after the mid-1990s; to be counted among that number, a person also must have once been on the payroll of a state-owned firm and must have been admitted to a "reemployment service center" (information obtained from the Chinese Academy of Social Sciences scholar Tang Jun, September 15, 2004), a privilege that an uncounted multitude of enterprises either could not afford or did not bother to install.

154. State Council, "White Paper on Employment, Social Security," *Asian Wall Street Journal,* April 29, 2002, 11.

155. Hu, "China's Present Economic Situation," 9, for the first figure; private communication, September 23, 2004.

156. Wang Depei, "San min yu erci gaige" [Three types of people and the second reform], *Gaige neican* [Reform Internal Reference] 7 (2001), 25. Hu also stated that China had laid off 55 million people from 1995 to mid-2002 (*China News Digest,* 9 July 2002).

157. Xue Zhaoyun, "Dui xiagang zhigong zaijiuye xianzhuang di diaocha, sikao yu jianyi" [Research, reflections, and suggestions about the reemployment situation of laid-off staff and workers], *Gonghui gongzuo tongxun* [Bulletin of Trade Union Work] 7 (2000), 8.

It is difficult, if not impossible, to disentangle policymakers' insistence on labor reduction from the worker displacement that was a by-product of other regime policy initiatives—or to distinguish the job loss that was politically induced from dismissals that took place without any prodding, as plants failed or tried to avoid doing so. Nor can the job-letting be neatly separated from the leaders' new understanding and acceptance of international economic norms and values enshrining profits, efficiency, and flexibility which undergirded the GATT by the 1980s and 1990s. But surely by the time China entered the WTO the many jobs that had disappeared had been sacrificed on its altar.

The Campaign to Join the GATT/WTO

China first signaled its interest in the GATT around 1980, almost immediately after its leaders determined that they would begin opening a portion of the country to the world market. As Pearson has written, "the government's desire to enter the GATT led it to initiate numerous concrete policy changes."[158] Elsewhere, she refers to "a negotiating strategy to make China seem more attractive to WTO member nations"; and she concludes, "The fact that China often made liberalizing reforms ahead of the deadlines imposed by foreign negotiators...has made these changes appear non-coerced. Yet the Chinese government clearly made them with an eye toward meeting externally imposed requirements."[159]

Aside from a wish to gain legitimacy at home from greater prosperity, leaders had a set of additional motives. Right from the start those in the top decision councils concluded that China could not advance without open markets for the country's exports, and without the expertise, technology transfer, and capital that would follow in the course of foreign investment in the Chinese market. Other motives included a desire to boost the chances of success for internal economic reforms by obtaining backing from international partners and, crucially, a wish to strengthen China's prestige and status in the world at large. There was also a hope of gaining the ability, which the overwhelming number of its trading partners possessed, to appeal to a supranational dispute resolution mechanism in cases of disagreement.[160] Leaders in Mexico and, to a somewhat lesser extent, in France shared

---

158. Pearson, "China's Integration," 169. Similarly, David Zweig alleges that "Deng Xiaoping's 1978 decision to strengthen China's security...and seek capital and technology from the West forced China to work within the rules of the world capitalist system." See Zweig, *Internationalizing China: Domestic Interests and Global Linkages* (Ithaca: Cornell University Press, 2002), 35.

159. Pearson, "Institutional," 92, 101.

160. Ibid., 165; Dorothy J. Solinger, "Globalization and the Paradox of Participation: The China Case," *Global Governance* 7, 2 (2001), 173–96; Jacobson and Oksenberg, *China's Participation,* 92; Banning Garrett, "China Faces, Debates, the Contradictions of Globalization," *AS* 41, 3, (2001), 419; Lampton, *Same Bed, Different Dreams,* 178–79, 184; Pearson, "Case of China's Accession," 359–60; Fewsmith,

many of these objectives when they linked their economies to others' abroad in the 1980s and 1990s.

As early as 1980, the same year that alterations to the labor regime were first put on the table, China started sending officials to take part in GATT-sponsored commercial policy cases. In the spring of that year, the country took a seat on the United Nations' Interim Commission for the International Trade Organization, which was charged with selecting the GATT secretariat.[161] In the next few years, China was allowed to be an observer at a GATT meeting on renewing the Multifibre Agreement, which governed the global trade in textiles, and at the end of 1982 to attend the ministerial-level session of GATT's Contracting Parties. After another year, it was admitted into GATT's Multifibre Arrangement, having already reached agreements on trade in textiles with the EEC four years before. In both 1984 and 1985, China had the legal adviser to the Director-General of the GATT come to China to convey information about the structure and functioning of the organization, and in mid-1986 the country formally applied to become a contracting member.

Throughout the next thirteen years, China's top politicians put every aspect of their economy and foreign trade framework through a series of alterations, often in response to foreign interactions. In 1991, for instance, the country initialed a market access agreement with the United States to lower tariffs and remove other barriers to trade.[162] According to Nicholas Lardy, the drawn-out nature of the talks owes much to heightening demands coming from its counterparts over time, even as the Chinese were continuously liberalizing their price and importing structures expressly in response to these conditions placed by outside powers.[163] Nonetheless, it was China's own choice to propose entry; absent that desire, no external pressure would have ordered the Chinese to change their ways.

On the eve of China's final acquiescence to the strict terms the United States set down in late 1999,[164] two special circumstances intervened, both of which added considerable urgency to China's desire to become a secure member of the global market. One was the 1997–99 Asian Financial Crisis, which badly disrupted the economies of Southeast Asia and Korea, countries that were among China's chief

---

China since Tiananmen, 205; Moore, "China and Globalization," 109–10; 117. Lardy, *Integrating China,* 11–16, adds that the leaders believed that their ability to hold onto power hinged on their ongoing generation of economic growth, which they presumed that WTO membership would provide. He offers additional reasons at 132–33. Zweig, *Internationalizing China,* 276, notes that top leaders hoped entry would force deregulation that could help in overcoming smuggling and corruption.

161. For this and the following information, see Jacobson and Oksenberg, *China's Participation,* 83–92.

162. Pearson, "China's Integration," 169.

163. Lardy, *Integrating China,* 9, 33, 63–65.

164. Pearson, "Case for China's Accession," 338, 344–45; Joseph Fewsmith, *Elite Politics in Contemporary China* (Armonk, N.Y.: M. E. Sharpe, 2001), 141; Lampton, *Same Bed, Different Dreams,* 183–84, 202; Zweig, *Internationalizing China,* 263.

trade partners and its major investors, as mentioned in chapter 3.[165] The other new factor was that by 1999 the Chinese domestic market had been stuck in a deflationary mode for several years, with domestic demand effectively stagnant. Those who had already lost their jobs—and those having qualms that their positions could soon disappear—were, reasonably enough, wary of spending money.[166]

Given these two factors, by 2001, the year China acceded to the WTO, its leaders were clearly ready to take any measures that appeared likely to increase receptivity to China's exports. The terms China accepted included allowing rigorous anti-dumping rules to be applied against its exports for fifteen years after admission and reducing production subsidies in agriculture to a rate below that to which other WTO members had submitted.[167] And, as was true in Mexico and France, the same irony about membership providing new prospects for employment seems to have influenced the decision to join: some of the advocates of acceding to the WTO supported the move in the expectation that it would create jobs.[168] But—again, as in Mexico and France—adhering to the rules of the supranational organization it joined (even before joining) often meant taking steps that, at least in the short term, to the contrary contributed to the release of millions of workers.

As opposed to the situation in Mexico, where World Bank and IMF loans put conditions on the leadership's decisions, there was often no direct external order demanding internal changes in China, other than China's authorities' own uncoerced decision to meet the standards of the WTO in order to qualify to enter it. Still, a case can be made that the protracted process of negotiating to be accepted in itself oriented the Chinese leadership to undertake one revision after another in their country's economy and its foreign trade system. These foreign trade reforms were occasionally adopted specifically as concessions under pressure during negotiations.

But many other times they came about on China's leaders' own initiative— to accord either with the basic principles of the GATT/WTO (i.e., to conduct commercial relations with a minimum of obstructions)[169] or to comply with

---

165. Dorothy J. Solinger, "Policy Consistency in the Midst of Crisis: Managing the Furloughed and the Farmers in Three Cities," in *Holding China Together: Diversity and National Integration in the Post-Deng Era*, ed. Barry Naughton and Dali Yang (New York: Cambridge University Press, 2004), 149–92; Moore, "China and Globalization," 109.

166. Naughton, "China's Economy," 54–55, and "The Chinese Economy: WTO, Trade, and U.S.-China Relations," in *U.S.-China Relations, Fifth Conference*, 18, 1 (January 17–23, 2003) (Washington, D.C.: Aspen Institute, 2003), 40; Cheng Li, "China in 2000: A Year of Strategic Rethinking," *AS*, 41, 1 (January–February 2001), 80–81; Li, "China's Macroeconomic Stabilization," 944–45; Lardy, *Integrating China*, 17, 20; Moore, "China and Globalization," 109; Lowell Dittmer, "Leadership Change and Chinese Political Development," *CQ* 176 (December 2003), 908.

167. Lardy, *Integrating China*, 80–81.

168. Moore, "China and Globalization," 110; Bhalla and Qiu, *Employment Impact*, 3.

169. Jacobson and Oksenberg, *China's Participation*, 89; Pearson, "China's Integration," 163; Lardy, *Integrating China*, 10.

explicit rules of that regime—all in advance of becoming a member. The moves included massive slashing of China's tariffs, opening up to foreign investors sectors previously closed to them, eliminating export subsidies, and removing strictures on quotas and licensing.[170] One prominent illustration is that China's average tariff rate was brought down from 56 percent in the early 1980s to 15 percent at the time of admission. A second example is that between the early 1980s and 2001, the number of imports subject to quotas or licenses was step by step cut down by 80 percent.[171]

As the leadership sought to fit the country's economic structures and practices into the WTO's regimen, it was to find that almost all the rules to which it had to acquiesce would require that China totally alter the conduct of its foreign trade. This held whether it meant reducing tariffs and nontariff barriers (such as quotas and licensing), treating foreign firms no differently than domestic ones (national treatment), cutting back subsidies for both exporting and production, or removing price distortions.[172] And every one of these measures had negative externalities for employment.

By the mid-1990s, the pointed impact on labor occasioned by these steps no longer greatly worried the Chinese leadership, for its chief members had already resolved to—and already managed to—substantially cut back the workforce by domestic fiat in any event. Lower tariffs and a lack of licenses became just more factors working in that same direction. In the end, as Mexico's Salinas also agreed to obligations not all of which served his nation's own best interests, China's leaders too jumped into the ring, conceding to what has been called "WTO-plus" conditions.[173] As they thereby similarly selected international commercial partners over their prior domestic alliance with the working class, this elite, like the ones in France and Mexico, readjusted the fulcrum within their political balances between the forces of capital (both at home and abroad) on the one side and domestic labor on the other.

170. Jacobson and Oksenberg, *China's Participation*, 83, 105, 141; Bhalla and Qiu, *Employment Impact*, 5–11, 114, 162–63; Lampton, *Same Bed, Different Dreams*, 181–83; Pearson, "China's Integration," 166–76, and "Case for China's Accession," 342–44, 355–56; Zweig, *Internationalizing China*, 35–36, 262.

171. Nicholas Lardy, "Adjustment of Foreign Trade Policies and Foreign Direct Investment," comment presented at the China Development Forum, Beijing, March 24–25, 2002. For a detailed listing of the gradual erasure of tariffs, see Lardy, *Integrating China*, 33–45. Ibid., 23, notes the cuts in nontariff barriers.

172. Bhagirath Lal Das, *The World Trade Organisation: A Guide to the Framework for International Trade* (London: Zed Books, 1999); Lardy, *Integrating China*, 81–104.

173. China's market-opening commitments were characterized as "sweeping" by the United Nations Conference on Trade and Development, in United Nations Development Program, *China Human Development*, 142, which also lists the benefits China should derive from membership. Lardy, *Integrating China*, 80–81, terms the conditions "WTO-plus," and on 22 sums up the commitments China made; Bhalla and Qiu, *Employment Impact*, 4, 11–12, 15, 72–73, 101, 104–5. For China's concessions and promises, see Wang, "Openness, Distributive Conflict."

Conclusion

China, France, and Mexico each entered and prepared to enter (or, in France's case, reconfirmed its participation in) a supranational economic organization between 1983 and 2001 in response to crises (or, in China's case, to a perceived or self-styled "crisis"), though the degree of severity of their positions differed. Of Mexico it could fairly be said that it was pushed into a corner by events almost totally outside its control. France's top politicians really did have two choices, even if the road not taken was likely to have led to further troubles down the path.[174] China's leaders also had a choice of the same sort—to continue along the course that had led to stagnation or to try another route. But of the latter two, France was under a much more specific and direct pressure from the outside, in the form of its European Community partners, when it made its selection. Thus there are some differences in the finer points of the plights of the three.

Nonetheless, the commonalities I have identified in the broad direction of the politicians' choices in each country, in the consequences of those choices for workers, and in the external and internal constraints under which the choices were fashioned enable me to conclude that these leaders operated in coinciding contexts with congruent macroeconomic coping strategies. All three gave up much of their accustomed modi operandi, vis-à-vis domestic labor and employment as well as styles of foreign trade and investment. After their analogous encounters with crisis around 1980, a common factor thus drove leaders in each country to behave as they did: they decided to join supranational economic bodies, which, in turn, meant submission to what for their nations were new rules of the game.

Such rules already appealed to these political elites—whether as a function of their own prior careers (in Mexico), their own educations (in France and Mexico), or their consultation of successful foreign experience (in China). In the end, all these leaders agreed to comply with these rules, as they had become convinced by the time of joining that they could contravene them only at grave economic peril to their countries. And though these regulations—of the WTO, the EU, and NAFTA—were not all precisely the same, the sudden unemployment that each country experienced in the course of entering or preparing to enter these bodies can be explained at least in part with reference to these rules. Having made a case for correspondence, I proceed to account for variant reactions by affected workers.

---

174. Levy, "France: Directing Adjustment," 324.

Part 2
DIVERGENCES

5

UNIONS AND PROTEST

Labor against the State and Global Forces

Once workers were severed from their posts and left the plants or were subjected to sudden cutbacks in their benefits, after 1983 in France and Mexico and in the 1990s in China, one would have expected a strong response. This chapter asks whether and where that occurred. The main question is whether there were changes in levels of protest in the face of abrupt deprivation, with the coming of unemployment surges and welfare cuts, as compared with the past. One might hypothesize—other things being equal—that the comparable historical features that had long linked workers' loyalty to and high expectations of their rulers, when joined to similar shifts in their post-1980 plights, should have called forth increases in protest among them all against acts of state disavowal. In other words, relative deprivation, compared with their own previous situations, should have led to the flaunting of grievances in each of them.

What happened, instead, was that Mexican and French workers protested far less than they had in the past. It was just in China that public marches, rallies, and struggles of all sorts rose exponentially in number after 1990. What can account for this puzzle? I propose that the "terms of attachment" that bound states to workers and their unions is the primary explanatory factor. These terms "mediated" the impact of globalization, to borrow a concept from Andrew Cortell.[1] Ironically, the upshot was that internationally fomented market forces produced the most commotion in the one state of the three where the unions were weakest.

---

1. Andrew P. Cortell, *Mediating Globalization: Domestic Institutions and Industrial Policies in the United States and Britain* (Albany: State University of New York Press, 2006).

Chapters 3 and 4 investigated the power of the economic imperatives of the new world order—of global economic forces—to compel similar state choices and moves in these three countries. Given the untenable situations into which each set of political elites had taken their states, when crisis hit, external forces were able to push troubled state leaders in all three to choose to join supranational economic organizations in their search for solutions, and then to engineer unemployment to meet the regulations of their new organizations. In those chapters, global forces were the independent variable.

Here and in the next chapter I argue that discrepancies among the three countries in the rise or fall of labor protest (and, in chapter 6, in new state welfare allocations that followed) were also in part conditioned by global economic forces (and by state policies of economic liberalization in response to those forces). But in this and the following chapter these forces are mediated, not sole, determinants of action. For the different terms of attachment in each country shaped the way in which similar global economic forces were processed internally in each place. That is, disparate terms molded the way in which global forces affected workers' protests (and their ability to protest) in the three states after the early 1980s. The dependent variable is the frequency of protest after the early 1980s, as compared with the level of activism in a given country stirred up by its workers in the past.

The basic contrast that emerges highlights the combined impact of two factors—similar global forces and older, seemingly similar, but ultimately unlike patterns of state-worker-union interactions—on worker activism. The comparison is one between, in China, a heightening of the original impotence of unions under the onslaught of marketization and privatization, which permitted workers to act autonomously; in France, a diminution of unions' appeal in workers' eyes and so a decline in their memberships, and thus of their earlier bargaining power (such as it was), in the face of *rigeur,* resulting in a reduction in workers' protests; and in Mexico, an ongoing, fundamentally unaltered repressiveness over workers by union bosses loyal to the PRI as Mexico liberalized and as that country's leaders aimed to satisfy foreign investors, producing a sizable setback for protest.

Admittedly, the protests in the three places had differing objectives: in China angry workers addressed job loss and wage and pension shortfalls whereas in Mexico and France the demonstrators were still-employed strikers agitating against wage levels, working conditions, and threats of benefit cuts. Nonetheless, I consider them together, for what interests me is variation over time in the level of activism in response to employment and welfare setbacks in each state.

Crude Measurements

To some extent these differences can be measured. But complete and accurate statistics on protest numbers and on trends are not available, for a number of reasons. In France and Mexico, annual data exist just for strikes and lockouts, not for protests over job loss. Moreover, in Mexico, while strikes themselves declined greatly, worker petitions (which were requests to demonstrate but whose submission required prior state approval) may have been numerous, but nearly all were later withdrawn. In China, the principal difficulty is that the regime works hard to keep bad news out of the media but from time to time releases figures on "social disturbances," a broad and ambiguous category. There are no known comprehensive compilations available for China either of strikes or of demonstrations over job loss.[2]

Nevertheless, the International Labour Office publishes a database on all strikes in a number of countries (a category that is different, of course, from demonstrations by workers aggrieved because of layoffs) which was compiled by its Bureau of Statistics from the early 1970s through the year 2000. These numbers reveal certain interesting trends in militancy over these years for France and Mexico. First of all, the number of strikes and lockouts in France over the years 1980–2001 reached a peak in 1982, the year before Mitterrand's U-turn toward the European Community's regimen. The numbers dropped to nearly half that in many of the following years up until 1999 (one exception being the year of a major society-wide movement in 1995, which still fell far below the level in 1982). Moreover, whereas the number of strikes and lockouts ranged from 3,121 to 4,348 in the 1970s in France, the range from 1985 to 1998 was just 1,391 to 2,040, contractions of more than 50 percent.

Indeed, Mark Kesselman comments that "prior to the strike wave of 1995, strikes were at their lowest level in the postwar period"; he adds that in 1970, there was an average of 1.75 days of work stoppage due to strikes each week, whereas by 1990 that statistic had dropped by more than two-thirds.[3] Even more notable, while the numbers of workers involved reached a high of 4,348,000 in 1976, those figures had fallen by about three-quarters by the late 1990s, with the one exception again being the year 1995. And the number of days not worked, which was as high as almost 4.4 million in 1980, dropped into the hundreds of thousands by 1985 and remained there until 2001 (with one exception, in 1988). See Figures 5.1–5.3.

In Mexico, the contrasts between pre-1982 and thereafter are sharper yet. Where in the first three years of the 1980s more than 1,000 strikes and lockouts occurred, reaching as many as 1,925 in 1982, immediately thereafter—just when the force of the debt crisis was felt the most—the numbers abruptly plummeted to

2. There was a report of 87,000 "public order disturbances" having taken place in the year 2005. But this category includes any event in which people gathered in a disorderly fashion, so it is not a record of worker protests. See Richard McGregor, "Data Show Social Unrest on the Rise in China," *Financial Times*, January 19, 2006, citing an official statistic released on the same date on the website of the Ministry of Public Security.

3. Kesselman, "French Labor Movement," 150

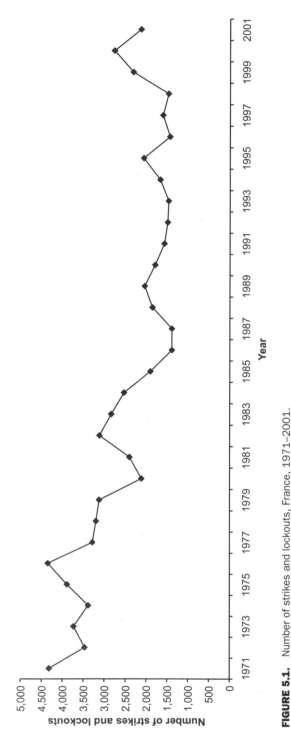

FIGURE 5.1. Number of strikes and lockouts, France, 1971–2001.

Source: Compiled from an International Labour Office database kept by the ILO Bureau of Statistics. The statistics are collected by the Sections de l'Inspection du travail. They are compiled by the Direction départementale du travail, the Direction régionale du travail, and the Administration central of the Ministère du Travail (Section des etudes et de la statistique). Accessed at http://laborsta.ilo.org/.

Notes: Localized strikes (the call to strike concerns only one establishment); one strike represents one establishment on strike; excludes agriculture and public administration.

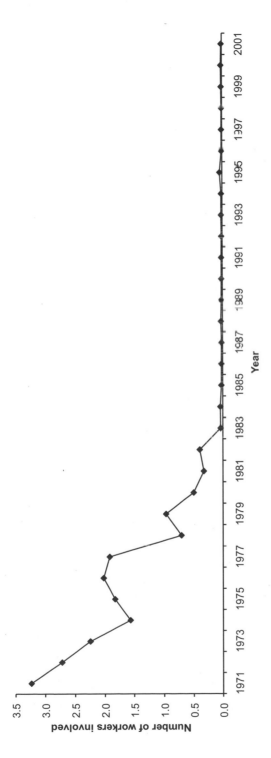

FIGURE 5.2. Number of workers involved in strikes and lockouts, France, 1971–2001.

Source: Compiled from an International Labour Office database kept by the ILO Bureau of Statistics. The statistics are collected by the Sections de l'Inspection du travail. They are compiled by the Direction départementale du travail, the Direction régionale du travail, and the Administration central of the Ministère du Travail (Section des etudes et de la statistique). Accessed at http://laborsta.ilo.org/.

Notes: Localized strikes (the call to strike concerns only one establishment); monthly average of workers involved in strikes in progress each month; excludes agriculture and public administration.

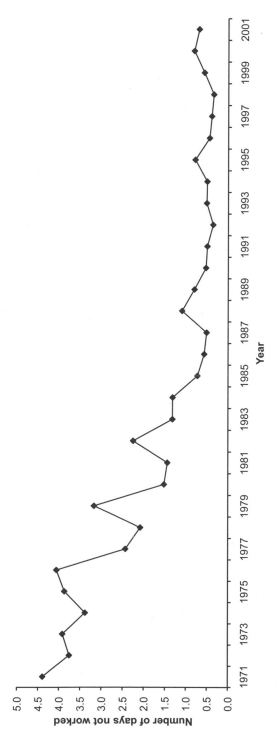

FIGURE 5.3. Number of days not worked because of strikes and lockouts, France, 1971–2001.

Source: Compiled from an International Labour Office database kept by the ILO Bureau of Statistics. The statistics are collected by the Sections de l'Inspection du travail. They are compiled by the Direction départementale du travail, the Direction régionale du travail, and the Administration central of the Ministère du Travail (Section des études et de la statistique). Accessed at http://laborsta.ilo.org/.

Notes: Localized strikes (the call to strike concerns only one establishment); figures rounded to nearest 100; excludes agriculture and public administration.

around a mere 100 per annum. By 1995, the counts had descended into the single digits. And while the number of days not worked because of strikes stood above 1.36 million in 1982, by the mid-1990s the statistics show a decline of 90 percent. See Figures 5.4–5.6.

From a different angle, figures from China and France provide some sense of the relative restiveness of their respective working classes. Timothy B. Smith reports that in Paris in 2001, 1,460 street demonstrations broke out over pay, working conditions, job security, and related matters, averaging four per day.[4] By contrast, Murray Scot Tanner, writing on the same period in one particular part of China, the northeastern province of Liaoning (the province that suffered the highest number of retrenchments of China's thirty-one provinces), saw 9,559 incidents between January 2000 and September 2002. This amounted to an average of ten per day over nearly three years.[5] This critical Chinese province, in short, saw a full two and a half times the number of protests as Paris. Thus, though neither the grievances nor the types of resistance are truly congruent, it is striking how dissimilar the incidence of open discontent was in these two sites.

The data are not strictly comparable, unfortunately. According to Smith, for the most part the protests in Paris—where such actions had long been normal events— were mounted by employed, well-compensated workers who enjoyed high levels of benefits and were objecting to what were only modest cutbacks; workers who had lost their jobs appear either to have been largely silent or to have attracted little attention from the data compilers.[6] In China, though, it was precisely those who had lately lost their jobs and were protesting unpaid wages and pensions who came forth. The figures themselves, nonetheless, are roughly comparable: the total urban-registered population of Liaoning was about the same size as the total urban and suburban one residing in Paris at around the same time.[7]

Documentary sources indicate that protest in China was indeed substantial and steadily increasing in and after the late 1990s. The Ministry of Public Security found that the numbers of "mass incidents…began a rise like a violent wind" from

4. Timothy B. Smith, *France in Crisis: Welfare, Inequality and Globalization since 1980* (New York: Cambridge University Press, 2004), 45.

5. Tanner, "China Rethinks Unrest," 140.

6. An example of one unemployment protest is Craig R. Whitney, "French Jobless Seize Unemployment Offices to Press for $500 Bonus," *NYT,* December 30, 1997.

7. According to Demographia, Paris Population Analysis and Data Product (24 March 2001), the total Parisian population was in the range of 11 million (10,952,011) in 1999 (http://www.demographia.com/db-parismet1921.htm). The urban-registered population of Liaoning province in 2002 was just over 14 million (14,160,030). Guojia tongjiju chengshi shehui jingji diaocha zongdui, bian [National statistics bureau, urban society and economy investigation general team, ed.], *Zhongguo chengshi tongji nianjian—2002* [China city statistical yearbook—2002] (Beijing: Zhongguo tongji chubanshe [Chinese Statistics Press, 2003), 37.

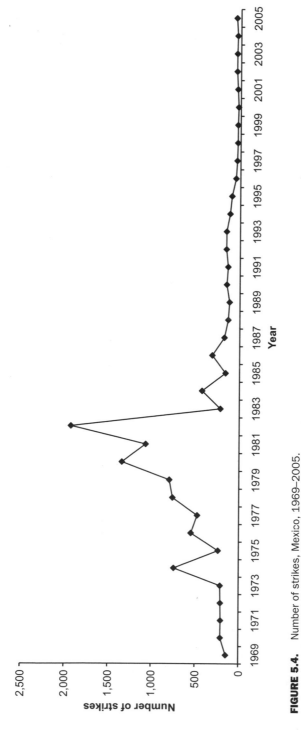

FIGURE 5.4. Number of strikes, Mexico, 1969–2005.

Source: Compiled from an International Labour Office database kept by the ILO Bureau of Statistics. The statistics are collected by the Sections de l'Inspection du travail. They are compiled by the Direction départementale du travail, the Direction régionale du travail, and the Administration central of the Ministère du Travail (Section des etudes et de la statistique). Accessed at http://laborsta.ilo.org/.

Note: Excludes enterprises covered by ocal jurisdiction.

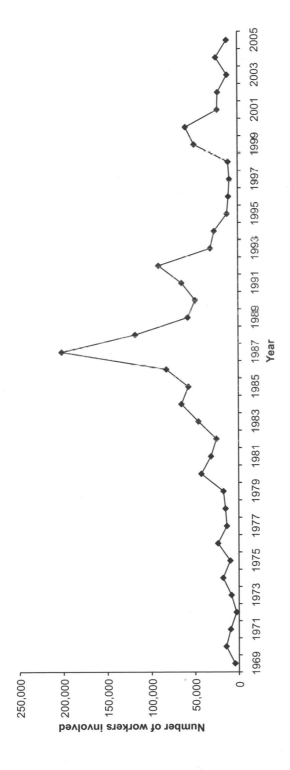

FIGURE 5.5. Number of workers involved in strikes, Mexico, 1969–2005.

Source: Compiled from an International Labour Office database kept by the ILO Bureau of Statistics. The statistics are collected by the Sections de l'Inspection du travail. They are compiled by the Direction départementale du travail, the Direction régionale du travail, and the Administration central of the Ministère du Travail (Section des études et de la statistique). Accessed at http://laborsta.ilo.org/.

Notes: Excludes enterprises covered by local jurisdictions; union members only (excludes workers indirectly involved and workers in positions of trust).

133

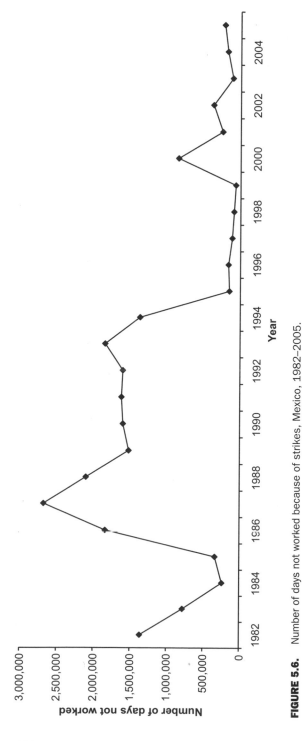

FIGURE 5.6. Number of days not worked because of strikes, Mexico, 1982–2005.

Source: Compiled from an International Labour Office database kept by the ILO Bureau of Statistics. The statistics are collected by the Sections de l'Inspection du travail. They are compiled by the Direction départementale du travail, the Direction régionale du travail, and the Administration central of the Ministère du Travail (Section des etudes et de la statistique). Accessed at http://laborsta.ilo.org/.

Note: Excludes enterprises covered by local jurisdiction.

1997, the year of the 15th Party Congress, which had pressed for factory firings.[8] Tanner attests to "incidents numbering in the tens of thousands each year";[9] he also cites a local Chinese report showing that in one province over 80 percent of the mass demonstrations were the result of dissatisfactions with the program of economic reform, which had radically undercut labor's position.[10] Another study characterized labor protests as having increased "by quantum leaps" in the 1990s.[11] And by the end of the decade, 100,000 labor protests had taken place (though certainly not all of them were waged by dismissed workers), according to the Center for Human Rights and Democracy, based in Hong Kong.[12]

How can we account for these differences of mounting outbursts in China, where nearly none had occurred in prior years, versus a sharp decrease in demonstrations in France and, even more so, in Mexico in the wake of similar losses? After reviewing several alternative hypotheses, I focus on the differential nature of the three countries' terms of attachment that connected states, unions, and workers as they all confronted challenging times.

Alternative Explanations

Before advancing alternative explanations, I want to dispel one possible objection: that the trajectory of protest in France as compared with China was much more sharply downward simply because the numbers of workers left to protest in France after 1981 might have decreased more rapidly, in proportion to the numbers of workers in 1981, than was the case in China. Perhaps, one might argue, this took place as manufacturing declined in the former country.[13] But this argument does not speak to my story, since the demonstrations were mounted precisely by those who were losing or had lost their jobs. In any event, as chapter 3 has documented, the proportion of the workforce in China that was affected by layoffs had already shot up to one-third of the total by 1998, with at least another 20 million or more being dismissed in the few years after that.

---

8. Gong'anbu dixi yanjiusuo "quntixing shijian yanjiu" ketizu [Ministry of Public Security Fourth Research Institute's "mass incidents research" group], "Woguo fasheng quntixing shijian de diaocha yu sikao" [Investigation and reflections on our country's mass incidents], *NBCY* 31 (576) (8/10/2001), 18. Party General Secretary Jiang Zemin's report to the congress is in *SWB* FE/3023 (September 13, 1997), S1/1–S1/10.

9. Tanner, "China Rethinks Unrest," 137.

10. Murray Scot Tanner, "Rethinking Law Enforcement and Society: Changing Police Analyses of Social Unrest," draft paper for the Conference on Law and Society in Contemporary China, Berkeley, Calif., September 2002, 10.

11. Chen, "Subsistence Crises," 41.

12. Jiang Xueqin, "Fighting to Organize," *FEER*, September 6, 2001, 72.

13. Thanks to an anonymous reviewer for the suggestion to consider this.

I began by reiterating that the workers in question were subsisting after the early 1980s in somewhat similar situations. Once-privileged workers in each of the three nations experienced sudden setbacks on two levels: all saw their material situations worsen rapidly and unexpectedly as their governments gave in first to global forces (chapter 3) and later to SEOs' rules (chapter 4)—which, in practice, amounted to a proxy for those forces. Even though I focus on these states' leaders joining different SEOs after 1980—each of which varied somewhat in its composition, goals, and partner members—the relevant regulations of all these bodies mandated behavior that was substantially congruent in its impact on workers and their jobs. And on a psychological plane, given that at least the elite among the workers had long entertained high expectations of, and a sense of dependency on, their states, their discontent and anger were apt to be mixed with a sense of betrayal in all these countries.

They all, in short, saw contractions of varying sorts in the physical, consumption-oriented conditions of their daily lives and, in all probability, also suffered corresponding psychological shocks. So because of like linkages with the state in the past (as laid out in chapter 2), and also because of comparable contemporary blows after 1980, one could expect a certain resemblance in laborers' responses to parallel—if not self-same—treatment and troubles at the hands of their once-generous governments.

I noted earlier that, were all else equal, one would expect more resistance when things got seriously worse for workers. But in fact, other things were *not* equal, though the variation was not in the expected direction. To start with, there was a set of what would seem to have been critical contextual differences that determined the objective *economic circumstances* facing aggrieved workers in the three countries (and thus, one might hypothesize, a variable likelihood of protest on material grounds, that is, with regard to the degree of sheer need).

There were also fundamental political differences in regime type among the three countries, and thus in the political opportunities and accompanying political calculations of the workers. These differences could have affected the probability on *political grounds* that aggrieved workers in one place would be more apt to express opposition publicly than those in another. Accordingly, I looked at the extent to which these contextual conditions—both economic and political— might have accounted for lesser protest over time in France and Mexico but a rise in unrest in China.

To begin with workers' objective *material circumstances*, the following variables could potentially account for differences in protest propensity. First, was there a possibility of obtaining welfare relief (specifically, unemployment insurance) to compensate for job losses? Second, did foreign-invested, private-sector, or informal labor markets exist, allowing dismissed workers to find new jobs if they had lost their state-sector ones? And third, were there opportunities to migrate to places where jobs were more plentiful? The supposition would be that where welfare relief, other jobs, or chances to leave were available, protest would be reduced. All these options would have given newly deprived laborers an "exit" from their plight.[14]

As for the *political environment* they confronted, one might hypothesize that regime type (along with ongoing regime change, in the case of Mexico) would be a critical factor. Here the option of "voice" would be relevant. But this factor can cut both ways. On the one hand, workers should have more space and scope for opposition in democratic contexts than in authoritarian or post-totalitarian ones, where repression is apt to operate as a serious obstacle to disruption. According to this argument, one could predict that protests would be most numerous in democratic France, where the political climate was most permissive, next most numerous in still-democratizing Mexico, and least of all in authoritarian China, where the risk of repression, one would assume, would have been greatest. But on the other hand, in democracies, though there is more openness and opportunity for demonstrating, there are also other, legitimate avenues for displaying discontent. These possibilities include elections, in which the discontented could try to empower opposing parties, and legal redress. Both factors might reduce the level of civil unrest. Thus it may be difficult to make firm predictions about the level of protest on the basis of political regime type alone.

On the *material level,* of the three countries it was only in France that workers had an extant unemployment insurance system to which they could turn for sustenance. And yet social expenditures themselves, like jobs, were also in decline in France, and indeed, these cuts were a prime motivation for demonstrators there. Already in the austerity budget of autumn 1982 severe reductions had been made; in 1987, Prime Minister Chirac put through legislation that allowed for the lowering of once legally enforced social benefits for workers.[15] As the 1980s unfolded, informal-sector jobs did steadily grow in number.[16] But this only meant that full-time, permanent, benefit-blessed jobs were being replaced more and more by part-time, unentitled work.[17]

Most of the strikes that did take place in France were aimed precisely at preventing layoffs or at blocking decreases in benefits.[18] This feature would suggest that a

---

14. Albert O. Hirschman, *Exit, Voice, and Loyalty* (Cambridge, Mass.: Harvard University Press, 1970).

15. Kesselman, conclusion to *French Workers' Movement,* 318, and "French Labor Movement," 150.

16. Part-time and temporary jobs increased by 30 percent the years 1988 to 1993, while the number of stable, permanent jobs declined by 15 percent. Kesselman, "French Labor Movement," 154.

17. Kesselman, "New Shape of French Labour," 172, and "French Labor Movement," 147–48, 153, 154.

18. Kesselman, "French Labor Movement," 150.

loss of employment—and of its attached welfare—was of critical importance to many workers of the period. At any rate, having unemployment insurance to fall back on would not have been a major deterrent to dissatisfaction. For the benefits themselves declined over time for a given worker and generally expired after just two and a half years. And as a leader of French unemployed workers remarked in 1997, "We should not forget that 80 percent of all the unemployed in France get less than $500 per month in benefits."[19] Not surprisingly, then, when demonstrations did break out, calls for job creation were prominent.[20]

As for the role of migration, the main issue among most of the jobless was not about whether they could leave the country, but about the marked discrimination that existed in France against hiring aliens (or even their first-generation descendants). This grievance was a raw one at the sites where levels of unemployment were most elevated: when unemployment stood around 10 percent in late 2005 in the rest of France, in immigrant neighborhoods it rose as high as 30 percent or even more.[21]

While formal unemployment insurance was not part of Mexico's political economy, public-sector workers had been the beneficiaries of all manner of subsidies and privileges—for housing, health care, and daily-use goods—in the days before 1982. But with the onset of the debt crisis there, Mexico saw a sharp decrease in the priority the government placed on social spending in education, health, and general social welfare, with a drop from 14.9 percent of the federal budget in 1982 down to only 9.2 percent five years later.[22] Thus, Mexico's relatively low rate of rebelliousness among its retrenched could not be attributed to labor's ability to rely on social insurance instead.

Informal labor markets were certainly present: as early as the late 1980s—a time when the unemployment rate was estimated to be 17.6 percent and the state was still the largest single employer—perhaps as many as a third of the working-age population was scraping out a living in what Kevin Middlebrook terms "marginally productive activities."[23] And by the end of the 1990s as much as half of the economically active population was relying on work in the informal sector. But the conditions there would have been of little consolation to the once-well-tended

19. Whitney, "French Jobless."

20. Adam Sage, "Day of Strikes a Test for Villepin," *Australian,* October 5, 2005; Craig S. Smith, "Chirac Appeals for Calm as Violent Protests Shake Paris's Suburbs," *NYT,* November 3, 2005, A11; Elaine Sciolino, "French Students Step Up Protests against New Job Law," *NYT,* March 15.

21. Smith, "Chirac Appeals for Calm."

22. Kevin Middlebrook, "The CTM and the Future of State-Labor Relations," in *Mexico's Alternative Political Futures,* ed. Wayne Cornelius et al. (San Diego: Center for U.S.-Mexican Studies, University of California, 1989), 293.

23. Kevin Middlebrook, "The Sounds of Silence: Organised Labour's Response to Economic Crisis in Mexico," *Journal of Latin American Studies* 21, 2 (1989), 198, and "CTM and the Future," 292.

state workers.[24] As for migration out of the country, this was surely an option for those without work in Mexico. But the rate of migration does not seem to have changed after 1982, and so would not explain the drop in demonstrativeness following that date.[25] So on material grounds, there are no easy answers for why protest lessened in France and Mexico in the 1980s and 1990s.

In China, unemployment insurance was initiated with new regulations for the first time only in the mid-1980s. But it did not go into meaningful operation until the late 1990s and so was not yet an option for the overwhelming majority of those detached from their workplaces as of the mid and late 1990s.[26] Even then, it served a very narrow segment of those whose jobs were gone. True, a special allowance was designed for laid-off workers (the *jiben shenghuofei* [basic living allowance]) and was implemented widely in 1998 and for a few years after, but its application was quite uneven, so workers in trouble could not count on it. On the other hand, as noted in chapter 4, the informal sector was rapidly expanding and existed as an alternative for workers who became laid off.[27] But this would not differentiate China from France and Mexico.

As for departing from the scene of job loss, this rarely occurred, for a former state worker was quite likely to be allowed to retain his or her housing even after having to forfeit the position. Accordingly, leaving one's hometown in search of another position elsewhere was a choice few were inclined to make. In China, thus, except for the possibility of moving to the informal sector, the potential for solving problems of sudden destitution through "exit" was not very great, and this might have disposed the dismissed to protest. But Chinese workers' lack of welfare insurance resembled what Mexican workers had to contend with, while the unlikelihood of their moving was similar to the situation in France.

Politically, the presence of democratic and democratizing regimes in the 1980s and 1990s in France and Mexico, respectively, also appears to have had little to do with their workers' decreased disposition to demonstrate after the early 1980s. In democratic France, there was, of course, little fear associated with fomenting disorder. And yet that disorder declined compared with pre-1982 there. And French with grievances certainly had the option of voicing their displeasure at the ballot

24. Levy and Bruhn, *Mexico*, 75; Dion, "Mexico's Welfare Regime," 22, 28.

25. According to a report in the *NYT*, "most of the men migrate to the U.S.," yet remaining workers nonetheless stirred up a protest in the autumn of 2001. See Ginger Thompson, "Mexican Labor Protest Gets Results," *NYT*, October 8, 2001.

26. Dorothy J. Solinger, "Path Dependency Reexamined: Chinese Welfare Policy in the Transition to Unemployment," *CP* 38, 1 (October 2005), 83–101.

27. Private companies already accounted for more than half of GDP by 2007 after their contribution had climbed steadily in the 1990s. Maureen Fan, "In China, a State Job Still Brings Benefits and Bragging Rights," *Washington Post*, May 29, 2007, A7.

box, and they used it.[28] But the ability to vote does not appear to have substituted for what was sometimes even simultaneous protest.[29] Besides, the top political issue going back to the early 1980s was judged by an influential, leftist newspaper, *The Liberation,* to be unemployment itself. This assessment indicates that despite the existence of unemployment insurance and private-sector jobs, the French have deep feelings about jobs.[30]

In Mexico, it is true that the left-oriented Democratic Revolutionary Party (PRD) nearly triumphed over the PRI in the 1988 presidential election, when a program of austerity was enervating the economy and depleting the job options in it in the late 1980s. But this did not mean that the voters among the newly unemployed found suffrage to be a solution to their woes, for the PRI managed to rig the returns, and its own candidate emerged as the victor. And when the PRI finally did lose the presidency in 2000, in what was then Mexico's most fair and open election ever, it was not to a candidate of the left. Within a year, disgruntled farmers who had had no part in the presidential victory of Vicente Fox, of the National Action Party (PAN), marched on the capital in anger against him.[31] So Mexican inclinations to express outrage were not quieted by the presence of an opportunity to cast ballots. In the next election, held in July 2006, voters' hunger for employment apparently overrode all their other concerns, even if there were plenty of jobs outside the state sector and even while people were departing for the United States in large numbers. In the run-up to the presidential polls, "jobs, jobs, and more jobs" was the chief platform of all three contenders.[32]

In China, there was no opportunity for an aggrieved worker to express his or her preferences on such matters as unemployment through the ballot, since only the most local units of urban society held elections, and the deliberations of these jurisdictions had no bearing on macro policymaking about the national structure of employment. As for regime type, as an authoritarian society it would seem that

---

28. An example is the Socialist Party victory in the 1997 general elections after the right failed to curb job loss. See Edmund L. Andrews, "The Jobless Are Snared in Europe's Safety Net," News of the Week in Review, *NYT,* November 9, 1997, 6. Another is the French vote against the European Union Constitution in May 2005, interpreted as a protest against French economic conditions, especially persistent high unemployment, plus the threat of cuts in social benefits that the EU represented to many French people.

29. In March 2004, teachers, hospital workers, scientists, and firefighters protested changes aimed at reducing retirement benefits and calling for harder work, even as the unpopularity of Chirac's domestic economic program led to losses for his party in regional elections. See Craig S. Smith, "In Setback for Chirac, French Veer Left in Regional Vote," *NYT,* March 29, 2004.

30. "For the past 25 years unemployment has been the French public's foremost concern and their prime voting motivation," according to an editorial in spring 2005, quoted in Elaine Sciolino, "The Continental Dream: Will the French Shatter It?" *NYT,* April 15, 2005.

31. Ginger Thompson, "Farm Unrest Roils Mexico, Challenging New Chief," *NYT,* July 22, 2001.

32. Sam Enriquez, "Candidates Pledge to Put Mexico to Work," *NYT,* June 11, 2006.

China would be a site where workers would be subject to repression if they dared to demonstrate. And indeed this was often the case. As layoffs mounted after the early 1990s, the police became implicated in the political management and oversight of demonstrations by terminated employees—sometimes simply for purposes of intimidation, other times to disperse marchers, and at yet other times resorting to violence, injuring the actors and detaining their leaders in the process.[33] This repression, however, while surely giving pause to many potential protesters, did not by any means bring street-based belligerence to a standstill.

Thus some aspects of the alternative explanations might yield insights for what happened in China, but most of them do not. And neither material circumstances nor political possibilities and opportunities explain why recently retrenched French and Mexican workers—or those in danger of losing some or all of their benefits—should have had a lesser propensity to go out on the sidewalks after 1982 than they did before. Nor can these factors lead us to an understanding of why Chinese laborers were more restive than those living in France and Mexico at a similar time and under somewhat similar circumstances. Having set aside these two forms of alternative explanation, I proceed to examine the place of unions in respect to the terms of attachment between workers and their states, and the way these terms affected the force of global market pressures.

China

The State and Its Workers

China's workers became far more demonstrative as the years of "economic reform," internationalization, and marketization went forward, as compared with their state of relative quiescence for most of the time during the preceding decades (except, of course, the years of generalized social turbulence during the late 1960s and early 1970s when the Cultural Revolution engulfed all of society, and on a few other, far briefer occasions, generally in conjunction with top leaders' initiation of nation-wide political movements).[34]

---

33. A few examples: Willy Wo-lap Lam, *SCMP*, March 2, 1994, 1, 8, reported the deployment of two armed police platoons to a strike of four thousand people, following the Ministry of Public Security's creation of a patrol police force in December 1993; *Hong Kong Standard*, September 27, 1994, 4; David Murphy, "Labour Unrest: Nothing to Celebrate," *FEER*, April 4, 2002, 32; Lisa Rose Weaver, "Taking on the State: China's Rustbelt Revolt," CNN.com, April 1, 2002; *SWB* FE/3885, July 6, 2000, G/9. Anti-terrorist exercises were held in autumn 2003 in a number of cities directed at preventing outbreaks of urban violence by aroused workers. Willy Wo-Lap Lam, "Beijing Faces Winter of Discontent," CNN.com, September 30, 2003.
34. Perry, "Labor's Battle."

That the job losses that came with market opening led to protests is at first glance surprising. After all, as is well known, in China the state's steps toward liberalization of the 1980s and thereafter were almost entirely limited to the economic realm, with only slight alterations to the political one. Top leaders repeatedly affirmed their determination to hold the underlying form of the regime constant, and even went so far as to erase the right to strike from the newly revised state constitution that appeared with the birth of marketization, in 1982. And critically, with new grants of autonomy and clout extended to factory management in the early 1980s, the capacities of unions were diminished.[35]

Yet after around 1995, workers in one place or another who had lost their jobs or their welfare benefits were out in the streets nearly daily. Although the government was determined to keep news of protests (and indeed of disturbances of any kind) out of the media, or to downplay their size and disruptiveness if they were reported, over the period 1994 to 2004 I was able to collect information on more than two hundred separate events, some from news sources in Hong Kong, some from the Western media, and a few from Chinese publications.[36] Descriptive data on these cases, along with a number of secondary sources,[37] inform my analysis of China.

---

35. Mary E. Gallagher, *Contagious Capitalism: Globalization and Politics of Labor in China* (Princeton, N.J.: Princeton University Press, 2005).

36. The news sources reporting these events are the following: two internal Chinese publications, Neibu canyue [Internal Consultations] (NBCY) and *Lingdao canyue* [Leadership Consultations] (*LDCY*); private letters from Chinese labor activists; one Chinese labor journal, *Zhongguo laodong* [Chinese Labor] (*ZGLD*); official Chinese news sources: Xinhua [News] (XH), *China Daily*, and Zhongguo xinwenshe [Chinese News Agency]); a range of publications from Hong Kong: the *South China Morning Post* (*SCMP*), *Hong Kong Standard*, *Wen Wei Po* [Cultural Paper], *Ming Pao* [Bright Paper] (*MP*), *Lien Ho Po* [United Paper], *Tangtai* [Contemporary Times], *Zheng Ming* [Contend], *Eastern Express* [now defunct], *Ping Guo Jih Pao* [Apple Daily], *Hsin Pao* [Information Paper], *Sing Tao Jih Pao* [Singdao Daily]; *Shijie ribao* [World Daily], the Hong Kong–based Zhongguo tongxunshe [Chinese News Report Agency], and Radio Television Hong Kong; the Central News Agency from Taipei; NHK TV from Japan; Radio Free Asia; *Far Eastern Economic Review* (*FEER*); news releases from human rights and labor groups, such as the Hong Kong Information Center for Human Rights and Democracy, *China Focus* (*CF*) (formerly published by exiles from the Chinese democracy movement at Princeton University, now defunct), *China Rights Forum* (*CRF*; the journal of the organization Human Rights in China), China Labor Watch, and the *China Labour Bulletin* (*CLB*); the online publication *China News Digest* [now defunct] (*CND*); the Western newspapers the *New York Times* (*NYT*), *Washington Post*, *Financial Times*, *Los Angeles Times* (*LAT*), and *Wall Street Journal* (*WSJ*); and the news agencies Agence France Press, Reuters, the Associated Press, and the British Broadcasting Corporation's Summary of World Broadcasts (*SWB*). I have all the citations on file but only occasionally, for important cases, note them here.

37. These include Marc Blecher, "Hegemony and Workers' Politics in China," *CQ* 170 (2002), 283–303; Ching Kwan Lee, "The Labor Politics of Market Socialism: Collective Inaction and Class Experiences among State Workers in Guangzhou," *MC* 24, 1 (January 1998), 3–33; Lee, "From Organized Dependence to Disorganized Despotism: Changing Labour Regimes in Chinese Factories," *CQ* 155 (1999), 44–71; Lee, "The 'Revenge of History': Collective Memories and Labor Protests in Northeastern

These secondary materials show that workers were generally slow to mount a demonstration and reactive and peaceable in their style. In one typical case, a reporter characterized the workers as "careful to avoid any activity that might be seen as illegal or presenting a political challenge to the government."[38] As another observer aptly noted, aggrieved workers demonstrate only "after the failure of all other mediation possibilities."[39] The typical pathway to protest was uncommonly cautious. An incident would begin with petitions to the management of the former employees' old firm. If no reply was received, or when negotiations bogged down, frustrated workers moved up the administrative hierarchy to their municipal leaders, usually to report the malfeasance or poor faith of their enterprise directors. If they found no satisfaction there, supplicants might proceed to writing petitions to send to even higher levels, first the provincial one. Some, in desperation, would travel to Beijing, as a last conciliatory resort. Another peaceable ploy was to work through the nascent legal system, beginning with arbitration and proceeding to the courts. As more and more workers became aware of their rights, use of this modality grew more common. But both petitions and calls to the courts were notoriously disappointing to those who experimented with them through the early 2000s.[40]

The steps to staging sit-ins—often before urban administration compounds, sometimes at factory gates—or to holding rallies and marches in which participants carried posters and shouted slogans, or to blocking traffic all signaled a further advance. As irritations and resentments persisted and escalated, and as

China," *Ethnography* 1, 2 (2000), 218; Lee, "From the Specter of Mao to the Spirit of the Law: Labor Insurgency in China," *Theory and Society* 31 (2002), 189–228; Lee, "Three Patterns of Working-Class Transitions in China," in *Politics in China: Moving Frontiers,* ed. Françoise Mengin and Jean-Louis Rocca (New York: Palgrave, 2002); Chen, "Subsistence Crises"; Feng Chen, "Between the State and Labour: The Conflict of Chinese Trade Unions' Double Identity in Market Reform," *CQ* 176 (December 2003), 1006–28; Yongshun Cai, "The Resistance of Chinese Laid-Off Workers in the Reform Period," *CQ* 170 (2002), 327–44; William Hurst and Kevin O'Brien, "China's Contentious Pensioners," *CQ* 170 (2002), 345–60; Jean-Louis Rocca, "Old Working Class, New Working Class: Reforms, Labour Crisis and the Two Faces of Conflicts in Chinese Urban Areas," first draft of a paper presented at the Second Annual Conference of the European Union–China Academic Network, January 21–22, 1999, Centro de Estudios de Asia Oriental, Universidad Autónoma de Madrid, Spain; Rocca, "Three at Once: The Multidimensional Scope of the Labor Crisis in China," in Mengin and Rocca, *Politics in China,* 3–30; Antoine Kernen, "Worker Protest in China: Toward a New Public Management of Social Conflicts" paper presented at the annual meeting of the Association for Asian Studies, April 4–7, 2002, Washington, D.C.; Antoine Kernen and Jean-Louis Rocca, "Social Responses to Unemployment and the 'New Urban Poor': Case Study in Shenyang City and Liaoning Province," *China Perspectives* 27 (2000), 35–51; Marc Blecher, "The Working Class and Governance in China," in *Governance in China,* ed. Jude Howell (Lanham, Md.: Rowman & Littlefield, 2004).

38. Philip P. Pan, "'High Tide' of Labor Unrest in China: Striking Workers Risk Arrest to Protest Pay Cuts, Corruption," *Washington Post,* January 21, 2002, A1.

39. Kernen, "Worker Protest," 15.

40. Mary E. Gallagher, "Mobilizing the Law in China: 'Informed Disenchantment' and the Development of Legal Consciousness," *Law and Society Review* 40, 4 (December 2006).

the hopelessness of appealing through official channels sank in, the numbers of participants would rise. In extreme and relatively rare cases, workers would throw themselves onto railway tracks (or even, in at least one case, onto an airport runway[41]), destroy machines, loot goods, detain or attack cadres, or burn police cars. The episodes were generally short, sporadic, spontaneous, and limited to one factory at a time. All in all, as of 2008, the wealth of incidents that unfolded remained far from constituting a labor movement.[42]

Not just the process but also the content of workers' pleas and plaints followed standardized patterns. Across the nation, the roots and the refrains of tribulation were the same: old unpaid wages and recently neglected pension payouts, sudden termination of medical care reimbursement, failure to deliver promised living allowances or unemployment insurance, insufficient severance packages. Simple appeals for food, work (whether new jobs or reinstatement in the old ones), and basic sustenance formed the core of their recitals. These straightforward cries for subsistence intensified when workers believed they had uncovered sordid stories of management embezzlement and alleged wrongful bankruptcies, plant closures, mergers, and takeovers. When these outrages occurred, participants demanded information and a chance for input.

Indeed, charges of corruption were nearly omnipresent behind the tales of hunger and other deprivations, as the processes of economic liberalization and privatization provided many opportunities for questionable exchange.[43] In one documented case workers suspected they were victims of a "fake bankruptcy," when—as is often the case in recent years in China—their managers hid their enterprise's assets, declared bankruptcy, and then bought the firm at a cut-rate price, using embezzled funds.[44] In another instance, over a thousand workers threw themselves on the trunkline of the Beijing-Shanghai railroad, suspending the line for up to eight hours because of a rumor that their old textile plant in the interior, burdened by heavy debts, obsolete equipment, and excessive personnel—as well as corrupt leadership—was to be announcing a reorganization and listing its shares on the stock market, after which it would be retrenching half its labor force and not paying the workers the money they were owed.[45]

The behavior of the authorities in the cities mirrored the goals of the central Party and state leaders in Beijing, but with some variation rooted in the differential

---

41. Elisabeth Rosenthal, "Workers' Plight Brings New Militancy in China," *NYT,* March 10, 2003.

42. Chen, "Subsistence Crises," 62; Blecher, "Working Class," 6; Kernen, "Worker Protest," 2; Rocca, "Three at Once."

43. Sun, *Corruption and Market.*

44. Pan, "High Tide."

45. The Hong Kong Information Center for Human Rights and Democracy, November 29, 2000, in *SWB* FE/4012 (December 1, 2000), G/2).

financial resources of the various localities, according to William Hurst.[46] As the site of final enforcement, the municipality was the place where choices had to be taken as to whether to soft-pedal official countermeasures when protests broke out, in the hope of not further inflaming impassioned protesters, or to quell disturbances with raw violence. Behind this choice lay a major incentive for urban officials to mollify protesters: a portion of the evaluation of a given local official's performance hinged on whether that person was able to preserve tranquility in his bailiwick.[47]

Urban authorities at the scene of disturbances in general feared provoking bigger conflagrations, and so they usually attempted, at least at first, to subdue the protesters. In some cases officials sent propagandists to meet with the demonstrators in the hope of changing their outlooks.[48] Municipal elites whose localities had the resources to do so would offer payoffs or extend promises—pledges that might never be fulfilled—or temporarily reverse the implementation of some reform measure that was especially disadvantageous to labor. Jurisdictions short on funds could appeal to the central treasury for emergency assistance, and, sensing the danger of not complying, central leaders often extended at least a portion of the funds requested. As a rule of thumb, both central leaders and their local deputies tended to tread lightly where the protest was small-scale, confined to one work unit, apolitical in its appeal, and nonviolent, and where it seemed to be spontaneous.[49]

Taken together, both the authorities—whether at central or local echelons—and the leaders of the demonstrations became locked into a tacit contract: though the protest went on, most of the time neither side was prepared to go beyond the limits of what the other would tolerate.[50] Thus older, popular presumptions about leaders' proper beneficence toward the state workforce, combined with politicians'

---

46. William Hurst, "The Forgotten Player: Local State Strategies and the Dynamics of Chinese Laid-Off Workers' Contention," paper presented at the conference "Reassessing Unrest in China," Washington, D.C., December 2003, 20.

47. Susan Whiting, *Power and Wealth in Rural China: The Political Economy of Institutional Change* (New York: Cambridge University Press, 2001), 115–16, 234; Lee, "Revenge of History," 218; Yongshun Cai, *State and Laid-Off Workers in Reform China* (New York: Routledge, 2005).

48. Lu Yu-shan, "CPC Guards against Mass Disturbances," *Tangdai* [Contemporary Times], 38 (May 15, 1994), 20–22; *MP*, April 4, 1998; Matt Forney, "We Want to Eat," *FEER*, June 26, 1997; Liu Binyan, "The Working Class Speaks Out," *CF*, August 1, 1997, 1; Craig S. Smith, "Workers in China Organize to Oppose Restructurings," *WSJ*, June 7, 1999; "Liaoyang Ferroalloy Factory Workers Protest and Petition Again Demanding the Release of Four Detained Workers' Representatives," China Labor Watch Press Release, October 3, 2002; *MP*, December 1, 1996, 6; and *SWB* FE/4012, December 1, 2000, G/3, from *Anhui ribao* [Anhui Daily], November 28, 2000, 2.

49. See Andrew G. Walder, "The Party Elite and China's Trajectory of Change," *China: An International Journal* 2, 2 (2004), 206.

50. Dorothy J. Solinger, "The Potential for Urban Unrest," in *Is China Unstable?* ed. David Shambaugh (Armonk, N.Y.: M. E. Sharpe, 2000), 79–94.

horror of societal disarray, on the one side, and worker expectations, on the other, often seemed to entwine the two within a dyad that resembled a static and repetitious tango.[51] And yet a perfect stalemate was not the outcome. Economic liberalization and the lackluster role played by unions modulated the reciprocally leery relationship between state and worker, invigorating Chinese labor protest and increasing its extent.

The Unions

The most significant variable affecting the nature of Chinese labor protest in the 1990s and after was the weakness and the circumspection of the All-China Federation of Trade Unions (ACFTU). These traits were a function of the federation's emergence after the 1949 Communist revolution as the Party's sole instrument for serving as the workers' overseer and putative delegate.[52] Union density in China remained exceptionally high into the 1990s, perhaps at more than 90 percent among the state sector workforce as late as 1992, according to the State Statistical Bureau.[53] But that figure simply reflected the fact that union membership in a state-run firm was compulsory and automatic; it had nothing to do with the relationship between the workers' official union and their own propensity to take to the streets.

In post-1949 China, labor unions had always been caught in a predicament between fulfilling their duties to the Party and honoring their obligations to their members; they were prevented by the Party from fully championing the workers, but at the same time were not entrusted with repressing them. Thus the mission of the unions at times of worker anger was little more than to promote and supervise conciliation among the parties involved and to defuse agitation.[54] As Chinese labor specialist Chang Kai has written:

> From the perspective of the trade union, because the law does not authorize them to organize strikes, trade unions are confronted with a dilemma situation when workers apply for strikes. If they stand on the opposite side of workers and oppose or dissuade workers from strikes, they would be criticized as "traitors of workers." However if they support and lead strikes by standing on the side of workers, they are afraid of violating the rules and are

---

51. Ibid.; Shue, "Legitimacy Crisis in China," 24–49.
52. Chen, "Between the State and Labour."
53. Gordon White, Jude Howell, and Shang Xiaoyuan, *In Search of Civil Society: Market Reform and Social Change in Contemporary China* (Oxford: Clarendon Press, 1996), 43.
54. Chen, "Between the State and Labour," 1019.

punished by their leaders. Thus trade union can only serve as an "outsider" by mediating between labors [*sic*] and the enterprise managers.[55]

The anemic quality of the unions is instituted in the provisions of the 2001 revised Trade Union Law, which posits "economic development as the central task" of these bodies in its fourth article. The following item calls on the unions to "assist the people's governments in their work and safeguard the socialist State power under the people's democratic dictatorship." It is not until the sixth article that, finally, the "basic duties and functions of trade unions" are listed as being "to safeguard the legitimate rights and interests of workers and staff members." But the very next dictum brings the unions back to their job of mobilizing and organizing workers and staff members "to take an active part in economic development and to strive to fulfill their tasks in production and other work." In case of a work-stoppage or slow-down strike, the union will "hold consultation," but especially "assist the enterprise or institution in properly dealing with the matter so as to help restore the normal order of production and other work as soon as possible." It is also notable that the full-time officials in the unions are paid by the units in which they work, thereby tying their principal interest to the success of their employer, not to the workers (Article 41).[56]

The upshot was that aggrieved Chinese workers in the People's Republic historically were in ordinary times unable to derive either succor or encouragement from their unions. But since they were not explicitly inhibited by the unions from protesting there were times—always times of apparent regime permissiveness spawned by political movements—that seemed to allow for labor to express itself. At such junctures, when workers did dare to act, they might command some supine support from the trade unions (as in the 1956–57 Hundred Flowers Movement and the 1989 Tiananmen demonstrations).

In the 1990s, though, the situation shifted. A heightened level of activism among the workers came in part simply from newfound freedoms workers experienced in the wake of job loss: without a secure workplace they became liberated from constant managerial oversight and enterprise schedules. Their dismissal, in addition, rendered pointless any worry that political involvement might endanger their positions or their perquisites, for these no longer existed.[57] And as state-owned

55. Chang Kai, "The Legislation of Right to Strike in China," paper presented at the conference "Globalisation, Migration and Labour Mobility in India and China," the Asian Business Economic Research Unit and the Institute for Global Movements, Monash University, Melbourne, Australia, September 29–30, 2005, 34.

56. "Trade Union Law of the People's Republic of China (Order of the President No. 62)," accessed at english.gov.cn/laws/2005-10/11/content_75948.htm.

57. Ching Kwan Lee, "The Politics of Working-Class Transitions in China." Paper prepared for the conference "Wealth and Labor in China: Cross-Cutting Approaches of Present Developments," Centre

firms that were suffering losses disappeared through mergers, foreign takeovers, and bankruptcy, the state's customary apparatuses of surveillance could no longer either oversee or restrain what individual workers were doing. Thus as marketization and internationalization both inflamed and inspired Chinese workers, they were essentially thrown back on themselves when they undertook to organize.

Internationalization and Marketization

As China opened up its markets and gradually reduced the role of the state in the economy from the early 1980s onward, the trade union became even weaker than it had been before. In the past (at least in theory), the union was charged by the state with serving as a model "transmission belt" association, relaying workers' sentiments upward to the leadership and then delivering official orders back down the line. Once the state plan lost its hold on the economy—and as the Party leaders chose, after the mid-1990s, to mount a huge push for international competitiveness—firms in the hundreds and thousands began to careen into bankruptcy, discarding millions of employees as they went. Worker grievances spiked upward significantly in response.[58] Political elites grew fearful of the havoc that frustrated workers might wreak, and therefore frequently urged the union to put all its energies into monitoring and attempting to mollify angry laborers.

Moreover, the ongoing privatization of enterprises loosened the grip of the Party, and thus of its lackey, the trade union, while the influx of foreign-invested firms not only introduced novel notions of worker empowerment but also provided an arena that the unions had difficulty penetrating.[59] As a consequence of these developments, unions became worse than useless as agencies for conveying to those at higher echelons—much less championing—the workers' sentiments and charges. All these factors compelled enterprise-based unions at the grass roots to put most of their efforts into attempting to appease (but, crucially, not to repress) workers who were involved in incidents of unrest.[60] Yet one more factor detrimental to unions' activities was their domination by local party branches bent on peaceful precincts, especially in an era where potential foreign investors might be scared away by instability and upheaval.

---

d'Études et de Recherches Internationales, December 6–7, 1999, Paris, 28; Chen, "Subsistence Crises," 62; Blecher, "Working Class."

58. Ching Kwan Lee, *Against the Law: Labor Protests in China's Rustbelt and Sunbelt* (Berkeley: University of California Press, 2007), 10.

59. See Gallagher, *Contagious Capitalism*.

60. Rocca, "Old Working Class," 16; Anita Chan, "Globalization, China's Free (Read Bonded) Labour Market, and the Chinese Trade Unions," *Asia Pacific Business Review* 6, 3–4 (2000), 274, 276.

International influences also made their mark in disseminating a language of "rights and interests" that began to inform workers' dissatisfaction. Initially this reference to legalism stemmed from the regime's own efforts to legitimize itself in the eyes of foreign investors, beginning with its first bid for outside capital in 1979. As the state progressively shifted its own discourse to incorporate legal references, protesters too adopted a frame that couched their more mundane demands for wages, pensions, and consultation in terms of justice, fairness, and rights.[61] Accordingly, legal language and practices supplied mistreated workers with a globally fashionable way to comprehend, reconfigure, and publicly announce their injured sense of fair deserts, along with their dashed expectations, as they began to style the goods they once received as their "entitlements."[62]

By the turn of the century, workers had started to move to civil and administrative collective lawsuits to address their grievances, especially when their petitions met with uncompromising silence from above. In one instance, in late 2004, workers went on strike at a Japanese factory supplying Wal-Mart, in part over abusive terminations of workers with seniority carried out to create posts for younger and cheaper replacements.[63] And so the global connection had perverse repercussions for Chinese workers: even as its rules had material outcomes detrimental to workers' subsistence interests, its conceptual baggage implanted ideas that energized and emboldened the jobless.[64]

In short, entering the world marketplace for China meant not just state obeisance to global economic rules, but also the country's opening to the currents of global rights talk and advocacy. Though this contact had yet to alter the regime's behavior significantly as of 2008, it lent new courage to protesters and heightened the temperature of the tension between labor and its state. Still, international forces—both for ill and for good—would have made scant headway among the members of the dismissed Chinese workforce were it not for the pusillanimous posture of the unions and their pitiful position when it came to protest. The weakness and effective absence of their so-called representative opened space for workers themselves to take charge.

---

61. For the working class, the most important new laws in the 1990s were the Bankruptcy Law of 1988, ordering firms to consult their Staff and Worker Congresses before going under and to pay employees' wages prior to settling debts; the Trade Union Law of 1992 (amended in 2001) and the Labor Law of 1995.

62. Hurst and O'Brien, "China's Contentious Pensioners."

63. *China Labour E-Bulletin,* Issue 17 (April 30, 2004); Howard W. French, "Workers Demand Union at Wal-Mart Supplier in China," *NYT,* December 16, 2004; Gallagher, "Mobilizing" and *Contagious Capitalism.*

64. Lee, "From the specter of Mao," 189.

Results

All these elements worked together to nullify any possibility of unions' representing, protecting, or even effectively supervising workers in the late 1980s and after, even for union cadres who were openly sympathetic to the plight of the workers. Local trade unionists in one city admitted that their principal function had become to maintain stability among the workforce in their jurisdiction, a task entailing dispute mediation, research on workers' attitudes, extra provisions for the needy, and keeping a watch over worker activities. This required collaboration with local security forces to forestall the formation of independent unions.[65]

The elevation of order maintenance over the unions' prior duties of assisting production, organizing recreation, and dispensing welfare[66] was a telling sign of the political elite's perception of an intimate tie between successfully achieving economic reform and productivity on the one hand and preventing, or at least placating, much of the resistance that reconstructuring occasioned, on the other. The chief effect of these several factors was that once the political elite chose to prepare the country for global entry and joining SEOs, the sheer impotence of the union—even more pronounced than it had been earlier—created an opening in the public space into which defiant workers (and former workers) could step.

In the absence of any genuine representation of or agency on behalf of their interests by the official union, worker activists themselves attempted at several junctures to establish their own, independent unions. The first such instance was during a brief moment of official liberality in the late 1980s, when such organizations sprang up throughout the country. These bodies were soon crushed, however, with the Tiananmen showdown of June 1989.[67] Yet the harsh repression on that occasion did not deter all later would-be activists. By 1992, an Association of the Urban Unemployed was one of a number of apparently spontaneous mass organizations uncovered by the public security.[68] With the default of their supposed delegate, the official union, representatives and leaders of such alternative groups were willing to undergo arrest and even imprisonment for their mission throughout the succeeding decade.[69]

---

65. Blecher, "Working Class." Also Chen, "Between the State and Labor," 1019, and Lee, "From Organized Dependence."

66. Morris, "Trade Unions," 64–65.

67. White et al., *In Search of Civil Society,* 49–50; Andrew G. Walder and Gong Xiaoxia, "Workers in the Tiananmen Protests," *AJCA* 29 (1993), 1–29; Sheehan, *Chinese Workers,* 211.

68. White et al., *In Search of Civil Society,* 35.

69. Ibid., 65–67. Reports on such organizations and their sorry fate include Lu, "CPC Guards against Mass Disturbances"; Willy Wo-lap Lam, "Dissidents Say Detentions, Sentencing Increase," *SCMP,* December 24, 1994, 1, 6; "Unemployment Committees," *CF,* 5, 4 (1997), 2; Henry Chu, "Chinese Rulers Fear Angry Workers May Finally Unite," *LAT,* June 4, 1999; "Buds and Blossoms: Labour

In general, in China the regime tended to act out its unease with protest in many ways, most often in a cautious style that delivered an implicit message that less disruptive and more limited protest was acceptable. A struggle between intertwined state aspirations—for economic restructuring, but also for the peace and order deemed necessary to push it through—bears witness to the leadership's perception of a symbiotic relationship between reform and stability. This relationship was ultimately one in which stability—sometimes achieved through coercion, other times by compensation, and most often by efforts at conciliation to be contrived by the trade unions—held the ultimate trump card.

The overall outcome of the interaction between governments (both in Beijing and at the grassroots) bent on enforcing order, on the one side, and disgruntled workers intimidated by the possibility of incarceration, on the other, was far from a stasis. Instead, the debility of the unions, and the absence of any other institutions that could mediate on behalf of the distressed, together served to bolster the workers' drive for expression on the streets in defense of what they deemed their just deserts. The inspiration and connections lent by global forces and new freedom growing out of reduced oversight—especially once workers had lost their jobs—contributed to both enabling and sparking activism. All told, the outcome of internationalization, marketization, and feeble unions was a high propensity for protest, in which the incidents were usually limited in size and scale, typically to the level of the individual workplace.[70]

France

The State and Its Workers

It would be incorrect to deny the facilitative impact of regime type on union behavior in democratic France. Certainly the liberal framework the political regime offered to disgruntled workers affected their behavior when they were faced with job or welfare cutbacks; it also colored the style of the regime's response. As in China, however, the shift in economic strategy toward liberalization after 1983,

---

Organising since 1989," *CLB* 46 (January–February 1999), 9; Susan V. Lawrence, "Risk Assessment: For Better or Worse," *FEER*, October 5, 2000, 60–61; John Pomfret, "Leaders of Independent Chinese Labor Union Fear Crackdown," *Washington Post*, December 15, 2000, A30; "Imprisoned for Organizing: Tong Shidong and Liao Shihua," *CRF*, Winter 2000–2001, 38–9; Trini Leung, "The Third Wave of the Chinese Labour Movement in the Post-Mao Era," *CLB*, June 5, 2002, 7; "Chinese Labor Activist Detained after Trying to Set up Federation," *Agence France Press*, August 11, 2002; Julie Chao, "Retiree Jailed for Trying to Organize China's Pensioners," Cox Washington Bureau, August 27, 2002; "Repression of Labour Activists," *China Labour Action Express* 26 (April 30, 2003).

70. Chen, "Between the State and Labour"; Lee, *Against the Law*.

when combined with the historical role played by the unions, affected the level of activity that was mounted.

Again like the Chinese state, as noted in chapter 2, the French one feared disorder, in part as a result of the prolonged and destructive outbursts of 1968, when almost every industrial plant in France fell under the sway of a nationwide movement.[71] That mobilization, though initiated by students, attracted the working class, whose members were already disturbed by the government's steps in the late 1960s to restructure industry. The outbreak of 1968 only served to strengthen French politicians' original conflict-aversion, to the extent of inducing them to write new legislation that aimed at assuaging workers' grievances.[72] Anthony Daley surmises that following the first oil shock the government prohibited layoffs out of nervousness over possible "social turmoil"; he also points to the French state's historical sensitivity to labor market destabilization, which, he believes, disposed bureaucratic and political actors to try to "calm" labor's reactions to unemployment.[73]

Among their efforts in this direction were the 1982 Auroux Laws, which had provisions supporting non-union channels of consultation and representation (such as workers' committees, health and safety committees, and expression groups). According to Mark Kesselman, the responsibility these laws bestowed on the unions to carry out collective bargaining in firms with more than fifty employees (which was not always observed, however) worked to dilute their confrontational customs.[74] Kesselman also holds that this legislation served as a plank in the new Socialist government's agenda after 1981 to cut back on the influence of the radical, contentious Confédération Générale du Travail (CGT) within the labor movement.[75]

Besides their historically rooted apprehensions, French politicians' concern with workers' discontent had another derivation, which was absent in authoritarian, Communist Party–ruled China. As members of a democratically elected elite who had to face the voters, political leaders were wary of alienating potential supporters at the polls. When in office, even right-wing politicians, not sympathetic to labor ideologically but hoping to avoid social disturbances that might undermine their own future electoral prospects, tended to use kid gloves to handle layoffs and the demonstrations and strikes that they occasioned.[76]

After winning at the polls, the Socialists under Mitterrand in 1981 and again under Jospin in 1997 spent several years attempting to shore up their base by

71. Boyer, "Wage Labor," 23; Bernard H. Moss, "After the Auroux Laws [AL]: Employers, Industrial Relations and the Right in France," West European Politics 11, 1 (January 1988), 71. "France: The Grand Illusion," Economist, June 5, 1999, 17, also mentions the "revolutions" of 1830 and 1848.

72. Levy, "France: Directing Adjustment?" 320; Howell, Regulating Labor, 209.

73. Daley, "Steel Crisis," 161, 180.

74. Kesselman, "New Shape of French Labour," 166, and "French Labor Movement," 145–47.

75. Kesselman, "New Shape of French Labour," 172–73.

76. Daley, "Steel Crisis," 154, 161.

promising and then enacting reforms to make workers' positions more palatable.[77] Even under a regime of the right, Prime Minister Juppé, who offended much of the nation when he attempted to gut the welfare system in 1995, softened his program in early 1997 in response to a major strike, in anticipation of elections to be held a few months later. A subsequent right-wing prime minister, Jean-Pierre Raffarin, hesitated on the issue of cutting pensions in 2003, anxious to avoid inciting a repeat of the vocal public opposition of 1995.[78] So in addition to their long-term discomfort with disorder, politicians in France—whether as candidates or as office holders, both on the right and on the left—had a clear political reason for sensitivity to labor.

The French working class had a long habit of looking to the state for resolving its grievances. Moreover, legal restrictions on unionization in firms for several decades after the World War II depressed the possibilities for trade union intermediation, a prohibition that served, until 1968, to thrust the workers directly into the arms of the state when they felt they were being mistreated. Even into the 1980s, half the private-sector workers were still employed in places that barred representation.[79] Thus the state, whether via legislation or administrative rulings, inserted itself in the unions' stead as the protector of the working class.[80]

Workers as a group were splintered in several ways, further frustrating union-based actions. This divisiveness meant, first of all, that their allegiance to often warring unions limited efforts at jointly coordinated action. Second, workers were separated by a dual labor market in which public-sector workers were far more likely to be organized than those in private firms (especially the smaller ones) and, consequently, to receive better working conditions and benefits.[81] These distinctions only grew with time. In and after the late 1970s, shocks from the world market produced an altered management strategy that resorted to flexible hours and part-time work, an approach that only deepened the segmentation within the already two-tiered workforce. In that new labor market, Robert Boyer notes, "only a fraction of workers could hope for a decent and reasonably permanent job."[82] The strikes that issued from this legacy of splits and disunity tended to be spontaneous, scattered and fragmented, brief, confrontational, and, after the mid-1970s, in defense of jobs and benefits.

77. Ross, "CGT," 71; Levy, "France: Directing Readjustment," 337ff.

78. Sidney Tarrow, "Center-Periphery Alignments and Political Contention in Late-Modern Europe," in *Restructuring Territoriality,* ed. Christopher K. Ansell and Giuseppe Di Palma (New York: Cambridge University Press, 2004); Elaine Sciolino, "France Seeks Pension Reform, Confronting Unions," *NYT,* May 9, 2003.

79. Kesselman, "New Shape of French Labour," 166, and "French Labor Movement," 145–47.

80. Kesselman, "French Labor Movement," 147, 145, 151, and "New Shape of French Labour," 166.

81. Kesselman, "French Labor Movement," 147; Howell, *Regulating Labor,* 211.

82. Boyer, "Wage Labor," 30–31.

Rather than take aim at their immediate bosses, as was the case in China, workers often specifically targeted the state, perhaps from a sense of betrayal by their one-time benefactor.[83] The differences notwithstanding, the hindrances to integrated action added up to a situation not so different from the one that obtained in the China of the 1990s and after, even if the genealogy of the obstacles was not the same. Instead of relying on coordinated battles organized by unions, French workers, like those in China, carried out a range of actions, from factory occupations to petitions, marches, and short demonstrations.

Unlike the Chinese, though, French labor was able to transcend this insulation and mobilize on a national scale on occasion, something that workers in China dared not do, for fear of certain state repression. The members of the French proletariat could reach out to and attract members of other occupations, as they did with success at several junctures, setting democratic France apart from authoritarian China.[84] Indeed, on rare occasions the unions cooperated enough to incite the entire French populace on a broad, cross-class scale. Workers achieved this arousal in 1968, to some extent in the mid-1980s (on behalf of the steel industry), in 1995, and in 2003. Each time, their activities went far beyond the typical plant- or even industry-centered "strike."[85]

The 1995 upheaval arose in response to Prime Minister Juppé's plans to prune the welfare system, as part of his attempt to diminish the public budgetary deficit in accord with the EU's criteria for monetary union membership. This unrest began to consolidate with President Jacques Chirac's call in early fall that year for a freeze on wages in the public sector, eventuating in a six-week shutdown. While the movement evinced the unions' ability, when united, to arouse French society, its major achievement was simply to compel the state to call off some of its chief proposals and to decelerate its program of cutbacks.[86]

More strikes in the spring of 2003—directed against a renewed attempt of the government to revamp its pension system—again brought together the unions nationwide in both the public and private sectors, as well as triggering more wildcat outbursts in several localities. This time, too, the episode produced only minor concessions.[87] But the government did choose to sustain an

---

83. Kesselman, "French Labor Movement," 150; Boyer, "Wage Labor," 27, 30; Ross, "CGT," 51–56; Smith, "Unemployment," 129; Wilson, "Trade Unions," 258.

84. Kesselman, conclusion to *French Workers' Movement*, 317; Moss, "After the Auroux Laws," 70.

85. Boyer, "Wage Labor," 23; Daley, "Steel Crisis," 168; Kesselman, "French Labor Movement," 144.

86. Kesselman, "French Labor Movement," 158–60; Levy, "France: Directing Readjustment," 336–37; Dani Rodrik, *Has Globalization Gone Too Far?* (Washington, D.C.: Institute for International Economics, 1997), 1, 41–43.

87. John Tagliabue, "Protest Strike in France Interrupts Travel," *NYT*, April 4, 2003, and "Militant Unions May Scuttle a French Pension Proposal," *NYT*, May 17, 2003; Sciolino, "France Seeks Pension Reform."

ongoing budget deficit, in defiance of the requirements of the European Union's Stability and Growth Pact of 1997, rather than force additional austerity on the working class. Indeed, the state honored domestic opinion in this case, even to the point of inviting censure from the European Union for its budgetary indulgences.[88]

So all in all, it would seem that the French state's trepidation about trouble from the workers, paired with labor's inclination to rely on the state, would normally have disposed workers to appeal their retrenchment-era tribulations directly upward through protest, in the absence of other effective channels.[89] But instead the workers' tendency to demonstrate was diminished after the early 1980s, in part as a result of features of the terms of attachment between workers and the state. For the efficacy of the intermediating agents that ought to have spoken for the workers and protected them had always been somewhat curtailed by their frequent incapacity to act in unison. Particularly critical in this period, however, was the fact that unions became less vigorous than earlier due to their shrinking memberships, as global economic forces—and the power of these forces to reshape state economic policy—reduced their clout.

Unions and International Influences

The strain in French history against intermediary associations, dating back to the Loi le Chapelier at the time of the French Revolution, continued to cast its shadow over unions' behavior throughout the twentieth century.[90] The French tradition of plebiscitarian rule, honoring an unbroken connection between social groups and the top leader (in lieu of appealing to intervening bodies), had a similar effect.[91] True, workers had their best chances for gains when they threatened or engaged in confrontation.[92] But they achieved their successes more often in spite of the unions than through their intervention.[93]

All told, French union politics were convoluted, the terrain they occupied furrowed by their complicated interrelations, their unpopularity with and lack of control over much of the workforce,[94] and the enmity with which employers

---

88. Richard Bernstein, "Europe's Lofty Vision of Unity Meets Headwinds," *NYT,* December 4, 2003, A1, A12.

89. Anne Stevens, *Government and Politics of France,* 3d ed. (New York: Palgrave, 2003), 247, writes of a "long tradition in France of direct action and confrontation with authorities."

90. Kesselman, "New Shape of French Labour," 166.

91. Peter Morris, *French Politics Today* (Manchester, U.K.: Manchester University Press, 1994).

92. Kesselman, "New Shape of French Labour," 170.

93. Kesselman, conclusion to *French Workers' Movement,* 2.

94. Wilson, "Trade Unions," 277.

viewed them. That the three leading unions—the CGT, the Confédération Française et Démocratique du Travail, and the Force Ouvrière—shifted their political agendas with some regularity was just one more factor that made it difficult for unions as a whole to coalesce around any one shared standpoint.[95] This disharmony had the unfortunate effect of putting off many workers, who realized that internecine conflict often lay at the core of labor's difficulties in winning a victory.[96] Inter-union rivalry meant not only that the unions all attempted to capture the same membership base, but also that they quarreled over ideology, tactics, and ultimate control. The tensions among them allowed employers and governments to manipulate the various confederations, even as the latter vied among themselves to out-bargain their competitors.[97]

Worse yet, combined with these problems in union politics, international competition and the structural obsolescence of much of French industry after the 1970s meant that, with time, the decline of the industrial sectors—smokestack ones in particular—in which unions had once had a foothold operated to drive union membership lower than in most of Western Europe. As Kesselman writes, "structural changes in the French and world economy have been the primary cause of the decline of organized labor."[98] From a high point in the early and mid-1970s, when unions absorbed one-quarter of the French workforce, membership dropped below 10 percent by 1992.[99] W. Rand Smith figures that overall membership density declined by more than half over a sixteen-year period, from 30 percent of the labor force in 1975, in his reckoning, down to 14 percent in 1991.[100] And by the early twenty-first century, unions existed in a mere 37 percent of the plants, mainly the larger ones.[101]

Problems within the union movement were exacerbated as labor became more impotent than ever with liberalization, privatization, and deregulation. And unlike in China, where unions' traditional style became attenuated with nothing much to replace it, unions in France took on a new role that empowered them but led them to switch to the use of a nonconfrontational manner, something novel there.

---

95. Ibid., 268–71; Smith, "Unemployment and the Left," 125–30; Kesselman, "New Shape of French Labour," 167–74.

96. Martin Schain, "Relations between the CGT and the CFDT: Politics and Mass Mobilization," in Kesselman, French Workers' Movement, 257; Wilson, "Trade Unions," 257–58; Smith, Left's Dirty Job, 219.

97. Kesselman, "New Shape of French Labour," 165; Ross, "CGT," 53; Wilson, "Trade Unions," 259; Schain, "Relations between the CGT," 257.

98. Kesselman, "French Labor Movement," 152; see also Kesselman, "Introduction," 1.

99. Kesselman, "French Labor Movement," 149; Daley, "Steel Crisis," 159.

100. Smith, "Unemployment and the Left," 130.

101. Chris Howell, "The State and the Reconstruction of Industrial Relations Institutions after Fordism: Britain and France Compared," paper presented at the 99th Meeting of the American Political Science Association, Philadelphia, August 28–31, 2003, 69.

With the passage of the Auroux reforms, organized labor became charged with promoting firm-level collective bargaining and, through that approach, the active enforcement of peace in the plants.[102]

France's new policies and its growing acquiescence with Community rules after 1983 worked to strengthen the hand of business against labor; they also undermined the state's customary capacity to use regulations and concessions to safeguard the working class.[103] At the end of the 1980s, Kesselman observed, "Unions have suffered heavy membership losses and severe setbacks in the face of state and business initiatives [beginning in 1982]; the labor movement is more divided than ever."[104] Robert Boyer concurs, noting that the impact of economic liberalization and austerity was principally to decimate the power of labor as against its counterpart, the business world, rather than to stimulate any new activism.[105]

As in China, there were influences from abroad which inspired workers. When the negative externalities of the EU's rules gave dismissed workers across the continent a common battle cry, cross-border organizing around the issue of joblessness began in the early 1980s. But it took more than a decade—until the mid-1990s, after the Maastricht Treaty specified its criteria for membership in the common monetary union—before a European Network of the Unemployed was even put into place. On this foundation, marches were held in 1997 and 1999. Jobless demonstrators took over employment offices, blocked trains, and occupied the tracks (reminiscent of the wildcat strike tactics so prevalent in China), as a result of which the government released some funds for the unemployed.[106] More of the same occurred in 1998. Organizations for fighting unemployment convened an EU-wide meeting attended by a representative of the French unemployed network, while thousands of the jobless went to the streets again in more than sixty French cities.[107]

Connected with this movement, French campaigns were organized on a nationwide basis in 1997 and 1998. At an EU Summit on Employment in 1997, Jospin's Socialist government proposed a plan for coordinating policies against unemployment throughout the Union. Unfortunately, however, these forays beyond the borders—both by workers and by their Socialist spokesman—in the end did little more than instill a feeling of camaraderie, as the resultant Pact for Employment

---

102. Kesselman, conclusion to *French Workers' Movement*, 313–14, and "New Shape of French Labour," 166–67.

103. Vivien A. Schmidt, *Democracy in Europe: The EU and National Polities* (Oxford: Oxford University Press, 2006), 127, 130; Kesselman, "French Labor Movement," 153.

104. Kesselman, "New Shape of French Labour," 169, 172, 174.

105. Boyer, "Wage Labor."

106. Craig R. Whitney, "French Jobless," and "French Unemployed Turn Their Ire on Socialists," *NYT*, January 6, 1998; *Economist*, "France."

107. "French Unemployed Protest to Demand Compensation Rise," *NYT*, December 22, 1998.

simply served to demonstrate a measure of support among collegial forces at the supranational level but made little material difference.[108]

Results

The historical peak of French protest (aside from the enormous marches and rallies of late 1995) passed with the mid-1970s, after which—with internationally generated economic setbacks for the French proletariat and an austerity program at home—labor's activism declined decisively. A political alliance between the Communists and the Socialists fell apart in 1977.[109] Then, following President Mitterrand's U-turn after 1982, workers and unions were reactive at first but then became silent for most of the rest of the decade.[110] The outcome was that in the years after 1980, outbursts of any sort were notably few, as workers became discouraged by their helplessness and frustrated by the lack of clear guidance or assistance from any sort of coherent or powerful mediating associations. The scattered, small-scale incidents that broke out occasionally, proving the rule, were often organized by independent groups outside the sphere of the unions.

Still, sensing impending loss—of their jobs or their welfare—laborers remained prone to demonstrate when the danger of deprivation appeared especially ominous, even in the absence of unified and effective union leadership. But the gains, not especially pronounced, were achieved only when the state became overwhelmed by widespread public outrage and sympathy for the working class from social groups of all sorts. As Kesselman observes, strikes "resulted neither in new policy initiatives favorable to labor's interests nor in a revitalization of the labor movement."[111] The propensity to strike, historically high,[112] remained present, but only at times of intense provocation. Both size and scale could be substantial on such (albeit infrequent) occasions, but only when the unions managed to collaborate in a general-strike, cross-societal mobilization.

---

108. Pierre Lefébure and Eric Lagneau, "Media Construction in the Dynamics of Euro-protest," in *Contentious Europeans: Protest and Politics in an Emerging Polity*, ed. Doug Imig and Sidney Tarrow (Lanham, Md.: Rowman & Littlefield, 2001).

109. Ibid.; Ross, "CGT," 55–65; Kesselman, "French Labor Movement," 144–45.

110. Wilson, "Trade Unions," 275–76; Smith, "Unemployment and the Left," 128–30; Vivien A. Schmidt, "Still Three Models of Capitalism? The Dynamics of Economic Adjustment in Britain, Germany, and France," in *Die Politische Konstitution von Maerkten*, ed. Roland Czada and Susanne Luetz (Opladen, Germany: Westdeutscher, 2000); Moss, "After the Auroux Laws," 74–76; Daley, "Steel Crisis"; Kesselman, conclusion to *French Workers' Movement*, 320; Smith, "Unemployment and the Left," 129; Schmidt, *From State to Market?* 127.

111. Kesselman, "French Labor Movement," 160.

112. Kesselman, "Introduction," 1.

So in the French case we see a withering of a habit that had once existed, a relative pacification of the unions in their past role as agitators, not a rise to a new challenge by labor under changed circumstances with altered possibilities, as in China. International forces buffeted them both. But the fragmented French unions that were a product of a liberal revolution—and yet depended on joint, unified action to pull off a grand protest—perhaps proved more equal to the job than did the subservient, servant-like unions attached to the Chinese Communist Party. Nevertheless, the Chinese workers broke free of their union and achieved a lot more in the way of disturbances without it.

Mexico

The State and Its Workers

After the formation of the present Mexican state in the postrevolutionary days of the 1920s, its leaders demonstrated, on one side, a responsiveness to labor, paired with a rhetoric of workers' rights, but, on the other, an effort to keep the unions under strict controls in order to preempt unrest.[113] The latter tendency was rooted in a fear of upheaval sparked during the Revolution of 1910–17 and never discarded.[114] As noted earlier, of the three states, it was the Mexican one whose constitution was the most generous and sympathetic to the working class, in principle offering the rights to engage in collective bargaining, to form unions, and to strike, in addition to granting social rights and benefits.[115] But in practice, the regime retained definite powers over labor and was equipped with the military and police power to bring order when it chose.[116]

The state sustained its rule—and the PRI upheld its own hegemony—through the implicit bargain, described in chapter 2, with the workers who were its allies. That is, such workers could count for decades on job security and favorable work conditions, so long as they kept up their end of the deal, which was to provide a support base for the PRI during elections and to keep quietly producing at other times. The government's economic achievements, paired with and often made more possible through this pact, secured a high measure of labor peace in Mexico, especially

---

113. Meyer, "Mexico," 19, 140; Teichman, *Privatization and Political Change,* 48–49, 195.

114. Coleman and Davis, "Preemptive Reform," 5; Haggard and Kaufman, *Political Economy,* 284.

115. Middlebrook, "Sounds of Silence," 202. The Federal Labor Code of 1931 elaborated on these principles. See Middlebrook, *Paradox of Revolution,* 63–64.

116. Teichman, *Privatization and Political Change,* 59–61, 67, 199; Robert R. Kaufman, "Democratic and Authoritarian Responses to the Debt Issue: Argentina, Brazil, Mexico," in *The Politics of International Debt,* ed. Miles Kahler (Ithaca: Cornell University Press, 1986), 198.

among the most protected tier of the workforce. These sheltered workers included those attached to the PRI: those in the large confederations, such as the CTM (Confederación de Trabajadores Méxicanos), the CROC (Confederación Revolucionaria de Obreros y Campesinos), and the CROM (Confederación Regional Obrera Méxicana), and those belonging to sectoral federations, which represented workers in state-owned firms.[117]

But this pact did not preclude restrictiveness and occasional ruthlessness on the part of the state. The law neither bestowed on unions any responsibility to represent workers nor authorized the unions to negotiate collective contracts or to wage strikes unless they had first acquired official recognition. This recognition and the right to register were both treated as privileges, moreover, and were not lightly bestowed. Even after a union had succeeded in becoming registered, there was no assured freedom to hold any given strike. Explicit state permission was required in every instance, while an array of prohibitions limited waging a strike, at the risk of immediate job loss for the participants.[118] At times of resistance, the regime was ready with rewards for those willing to abandon the effort and with repression against those who were not, sometimes including arrests and imprisonment.

These latter tactics were to assist the state in preventing labor discontent from interfering with its program of privatization, economic liberalization, and retrenchment in and after the 1980s.[119] Such measures were also drawn on to quell opposition to PRI candidate Carlos Salinas's bid for the presidency, and to prevent protest in anticipation of the stifling continuation of austerity, liberalization, and internationalization that his rule would promise, in 1988. Thus a potential refuge from coercion, available to a subset of the workforce and conditional upon loyalty and compliance, sustained the broad outlines of the Mexican labor regime and the state's economic strategy historically and into the present.

Additionally, the semi-authoritarian nature of the government meant that elections—if highly rigged and corrupted ones—went on, and their presence had an effect on the governing party's politicians, if a less critical one than in fully democratic France. Unions that joined in ensuring PRI victory at the polls, by means of corralling votes, handing out money, arranging marches, and falsifying votes during and after polling, were favored by the party. But apparently the PRI did not believe itself altogether immune to a loss of power;[120] its politicians could never be entirely certain that their methods would always achieve success. Consequently, on

---

117. Collier and Collier, *Shaping the Political Arena*, chap. 7.

118. Middlebrook, *Paradox of Revolution*, 64–65, 68–69, and "Sounds of Silence," 197; Teichman, *Privatization and Political Change*, 52–53.

119. Collier, *Contradictory Alliance*, 137; Teichman, *Privatization and Political Change*, 212; Middlebrook, *Paradox of Revolution*, 295, 300–301.

120. Teichman, *Privatization and Political Change*, 66–67; Middlebrook, *Paradox of Revolution*, 30, 153, 301.

more than one occasion the PRI-backed government either caved in to workers' demands or at least pulled back from some of its more worker-unfriendly proposals on the eve of an election, after but also even before the state could in any way be considered democratic.[121]

Workers advantaged by this system developed a sense of deserts and expectations and were often able to rely on their party bosses to supply the goods they counted on. As Judith Teichman, writing in the mid-1990s, remarked, "Expectations among those who might later benefit induces potential clients to see their economic salvation in winning a patron's favor rather than in collective political action to overturn the status quo."[122] Thus the legacy of favorable treatment that PRI-connected workers had experienced for dozens of years shored up their loyalty. This faithfulness disposed them to stick with the PRI in the wake of austerity, even as the party progressively reversed its historical connection with labor after the early 1980s.[123]

Unlike ordinary workers, the labor bosses in the PRI-connected unions, a tiny proportion of the Mexican working class, had access to formal channels of interest articulation and opportunities to engage in negotiations on occasion.[124] But by and large, mediation between the political regime and the workers was controlled by the PRI, even if it operated through its affiliated confederations of unions. And it was just the bosses who had any hope of exerting some influence and who derived special benefits, especially in their eligibility for nomination by the PRI to run for public office and sometimes in their input into the choice of the PRI presidential candidate. According to Katrina Burgess, "the relative autonomy of the CTM leaders from workers encouraged them to value leadership privileges such as party posts and elected office independently of their impact on workers."[125]

Another feature of state-labor ties in Mexico was the contingency of even privileged workers' status, as compared with the situation in China. In the greater room for maneuver in Mexico's more pluralist trade union environment,[126] public-sector Mexican workers' elite standing was more conditional than in China. Any sign of

---

121. This occurred in the 1970s (Haggard and Kaufman, "Political Economy of Inflation," 292); in 1985 (Collier, *Contradictory Alliance*, 83); at the end of 1987 (ibid., 110, and Middlebrook, "CTM and the Future," 297); in 1993 and 1994 (Katrina Burgess, "Loyalty Dilemmas and Market Reform: Party-Union Alliances under Stress in Mexico, Spain, and Venezuela," *WP* 52, 1 [1999], 124); and in 1999 in preparation for the presidential succession of 2000 ("Mexico's Trade Unions Stick to the Same Old Tune," *Economist*, October 23, 1999, 35–36).

122. Teichman, *Privatization and Political Change*, 62. See also Middlebrook, "CTM and the Future," 293, and Burgess, "Loyalty Dilemmas," 116.

123. Collier, *Contradictory Alliance*, 110.

124. Middlebrook, "Sounds of Silence," 213.

125. Burgess, "Loyalty Dilemmas," 122; Middlebrook, *Paradox of Revolution*, 101–2.

126. On a sort of pluralism among the unions in Mexico, see Collier and Collier, *Contradictory Alliance*, 597.

opposition on the part of a particular worker could bring trouble with the PRI and put his or her job or rank at risk. Thus the opportunity that workers in Mexico (unlike those in China) had to affiliate with a union other than the PRI-blessed one could expose the potentially vindictive nature, and the ultimately uncertain protection, of the PRI.[127] In time, feelings of betrayal among a portion of the proletariat paved the way for the PRI's poor showing in the presidential election of 1988 (the PRI candidate, Carlos Salinas, was proclaimed the victor, but much evidence of fraud cast doubt on the outcome). For their leadership of this opposition, several union bosses suffered retribution from the regime.[128] These events eventually set the scene for something novel in the country: the appearance of untrammeled, independent unions by the 1990s.[129]

The Unions

In 1978, even before the debt crisis hit, labor unions represented just 16.3 percent of Mexico's economically active population, and the CTM was the putative agent for a third of all unionized workers.[130] But despite its place in the sun, even the CTM was ultimately vulnerable.[131] For the PRI might at any time play this confederation off against two rival ones—the CROC and the CROM[132]—when the party leadership was displeased with some stand or other that any one of them took temporarily, or when it was angered by a confederation's short-term failure to march in lockstep with every policy the PRI proposed. There were alternative options for workers before the 1990s—especially in the precariously placed independent unions that did exist, particularly in the 1970s—but the outcome for a worker who took part in them was unpredictable and could often be brutal. Indeed, in the hope of ensuring its pride of place, the CTM performed a critical role in assisting the party to suppress attempts at forming independent unions, which—had they

---

127. Teichman, *Privatization and Political Change,* 62–67.

128. Collier, *Contradictory Alliance,* 110.

129. Independent unions had existed before, especially in the 1970s, but they were frequently the targets of PRI repression. Levy and Bruhn, *Mexico,* 76, state in 2006 that "the number of independent unions has grown dramatically."

130. Middlebrook, "Sounds of Silence," 212. Levy and Bruhn, *Mexico,* 74–75, however, basing their estimate on ILO figures, state that about 43 percent of nonagricultural salaried workers belonged to unions as of 2000 (www.ilo.org). But Teichman, *Privatization and Political Change,* 48, writes that "the industries of highest state participation have experienced the most advanced unionization...where the rate of unionization in industry in general was 26 percent in 1975, it was 78.6 percent in the extraction industries, 97.9 percent in electricity and gas and 84.9 percent in transportation."

131. Collier, *Contradictory Alliance,* 35; Middlebrook, *Paradox of Revolution,* 35; Camp, *Politics in Mexico,* 3d ed., 142; Haggard and Kaufman, *Political Economy,* 287.

132. See Collier, *Contradictory Alliance,* 83; Ian Roxborough, "Organized Labor: A Major Victim of the Debt Crisis," in *Debt and Democracy in Latin America,* ed. Barbara Stallings and Robert Kaufman (Boulder: Westview Press, 1989), 104–5; Middlebrook, "CTM and the Future," 294.

had the space to do so—would have championed rights and benefits for groups beyond the selected elite.[133]

After austerity set in, the position of the CTM and some of its bosses shifted somewhat. But as Katrina Burgess points out, even as the union leaders who were affiliated with the PRI castigated the party's stance in the 1980s, they remained its partner; for the most part, they also refrained from arousing their workers in protest against the liberalization initiative. Indeed, the ongoing power of many union bosses to subdue their workforces in the PRI-related firms, and the unchanged connections binding these bosses to the state, seriously undermined protest in the era of cutbacks after 1980.[134] Consequently, though strikes in Mexico were never plentiful, their numbers dropped by 80 percent in the decade following the accession to power of President de la Madrid in 1982, according to Barry Carr.[135]

Union bosses submitted a fair number of strike petitions during the 1980s and 1990s, but critically, they ultimately refrained from taking their discontent out onto the streets.[136] Meanwhile, up until the mid-1990s, the regime was increasingly indiscriminate in its impulse to subvert and quash worker opposition from any quarter at all, willing even to turn its back at times on its long-time ally, the CTM, rather than accede to demands that would threaten the austerity program.[137] Unlike in China, where only the leaders of protests were apprehended in demonstrations, in similar instances in Mexico ordinary followers as well stood in danger of forfeiting their jobs.[138] So while seemingly leaderless demonstrations were plentiful in China, such actions were rare indeed in Mexico.

Marketization and Internationalization

As in China and France, Mexico's economic reforms and liberalization had an impact on protest possibilities in ways other than at the polls. As Teichman observes, "the process of privatization set in motion…the disintegration" of the modalities that the government, working through the PRI, had utilized for decades to bind the state-sector unions to the state apparatus by way of discriminatory benefits.[139]

---

133. Sklair, *Assembling for Development*, 58, 61–62.

134. Meyer, "Mexico," 144.

135. Barry Carr, "Crossing Borders: Labor Internationalism in the Era of NAFTA," in *Neoliberalism Revisited: Economic Restructuring and Mexico's Future*, ed. Gerardo Otero (Boulder, Colo.: Westview Press, 1996), 222. Carr counted the number of strikes that occurred between January 1982 and December 1991. Personal communication.

136. Dion, "Mexico's Welfare Regime," 20; Middlebrook, "CTM and the Future," 293–96.

137. Collier, *Contradictory Alliance*, 106–7, 139; Middlebrook, *Paradox of Revolution*, 260, and "CTM and the Future," 293–94.

138. Middlebrook, *Paradox of Revolution*, 69; Burgess, "Loyalty Dilemmas," 12.

139. Teichman, *Privatization and Political Change*, 50; Levy and Bruhn, *Mexico*, 77; Middlebrook, *Paradox of Revolution*, 287.

Back in the 1980s, the PRI was forced to relinquish some of its ability to privilege a set of incorporated unions when the state undertook a massive sell-off of public firms. Trade internationalization, too, was detrimental to the unions in that it meant that state leaders were well aware that foreign investors could withdraw their funds if the state was too sympathetic to worker demands.[140] This consciousness naturally tempered the old state benevolence toward the unions.

And in part the PRI lost some of its dominance because of a set of policies initiated in the Ministry of Finance under the influence of internationally prevalent patterns, including a reformulation of the terms under which those enterprises that remained in state hands operated. In particular, this entailed cutting back state funding for the unions. The ministry also prevailed in getting workers' contracts rewritten and engineering decreases in the state's investments in its plants—in sync with a series of larger reforms that spelled reductions in wages and benefits. All these modifications in the state's role in the economy, made in the name of international competitiveness and efficiency, combined to undermine the powers of patronage and clientelism that had formerly incorporated the "official" unions into the regime.[141] In short, the reforms eroded—though they did not eliminate altogether—the special perquisites that bound the most privileged workers to the dominant party, through their unions. So with the arrival of these new measures, Mexico's chief mediating arrangements began to unravel.

There were in addition, as in France and China, international influences on the working class and its unions that might have encouraged activism. But these influences proved inadequate to the task of breaking through the ferocity of the PRI's determination to streamline the industrial sector and win foreign approval for the Mexican economy in the 1980s and 1990s. Forces from outside the country at least managed to rebalance a bit the lopsided battle that labor occasionally tried to wage against the state in the 1990s, however, and to awaken interest in the plight of Mexican workers in the United States and Canada.

The inauguration of NAFTA heightened the awareness in these countries of the problems of Mexican labor, while inspiring some organizing across the borders.[142] In the early 1990s, several Mexican unions signed on to support the NAFTA agreement only if it incorporated a labor rights charter, and a North American Worker Bloc arose with the aim of serving as a forum for communication over

---

140. Dion, "Mexico's Welfare Regime," 10–11.
141. Teichman, *Privatization and Political Change*, 199–200, 205; Roxborough, "Organized Labor," 91; Rochlin, *Redefining Mexican "Security*," 30; Collier, *Contradictory Alliance*, 107; Middlebrook, *Paradox of Revolution*, 161, 256, 297; Burgess, "Loyalty Dilemmas," 106; Judith Adler Hellman, review of *Social Movements and Economic Transition: Markets and Distributive Conflict in Mexico*, by Heather L. Williams, *American Political Science Review* 96, 2 (2002), 457.
142. Samstad, "Unanticipated Persistence," 28–29; Sam Dillon, "After Four Years of Nafta, Labor Forging Cross-Border Ties," *NYT*, December 20, 1997, A1, A7.

labor issues.[143] NAFTA's provisions also carved out space for independent organizations, even among the assembly plant workers, where unionization had been particularly weak historically.[144] In late 1997, demonstrators in twenty-five cities across the United States protested at Hyundai dealerships and organized a consumer boycott against the firm at home when a group of workers struck at a Korean factory in Tijuana, something that may never have occurred absent the NAFTA connection.[145] Four years later, a cafeteria boycott at another assembly factory that supplied college sweatshirts to Nike and Reebok attracted the active support of some eighty-five American colleges and universities. This movement managed to prompt investigations within the offending plants and to win changes that strengthened the independent labor movement in Mexico.[146]

Results

All told, protest in Mexico after 1980, like that in France, became infrequent, as compared with the past. Compared with the French pattern, the expression of grievances that did occur was much more limited in duration and far more contained in scale than in former times. The effectiveness of this opposition, moreover, was minimal to negligible. Insofar as there were any achievements at all—such as the 1987 Economic Solidarity Pact, in which income taxes were cut and inflation arrested—only the affiliates of the CTM received benefits, while workers as a group continued to suffer from the government's wage policy and its program of retrenchment. Other outcomes issuing from protest included at best delays of unfavorable policies. The CTM's greatest accomplishment was its prevention of the Salinas administration's rewriting of the federal labor code, a reform yet stalled as of 2008. But even in this instance, in the view of one observer, the government managed to implement labor policy as if the law had indeed been altered.[147]

Thus as neoliberal international examples and formulas entered Mexico, they found a welcome climate despite the dissatisfactions of the working class, for the duet that defined the terms attaching the chief union to the ruling party remained largely undisturbed. As a result, CTM bosses buttressed the platform of the PRI, much as they always had. In Mexico, as in China and France, the old terms of attachment continued to cast their shadows, even if the shadows were refracted somewhat by international dealings and demands.

---

143. Carr, "Crossing Borders," 222–23.
144. Camp, *Politics in Mexico,* 3d ed., 141; Sklair, *Assembling for Development.*
145. Sam Dillon, "Workers Win Showdown with Factory in Mexico," *NYT,* December 14, 1997.
146. Thompson, "Mexican Labor Protest."
147. Middlebrook, *Paradox of Revolution,* 264–65, 295–99.

Conclusion

In these three stories, neither the density of unions nor the type of regime controlling the state was able to account fully for the way workers reacted to job terminations and welfare cutbacks. Asking how much power the central government wielded or determining which political party was in power was similarly unhelpful. It turned out that what was important in these three countries was not so much whether a labor regime could be labeled a "weak labor political economic" one, whether it was paired with a leftist party, or even whether there were a high number of strikes historically in a given country. Instead, what yielded explanatory power in assessing changes in the propensity of workers to strike after cutbacks—as compared with their own past—is a less quantifiable variable: it is *the extent and nature of the power that labor unions exercised over and against—rather than for—the workers,* in line with the terms of attachment forged by revolutions and the respective states and in reaction to global forces.

In the end, unions turned out to be less significant in the traditional ways scholars expect them to be: it was not that they initiated more strikes and demonstrations in China than in France or Mexico or that in other ways they fought for their members there in the face of regime reversal on labor issues. After all, all three of these countries were places where unions were historically inadequate entities for taking in and transmitting workers' needs and desires. Instead, it was the *absence* of active, assertive unions in China—the union there was neither repressive, as in Mexico, nor one of several quibbling, competing unions losing members, as in France—that gave Chinese workers an opportunity to demonstrate on their own.

Besides the role of unions, I considered the part played by internationalization and concomitant economic reforms in shaping workers' situations. I was interested first in the power of privatization, induced in all three cases by influences from abroad, to release workers who were once tied to and dependent on the state and its largesse. The retreat of the state (or of its partner union), a feature particularly marked in China, enabled labor to achieve a new measure of freedom to express its needs and grievances. But economic liberalization and international trends and pressures did not produce a standard measure of political opening for workers' resistance. Whether or not the new openness in the economy mattered for activism depended on how the relevant unions behaved both toward the state (and its ruling party) and toward the workers in the wake of that liberalization. Thus the power of economic liberalization to activate labor's proclivities to demonstrate and to demand hardly depended, in these cases, on the type of regime in which such reform was taking place. It depended much more on the role and the power (and absence of power) of the unions in a country.

Another dimension of internationalization was support from comrades across the borders and from new ideas that might have fostered workers' friction and combativeness with the state. But such international forces did not automatically and significantly bolster workers' resistance at home, though the cross-border sympathy they facilitated was surely encouraging. Whether international forces of this type made major inroads had much to do with the amount of interference that met them, which in turn was related to the extent other forces in a country were organized and poised to counter them. It was in China that new notions and consciousness of rights among workers had the greatest impact, probably because the state itself promoted such concepts in its bids for foreign capital and domestic legitimacy.

In understanding the possibilities for worker demonstrations to break out, it turned out that the concept of "union" needed to be interrogated, since unions performed quite differing roles in these three different contexts. And in none of them did unions behave as standard accounts presume they will. Ultimately, I found most critical the extent to which unions had to answer to the state, but perhaps even more important, the degree to which they had clout—whether coercive, as in Mexico, or insufficiently collaborative, as in France—with respect to the workers.[148] Having little to no clout, as in China, turned out to be the most conducive of all for resistance in the face of the incursion of foreign economic forces.

Thus these three cases suggest the following conclusions. Where marketization has disengaged workers from the clutch of the state; where the state is especially chary (for historical reasons) of chaos in the streets, particularly when it is also uneasy about the possibility of its own loss of power; where workers have a high level of expectation; where international forces are supportive and vocal on behalf of workers facing hardships; and—most critically—where unions are largely impotent (whether under their administrative superiors, as in Mexico; among themselves, as in France; or over the workers themselves, as in China), the outcomes for protest may not be so easily predicted by regime type, as has often been thought. And critically, weak unions can be weak in a number of ways, some of which may actually facilitate protest under particular conditions. As for the effects produced by protest, what matters most, in the end, is the response of the regime to the demonstrators and their causes, and that is where the argument turns next.

---

148. Murillo, *Labor Unions,* chap. 9. Looking at subnational as well as national variation, Murillo elegantly extends and explains these distinctions.

6

THE WELFARE OUTCOME

States' Responses to Labor's Laments

Now I investigate the linkage, if any, between new and widespread resistance in China versus its relative absence or downswing in France and Mexico, respectively, on the one hand, and state welfare response on the other. Certainly the components of governmental "social expenditure" vary with governments and compilers. Nevertheless, it is still possible to track the extent to which there was a correlation between a sudden surge in resistance in China and novel silence in France and Mexico, and variation in state welfare action.

Both the French outlays as a percentage of gross domestic product and the Mexican ones changed very little in the postcrisis years, according to various calculations.[1] To rely on just one source, in the interest of comparability, the

---

1. For France, Martin Hutsebaut, "The Future of Social Protection in Europe: A European Trade Union Perspective," 3, has France's expenditure at 25.4 percent in 1980, 27.7 percent in 1990, 31.2 percent in 1993, and 30.8 percent in 1996 (http://pre20031103.stm.fi/english/tao/publicat/financing/hutsebaut.htm, accessed July 25, 2007). But Australian Government, Department of Family and Community Services, Policy Research Paper No. 4: "Changes in Social Expenditures" (http://www.facsia.gov.au/research/prp04/sec2.htm, accessed July 25, 2007), 5, shows France at 23.5 percent in 1980, 27.0 percent in 1985, 26.0 percent in 1990, and 28.8 percent in 1995. Also see Scharpf, "Economic Changes," 107–8, and Hemerijck and Schludi, "Sequences of Policy Failure," 171. France's level of social spending placed it number three globally in this category, following Sweden and Denmark. Gordon and Meunier, *French Challenge,* 99. Australian Government, "Changes in Social Expenditures," gives 2.1 percent for Mexico in 1985, 2.9 percent in 1990, and 4.0 percent in 1995. But Manuel Pastor and Carol Wise, "State Policy, Distribution and Neoliberal Reform in Mexico," Paper no. 229 (Washington, D.C.: Latin American Program, Woodrow Wilson International Center for Scholars, August 1997), 31, 45, show that social spending fell as a percentage of GDP, from 6.10 percent in 1980, down to 5.62 percent in 1985, and then to 4.89 percent in 1990. Jonathan Schwabish et al., "Income Distribution and Social Expenditures: A Crossnational Perspective," unpublished paper, October 2004, demonstrate that

Table 6.1. Public social expenditure as a percentage of GDP, France and Mexico, 1990–2001

	1990	1991	1992	1993	1994	1995	1996	1997	1998	1999	2000	2001
France	26.61	27.23	28.03	29.48	29.27	29.24	29.38	29.42	28.96	28.91	28.34	28.45
Mexico	3.84	4.33	4.61	4.92	5.44	5.43	4.91	4.97	4.89	4.96	4.97	5.10

Source: OECD Factbook 2006-ISBN 95-64-03561-3 @ OECD 2006.

Organization for Economic Cooperation and Development found that in the eleven years between 1990 and 2001 the French government's social expenditures rose from 26.61 percent to 28.45 percent of GDP, or 1.84 percent, while Mexico's grew from 3.84 to 5.10 percent, or 1.26 percent. In China, however, the central government increased its expenditures in this category as a percentage of GDP from under 2 percent in 1980 to about 8.3 percent in 2005 (see Tables 6.1 and 6.2 and Figures 6.1 and 6.2).

Besides the numbers, there are other indicators that a tight bond existed between demonstrations and welfare disbursements in China. Officials there often admitted as much in and after the mid-1990s. For example, in April 2000 then-premier Zhu Rongji stated during a brief sojourn in the province of Liaoning, where job losses were massive: "Some laid-off workers could not receive the regulated amount of subsistence allowance, and others failed to get it at all. Collective petitions and instances of social unrest have occurred repeatedly. Hence, the party committee and government at each level must see it as an unshakable duty to establish an adequate welfare system and a stable social environment."[2] Given that China was the only case of the three where budgetary allocations for welfare shot upward as a percentage of GDP between 1980 and 2005, and was also the only one where worker demonstrations clearly escalated, I hypothesize a linkage between these two phenomena. I justify advancing this proposition on the basis of the similarities among these states posited in chapters 2 through 4.

What is often ignored in looking only at democracies—the research site for most work on politics and welfare—is that popular opposition can be at least as threatening to power holders in nondemocratic states as in democratic ones; indeed, popular disapproval can be every bit as potent when expressed in action outside the framework of the regular political process as when articulated in action

---

Mexico's total nonelderly social expenditures as a percentage of GDP rose a bit over these years, never going over about 1.7 percent, and remaining under 1 percent of GDP, as of 1999. For China, see Wang Shaoguang, "The Great Transformation: The Emergence of Social Policies in China," paper presented at the University of Southern California USC US-China Institute conference, "The Future of U.S.-China Relations," April 20, 2007.

2. *RMRB*, May 28, 2000.

Table 6.2. Government expenditure for social security as percentage of total government expenditure, China, 1978–2005, selected years (Unit: 100 million yuan)

Year	Total expenditure	Expenditure on Social Security	Social Security as % of total expenditure
1978	1122.09	18.91	0.017
1980	1228.83	20.31	0.017
1985	2004.25	31.15	0.016
1990	3083.59	55.04	0.018
1991	3386.62	67.32	0.020
1992	3742.20	66.45	0.018
1993	4642.30	75.27	0.016
1994	5792.62	95.14	0.016
1995	6823.72	115.46	0.017
1996	7937.55	182.68	0.023
1997	9233.56	328.42	0.036
1998	10798.18	595.63	0.055
1999	13187.67	1197.44	0.091
2000	15886.50	1517.57	0.096
2001	18902.58	1987.40	0.105
2002	22053.15	2636.22	0.120
2003	24649.95	2655.91	0.108
2004	28486.89	3116.08	0.109
2005	33930.28	3698.86	0.109

Source: Zhonghua renmin gongheguo guojia tongjiju, bian [Chinese People's Republic National Statistical Bureau, ed.], *Zhongguo tongji nianjian—2007* [Chinese statistical yearbook] (Beijing: Zhongguo tongji chubanshe [Chinese Statistical Publishing Co.], 2007), 280, 281.

Note: Includes expenditures on pensions and social welfare relief, on social security subsidies, and for retired government officials. Pensions were not included before 1996.

within it (such as by defeat at the polls).[3] Below I suggest a set of dynamics of deprivation, reaction, and counterreaction that appeared in places that were not democratic, as well as in one that was.

I assume that politicians are well aware of the level of restiveness in their realms and that their gamut of reactions is generally limited to three. In the words of Frances Fox Piven and Richard A. Cloward, elites can "ignore [what they term 'institutional disruptions'], employ punitive measures, or try to conciliate" the perpetrators.[4]

---

3. Paul Pierson, *Dismantling the Welfare State: Reagan, Thatcher, and the Politics of Retrenchment* (New York: Cambridge University Press, 1994), 16.

4. Frances Fox Piven and Richard A. Cloward, *Poor People's Movements: Why They Succeed, How They Fail* (New York: Vintage Books, 1979), 27.

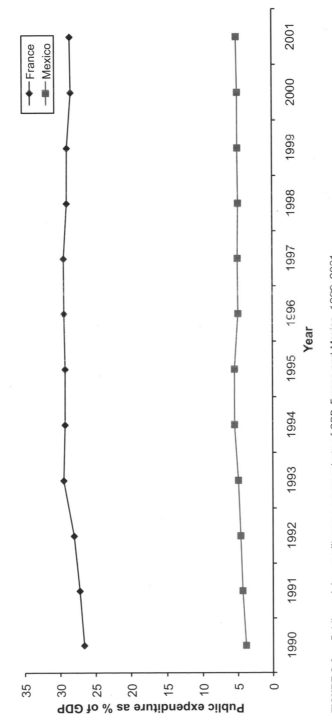

FIGURE 6.1. Public social expenditure as a percentage of GDP, France and Mexico 1990–2001.

Source: OECD Factbook, 2006–(Paris: OECD, 2006).

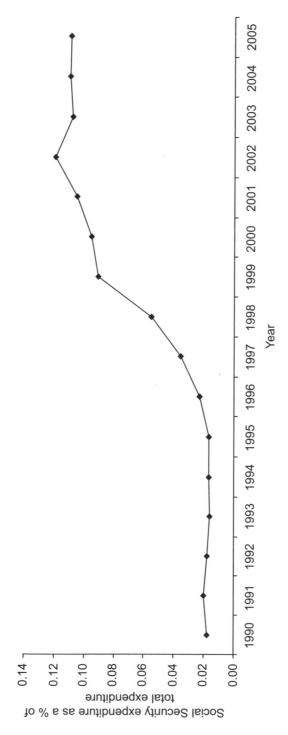

FIGURE 6.2. Government expenditure for social security as a percentage of total government expenditure, China, 1990–2005.

Source: Zhonghua renmin gongheguo guojia tongjiju bian [Chinese People's Republic National Statistics Bureau, ed.], *Zhongguo tongji nianjian* [Chinese statistical yearbook] (Beijing: Zhongguo tongji chubanshe [Chinese Statistical Publishing Co.], 2007), 280, 281.

Note: Includes expenditures on pensions and social welfare relief, on social security subsidies, and for retired government officials. Pensions were not included before 1996.

In none of the three cases here did the leadership pick the first option, that is, none simply disregarded the unrest. The variation, instead, was between Mexican repression, France's milder conciliation, and China's activist rejoinder, the goal of which aimed for—but went beyond—pure placating: in China, not only did disbursements shoot up significantly, but brand-new welfare programs were established in reply to the demonstrations of distraught workers (mainly ex-workers). The French government in the 1990s shored up programs that already existed and made several small advances that helped certain groups—but not the newly unemployed.[5]

For the most part, however, French leaders' positive efforts were preemptive rather than reactive to dissent. Besides, the steps taken by the French state tended only to delay or cancel proposed designs that would have undercut the "corporatist privileges" of "the most comfortably employed workers."[6] In Mexico, where in the late 1980s the PRI for the first time ever had to battle electorally in earnest for its political place, any new benefits the state extended went to the poor—people who were not even out on the streets demonstrating—in search of their votes, and not to the silenced proletariat.[7] Repression was used against the latter.

I focus on protest—thus on worker agency, whereby the aggrieved vent their anger—as the prod affecting (or not affecting) social programs when these three states' economies became more involved globally. One alternate approach explains state reaction with reference to the abstract, faceless process of "globalization," the degree of states' changing enmeshment in the world economy, taking that process as the determinant of shifts in governments' handling of benefits for workers. Thus the external market and—since democracies are generally the target of that brand of analysis—the political color of the party in power are often given pride of place as the chief relevant variables.[8] The debate in such studies is over whether rulers are more apt to cut benefits in an effort to help firms become more competitive—and also more easily to attract foreign investment—or whether, to the contrary, politicians increase welfare outlays in order to make up for what groups suffering losses have had to forfeit.[9] Scholars taking that angle put the question in

---

5. Levy, "France: Directing Adjustment?" 339.

6. Smith, *France in Crisis,* 38.

7. Katrina Burgess, *Parties and Unions in the New Global Economy* (Pittsburgh: University of Pittsburgh Press, 2004), 24.

8. Garrett and Lange, "Political Responses to Interdependence. Katzenstein, *Small States in World Markets,* distinguishes among advanced, industrial, democratic, Western European states on the basis of their size and the relative weight of differing social classes within them to account for the handling of social welfare. But he does not examine states of other types, nor does he focus on the behavior of the working class and their protests, especially since the countries he covers are more or less quiescent.

9. Brian Burgoon, "Globalization and Welfare Compensation: Disentangling the Ties that Bind," *International Organization* 55, 3 (2001), 509–51. An exception is Nita Rudra, "Globalization and the Decline of the Welfare State in Less-Developed Countries," *International Organization* 56, 2 (2002), 411–45, which does consider the impact of social forces.

terms of whether governments, once they are ensconced in the global economy, become more prone to put economic "efficiency" objectives ahead of other goals, or whether they direct their energy and resources to "compensating" victims suffering from the effects of competition.[10] Most of this research is quantitative, and it sometimes fails to explore the pathways along which—or the political mechanisms by which—globalization promotes a heightened or a lessened welfare effort.[11] Here I home in on these pathways and take into account issues often left out.

A different line of inquiry concerns not whether or not programs are expanded but only whether they are scrapped, crediting the electoral power of interest groups that had been the beneficiaries of relevant policies for preventing program cuts or cancellations.[12] But looking to groups that had been recipients of state largesse and at their electoral power cannot explain the workings of a situation in which a social group that was previously privileged loses its perquisites, goes out to protest, and is finally mollified a bit. Neither is this logic useful for cross-regime comparative analyses of states in which only one party holds hegemonic position, such that elections become empty exercises, as in China, and in Mexico through most of the 1980s. Nor is it helpful when the parties capable of capturing elections are largely in agreement about the thrust of economic and social policy, as in France after 1983. In short, what I am investigating is precisely how once empowered social forces in fact lost jobs or benefits or both and what happened next.

In the cases under consideration here, those one-time recipients not only lacked the backing of strong labor movements, but in addition found that their previous

---

10. See Geoffrey Garrett, "Globalization and Government Spending around the World," *Studies in Comparative International Development* 35, 4 (2001): 3–29; Markus M. L. Crepaz, "Global, Constitutional and Partisan Determinants of Redistribution in Fifteen OECD Countries," *CP* 34, 2 (2002), 169–88; Kaufman and Segura-Ubiergo, "Globalization, Domestic Politics"; Alexander Hicks, *Social Democracy and Welfare Capitalism: A Century of Income Security Politics* (Ithaca: Cornell University Press, 1999).

11. Burgoon, "Globalization and Welfare Compensation."

12. Huber and Stephens, *Development and Crisis.* "Cohesive," robust labor movements are touted in Evelyne Huber et al., "Social Democracy, Christian Democracy, Constitutional Structure, and the Welfare State," *American Journal of Sociology* 99, 3 (1993), 711–49; Lowell Turner, *Democracy at Work: Changing World Markets and the Future of Labor Unions* (Ithaca: Cornell University Press, 1991), 17. Huber and Stephens, *Development and Crisis,* 314, term "partisan incumbency" the "key factor for welfare state construction"; on this, see also Huber et al., "Social Democracy," 716. On Western Europe, see Geoffrey Garrett, *Partisan Politics in the Global Economy* (New York: Cambridge University Press, 1998); Walter Korpi and Joakim Palme, "New Politics and Class Politics in the Context of Austerity and Globalization: Welfare State Regress in 18 Countries, 1975–95," *American Political Science Review* 97, 3 (2003), 425–46; Stephens et al., "Welfare State," 178–79 and 190; Crepaz, "Global, Constitutional and Partisan"; on Latin America, see Kaufman and Segura-Ubiergo, "Globalization, Domestic Politics." See Pierson, *Dismantling the Welfare State,* for the argument about interest groups and the vote; also Stephens et al., "Welfare State," 167, and Bo Rothstein and Sven Steinmo, "Restructuring Politics: Institutional Analysis and the Challenges of Modern Welfare States," in *Restructuring the Welfare State: Political Institutions and Policy Change,* ed. Rothstein and Steinmo (New York: Palgrave Macmillan, 2002), 2.

status as support bases of leftist political parties meant little when their centralized, powerful states became willing to sacrifice these bases on the altar of productivity and competitiveness on global markets.[13] In all three, the state concentrated enough power centrally to render it relatively autonomous from social groups in opposition, even when those social groups had once been at the core of their power bases.[14] These postrevolutionary states shared two further features pertinent to this piece of the story. These were (as reviewed in chapter 2) the states' panic over instability and their state-designed, deeply segmented labor markets. The dual labor market, when combined with leaders' fears of eruptions, enabled and disposed all three regimes—if to varying degrees of new generosity—to pair shortchanging the old workforce as a whole with a state effort to retain at least a modicum of the loyalty, and thereby at a minimum to achieve the passivity of, an elite portion of labor.

The existence of a long-standing tiered market in labor in all three countries thus allowed politicians preferentially to relieve (at least partially) certain segments of the working class.[15] This was a choice that saved on funding, even as it demonstrated a measure of caring to the recipients—those workers who had earlier enjoyed the highest level of protections (and so sustained the greatest expectations). Dual labor markets meant that when state policies shifted, the workforce did not simply turn into a group of losers. Instead relative winners and relative losers were both created within each workforce, even if both lost as compared with business and with the past.[16] The relative winners also happened to be those whom the regime suspected of being not just most prone to but also most capable of inciting disorder.[17] Regime-crafted segmentation among the workers thus allowed the leadership to fine-tune its benefits, in the hope of preserving order while shoring up its own legitimacy. The concern at the top with regime credibility and legitimacy in China appeared in a speech in 2000 by then-premier Zhu Rongji,

---

13. Kaufman and Segura-Ubiergo, "Globalization, Domestic Politics," 582.

14. Haggard and Kaufman, "Introduction," 8; Levy, "France: Directing Adjustment," 326.

15. Jonas Pontusson, "Introduction: Organizational and Political-Economic Perspectives on Union Politics," in *Bargaining for Change: Union Politics in North America and Europe,* ed. Miriam Golden and Jonas Pontusson (Ithaca: Cornell University Press, 1992), 36, speaks of the increasing significance of duality in labor markets in Western Europe in dividing up the workforce since the mid-1970s, and Kaufman and Segura-Ubiergo, "Globalization, Domestic Politics," 583, say much the same thing about Latin America.

16. On winners and losers, see Ethan B. Kapstein, "Conclusion: Toward a Political Economy of Social Policy," in *Sustaining the Transition: the Social Safety Net in Postcommunist Europe,* ed. Ethan B. Kapstein and Michael Mandelbaum (New York: Council on Foreign Relations, 1997), 182.

17. For China, see Antoine Kernen and Jean-Louis Rocca, "The Reform of State-Owned Enterprises and Its Social Consequences in Shenyang and Liaoning" (ms., 1999), 23. The published version is Antoine Kernen and Jean-Louis Rocca, "Social Responses to Unemployment and the 'New Urban Poor': Case Study in Shenyang City and Liaoning Province," *China Perspectives* 27 (2000), 35–51. See also Jane Duckett, "China's Social Security Reforms and the Comparative Politics of Market Transition," *Journal of Transition Politics and Post-Communist Studies* (March 2003), 12; and Lee, "Revenge of History."

in which he said, "This year no matter how, we can't again see new delays. We must definitely pay out the arrears of the past several months within this year and do it as fast as possible, in order to obtain the people's confidence."[18]

Of course, the baselines of the welfare regimes differed considerably, with France for decades already boasting a substantial and generous set of entitlements; China's former, welfare-dispensing work-unit system in disintegration by the late 1990s; and Mexico's targeted beneficence meant just for state-employed labor. Nonetheless, changes in the magnitude of worker protests in the wake of job loss and benefit retraction appear to have been correlated with these states' welfare response in all three countries. Thus, I posit a link between protest level and welfare. The behavior of the unions (in relation to workers' protest) served as an intervening, or mediating, variable between the effects of global involvement on jobs and benefits, on the one hand, and the state's welfare effort (my dependent variable in this chapter), on the other. That is, in China, where unions' behavior allowed for and facilitated open opposition, the effects of states' global involvement (heightened unemployment and lowered benefits) prodded protest. Other things being equal, such protest stimulated state welfare allocations.

France

The EU's former incarnation, the European Community, promulgated social policies; later the composers of the Maastricht Treaty appended to it a supranational Social Chapter.[19] But regardless of these community-wide measures, some years after the Union had come into being Martin Rhodes concluded, "National governments may have lost their power to expand social spending at will, due largely to their [EU-mandated] inability to sustain growing public deficits, but they remain the architects of welfare states and employment systems."[20]

France in particular has long been the home of state-supported welfare. The historical roots of its contemporary social security system trace back to the end

---

18. "Zongli zai guoyou qiye xiagang zhigong jiben shenghuo baozhang he zaijiuye gongzuo huiyishang di zongjie jianghua" [Premier Zhu Rongji's summary speech in the work conference on state-owned staff and workers' basic livelihood guarantee and reemployment work], *LBT* 3 (January 13, 1999), 6.

19. Roberts and Springer, *Social Policy;* Jackman, "Impact of the European Union," 60–78; Bastian, "Putting the Cart,"; Martin Rhodes, "Defending the Social Contract: The EU Between Global Constraints and Domestic Imperatives," in Hine and Kassim, *Beyond the Market,* 36–59; and Symes, *Unemployment in Europe,* all discuss European Union policies toward unemployment.

20. Rhodes, "Defending the Social Contract," 50; Wolfgang Streeck, "From Market Making to State Building? Reflections on the Political Economy of European Social Policy," in *European Social Policy: Between Fragmentation and Integration,* ed. Stephan Leibfried and Paul Pierson (Washington, D.C.: Brookings Institution, 1995), 389–431.

of the Second World War, when a left-wing coalition held power. At that point a new welfare program became entrenched in a way that, for Europe, was unusually centralized and highly state-funded,[21] and the manifold benefits and entitlements it offered grew to be seen as inviolable birthrights in the eyes of the public.[22] The legacy of that provisioning largesse was worker dependence on the state for protection, and an expectation of ultimate sustenance from it.[23]

Thus, compared with other Community members, the French state spent proportionately more of its budget on welfare and tried harder to deal with the fallout when unemployment first rose across Europe, beginning in the 1970s. Following the initial oil shock of 1973 and throughout the rest of the century, French governments—both left and right—promoted an impressive array of labor market policies, both active and passive, including during times of austerity and even while battling inflation.[24] In the 1990s, France not only refrained from cutting back its expenditures, even as other countries around it—such as Germany, Belgium, and Ireland—reduced social spending as a share of their own GDP.[25] From a related angle, through the late 1980s and beyond, the country was among the OECD member states that did most to pass legislation directed at protecting jobs.[26] Nonetheless, as I document below, France did very little by way of investing funds for the jobless—apparently much less than it might have done—if we compare its effort with that of China.

Political parties in France had somewhat differing approaches to social policy, disagreeing sometimes as to the specific groups to target for funding and the modes of providing relief.[27] Nonetheless, parties on both ends of the mainstream spectrum were historically in accord on the fundamental necessity of a robust set of protections. This common inclination was a function of a shared view of untrammeled capitalism as an uncivilized affront to society, a traditional orientation that has been referred to as a "mix of old French paternalism and Social Catholicism,

---

21. Schmidt, "Values and Discourse," 269; Symes, *Unemployment in Europe*, 62.

22. Bell and Criddle, *French Socialist Party*, state that the levy charged to employers amounted to one-third of the wage bill. Rodrik, *Has Globalization Gone Too Far?* 42, notes that as of late 1995 the system accounted for half of all public-sector spending. See also Craig R. Whitney, "Why Blair's Victory May Not Travel Well in Europe," News of the Week in Review, *NYT*, May 4, 1997, 3.

23. Tony Judt, "The Social Question Redivivus," *Foreign Affairs* 76 (5) (1997), 103. Levy, "France: Directing Readjustment," 345, notes that it is "popular expectations" that "nurture" state activism.

24. In the immediate aftermath of that first oil shock, even in a climate in which fiscal conservatism prevailed, the percentage of GDP allocated to social security rose by .86 percent per year throughout Giscard's presidency (1974–81). After Mitterrand came to power, the advances were slower, but an annual rate of increase of .51 percent held for several years (Stephens et al., "Welfare State," 188), though some cuts were made (Kesselman, conclusion to *French Workers' Movement*, 317–18; Schmidt, *From State to Market?* 107, 110–12; Bell and Criddle, *French Socialist Party*, 154–61, 190).

25. Bastian, "Putting the Cart," 96.

26. Scharpf, "Economic Changes, Vulnerabilities," 115–16.

27. Levy, "France: Directing Adjustment," 340–43. Stephens et al., "Welfare State," 188.

with a trace of French socialism."[28] Societal values of social solidarity and social justice,[29] harking back to the Revolution, disposed politicians to take it for granted that it was up to the state to shelter potential victims from the offenses wrought by the naked market. So despite the austerity that became enshrined in France and the growing debility of the unions after 1983, over the ensuing decades the parties of the right as well as the left (if each with their own distinct approaches), maneuvered to commit some funds and to initiate a few programs aimed at the working class and for welfare. Both parties took the grievances of those who were one way or another disadvantaged into account in writing new legislation.[30] Thus, with the leadership as a whole ideologically committed to helping the needy and the noisy, politically inclined to win the support of the discontented,[31] and tactically touchy about disorder, when sufficiently aroused and united the trade unions (though split, mutually competitive, and quarrelsome, and though beset by shrinking memberships) could pry out certain victories through societal mobilization.[32]

The regime's early 1980s moves toward compensating workers who had fallen victim to rising unemployment were those of a leftist president. A good example was the program of "conversion poles," with handouts for retraining and modernizing in regions where adjustment had left many without work.[33] But rightist regimes remembered the working class as well, though attacking problems in a distinctly business-friendly fashion. In the mid-1990s, for instance, under the administration of conservative prime minister Édouard Balladur (and the presidency of Socialist Party leader Mitterrand), the government delivered a 60-billion-franc program aimed at creating some 700,000 new jobs before the end of 1996. This was to be accomplished first by cutting employers' mandatory contributions to social security, thereby supposedly encouraging more hiring, and by offering incentives aimed at reducing by 10 percent the costs of taking on low-wage workers and by 40 percent were a firm to recruit the long-term unemployed.[34] In 1997, under

---

28. Roberts and Springer, *Social Policy,* 69.

29. Miura and Palier, "Veto Players," 10.

30. Roberts and Springer, *Social Policy,* 69; Howell, *Regulating Labor,* 215. Mark Vail, writing in 2003 of the period after Howell's book was published, sees the same trend continuing. Vail, "Institutional Legacies, Political Discontinuities, and the Dynamics of French and German Social-Protection Reform," paper presented at the annual meeting of the American Political Science Association, August 28–31, 2003, 15–19. Scharpf, "Economic Changes, Vulnerabilities," 67, also speaks of French governments at both ends of the continuum acting on a perceived need to enact civic equality, which kept them from pursuing radical liberalization and extreme labor market deregulation. See also Levy, "France: Directing Readjustment," 326.

31. Levy, "France: Directing Readjustment," 331, states that social policy figured heavily in the politics of the late 1990s.

32. Miura and Palier, "Veto Players," 6, 11.

33. Smith, "Unemployment and the Left," 115–16; Levy, "France: Directing Adjustment," 326–27.

34. Schmidt, *From State to Market?* 195.

Socialist prime minister Lionel Jospin, the French government laid out 27.7 billion francs per year for financing early retirement packages and other measures of job support.[35]

The story of retraining programs was a similarly bipartisan one. This initiative, initially emphasized under the early 1970s conservative government of President Georges Pompidou, was continued not just by the Socialists under Mitterrand (1981–95) but also by his conservative successors, and again later by the Socialists once more.[36] All told, this effort permitted a full 95 percent of those retrainees who had been made redundant in the steel industry to obtain work as of early 1989.[37] Moreover, as of the year 2000, France had one of Europe's highest tax rates, at over 5 percent of GDP.[38]

But it must be noted that French generosity to labor had its limits and its logic. Two features of the relation among the state, the workers, and the unions played critical roles in restricting the largesse of state initiatives. The first of these was the segmentation of the French labor market, according to which those in state firms, where the trade unions were strongest, fared best. The relatively forceful position of the state enterprises can be traced back at least several decades. As the shocks of the 1970s began to cause unemployment, state-owned firms were utilized to protect jobs.[39] Later Mitterrand's nationalizations of 1981 were expressly aimed not only at job formation of any sort but also—by specifically supplying new *state* jobs—at creating positions that would come with social benefits.[40] At the same time, workers let go from state jobs were to be given first priority in future hires.[41]

A decade later, President Jacques Chirac's conservative prime minister Édouard Balladur managed to reduce pensions in the private sector in 1993. Yet just two years later, massive strikes instigated by the public-sector unions prevented a later rightist prime minister, Alain Juppé, from achieving the same thing in the public sector.[42] That the public sector unions and their charges absorbed by far the bet-

---

35. Vivien A. Schmidt, "Democracy at Risk? France, Great Britain, and Germany between Globalization and Europeanization," paper presented at the conference "State and Sovereignty in the World Economy," Laguna Beach, Calif., February 1997, 19. The final version of this paper was published as Vivien A. Schmidt, "Convergent Pressures, Divergent Responses: France, Great Britain, and Germany between Globalization and Europeanization," in *States and Sovereignty in the Global Economy*, ed. David A. Smith, Dorothy J. Solinger, and Steven C. Topik (New York: Routledge, 1999), 172–92, but without that statistic.

36. Moss, "After the Auroux Laws," 68, 71; Smith, "Unemployment and the Left," 117.

37. Daley, "Steel Crisis," 177.

38. Thomas Sancton, "The French Connected," *Time*, June 12, 2000, 44.

39. Scharpf, "Economic Changes, Vulnerabilities," 37.

40. Ibid., 66. Twelve industrial conglomerations and thirty-eight banks were taken over by the state. Levy, "France: Directing Change," 321.

41. Smith, *France in Crisis*, 115.

42. Hemerijck and Schludi, "Sequences of Policy Failure," 170. Vail, "Institutional Legacies," 23, attributes this to the difference in political style adopted by the two men, as well as to the veto power

ter part of the state's attention was certainly a rational response on the part of the politicians, for by the late 1980s, unionism was nearly entirely concentrated within the public sector. With the turn of the century, the unions were able to draw in a mere 6 percent of the private sector's employees, the lowest rate in all the European Union member states.[43] And strikes mounted by workers in the public sector numbered about ten times more than those in the private sector over the years 1995 to 2000.[44]

Probably for these reasons, those working in formal jobs, but especially those on the state payroll, traditionally drew a far better package of benefits than those laboring elsewhere.[45] Many unemployment benefits (or their most favorable terms) continued in the 1980s and 1990s to be directed primarily at those formally a part of the employment-based system, thereby excluding from assistance over half of the unemployed as of the late 1990s.[46] It would appear that the state's generosity to those already secure could have been responsible for the deprivation of the rest.[47] The outcome of this closed and segmented labor market was an "insider effect," a pattern particularly strong in France.[48] In the words of Timothy B. Smith, "The vast majority [of social spending funds] goes to the rich and to the middle class, to the comfortably employed 'insiders'...very little of it goes to the 'outsiders' (the unemployed, low-income workers, the poor, youth, immigrants)." Based on sources from the early years of the twenty-first century, he also asserts, "Up to 40 percent of the working-age population...is either poor, unemployed, or underemployed with access to limited social benefits."[49] This pronounced segmentation in the labor market means that it is inappropriate to theorize about "workers" as if they were a uniform group, as is often done.

The second distinctive feature of the French state's stance toward workers was its prophylactic approach to programming for the unemployed, a function of its pronounced fear of disorder. Jonah Levy, Mari Miura, and Gene Park characterize

---

of the unions, which, presumably, was either more well coordinated or mattered more in 1995 than in 1993. As Kesselman, "French Labor Movement," 159; Rodrik, *Globalization*, 42–43.

43. Roberts and Springer, *Social Policy*, 70. Howell, *Regulating Labor*, 181.

44. Smith, *France in Crisis*, 165.

45. Vivien A. Schmidt, "Three Models of Capitalism," ms. copy, 27, and *Economist*, June 5, 1999, 5, make the case that public-sector workers were in 1999 receiving pensions worth 75 to 85 percent of their final salary, while those in private firms got just 50 percent.

46. Richard Hauser and Brian Nolan with Konstanze Morsforf and Wolfgang Strengmann-Kun, "Unemployment and Poverty: Change over Time," in *Welfare Regimes and the Experience of Unemployment in Europe*, ed. Duncan Gallie and Serge Paugam (Oxford: Oxford University Press, 2000), 31.

47. Smith, *France in Crisis*, 10.

48. Paolo Barbieri with Serge Paugam and Helen Russell, "Social Capital and Exits from Unemployment," in Gallie and Paugam, *Welfare Regimes*, 201–11. The terms come from Assar Lindbeck and Denis Snower, *The Insider-Outsider Theory of Unemployment* (Cambridge, Mass.: MIT Press, 1988).

49. Smith, *France in Crisis*, 6.

this strategy as being aimed specifically "to pacify and demobilize potential oppo-
nents of market-led adjustment."[50] Thus, various administrations put forward a
set of policies clearly geared to preempt social upheaval.[51] So even as the state was
increasing the numbers of those who fell into joblessness, it was also attempting to
forestall and deal with their likely grievances.[52]

Steps to stave off the anger that redundancy was certain to stir up included
the state's contribution of funds to failing enterprises to keep them afloat[53] and
its mid-1970s legislation restricting layoffs. That law demanded that firms dismissing more than ten workers for economic reasons obtain the approval of an
inspector from the Ministry of Labor. This requirement, however, was eliminated
in 1986 under premier Chirac's program of austerity. Still, in 1993 the conservative premier Balladur requested that public-sector firms delay layoffs, and in late
1999 Jospin proposed withholding state aid from profit-making enterprises that
fired workers.[54] There was also much state investment in public infrastructure construction, all in the interest of seeing the maximum possible number of French
people at work and, correlatively, the minimal number poised in opposition to the
state. Prime Minister Jospin's famous initiative to reduce the work week was clearly
directed at retaining existing but threatened jobs and, ideally, furnishing new ones
in the process.[55]

Passive measures, those aimed at income maintenance, existed as well. These
included a lavish minimum wage when compared with elsewhere in the Union[56]
and, in the 1970s, liberal severance payments for discharged workers, such as a
handout of 50,000 francs to speed along the exit of workers from industries to

50. Jonah D. Levy, Mari Miura, and Gene Park, "Exiting Étatisme? New Directions in State Policy
in France and Japan?" paper presented at the workshop "The State after Statism: New State Activities in
the Age of Globalization and Liberalization," University of California, Berkeley, November 1–15, 2003,
3, 18; Levy, "France: Directing Readjustment."

51. Schmidt, From State to Market? 195; Levy, "France: Directing Readjustment"; Daley, "Steel
Crisis"; Bell and Criddle, French Socialist Party, 154–61; Bastian, "Putting the Cart," 102. See also Kesselman, conclusion to French Workers' Movement, 320; Levy, "France: Directing Readjustment," 312.
Andrews, "Jobless Are Snared," 6, claims that in France, something like two-thirds of all newly hired
workers were on temporary contracts of less than one year. Economist, "France: The Grand Illusion," 6,
states that in 1998 four-fifths of the jobs created in the private sector involved short-term contracts.

52. Daley, "Steel Crisis," 170; Bell and Criddle, French Socialist Party, 157. Scharpf, "Economic
Changes, Vulnerabilities," 67; Hemerijck and Schludi, "Sequences of Policy Failure," 16; and Levy,
"France: Directing Readjustment," 328.

53. Levy, "France: Directing Readjustment," 323; Schmidt, From State to Market? 175; Bell and
Criddle, French Socialist Party, 158–59.

54. Schmidt, From State to Market? 192; Suzanne Daley, "Under Attack, Premier Offers France's Left
an Embrace," NYT, October 3, 1999.

55. Levy, "France: Directing Readjustment," 338–39; Gordon and Meunier, French Challenge, 36,
100; Bastian, "Putting the Cart," 92–93; Economist, January 6, 2001, 47.

56. Jackman, "Impact of the European Union," 72–73.

be phased out.[57] A liberal plan providing benefits for unemployment originated in the mid-1970s under the rightist presidency of Giscard, even as he was getting industrial restructuring under way. At the time, this outlay bestowed an allowance equivalent to 90 percent of the worker's prior wages for up to one year.[58] True, once the post-1980 crisis hit, the amount of the benefit was lowered substantially, though it was still extended for a minimum of three and a maximum of forty-five months, depending on the length of a worker's contribution to the program and his or her age.[59] In the late 1980s, after the Socialists returned to power, a minimum income plan was introduced to assist people normally outside the welfare system, such as the long-term unemployed, though its means-testing bespoke conditionality.[60]

So overall, despite the watchfulness of the regime and its apparent magnanimity (at least for state-connected workers), the France of the 1980s had long been equipped with a full-fledged welfare system, and for this reason alone it might seem that there was not much room for enhanced benevolence. But, I would argue, given that the level of disturbances coming from labor was not so terribly threatening, appearances to the contrary, state programs for the unemployed were not particularly costly; besides, in subtle ways they were being undermined. Aggregate spending on labor market policy rose from just over 2 percent of GDP in the mid-1980s to only 4.2 percent in 1999. Not only was the portion of spending reserved for labor-related matters relatively small, the two largest relevant programs pertained not to employment issues at all but to pensions and health care. The true amount spent on health and the 35-hour work week amounted to 27 billion francs instead of the 119 billion advertised.[61] Throughout the 1990s, moreover, unemployment compensation taken by itself hovered around a mere 1.5 percent of GDP.[62]

57. Daley, "Steel Crisis," 169.

58. Levy, "France: Directing Readjustment," 320.

59. More details (as of the mid-1990s) are in Symes, *Unemployment in Europe,* 63–64.

60. Stephens et al., "Welfare State," 189, and Levy, "France: Directing Readjustment," 328. But according to Vail, "Institutional Legacies," 19–20, since 1984 those whose right to benefits had expired or who had inadequate contribution histories had access to the means-tested "allocation de solidarité spécifique." As of the mid-1990s, the basic rate of income maintenance for those outside the system was about half the level of the minimum wage for adults. Symes, *Unemployment in Europe,* 64.

61. Miura and Park, "Veto Players," 13–14. Levy, "France: Directing Readjustment," 339–40, states that although it appeared that as much as 154 billion francs were committed to three programs under the Jospin administration for health insurance, youth employment, and a reduction in the work week from 39 to 35 hours, in fact the state was already underwriting health care at the local level, older youth employment programs were being phased out, and employers were already being paid to shorten the work week.

62. OECD, *Employment Outlook: Statistical Annex,* 1991–99.

And in preemptively steering these more ample benefits to the upper crust of the workforce, and thereby positioning itself to ward off the possibility of that segment's belligerency in the boulevards, the French democratic government was both less directly reactive and less bold in its spending than the Chinese communist regime under the impact of similar circumstances. Accordingly, Kesselman concluded, "the strikes [of the autumn of 1995] demonstrated that the state cannot ignore unions but resulted neither in new policy initiatives favorable to labor's interests nor in a revitalization of the labor movement."[63] All told, however, France far outdid the Mexican state, even when the latter's hegemonic party stood in danger of losing its political power.

Mexico

Throughout Latin America in the 1980s, social spending dropped precipitously in response to huge foreign debts and the attendant pressure to cut back on state expenditures of all kinds. Indeed, social welfare was a sector specifically targeted for economizing across the region.[64] Mexico did not simply follow a trend: it was Mexico's debt crisis that paved the way. Here too, as in France, a tradition existed of helping the state-affiliated workforce before the crisis struck. As early as 1943, legislation gave workers in the formal sector social insurance, consisting of pensions, disability benefits, health insurance, and workers' compensation. In later decades, other categories of workers, such as the self-employed, were permitted to enroll, but only at their own expense. In 1960, all federal government employees received an attractive coverage package.[65]

But the tacit corporatist contract which had long bound union leaders with the PRI—and which had lent the state, via its ruling party, a fair measure of legitimacy among the laboring people who benefited—crumbled for the workers once national economic crisis set in, much more dramatically than in France. For example, state-financed per capita health and welfare spending fell 34 percent between 1981 and 1989, and by the late 1980s only a little over half the population possessed public social security benefits for health care, old age, disability, and widowhood.[66]

---

63. Kesselman, "French Labor Movement," 160.

64. Stallings and Peres, *Growth, Employment, and Equity,* 67.

65. Dion, "Mexico's Welfare Regime," 7–10.

66. Levy and Bruhn, *Mexico,* 175; Fleck and Sorrentino, "Employment and Unemployment," 3. Rudolfo Tuiran, "The Sociodemographic Effects of the Crisis in Mexico," found at http://lanic.utexas.edu/project/etext/mexico/selby/chap4.html, accessed on September 15, 2005, notes that public expenditures decreased by an average rate of 10 percent per year between 1982 and 1988, with the chief impact on education, health, and housing.

New technocratic, economically sophisticated politicians easily adjusted to the restructuring agenda the International Monetary Fund laid down—one that demanded that the Mexican government cut deeply into its social spending—in exchange for loans.[67] Reductions began under de la Madrid in 1983; in his last five years in power, government expenditures on education and health fell by a cumulative 29.6 and 23.3 percent, respectively.[68] Substantial shaving away of subsidies for basic commodities, transport, electricity, natural gas, and gasoline also occurred under the rule of Miguel de la Madrid (1982–88).[69]

Meanwhile, social development dropped from 25 percent of total federal spending in 1976 to under 10 percent in 1988.[70] Mexico increased its spending in this arena at the end of the decade and into the early 1990s, but that move was made to meet a short-term electoral goal. Later, in the one year from 1994 to 1995, social spending contracted by 12 percent in real terms as it competed for funds with debt servicing.[71] Moreover, there was virtually no programmatic repositioning, let alone any increase in outlays for workers by the state in response to union mobilization. Labor bosses saw to it that nearly none of that took place.

Indeed, the linkage between the PRI, a self-proclaimed leftist party, on the one side, and unions whose bosses possessed influence, on the other, flatly failed to yield protection—at least for most of the workforce—against the new global forces when their repercussions hit the country in and after the early 1980s. As the economic crisis unfolded and enormous bills had to be paid off by the state, privatization of thousands of state-owned firms became one of the primary means the government had at its command for raising capital. The extent of this auction is apparent in the statistic that the government gained US$24 billion in the sale of state assets just in the four years between 1989 and 1993.[72] Such shunting off of firms often led at the least to the slashing of wages and benefits for the employees and at the most to the loss of state workers' jobs.[73] Shutdowns and sales of large state-owned firms throughout the 1980s cut down on the command once pos-

67. Rochlin, *Redefining Mexican "Security,"* 25.

68. Middlebrook, *Paradox of Revolution,* 258.

69. Dion, "Mexico's Welfare Regime," 32; Middlebrook, *Paradox of Revolution,* 161, 286, 287; Peter M. Ward, "Social Welfare Policy and Political Opening in Mexico," *Journal of Latin American Studies,* 25, 3 (1993), 626.

70. Ward, "Social Welfare Policy," 617–18.

71. Lustig, *Mexico,* 210.

72. Manuel Pastor and Carol Wise, "State Policy, Distribution and Neoliberal Reform in Mexico," *Journal of Latin American Studies,* 29, 2 (1997), 429. The term "auction" for selling off state assets is borrowed from Jozsef Borocz, "From Comprador State to Auctioneer State," in *States and Sovereignty,* ed. Smith et al., 193–209. Rochlin, *Redefining Mexican "Security,"* 30, refers to 766 sales in the years 1983–88.

73. Rochlin, *Redefining Mexican "Security,"* 30; Collier, *Contradictory Alliance,* 105–6; Middlebrook, *Paradox of Revolution,* 256, 286.

sessed by important industrial unions, rendering them increasingly incapable of fighting effectively against the state's watering down of old benefits for workers, even on those few occasions when unions attempted such defenses.[74]

Simultaneously, debt-induced austerity policies led to bankruptcies that threw people out of jobs, concurrently, of course, spelling the elimination or the reduction of generalized subsidies and welfare benefits. In cases in which a firm lumbered on, the level of contributions demanded from the insured rose considerably.[75] A new rift developed with the desertion of some critical sections of labor in Salinas's 1988 election. What the new president viewed as a betrayal led his yet PRI-controlled state to retaliate by unseating labor leaders as well as by reducing the resources in bosses' hands; downgrading the attractiveness of workers' contracts was another punitive tactic. A severe drop in oil prices on the international market in 1998 meant several billion dollars' worth of new cuts in social and educational expenditures; by 1999, all subsidies had been eliminated.[76]

The style of the relationship that unions had fashioned with the workers, especially the decidedly superior position commanded by the labor chiefs as opposed to their charges,[77] accounted for this welfare outcome. For the most part, the primary power that labor leaders enjoyed was not one *for*, but one *over*, the working class, as already discussed.[78] Insofar as any sort of alliance survived between the PRI and the big unions after the early 1980s, it was a bond based on preserving the status of bosses willing to present the PRI with their unions' backing for the regime's harsh measures of restructuring.[79] At least up through 1988, while wages fell, social spending dropped, and subsidies disappeared for the rank and file, union leaders in good standing with the PRI continued to benefit from privileges.[80]

The pension reform program of 1995 is a good example of the nature of the transformation that came about: this policy entailed the replacement of an old collective account system with an individual account one, with the new system man-

74. Teichman, *Privatization and Political Change*, 199–200; Middlebrook, *Paradox of Revolution*, 161, 256, 287.

75. Michelle Dion, "Neoliberal Reform of Mexico's Welfare Regime, 1980s–1990s," paper delivered at the annual meeting of the American Political Science Association, Boston, August 31, 2002. This is chap. 4 of her Ph.D. dissertation, "Progress of Revolution? Mexico's Welfare Regime in Comparative and Historical Perspective," University of North Carolina, Chapel Hill; see 165, 167, 168, and 180 on the rise in individual contribution rates. See also Dussel Peters, *Polarizing Mexico*, 150.

76. Dussel Peters, *Polarizing Mexico*, 149 and 68.

77. Burgess, *Parties and Unions*, 34.

78. This is similar to Burgess's argument in "Loyalty Dilemmas." See also Toledo, "Free Trade and Labor Relations," 31–32. Dussel Peters, *Polarizing Mexico*, 145–46, 203, emphasizes the continuing stance of the corporatist unions behind the PRI's program of liberalization, even to the point of using physical coercion to break up strikes against provisions of reform.

79. Middlebrook, *Paradox of Revolution*, 287, 299.

80. Burgess, *Parties and Unions*, 20–21; Teichman, *Privatization and Political Change*, 64–66.

aged not by the state but by private firms.[81] Thus the inexorability of the economic downturn severely undermined the fortunes of workers as a group. And while official union heads could not block pension privatization altogether in 1995, they managed to make it less offensive to their own interests.[82]

The duality of the Mexican labor market was at least as pronounced as it was in France. For years before the debt crisis imposed constraints on the government's ability to provide welfare benefits, organized urban workers were a privileged section within the workforce. President Luis Echeverria (1970–76) offered special benefits for those who were union members and took measures to protect their purchasing power, but his emergency salary increments probably missed those outside the unions.[83] For decades, those party to the coalition between the PRI and its favored affiliates, as well as those who were members of strong, independent public-sector unions, such as the electricity union, thrived as insiders. At the same time, many workers, particularly those in the informal sector,[84] were excluded altogether from the benefits of which others were assured.[85] Those in the public-enterprise unions were the most privileged component of the working class, enjoying their own state-underwritten hospitals, clinics, and recreational facilities, among other perquisites.[86]

As economic austerity and adjustment proceeded, laborers who either had been or who landed on the outside of this system of entitlement were particularly hard hit. In the absence of any state-sponsored welfare or government unemployment insurance, the laid-off had no recourse but to drop into the informal sector to make a living. Concurrently, mounting foreign investment in the maquiladores along the U.S. border often meant the only wage work available came with a low level of benefits, if any.[87] The same was true of the service jobs that made up the largest component of the informal sector.[88]

With Mexico's gradual acquiescence to NAFTA-like principles, the overall result was a steadily expanding segment of the populace thrown not just out of work

---

81. Dion, "Neoliberal Reform," 232; Dussel Peters, *Polarizing Mexico,* 150.

82. Dion, "Neoliberal Reform," 159, 178, 191, 194–97, 202–3, and 206–12. Fabrice Lehoucq, "Structural Reform, Democratic Governance, and Institutional Design in Latin America," *CP* 39, 2 (2007): 240, remarks, "Only when pension system members belonged to…public sector unions [as in Mexico] did technopols have to modify pension privatization bills."

83. Coleman and Davis, "Preemptive Reform," 8.

84. Tardanico, "From Crisis to Restructuring," 244, defines the private sector simply as "the segment of employment that has escaped state regulation."

85. Only in 1973 did some groups in the informal sector become eligible to enroll in the social security program that had served formal labor since the 1940s. Dion, "Mexico's Welfare Regime," 8.

86. Teichman, *Privatization and Political Change,* 65.

87. According to Pastor and Wise, "State Policy," 433, average real wages and benefits in these firms was about half the Mexican manufacturing average in the mid-1990s.

88. Samstad, "Unanticipated Persistence," 11.

but into a totally unprotected realm. These alterations to meet external principles meant that previous governmental programs supporting price controls and granting food subsidies for the general public disappeared as well, victimizing the poor even further. Meanwhile, health, education, and social security became managed on a basis of efficiency and profit.[89]

Even as the rate of poverty climbed among the populace as a whole, and as wages fell across the working class, the distinction between formal and informal labor, insiders and outsiders, persisted and, indeed, deepened. In 1987, in the midst of austerity, a pact on wage and price stabilization preserved advantages just for state-affiliated unions, giving them special access to subsidized food, housing, and bank credit,[90] and the right, if dismissed, to a moderately attractive severance package: three months of pay plus twenty days of pay for each year of service.[91] And the 1995 "reform" noted earlier exempted state employees from its provisions, so that their significantly higher and better pension and health care benefits continued intact. That special segment of the labor force also continued to be the beneficiary of consumer loans, vacation discounts, and other subsidies; those in the armed forces and the petroleum industry held onto their separate, and superior, social security systems as well.[92]

The government took some note of these inequities, but the dynamic was distinctly different from the ones operating in France and China. As poverty and the numbers of people stripped of their means of sustenance rose,[93] elections began to turn threatening for the first time for the leaders of the PRI. Beginning with the period just after the 1988 presidential election, which PRI candidate Carlos Salinas barely won (and in which he prevailed probably more because of sleight of hand than because of an honest count), welfare expenditures increased. But the new funds were concentrated in a means-tested program—like the French Socialists' late 1980s plan for the long-term unemployed—targeted just at the poor in regions where the PRI had lost votes.

This initiative, called PRONASOL, or the National Program of Solidarity (Programa Nacional de Solidaridad), was funded in part from the proceeds of

---

89. Dussel Peters, *Polarizing Mexico,* 148–49.

90. Middlebrook, *Paradox of Revolution,* 264–65.

91. Fleck and Sorrentino, "Employment and Unemployment," 20. See also Roberts, "Dynamics of Informal Employment," 107; Ward, "Social Welfare Policy," 624.

92. Dion, "Neoliberal Reform," 231.

93. According to Rochlin, *Redefining Mexican "Security,"* 27, the minimum wage lost 53 percent of its purchasing power between 1982, the year of the advent of the debt crisis, and 1988, and dropped another 28 percent over the following six years. Lustig, *Mexico,* 201, notes that between 1984 and 1989 moderate poverty rose from 28.55 to 32.6 percent of the population while extreme poverty increased from 13.9 to 17 percent. Polaski, "Jobs, Wages, and Household Income," 26, found that 41 percent of the population was living in poverty by 1989, while the extreme poverty rate was 31 percent of the population by the time NAFTA went into effect in 1994.

the privatization of state enterprises and in part from the World Bank. Its initiation represented an effort to win back votes in regions that had gone to the newly minted, more leftist Party of the Democratic Revolution.[94] PRONASOL sponsored the formation of tens of thousands of neighborhood committees charged with supplying electricity, drinking water, sewage disposal, road paving, and schools in their communities, and the two to three billion dollars that went to the program annually accounted for a significant portion of the increase in social spending that Mexico saw in the early 1990s.[95] Even still, the sums of money allocated to this policy never surpassed 1 percent of GDP.[96]

Although this measure may have seemed a corrective to the PRI's new neoliberal tilt away from its past alliance with those who toil, in fact the beneficiaries were not former workers or even workers at all, and certainly not union members.[97] And the program's focus on places where the party had lost support demonstrated the growing salience of electoral competition in the PRI's calculus; the program, accordingly, was neither a response to actions from the working class (as in China) nor a move to forestall such actions (as in France). For, as noted before, in Mexico the power of the most prominent unions ensured there would be few disruptive actions.

Under Salinas's successor, Ernesto Zedillo (1994–2000), PRONASOL was terminated and a somewhat different project, PROGRESA, was created in its place, this one also means-tested and also directed at a particular constituency, the extreme poor. Set up in 1997, PROGRESA, or the Program in Education, Health and Nutrition (Programa de Educación, Salud y Alimentación), unlike PRONASOL, was aimed just at families in the countryside, so it obviously had nothing to do with urban unemployment, workers' demonstrations, or workers' interests. The targeted population was to receive a sum of about US$30 per month, with the goal of improving diets, health care, and educational opportunities.[98] Within its first year, though nearly two million families received benefits, it did little to undercut poverty in Mexico, which in fact increased by 4.5 million persons over the period 1989–96, to reach a total of 67.8 million at the period's end.[99] Appraisals of the effects of this initiative are mixed: though at under 1 percent of GDP it was at

94. Ward, "Social Welfare Policy," 627; Reynolds, "Power, Value, and Distribution," 86.

95. Ward, "Social Welfare Policy," 626–28; Meyer, "Mexico," 148; Heath, "Original Goals," 48; Haggard and Kaufman, *Political Economy,* 300–303; Stallings and Peres, *Growth, Employment, and Equity,* 35.

96. Pastor and Wise, "Long View."

97. Burgess, *Parties and Unions,* 24.

98. Lustig, *Mexico,* 212.

99. Dussel Peters, *Polarizing Mexico,* 151–57, 160, points out that extreme poverty in Mexico has been relatively high since 1984, accounting for over 30 percent of total households in the years 1984–96, with the poorest concentrated in the rural areas.

least as poorly endowed as PRONASOL had been, it has been said to have affected almost 40 percent of rural households, reducing poverty by almost 8 percent for those it served.[100] Still, being means-tested, both of these programs were targeted at specific, limited groups, in a bow to neoliberal welfare approaches.[101]

In their goal of winning ballots, neither of these programs constituted a reaction to protests from dismissed workers, for, as noted, such voices were largely lacking. What happened in Mexico was just the creation of broad-based, active labor market, remedial activities, such as retraining or job creation. Such responses were devised only in the wake of the 1995 peso crisis and were nowhere in evidence over the preceding decade and a half, as the numbers of positions plummeted nationwide.

The government's retraining program for the unemployed following the 1995 peso crisis was far from adequate to serve the numbers laid off, provided only very short courses geared toward upgrading skills, and excluded many of those in need through its strict qualifications for participation. The state also moved funds from other poverty programs in order to establish a short-term employment program in 1995, creating half a million short-term jobs, but nearly three-quarters of these were in rural areas. A minimal effort was undertaken to create urban jobs in the wake of that crisis, but there were no such programs operating on a regular basis.[102] Most of the newly installed ongoing employment programs, moreover, were funded not by the regime but by the World Bank.[103] Nor did state leaders adopt any passive approaches to unemployment, such as severance pay packages or income subsidies, except for a brief time in 1995.

Thus in Mexico, in a time of hardship, union leaders played out their traditional functions of ministering to the ruling party and serving themselves more than the workers. At the same time, the state accentuated its customary role of provisioning the formal sector, comprised of state-employed laborers, to the detriment of those on the outside of that charmed circle. The big picture is one in which the segmentation of the labor market and the loyal labor bosses were critical to allowing the state (and the PRI) to retain its old supporters even as, in comparison with the past, it shortchanged them.

A conclusion at this stage is that the French welfare state, historically already far more generous than the Mexican one, and also unable to count on coalition partners to keep its workers quiet (and, as a democratic regime, not inclined to do so), disbursed a few supplemental, well-publicized new sums (but without a sizable resource outlay) at the appearance of occasional worker demonstrations. Compared with Mexico, French leaders were trained in preempting protest, rather

100. Pastor and Wise, "Long View."
101. Dion, "Neoliberal Reform," 230–33; Burgess, *Parties and Unions,* 22–23.
102. Lustig, *Mexico,* 210–11; Pastor and Wise, "State Policy," 439.
103. Dussel Peters, *Polarizing Mexico,* 149.

than in nurturing and then using labor boss collaborators to suppress any hint of protest in their time of austerity.

China

As in the other two countries, in China unionized workers belonged to an organization that even in normal times had only a very limited, if any, ability to influence the large sweep of events that touched its members' interests. In the face of the economic crisis following 1980 (in China's case, more a purported crisis) and the leadership decisions forged to cope with it, this regime-linked body was more or less impotent. Indeed, in China the chance for workers to use institutional mechanisms to defend their interests surely was the very slightest of all three. Yet also as in France and Mexico, Chinese labor—or, better put, favored sections thereof—continued to receive a measure of regime protection from the onslaught of the market's perturbations once layoffs surged into the 1990s and even beyond, indeed even after China joined the WTO, despite the WTO's anti-protectionist credo. And even the less elite portion of the workforce was neither always nor altogether left aside.

But regardless of the lingering care in these countries, it cannot be denied that in all of them workers experienced a clear diminution of their social security benefits, beginning in Mexico in the mid-1980s, next in France in the early 1990s, and last of all in China from the mid-1990s, in each case at and after the moment of the political elite's choice for intensified global immersion through SEO membership. In a comparison of labor's losses among the three countries, China's workers were at once the politically weakest but also shielded the longest. They also elicited from the political elite the most concern and, correlatively, the most effort at official compensation.

The two relevant traits that the three polities shared—state-fashioned segmentation within the labor market and regime insecurity about disorder—were especially pronounced in China's case. The protected portion of the labor force was made up of workers with a particularly strong sense of entitlement: it was the only country of the three, in fact, where state rhetoric had specifically enshrined and ennobled the working class (especially its state-employed component) from the very inception of the regime. And that rhetoric was actually realized for decades, as the state liberally provided for the proletariat's urban members (especially those in state firms), as compared with Party treatment of any other nonofficial occupational section of civilian society. China was an extreme case of elite apprehensiveness as well. For the Communist Party, which had long rooted its legitimacy precisely in its allegiance to the working class, was the only political actor at the elite level, and its bosses believed deeply in the necessity of that hegemonic party's persisting rule. But despite the leadership's having shored up the top tier of the workforce, and regardless of the elite's anxieties over its own legitimacy, the Party was never inclined to let the trade union act as the true representative of the working class. And what little authority the union had steadily slipped away with the rise in the private and foreign sectors of the economy, for in these arenas its branches largely failed to penetrate.

In pre-reform-era China, after the early 1950s, urban state-employed workers received labor insurance and cradle-to-grave welfare benefits for decades.[104] Not just during the period dominated by the rule of Mao Zedong (1949–76), but even into the 1990s the allocation of benefits was the responsibility of the cellular work unit, called the *danwei*, through which each employed individual and his or her dependents could count on receiving social security, including pensions, medical care, workers' compensation, housing, and schooling.[105] But this list of perquisites had no place for unemployment insurance (UI), since even the concept of unemployment, much less the reality, was taboo in pre-reform-era China after the very early post-takeover years.[106]

Thus new programs instituted in the 1980s and 1990s to cater to those deprived of their jobs were unprecedented in the PRC and had to be forged from scratch. From the early 1950s until 1969, workers in urban, state-owned firms turned over 3 percent of their payroll to a labor insurance fund, whose management was shared between their firm and its trade union branch. Factory unions then gave about one-third of these contributions to their superior-level union, resulting in some minimal redistribution among the enterprises under the same higher-level union. But it was the workers within this system—those employed by state-owned enterprises—and they alone, who received union benefits. During the Cultural Revolution (1966 to the early 1970s), when the unions were disbanded, expenditures for welfare became the responsibility solely of the firms themselves. At that point, whatever pooling had been done above the level of the work unit ceased and the nature of one's *danwei*—its size, its industrial sector, and, of course, as before, whether or not it was state-owned—became the determinant of one's welfare level.[107]

In linking state beneficence to workers' employment status and to that of the form of ownership of their employer, and in favoring only the formally state-employed, the system clearly practiced exclusivity, rendering the urban labor

104. Walder, "Property Rights," and "Remaking of the Chinese Working Class."

105. Athar Hussain et al., *Urban Poverty in the PRC,* Asian Development Bank Project No. TAR: PRC 33448, 2002, 154.

106. Wong, *Marginalization and Social Welfare,* 66. Some exceptions are discussed in Perry and Li, *Proletarian Power.* Perry and Li demonstrate that the taboo was sometimes broken in practice, in the case of the most marginal urbanites.

107. Chow, *Social Security in China,* 53; Walder, "Property Rights."

market an overtly and explicitly dual one, with one tier kept generally placid at comparative cost. Though some of the larger "collective" firms were operated like state-owned ones, those in the inferior portion of the urban dual labor market—workers in smaller collectives and contract, temporary, and peasant workers employed in city factories—were shut out of the welfare system altogether, and the small enterprises that were located in the rural areas were also barred from partaking in these arrangements. There was no private sector or any foreign-invested firms during the Mao era, so the issues of welfare and inclusion for those realms were effectively moot.[108]

As for the regime's special sensitivity to unrest, Chinese party-state leaders' proclivity to link stability with welfare was openly and regularly enunciated. In early 1997, before their major thrust to clear out the ranks of what they considered excess workers from the factories was even under way, Beijing authorities emphasized that "subsidizing enterprises in financial difficulties to reassure and pacify workers and staff is absolutely vital to social stability."[109] In late 1997, just after the 15th Party Congress called for cutting back the workforce, central-level political figures demanded that localities devise a "responsibility system" to stave off the potential "social chaos" they considered likely to issue from what was then termed the "daily increasing army of the unemployed."[110]

In May 2000, a State Planning Commission research group published an internal piece titled, "Establishing a social protection system is the key to our country's social stability."[111] Around the same time, a book on employment and social security plainly acknowledged, "Growing out of our concern for social stability, we have made very great government expenditures in social security."[112] The next year a writer from the Planning Commission's research group proclaimed, "Social security and social stability are tightly interlinked."[113] Also in 2001, the minister of labor and social security spoke of using the social security system under construction to "stabilize society" and warned of a "very great risk" if social security benefits were reduced, reasoning that a decrease would virtually invite social turmoil.[114]

---

108. Croll, "Social Welfare Reform," 686–87.

109. SWB FE/2824, January 23, 1997, S1/3, from *Sing Tao Jib Pao* (Singapore).

110. *Shijie ribao* [World Daily] (New York), December 8, 1997, A12.

111. Guojia jiwei hongguan jingji yanjiuyuan ketizu [State Planning Commission, Macroeconomic Research Group], "Jianli shehui baohu tixi shi wo guo shehui wending de guanjian" [Establishing a social protection system is the key to our country's social stability], *NBCY* 511 (May 5, 2000), 8–14.

112. Gong Li, *Kuashiji nanti: jiuye yu shehui baozhang* [A difficult issue straddling the century: Employment and social security] (Kunming: Yunnan renmin chubanshe [Yunnan People's Publishing], 2000), 215.

113. Yang Yiyong, "Wanshan shehui baozhang tixi shi shehui jinbu di xuyao" [Perfecting the social security system is the demand of social progress], *NBCY* 550 (February 9, 2001), 15.

114. Zhang Zuoji, "Guanyu shehui baozhang tixi jianshe di youguan wenti" [Some relevant issues in the construction of the social insurance system], *LBT* 7 (2001), 6, 11.

Near the end of 2001, on the eve of China's accession to the World Trade Organization, when queried as to whether disbursements of a minimum livelihood allowance for the city's poorest might increase after entry, the head of social security operations at the Wuhan city trade union replied, "They definitely will [as indeed they did]…because the government takes this segment of the populace particularly seriously, on account of social stability" [kending hui…yinwei weile shehui wending, zhengfu feichang zhongshi zhe yikuar ren].[115] Thus the preoccupation with outbreaks of unrest was clearly linked with liberal allocations of funds. In 2002, Party boss Jiang Zemin admonished the members of the Party's Politburo that China "must tackle poverty to ensure social stability."[116] And perhaps most bluntly of all, the deputy director of the central government's Northeast Revitalization Office acknowledged in a 2005 interview on new state welfare efforts in that region that "if the Northeast had remained stable, we would not have to take such care of it now."[117] In short, the nagging fears of the authoritarian Chinese political elite had a great deal to do with the regime's prolonged sheltering of the urban laboring class, especially of its upper tier.

As the 1980s wore on, the factories were told to operate on the basis of their own profits and loss, without the security of bailouts by the state. Multitudes of state and urban collective firms, suffering losses, had to renege on their welfare responsibilities to their employees, lay off much of their workforce, or disappear entirely, as already discussed. Enterprises' financial responsibilities for their labor became progressively more unmanageable as the aging of the workforce meant the numbers in need of pensions grew with time and as more and more firms, falling prey to competition from rivals in the now-sanctioned nonstate sector—or from brand-new firms that were foreign-funded (many of which, purely market-driven, provided no welfare benefits at all)—were overcome by losses.[118] As one analyst remarked in the late 1990s, "the cost of maintaining the current level of social programs would bankrupt the state-owned enterprises."[119]

---

115. Interview with local trade union official, Wuhan, October 31, 2001.

116. CND, February 8, 2002, GL02–006, taken from Agence France-Presse, which quoted RMRB.

117. Quoted in Tom Miller, "Up from the Abyss: Reviving the Northeast," China Economic Quarterly Q2 (2005), 23.

118. Croll, "Social Welfare Reform," 692; Lee, Chinese Occupational Welfare, 144; Wong, Marginalization and Social Welfare, 66.

119. Wei Yu, "Financing Unemployment and Pension Insurance," in Dilemmas of Reform in Jiang Zemin's China, ed. Andrew J. Nathan et al. (Boulder, Colo.: Lynne Rienner, 1999), 128. See also Stephen Philion, "Chinese Welfare State Regimes," Journal of Contemporary Asia 28, 4 (1998), 529. Wong, Marginalization and Social Welfare, 66, notes that in 1978 labor insurance and welfare funds for urban workers (covering pensions, health care, hardship subsidies, allowances, and collective welfare amenities) amounted to 7.81 billion yuan per year but skyrocketed quickly once reforms were under way: to 65.3 billion in 1988 and then to 236.1 billion in just another seven years.

Another consequence of the new fiscal regime was that firms owned by urban governments began to provide greatly reduced tax revenue to their local governments as compared with the past. This change stemmed from one of two causes: firms' own penury or because many managers of successful factories refused to turn over the funds, preferring to hoard their holdings and having no incentive to share their proceeds. All this transpired even as the job of financing welfare was increasingly transferred from enterprises to the urban administrations.[120] These developments only compounded city officials' usual proclivity to court and favor successful, money-earning firms and their workers, just as the poorer, money-losing enterprises and their staff needed the wherewithal for sustenance and welfare more than ever.

In the 1990s, with the market steadily extending its reach, China's relatively egalitarian welfare arrangement in the urban areas became inadequate in any event. For one thing, the state-governed arrangement of unit-attached welfare prohibited the geographical mobility required in a market economy. For another, as marketized housing and a multifaceted set of employment options outside the state became available, the *danwei*'s place in urban society began to recede.

After the 15th Party Congress, because of the pronounced upsurge in urban poverty, inequality, and joblessness that its policies fostered, the political elite was soon forced by a rising tide of protests to unveil a brand-new social security system. For with that convention's decision on layoffs, dismissed employees whose benefits had been attached to their jobs suddenly found themselves not just without work but without any social assistance as well.[121]

An attempt to establish a contributory system that could cater to the displaced and that was also fully independent from the enterprises (in the hope of giving the firms a greater chance of surviving in the new marketplace) led to the creation of three programs, all targeted just at the urban areas: one for unemployment insurance, one to provide basic living allowances to workers let go from state-owned firms, and one to supply a minimal livelihood subsidy to those living in dire poverty.[122] These three initiatives were first devised as early as the mid-1980s in the case of unemployment insurance and into the early 1990s for the latter two. But they were barely implemented before the late 1990s, when

---

120. Christine P. W. Wong, "Central-Local Relations in an Era of Fiscal Decline: The Paradox of Fiscal Decentralization in Post-Mao China," *CQ* 128 (1991), 691–715. *LBT*, "Zhongli zai guoyou," 6–7; Li Shigeng and Gao Ping, "Shiye baoxian zhidu cunzai di wenti he duice" [Existing issues and how to deal with them in the unemployment insurance system], *LBT* 6 (2000), 32.

121. Duckett, in "China's Social Security Reforms," agrees.

122. State Council, "White Paper on Employment, Social Security." *Asian Wall Street Journal*, April 29, 2002, 20.

they were finally seriously and widely applied nationwide as job losses spiraled upward.[123]

At the start of 1997, the State Council apportioned the relatively sizable sum of 30 billion yuan to be held as a reserve fund for mergers and bankruptcies of state firms and to help reemploy workers displaced by those regroupings.[124] But this sum was soon found to be grossly insufficient for the task. Shortly after the 1997 Party Congress, in May 1998 the central leadership convoked a major meeting focused on extending livelihood guarantees to and devising reemployment opportunities for state workers whose jobs had disappeared.[125] Premier Zhu Rongji addressed the convention, pledging that the assurance of the basic living needs of laid-off state workers and their reemployment was "a matter of utmost importance," indicating explicitly that state workers were to be the sole recipients of state beneficence.[126] A few weeks later, the State Council passed an urgent decision on these laid-off workers which expressly mandated accelerating the perfection of a social security system.[127]

Thus, China's response was different from that of France, where a long-standing and well-entrenched welfare system was simply supplemented by anticipatory initiatives, and where the best that was done was to cancel proposed cutbacks in benefits for the already privileged in the wake of society-wide street marches and rallies. Likewise, in Mexico, the state-connected workers remained better off than others (but still had to face cuts in welfare), and unions were able only to beat back plans to undo or revise old regulations that had helped them (such as the labor law and the social security system). But the wary Chinese government created three welfare programs entirely de novo. I review these below, highlighting their exclusivity but also noting the state's comparative generosity.

---

123. Christine P. W. Wong, Christopher Heady, and Wing T. Woo, *Fiscal Management and Economic Reform in the People's Republic of China* (Hong Kong: Oxford University Press, 1995), 14, comment, "The draw on unemployment insurance funds has been small to date, because state-owned enterprises are under great pressure to hold on to their surplus workers, receiving tax exemptions and bank loans to do so when necessary."

124. SWB FE/2860, March 6, 1997, S1/1, from XH, March 3, 1997.

125. *Jingji ribao* [Economic Daily], May 18, 1998, 1. The program initiating these measures was entitled the Reemployment Project, discussed below.

126. On February 7, 2002, the official *RMRB* announced an urgent circular put out by the Ministry of Labor and Social Security ordering that local governments set aside at least 15 to 20 percent of their annual budget for unemployment subsidies and retirement pensions for workers from state enterprises. Josephine Ma, "Campaign Aims to Pacify Poor as Anger at Wealth Gap Grows," *SCMP*, February 8, 2002; Barry L. Friedman, "Employment and Social Protection Policies in China: Big Reforms and Limited Outcomes," in *Changes in China's Labor Market: Implications for the Future*, ed. Gregory K. Schoepfle (Washington, D.C.: U.S. Department of Labor, Bureau of International Labor Affairs, 1996), 157.

127. *Guangming ribao* [Bright Daily], June 23, 1998, 1, 4.

Unemployment

As detailed in chapter 4, long after the central government began devolving funds and fiscal responsibilities to local levels of administration in 1980 in the hope of stimulating productivity, and even after the enterprises were told to become market actors responsible for their own profits and losses, party leaders remained remarkably queasy about firing the members of the old urban proletariat.[128] Their tentativeness can be attributed in part to concerns about abandoning socialist proletarian principles that were the Party's birthright; it was also a function of the Party elite's certainty that some degree of social upheaval would follow such a move, given the workers' long-term receipt of state largesse and their related expectations and conceptions of their deserts.

Once workers were finally let go in large numbers, protests became a regular occurrence in many cities and their numbers quickly escalated, as chapter 5 documents. The regime proceeded to divide the affected potential recipients into separate segments, along the lines of the original dual labor market. Those to be categorized as "unemployed" were workers from lesser state firms that had been allowed to dissolve but where the employer had previously contributed to the unemployment insurance fund;[129] a second group, the "laid-off," or *xiagang,* was composed of workers who hailed from the stronger, more profitable enterprises still in existence. That separation of the discharged into the "unemployed" and the "laid-off" amounted, in effect, to the customary practice of preferential treatment for the better-off firms and their employees, those enterprises prosperous enough to continue operating, those producing something the authorities considered essential, or those whose managers were sufficiently in favor with administrators at one level of government or another that they could continue to acquire the state subsidies requisite to their survival.[130] Needless to say, many former laborers, probably numbering in the tens of millions, did not qualify for either one of these labels.

In theory, those in the "laid off" group were to be furloughed only temporarily, though in fact a return to one's original plant was practically speaking impossible. While ostensibly just those in that cohort of the proletariat were said to be still attached in some manner to their original enterprises (it was only they whose firms still remained intact), the fate of the "unemployed," the second-tier group, came to

---

128. White, "Changing Role."

129. This and the next five paragraphs draw from Nelson Chow and Xuebin Xu, *Socialist Welfare in a Market Economy: Social Security Reforms in Guangzhou, China* (Aldershot, U.K.: Ashgate, 2001), 59–62, unless specified otherwise.

130. The following several paragraphs are slight revisions of Dorothy J. Solinger, "Labor in Limbo: Pushed by the Plan Towards the Mirage of the Market," in *Politics of China: Moving Frontiers,* ed. Francoise Mengin and Jean-Louis Rocca (New York: Palgrave, 2002).

be much affected by the situation of their former home plants as well. The lowest level among the workforce was populated by those from firms that had fully failed, whether they collapsed under the weight of their debts or whether, as collectives, they had never been linked to the state in any guise. Those in that last and certainly largest set of laborers were effectively left to their own devices.[131]

The first of the new welfare programs to appear was the one for the "unemployed."[132] A 1986 Regulation on Labor Contracts specified that all new workers were to be hired on limited-term contracts, though to illustrate how awkward the concept must have seemed, as of 1993 a mere 20 percent of state industrial workers had ever signed a fixed-term contract.[133] Along with that ruling came the first Regulations on Unemployment Insurance, designed to assist the new contracted laborers when their terms were up, so long as they met the necessary conditions. In that same year a Regulation on Discharging Employees was announced as well. But none of these decrees had much if any impact at that time.[134]

Eligible workers had to meet restrictive conditions,[135] the most significant of which was that they were to be cared for, in the inability of their firms to do so, by their local government.[136] But it was precisely those firms no longer able to sustain their previous, probably bloated workforces that were the self-same ones unable to afford to contribute to the local UI fund.[137] Further favoring those better placed within the labor market hierarchy, revised regulations in 1993 that aimed to deal with the rising numbers of workers losing their jobs specified explicitly that benefits should go only to former state enterprise workers.[138] Tellingly, the percentage of the workforce covered by UI dropped as the proportion of the urban labor force moving to jobs in the nonstate and foreign-funded sectors, both of which offered no protection to their employees, grew.[139] In one accounting, the share of

---

131. Solinger, "Why We Cannot Count the Unemployed."

132. Gordon White, *Riding the Tiger: The Politics of Economic Reform in Post-Mao China* (Stanford, Calif.: Stanford University Press, 1993), 138–43, 159.

133. Sheehan, *Chinese Workers*, 207.

134. Lim and Sziraczki, "Employment, Social Security," 51–52.

135. The conditions were these: the workers had to be from a bankrupt firm; be a redundant worker in an insolvent firm on the verge of bankruptcy that was undergoing streamlining; be a contract worker not reappointed at the end of the contract term; or have been let go for disciplinary reasons.

136. Clarifying the promise in Article 4 of the bankruptcy law of 1986, which holds that the state will guarantee the basic living needs of workers of bankrupt firms, a State Council circular of 1997 called on local governments to "pay for the arrangement of employees if a bankrupt enterprise cannot afford the arrangement." Thanks to Stephen Green for alerting me to the provision in the law; the circular is quoted in SWB FE/2899 S1/3, April 22, 1997, from XH, April 20, 1997.

137. Yu, "Financing Unemployment," 130.

138. Li Hong, *China Daily*, February 10, 1992, reprinted in *FBIS*, China Daily Report, February 10, 1992, 27, on the 1986 regulations and the need for revision. For the 1993 set, State Council Document 110, see Herald Translation Service, Chinalaw Web, http://www.qis.net/chinalaw/prclaw66.htm.

139. Chow and Xu, *Socialist Welfare*, 60.

employment in non-public-sector firms over the years 1994 to 2000 rose from just 21 percent to a high of 54.9 percent.[140]

Throughout the 1990s, as the numbers of workers without an extant work unit—and the sum total of official bankruptcies—both continued to mount, the UI fund was beset by shortages resulting from the rising percentage of loss-making state firms. To address this quandary, officials attempted in 1999 to expand the funding base for UI by extending coverage to all work units of any ownership type in the cities[141]. But this time again the localities could set the standard for benefit payments in accord with what each estimated could be raised in its area, thereby maintaining the dual labor market in yet one more way.[142] Such measures, in saving the state funds (at both central and local levels), enabled the program to go into effect for at least some workers.

The Reemployment Project for the "Xiagang"

Every one of the three sets of UI regulations (1986, 1993, and 1999) excluded from the benefits of UI the so-called laid off, or *xiagang* (off-post), workers. But they got something better than the "unemployed" did. "Laid-off" workers, who generally came from the better-off state-owned enterprises—those still surviving after the losses that pulled many thousands of others under—were treated as an elite group among those who had lost their jobs. They became eligible temporarily (officially, for three years) for a sum called the "basic living allowance," (*jiben shenghuofei* or *jiben shenghuo baozhang*), which was higher than UI.[143] These sums, a kind of payoff, were part of a program labeled the "Reemployment Project," which was initiated earlier in the decade and widely promoted at the end of the 1990s, precisely when worker protests had become commonplace.[144]

140. Hussain, *Urban Poverty,* 84.

141. State Council Document No. 258, in "Shiye baoxian tiaoli" [Unemployment insurance regulations]: Zhonghua renmin gongheguo guowuyuan ling di 258 hao [PRC State Council Order No. 258], February 3, 1999, *ZGLD* 3, 1999, 44–45.

142. Hussain, *Urban Poverty,* 98.

143. Hu Angang, "Chuangzhaoxing de cuihui: Zhongguo di jiegou biange (1996–2000 nian)" [Creative destruction: China's structural evolution (1996–2000)], unpublished manuscript, 2001, 16–17. In 1999, the average living allowance for laid-off workers was 18.5 percent of that of employed workers, while the UI amounted to only 14.1 percent of employed workers' wages.

144. "Nationwide Employment Project to Be Launched," *FBIS,* January 25, 1994, 69, from XH, January, 24, 1994; Chengzhen qiye xiagang zhigong zaijiuye zhuangkuang diaocha ketizu [Investigation of urban enterprises' laid-off staff and workers' reemployment situation project topic group], "Kunjing yu chulu" [A difficult pass and the way out], from *Shehuixue yanjiu* [Sociology Research] 6/97 (reprinted in *Xinhua wengao,* shehui [New China draft, society] 3/98, 21–28); *1998 nian: zhongguo shehui xingshi fenxi yu yuce* [1998: Analysis and prediction of China's social situation], ed. Ru Xin, Lu Xueyi, and Dan Tianlun (Beijing: Shehui kexue wenxian chubanshe, 1998), 86; SWB FE/3231 (May 20, 1998), G/3, from XH, May 17, 1998.

The project called on each firm that had laid off some or all of its workers to create a "reemployment service center," to which its *xiagang* workers were to be entrusted for a period of up to three years.[145] The center was to train the workers for a new profession and help them locate new positions. It was furthermore charged with contributing to the pension, medical, and social security funds on behalf of each laid-off worker assigned to it. It is obvious that only flourishing firms could have managed to fulfill this list of charges. So the program as a whole ensured, once again, that those who had been employed in the factories most patronized by the polity were, as a class, to be treated best.

Beyond the centers, much of the program's content entailed active labor market policies, perhaps not just coincidentally much like programs instituted in France for the unemployed there, though rather more generous.[146] Its additional charges included computerizing information on local job markets; setting up job introduction offices; forming "reemployment bases" to offer jobs and free training; and building new marketplaces where traders were to receive preferential policies in taxes and fees. By no means were all these obligations met; still, the munificence behind the conception is notable. Once their three-year terms were over, just a select set could become eligible to rely on UI should they not succeed in finding work,[147] for movement into the UI system depended on the financial condition and the priorities—and thus the ability and/or willingness to contribute to the fund—of their former firms.

A Program for the New Indigent

A sudden upsurge in the numbers of the urban poor occurred after the mid-1990s,[148] at the same time that masses of state manufacturing workers began to

---

145. Yang Shucheng, "Zaijiuye yao zou xiang shichanghua" [In reemployment we must go toward marketization] *ZGJY*, March, 1999, 19.

146. Zhao Zhongheng and Wei Zhikui, "Yanglao baoxian zhidu chuangxin yunxingzhong di san da nanti" [Three big difficulties in blazing a trail in running a pension insurance system], *ZGLD* 1 (2000), 12, and SWB FE/3925 (August 22, 2000), from XH, August 20, 2000, G/8, discuss learning from international experience. "Faguo de peixun yu jiuye" [France's training and employment], *ZGJY* 1 (2000), 41–44, and "Fanshiye: Faguo di xilu he cuoshi" [Combating unemployment: France's thinking and measures], *ZGJY* 1 (1998), specifically discuss the French system.

147. Wang Dongjin, "Shehui baozhang zhidu gaige de zhongdian" [Critical points on the reform of the social security system], *Gaige neican* [Reform internal reference] 10 (2001), 5; "2001 nian laodong he shehui baozhang gongzuo yaodian" [The gist of the labor and social security work for the year 2001], *LBT* 2 (2001), 9; Zhang Zuoji, "Guanyu shehui," 9–10; and Yang Shengwen, "Kexi de yibu: Cong Beijing deng bashengshi xiagang zhigong lingqu shiye baoxianjin renshu chaoguo jin zhongxin renshu kan chu zhongxin gongcuo" [A heartening step: Look at the work of exiting the center from Beijing and eight provinces and cities' numbers of laid-off staff and workers getting unemployment insurance money has surpassed the numbers entering the center], *LBT* 9 (2001), 27–31.

148. In 1995, 41 percent of urban households saw an income decline. Wong, *Marginalization and Social Welfare*, 124.

be pruned from their posts; indeed, there is a clear correlation between these two phenomena.[149] One source estimated that the newly urban indigent numbered somewhere between 15 and 30 million as of the year 2002, depending on how the count was conducted.[150] Another study arrived at much more startling figures: that nationwide 20 to 30 million urban-registered workers had fallen into poverty in the late 1990s, and that, with their family members, they added up to about 40 to 50 million people altogether, or almost 13 percent of the urban population.[151]

As the numbers of people subsisting in straitened circumstances rose with the progression of marketization, the leadership determined that a broad-based, inclusive system had to be devised for them. The idea behind the plan was twofold: to sever the bond between firms and their most indigent staff and ex-staff, since often the very most poverty-stricken people were attached to enterprises doing too poorly to help them; and to extend the scope of the population eligible for sustenance relief. In 1994, Shanghai pioneered the new system, named the "minimum livelihood guarantee" [*zuidi shenghuo baozhang*, colloquially, the *dibao*], as an experiment.[152] By September 1997, after spreading nationwide, it was formalized, with orders that localities must lodge this item in their budgets to be managed as a special account.[153] In September two years later, the State Council's "Regulations for Safeguarding Urban Residents' Subsistence Guarantees" transformed the program into law.[154]

Urban bureaucracies were again to determine their own local standard of relief, in accord with the amount of money they claimed was needed to maintain a mini-

149. Sarah Cook, "Politics, Policy Processes and the Poor: Responding to Poverty in China's Cities," report on a research project, "The Political and Social Dynamics of Poverty in China," undertaken as part of the DFID funded IDS Poverty Research Programme, December 2000, 5. Song Xiaowu, *Zhongguo shehui baozhang zhidu gaige* [The reform of China's social security system] (Beijing: Qinghua daxue chubanshe, 2001), 137–38.

150. Li Peilin, "Dangqian zhongguo shehui fazhan de rogan wenti he xin qushi" [Current issues and new trends in social development], in *Shehui lanpishu: 2003 nian; Zhongguo shehui xingshi fenxi yu yuce* [Social blue book: 2003 analysis and predictions of China's social situation], ed. Ru Xin, Lu Xueyi, and Li Peilin (Beijing: shehui kexue wenxian chubanshe [Social Science Documents Co.], 2003), 23. Wong, *Marginalization and Social Welfare*, 124, also estimates the total people living in poverty at around 30 million as of 1997.

151. Zhonggong zhongyang zuzhibu ketizu [Chinese central organization department research group], *2000–2001 Zhongguo diaocha baogao—xin xingshixia renmin neibu maodun yanjiu* [2000–2001 Chinese investigation report—research on internal contradictions within the people under the new situation], (Beijing: Zhongyang bianyi chubanshe [Central Compilation and Translation Press], 2001), 170–71. Here the urban population of about 390 million is calculated without including peasant migrants unless they had lived there for at least one year.

152. Wong, *Marginalization and Social Welfare*, 124.

153. Song Xiaowu, "Zhongguo shehui," 149–50.

154. Tang Jun, "The New Situation of Poverty and Antipoverty," in *2002 nian: Zhongguo shehui xingshi yu yuce (shehui lanpishu):* [Year 2002: Analysis and Forecast of China's Social Situation (Blue Book on Chinese Society)], ed. Ru Xin, Lu Xueyi, Li Peilin et al., January 1, 2002. [FBIS Translated Text].

mum livelihood in their cities.[155] From the outset, the boundaries encompassing those to be covered kept duality at work: recipients had to be holders of permanent household registration in the city (that is, born there), thereby barring migrant rural immigrants—people whose households were registered in their home villages—from its benefits.[156] But unlike the other two new welfare measures, the *dibao* was meant to ignore the status of one's work unit, and instead to service anyone at all whose income did not reach a locally-set standard.[157]

Although the localities were in theory to be the agents underwriting the program, many cities could not afford to finance it on their own. That the central government took on a growing share of the cost was a response to this problem; it was also, plainly, an emblem of the state's firm commitment to tamp down expressions of discontent and prevent further unrest.[158] No doubt alarmed at the growing extent of urban poverty as well as the increase in disturbances, top officials had the national treasury raise its allotments for social security as many as five times between 1998 and 2002; in 2002 funds for the *dibao* rose from 0.2 percent of government expenditures to almost 0.5 percent.[159] Meanwhile, across China, many localities' inability to finance the program was such that by the year 2002, cities were making only slightly more than half the contributions to this program, originally envisioned as one to be provisioned locally.[160]

---

155. Song Xiaowu, "Zhongguo shehui," 148; "Guowuyuan bangongting fabu tongzhi: Jiaqiang chengshi jumin zuidi shenghuo baozhang gongzuo" [The State Council Office announces a circular: Strengthen urban residents' minimum livelihood guarantee work], *Renmin ribao haiwaiban* [People's Daily Overseas Edition], November 19, 2001 (from XH, November 17, 2001), states that localities were to manage every dimension of the system, including raising the necessary funds.

156. SWB, FE/3016, September 5, 1997, G/6, from XH, September 3, 1997. From 1960 until the early 1980s, the government prohibited people from the countryside from entering the cities and barred any who might come from obtaining benefits accorded urban residents. Dorothy J. Solinger, *Contesting Citizenship in Urban China* (Berkeley: University of California Press, 1999).

157. Cook, "Politics," and Croll, "Social Welfare Reform."

158. Hussain, *Urban Poverty*, 70. See also "Circular from the State Council General Office on Further Enhancing Work on the Minimum Livelihood Guarantee for Urban Residents" (from XH, November 17, 2001), in FBIS-CHI-2001–1117.

159. Duckett, "China's Social Security," 13, based on a statement made by Hu Angang which was cited in *SCMP*, August 10, 2002. For announcements of some of these increases, see Information Office of the State Council of the People's Republic of China, "Labor and Social Security in China," pamphlet, Beijing, April 2002; SWB FE/4092, March 11, 2001, G/5, from XH, March 10, 2001. On the increase in the *dibao* funds, see Dorothy J. Solinger, "*Dibaohu* in Distress: The Meager Minimum Livelihood Guarantee System in Wuhan," in *China's Social Welfare Mix*, ed. Jane Duckett and Beatriz Carrillo, table 1, forthcoming.

160. In that year the total fund for the program had reached 10.53 billion yuan, nearly double the amount spent in 1991. Of this, 4.6 billion came from the central treasury and 5.93 billion from the local governments (just over 56 percent) (Xinhuanet, 7/19/2002, Beijing). Thanks to Jane Duckett for this citation.

Other Budgetary Allocations

Besides these three major initiatives, there were many other indications, beginning in the late 1990s, of the leadership's determination to underwrite welfare payments, even if not for everyone. Among them were its move to continue subsidizing loss-making state firms via forcing state banks to distribute credit to them (so-called policy loans);[161] its inauguration of a National Social Security Fund in 2000, which was to offer support to indebted provinces;[162] periodic increases in the *dibao* allowances and in payouts to workers whose positions had been cancelled;[163] its 2001 choice to aid some three million persons whose three-year stint in "reemployment centers" had come to an end, including extending a benefit card and offers of tax and fee exemptions were they to set up their own businesses;[164] and a pledge to bestow low-income allowances on employees in troubled state firms that suffered continuous losses or had ceased production. In the last of these programs, targeted people were categorized as being "currently out of the reach of government subsidies."[165]

In this same vein, in mid-2001 the minister of labor and social security promised ongoing sustenance to areas where a gap in finances persisted.[166] At the same time, as the nation confronted its soon-to-be-realized accession to the World Trade Organization, then-head of the State Development and Planning Commission Zeng Peiyan announced that "solving the problem of unemployment" had been "moved toward the top of the agenda," no doubt in expectation of the loss of additional jobs portended by this move.[167] Simultaneously, references to sympathy for the "weak masses" [*ruoshi qunti*] in society began to pepper the speeches of the top leaders,[168] a sentiment espoused in the very first Politburo Standing Committee gathering following the ascension to power of a new set of leaders in December

---

161. Dennis Tao Yang and Cai Fang, "The Political Economy of China's Rural-Urban Divide," in *How Far Across the River? Chinese Policy Reform at the Millennium*, ed. Nicholas C. Hope, Dennis Tao Yang, and Mu Yang Li (Stanford, Calif.: Stanford University Press, 2003), 410; Chow and Xu, *Socialist Welfare*, 26.

162. Mark W. Frazier, "China's Pension Reform and Its Discontents," *CJ* 51 (January 2004), 103.

163. For example, in summer 1999, on the eve of the fiftieth anniversary of the establishment of the People's Republic, this occurred, very likely to stave off public demonstrations by the disadvantaged. Wu Yan, "Laid-Off Workers to Get Extra Pay," *China Daily*, August 31, 1999.

164. *CND*, June 8, 2001, GL01–045.

165. "For Workers, Parting Is Painful," *China Daily*, February 2, 2004.

166. Zhang Zuoji, "Guanyu shehui."

167. *CND*, March 8, 2002, GL02–010, from *SCMP*, March 7, 2002.

168. At the annual session of the National People's Congress held in March 2002, Premier Zhu Rongji spoke on their behalf (as cited in Wang Shaoguang, "Shunying minxin de bianhua: Cong caizheng zijin liuxiang zongguo zhengfu jinqi de zhengce tiaozheng" [A change that complies with popular sentiments: A recent policy readjustment in the flow of financial funds toward the Chinese government], paper presented to the Center for Strategic and International Studies, Washington, D.C., unpublished manuscript, January 16, 2004, 6).

2002.[169] And in 2004, an official document published on the country's employment situation urged the stimulation of domestic demand and the maintenance of the rapid and healthy development of the national economy, expressly in order to boost employment.[170]

Another sign of the state's dedication to calm down displaced workers was its constant infusion of funds for them. According to a State Council "White Paper" on Employment and Social Security from spring 2002, in 2001 the central treasury allocated 98.2 billion yuan for social security payments, a figure that amounted to 5.18 times that expended just three years before. Over the years 1998 through 2001, it went on to note, the central treasury injected a total of 86.1 billion yuan in subsidies for pension insurance.[171] Total subsidies to laid-off and unemployed workers reached 50 billion yuan in 2001 and exceeded that figure in 2002.[172] In 2002, the head of the People's Bank of China announced that another 86 billion yuan would be earmarked for social security payments for that year alone, an increase of 28 percent over 2001, to "assist in maintaining social stability" in the wake of entry to the World Trade Organization;[173] soon thereafter, the bank issued an urgent notice to managers and local governments to "step up efforts to reemploy laid-off workers and ensure [the delivery of] pensions and allowances to safeguard social stability."[174]

A bit later, in early 2004, Premier Wen Jiabao announced that the central government had contributed 4.7 billion yuan of subsidies the previous year just for the purpose of job creation, while spending 70 billion for laid-off workers' and poor people's allowances, 20 percent more than in the previous year. Of that amount, the monies for the urban indigent doubled in one year, from 4.6 billion in 2002 to

---

169. "Zhonggong zhongyang zhengzhiju changwu weiyuanhui zhaokai huiyi yanjiu jinyibu jiejue hao kunnan chunjong shengchan shenghuo wenti de gongzuo" [Chinese Communist Party Central Committee Politburo Standing Committee convenes a meeting to research work on the progressive solution to the production and livelihood problems of those in difficulty], chinesenewsnet.com, December 12, 2002.

170. "China's Employment Situation and Policies," issued by the Information Office of the State Council, April 26, 2004. http://english.peopledaily.com.cn/200404/26/eng20040426_141553.s.

171. State Council, "White Paper," 21, 24. Jane Duckett, "Research Report: State, Collectivism and Worker Privilege: A Study of Urban Health Insurance Reform," CQ, 177 (March 2004), 156, claims that between 1998 and 2001 the central government increased its spending on social security (including pensions, laid-off worker allowances, and urban poverty relief) more than fivefold (data are from RMRB, March 7, 2002).

172. Susan H. Whiting, "Central-Local Fiscal Relations in China," China Policy Series No. 22 (New York: National Committee on United States-China Relations, April 2007), 14.

173. Feng Lei, Bao Shenghua, and Chen Mengyang, "Liaoning shebao gaige chongguan" [Liaoning's social security reform's important period], Liaowang [Outlook], 11 (2002), 26.

174. CND, March 7, 2002, and Reuters, April 19, 2002, respectively.

9.2 billion in 2003, and continued to rise thereafter.[175] And in the five-year period from 1998 to 2003, the central budget designated a grand total of 73.1 billion yuan for the basic subsistence needs and reemployment of workers furloughed from state-owned firms.[176] Though these figures are difficult to interpret, as it is not clear to what extent the categories named overlap or are additive, the point is the steady escalation in central government disbursements as time went on.

In any event, Wang Shaoguang calculated that social welfare and social security as a percentage of GDP rose from under 2 percent in 1980 to about 8.3 percent in 2005.[177] Mark Frazier's findings more or less corroborate Wang's. If the funds allocated to pensions and health insurance from provincial social insurance funds are included in the 2004 national social expenditures-to-GDP ratio, he calculated, the national percentage climbed to 6.8 percent over the years 2000 to 2004.[178] At the provincial level, social expenditures amounted to an average of 8.7 percent of GDP in those years,[179] far from France's 28-or-so percent, but well above Mexico's 5 percent (see Table 6.1). And in comparative terms, the leap is notable.

Another, more specific indication of the central government's exertions to keep the peace was its special attention to Liaoning province in the rustbelt Northeast. Not coincidentally the locale where the most retrenchments in the nation and, accordingly, the most protests, had occurred, this place became the venue for the central government's trial operation of a full-fledged social security system. Because of the regime's aim of contriving a successful model for this reform, in

---

175. "Premier Wen delivers government work report," http://english.peopledaily.com.cn/20040305/eng20040305_136592.s. Full text, last updated at BJ time, Tuesday, March 16, 2004. Delivered at the Second Session of the 10th National People's Congress, March 5, 2004. Tang Jun, "Zhongguo chengshi jumin zuidi shenghuo baozhang zhidu de 'tiaoyueshi' fazhan" [The 'leap forward style' of development of Chinese urban residents' minimum livelihood guarantee], in *Shehui lanpishu: 2003 nian: zhongguo shehui xingshi fenxi yu yuce* [Social blue book: 2003 analysis and predictions of China's social situation], ed. Ru Xin, Lu Xueyi, and Li Peilin (Beijing: shehui kexue wenxian chubanshe [Social Science Documents Co.], 2003), 243–45.

176. "China's Employment Situation and Policies," issued by the Information Office of the State Council, April 26, 2004. Christine Wong, "Can China Change Development Paradigm for the 21st Century? Fiscal Policy Options for Hu Jintao and Wen Jiabao after Two Decades of Muddling Through" (Berlin, unpublished manuscript, January 2005), 17, calculates that RMB177.7 billion was transferred from the central government to subsidize local governments' payouts of state enterprise workers' living stipends, unemployment allowances, and the minimum living support. Another RMB51.2 billion was budgeted for subsidies to local social security schemes.

177. Wang, "Great Transformation."

178. Mark W. Frazier, "Welfare State Building China in Comparative Perspective," presented on the panel "Asian Welfare States," at the annual meeting of the American Political Science Association, August 31–September 3, 2006, Philadelphia. Wong, "Can China Change?" 7, notes that the social expenditures that in the past were the responsibility of the state-owned firms were by the late 1990s transferred to local governments. Retrenchments in this sector meant that safety net costs jumped quickly, for unemployment and layoff allowances and for pension payouts.

179. Frazier, "Welfare State."

the program's first year the central government contributed a full 80 percent of the necessary funds, thereby showering the province with 12 percent of total central governmental social security subsidies, despite Liaoning's housing just 3 percent of the nation's urban labor force.[180]

Yet one more initiative was Beijing's relentless drive to create jobs and its promotion of training programs on both local and national scales. Especially in the midst of the Asian financial crisis and the simultaneous push for labor cutbacks in 1997 98, huge investments were made in infrastructural construction, in large part to create jobs.[181] And in early 1998, almost immediately on the close of the fateful 1997 Party Congress, Minister of Labor Li Boyong made public a plan to organize vocational training over the following three years—through technical schools, labor departments, and employment centers—for as many as ten million of the workers pushed aside.[182] Allegedly, over the years from 1998 to 2000, more than 13 million laid-off and unemployed persons nationally participated in state-sponsored retraining courses.[183]

In sum, China's uneasy government undertook an ongoing and multipronged series of attempts to keep its retrenched and restive proletariat at bay. The persistent duality of the labor market in the cities must have kept the outlays more manageable than they would otherwise have been.

Conclusion

In China, Mexico, and France, in the wake of sudden spurts of unemployment and welfare retrenchment, leaders were similarly unsettled by visions and/or the reality of resentful and righteous laborers confronting their regimes. But the varying scale of protest in these places—a function, I have argued, of disparate terms of attachment, that is, the nature of the ties unions had with their workforces and their states—presented the politicians in the three places with differential degrees

---

180. Jackson and Howe, "Graying of the Middle Kingdom," 22. "New Social Security System Draws up Its Curtain in Liaoning Province," *Nanfang zhoumo* [Southern Weekend], July 26, 2001. Interview, Beijing, August 29, 2004, with Tang Jun, vice director of the Social Policy Research Center of the Institute of Sociology, Chinese Academy of Social Science.

181. William H. Overholt, "China in the Balance," Nomura Strategy Paper, Hong Kong, May 12, 1999. Francesco Sisci, "Another China," unpublished manuscript, 2001, states that in 1998 and 1999 the state invested 700 billion yuan, the equivalent of approximately 10 percent of GDP in 1999, in infrastructural construction. Hu, "China's Present Economic Situation," claims that infrastructural investment over the years 1998 to 2001 added up to 3.7586 trillion yuan.

182. SWB FE/3147, February 10, 1998, S1/4, from Zhongguo tongxunshe [Chinese News Agency], February 6, 1998, and SWB FE/3162, February 27, 1998, G/5, from XH, February 20, 1998.

183. State Council, "White Paper on Employment," 10.

of disorder. This disparity goes a long way toward explaining the differing welfare responses of the three governments, I argue.

In China, once the program of marketization allowed work units to relinquish their customary welfare responsibilities, the lack of any prior nationwide welfare network, when combined with widespread and frequent worker protests, made the construction of a brand-new system a much more urgent affair than it was in France. Of course, France was already equipped with an ample welfare system. But I emphasize a different variable: that French postcrisis protests were less numerous and—because of the labor movement's fractured organization and the near decimation of the unions with the liberalization of the economy—harder to pull off. These differences contributed significantly to the disparity in levels of funding and development of new initiatives between France and China. Furthermore, the French political elite had long had its share of workers in the streets and was therefore primed to put forward preemptive programs of just a supplemental nature.

But in Mexico, as in China, there had never been any unemployment insurance. And yet, in the former country, very little in the way of either new money or new measures was proffered to address the massive unemployment and welfare cutbacks that came with market openness. There the power of the union bosses to keep protest to a minimum apparently convinced the leadership that it could afford to go forward with its policies of liberalization, tending only to spots where votes had been lost. Those in command of the polity were also careful to keep union bosses on board, so long as they fell in line with the leaderships' policies.

All three states presided over a segmented labor force in which the numbers consigned to the lower portions rose steadily as the governments made deeper and deeper moves into the global market over time. The steady state-sponsored catering just (or mainly) to the shrinking upper tiers helped to keep the costs to the regimes comparatively low in all three cases as against what they could have been were entire workforces assisted. Given the similarities in these regimes' stances toward the more privileged portions of their proletariats—along with their trepidation over workers' turning out on the streets—and the analogies in the plights suffered by those thrown out of work in the 1980s and 1990s in all three countries, the differential welfare outcomes in the three cases for those dispossessed of their jobs needed to be explained.

The story here is that these outcomes had less to do with the type of regime under which the former workers lived or with the political leanings of the parties in power at the time. Instead, because of the wariness of each state in the face of labor opposition and unrest, where the expression of this discontent was most pronounced (a function of the abdication of any meaningful or substantive advocacy for the workers—and of the absence of overt repression—on the part of the unions), so too was the official response.

7

CONCLUSION

With globalization both besetting and blessing the planet, the issue of the respective roles of the state, the proletariat, and the new forces driving the world economy has been a critical one for scholarship for several decades to date. Taking it as a given that workers are losers, which one of the other two actors comes out on top, many observers have queried? What is the status of the state at the start of the new century? Does labor have any leverage at all in the interplay? And which is it—domestic or international politics and economics—that sets the agenda? This book addresses these large concerns.

Using entry into supranational economic organizations as a proxy for the forces of the global market, I grappled with these problems. My method was to examine similarities and differences in the interrelationships among these three types of players in three seemingly quite disparate countries, China, France, and Mexico, as their elites opted to enter the global economy in force after many decades of eschewing it, to greater or lesser degrees. In the course of the research, I sought propositions to address what happened in these places with respect to this drama.

I set my study at a time when politicians around the world urgently maneuvered in response to external events. In my story the leaderships in ostensibly unlike domains managed to follow the same sequences of policy choice and action toward their macroeconomies and their place in the world economy. The three countries I chose represented different, broad categories, each emblematic of a distinctive economic developmental model and regime type. Clearly, East Asia's China, Western Europe's France, and Latin America's Mexico appear at a glance to vary in a multitude of ways. As of the early 1980s, when the crucial shifts in them all took place, we find one a democratic, one a semi-authoritarian, and one a post-totalitarian state; one each practicing a capitalist, a mixed, and a socialist economy; and one each a multi-party, a one-party-dominant, and a one-party system.

Despite these contrasts, the three places all traveled pathways that were remarkably alike both before and after the year 1983, by which time all three of them had decisively shifted course. By that point, all were in the midst of turning from the inward-oriented, worker-friendly, supernationalistic states they had been as of 1979 (and for some decades before) to the outward-directed, worker-rejecting, and internationalist entities they had irrevocably become by 2000. I showed how and why this came to be the case. Most simply, they all suffered from capital scarcity by the early years of the 1980s, as their former, generically analogous tracks had led each one of them into collision with the new workings of the economy outside.

In their search for foreign funds to make up their shortfalls, a changed political elite in each of them—one disposed to dive into the waters of the world's exchange—opted to enter extranational economic organizations. Following that decision, these leaders found their subsequent policy choices dictated either by the desire to belong to (or by the demands of the other members in) these organizations. One critical, and common, corollary of that large choice was to jettison the labor allies who had long bolstered their regimes. For this first portion of the story I emphasized the similarity of both their old pathways and the clash between those paths and changed global forces; I also showed how the regimens and strictures of the organizations they joined constituted the main reason behind this abandonment. Thus once these countries' congruous, accustomed developmental trajectories all ran up against new international economic modalities, it was the supranational economic organizations that these states' officials entered and, in particular, the stylized *rules* of these bodies, that drew what were apparently divergent countries onto a common road.

As is generally the case in political research, I took up a puzzle. What was it that made the ensuing dynamics among relevant domestic players in each polity so disparate, one from the next? Why were the results—in labor activism and in state-dispensed welfare—so dissimilar among them? For what transpired was that civil unrest burst out with a vengeance and rose exponentially only in post-totalitarian China, where, in return, the government rather quickly came up with a great deal of cash and several brand-new welfare programs. Meanwhile, occasional outbreaks of discontent called forth only tinkering at the governmental level in democratic France; and near silence from workers summoned up next to nothing from the authorities in semi-authoritarian Mexico. What shaped these results?

I found that none of the explanations to which the majority of analysts have appealed in the past provided assistance. Usually scholars have pointed to one or more single domestic institutions to uncover the operative mechanisms. But in my cases the best interpretation called instead for questioning not the workings of solitary variables but the nature of the interactions among several crucial agents.

For neither regime type nor the color of the ruling parties at the time of critical decisions, nor the level of economic development, nor explicit legalistic modes of accountability, nor political party systems—all factors at the forefront of others' analyses—were able to make sense of the outcomes in these systems characterized by a strong but protective state and weak unions.

Two other potential determinants that I eliminated as causal for comparative purposes were the extent of the crisis and the vitality of the labor movement in a given country. A crisis of a kind common to many states as of the 1980s occurred in each of them—whether sparked by debt, by terms of trade, or by a political decision to denounce anachronisms bequeathed by a once productive planned economy. And yet it was not the degree of crisis that determined the outcomes. For though Mexico's debacle was the most disastrous, its leadership was least inclined among the three to satisfy and thereby buy the cooperation of its workforce. China had the least pressing economic crisis and yet responded most vigorously to labor.

Nor was it the robustness of the labor movement that stirred up the politicians, especially since in none of these cases was labor on its own particularly potent. If anything, Mexico's most dominant union had the best access to the corridors of power and the most input into policy of the three countries' labor associations. But in Mexico, workers clearly fared the worst among these states' proletariats. I was therefore compelled to seek out another sort of explication.

My most fundamental finding is that under the sway of the radical restructuring that the dictates of globalization have come to demand, the manner in which labor unions were connected to the state and to the workers who were their members—a matter of a mission tied to old, revolutionary historical traditions—had repercussions, both for the rise of protest among the workers and for the style of welfare response that emerged from the state. Accordingly, it came to be that where unions were feeble, which was the case most of all in China—because of their total subservience to the Communist Party—workers became freest to fight for their needs as the foreign incursions and the privatization that globalization introduced set in. Both of these new forces operated to vitiate the union even more than the Party had already done long before.

The nearly total ineffectuality of Chinese unions by the 1990s meant that labor in that country was not bossed or repressed as in Mexico; neither were workers there fed up with bickering, competitive labor leagues once able (but no longer) to command at least a respectable portion of the working class, as in France, for only one Chinese union existed. Thus, to be truly comparative, the analyst must take the content of the term "union" and, correlatively, its tasks as things to be interrogated and not assumed. This is a novel finding.

In short, it was the nature of the job that the states permitted—or coerced—their unions to perform that liberated the workers (in China), left them relatively passive (in France), or clamped down on them (in Mexico), once the elimination of formerly protective regulations meant removing workers from their positions and once the restrictiveness imposed by austerity rewrote the terms of old welfare contracts. I conclude that while global forces were an independent variable in reshaping state macrostrategies, both at home and abroad, in accounting for what happened to workers directly I view them as having been refracted: In that interaction, the power of global forces was bent by or subjected not to workers themselves, and not precisely to unions either, but instead to what I call unions' terms of attachment—their ties to their states and to their worker charges.

At first blush, these findings might suggest that states like these, whose prior developmental modes entailed expensive protective measures that ultimately produced clashes with the post-1970s global economy—and which were then obliged to relinquish old alliances—emerged from these episodes battered and weakened. Blows came first from their submission to prescriptions decreed by supranational agents. And then such states had to yield at times, when labor had the chance to challenge them, to workers on the streets. Yet there is more to the tale than this simple ending, more to it than a crushing conquest over states and workers by the global economy, and also more than a new empowerment for workforces on their own over their states.

Looking closely, we see that the full picture of what has become of these states and their workers is not so clear-cut. Instead, the fact is that the governments in all three countries remained capable of and disposed to stand up to and against the SEOs they had joined, perhaps at least partly to placate their proletariats or, at a minimum, the privileged parts thereof. For example, China's leaders openly admitted to a connection between their reluctance to alter the relative worth of their currency—spurning much international urging to devalue it—on one hand, and the nagging problem of providing sufficient jobs for its populace, on the other. A vice minister of labor and social security remarked in mid-2006, "It is hard to create new jobs in large numbers because of surplus production capacity, more trade frictions, and [demands for] reevaluation of the *yuan*."[1] Thus, despite insistent entreaties and ongoing signs of frustration from their trade partners in the West, China effectively ignored external pressure to devalue into the middle of the first decade of the twenty-first century.

More to the point, China has been charged with a litany of misbehaviors in its trade practices, all pertinent to its initial commitments on entry into the WTO. Among these were its tardiness in permitting foreign companies to distribute their products through Chinese wholesale and retail channels as it had agreed to do by the end of 2004; its maintenance of secrecy in its regulatory regime; and its failure to abide by internationally accepted product standards, instead setting up rigid

---

1. Quoted in "60 pc of graduates to be jobless," *SCMP,* May 8, 2006.

ones of its own.[2] All these actions left open space and opportunity for domestic firms and their workers. In succeeding years, the list of disputes only lengthened.[3]

Arguably, some of China's questionable or flagrantly inadequate observance of its World Trade Organization membership requirements—such as its importing delays and the seemingly arbitrary phytosanitary barriers it erected against imported soybeans, or its continuing supportive measures for domestic automobile production—amounted to industrial policies geared to placate domestic farmers and workers in unstable provinces that specialize in these commodities, all in the interest of preventing turmoil. Indeed, the 2004 open door to foreign soybeans after months of roadblocks that had inconvenienced and outraged external dealers came only in the wake of central governmental welfare fund transfusions into the demonstrations-prone Northeast, where soybeans are a local specialty.[4]

Officials must have reasoned that further unrest in that region's cities could be forestalled were measures taken to undermine the import of a major product of the Northeast, for fewer soybeans entering the country would mean lower numbers of hard-up farmers poised to march into nearby urban areas in search of work. In general, it is quite likely that these and other practices were expressly intended to insulate certain sectors or regions from further job-threatening competition from abroad, even if such practices contravened pledges China made to secure entry into the WTO in 2001.

Mexico has been faithful to the agreements it made on joining NAFTA, not raising its tariffs beyond the limits negotiated with its treaty partners, the United States and Canada.[5] But in 2001, as trade with its principal trade associate, the United

---

2. "China Shirking WTO Obligations—US Manufacturers," Reuters, September 6, 2005. Margaret M. Pearson, "The Business of Governing Business in China: Institutions and Norms of the Emerging Regulatory State," *WP* 57 (January): 313–14, provides a theoretical explanation of China's regulatory behavior in the early 2000s that includes reference to its norm favoring "the achievement of employment, universal services and social security goals."

3. For instance, in March 2007 the U.S. Department of Commerce decided to apply U.S. antisubsidy law to imports of coated paper from China, after already charging in early February that China was offering improper subsidies in steel, paper, semi-conductors, and other sectors to make its companies more competitive in world markets. Congressional leaders and manufacturers in the United States attributed the U.S. trade deficit with China to China's offering cheap loans, tax rebates, and other governmental help. See "China Protests at US Tariffs on Paper Imports," XH, April 2, 2007; Evelyn Iritani, "U.S. to Slap Duties on China Paper," *LAT,* March 31, 2007; and Andrew Yeh, "China Demands US Rethink on Duties," *Financial Times,* April 1, 2007.

4. On soybeans, see Daniel Goldstein, "U.S. Presses Soy Case as China Retains Ban," Bloomberg News, August 26, 2003; Peter Wonacott and Phelim Kyne, "In Shift, U.S. Investors Intensify Criticism of China Trade Policies," *WSJ,* October 6, 2003; and Peter S. Goodman, "China Trade Policy's Ripple Effect: Limit on Soybean Imports Is Felt Widely around the Country," *Washington Post,* November 11, 2003; on autos, see Myron A. Brilliant and Jeremie Waterman, "China's WTO Implementation: A Three-Year Assessment," (U.S. Chamber of Commerce, September 2004), 20, 21.

5. Communication from Carol Wise, an expert on the country's foreign trade, August 12, 2005.

States,[6] slumped with falling U.S. demand in a time of recession, Mexico's policy-makers increased its tariffs outside of NAFTA, hiking the average applied rate by about three percentage points, to 16.5 percent. Tariff protection was extended especially to agricultural products, since farming was the sector of the economy most vulnerable to U.S. imports and thus the one most prone to job loss; the Mexican government also continued to require import permits for products whose entry into the country would dangerously expose domestic industry.[7]

Of the three, the case of France is the most conspicuous instance of resistance to the rules of the SEO it joined. In the words of Ben Clift, French policy elites "successfully played a long-run game, signing up to the establishment of tough rules to build credibility, then using the policy space so created to pursue policies that might otherwise be unsustainable."[8] In particular, French governments going back to at least the mid-1990s insisted on bringing political considerations such as employment and growth into the discussions over the 1997 Stability and Growth Pact (SGP),[9] eventually managing to revise that protocol to allow more room for the role of national-level policy.[10]

Even under the centrist-right administration of Premier Jean-Pierre Raffarin in 2002, a determinedly expansionary fiscal policy violated the aims of the European Union's rules, as promulgated in the 1992 Maastricht Treaty and reiterated in the SGP, against sustaining a deficit over 3 percent of gross domestic product. This recalcitrance even prompted the European Commission to initiate excessive deficit proceedings against the country (and, at the same time, against Germany).[11]

The French strategy—of agreeing to terms that were necessary for the purpose of securing admission to the EU but then behaving in accord with the leadership's own perception of its national needs—appears to be one that fits the Chinese actions as well. As one analyst wrote, borrowing from a September 2005 report prepared by the U.S.-China Business Council, "backtracking may indicate that Chinese officials believe they have made enough significant progress on WTO

---

6. In 2000, the United States supplied 73 percent of Mexico's imports and absorbed a full 89 percent of its exports (WTO Trade Review, by the Trade Policy Review Body of the WTO, April 16, 2002).

7. Ibid. China also increased state assistance to farmers substantially in the years after joining the WTO. Han Donglin, "Why Has China's Agriculture Survived WTO Accession?" *AS* 45, 6 (November–December 2005), 931–48.

8. Ben Clift, "The New Political Economy of Dirigisme: French Macroeconomic Policy, Unrepentant Sinning and the Stability and Growth Pact," *British Journal of Politics and International Relations* 8 (2006), 1–22.

9. Other partners, especially Germany, emphasized tight monetary and fiscal discipline and overall austerity (see Clift, "New Political Economy," 6, 7). Lintner, "European Monetary Union," 329, also discusses the principle of fiscal rectitude that was involved in composing this pact.

10. Clift, "New Political Economy," 11.

11. Ibid., 10, 12.

compliance that they can now yield to domestic pressures to protect vulnerable industries."[12]

Thus these states have not fully caved in either to their SEOs or to their workers. Even states such as the three examined here—regimes whose capital shortages forced them into seemingly undoing old alliances with their workers—have not entirely surrendered to the SEOs they joined. It would appear that these governments, while reducing their commitments to their proletariats and renouncing the priority they had in the past assigned to workers' issues, in joining SEOs did not at the same time fully relinquish their sovereignty over domestic economic and social policy. It seems that they chose to retain that power in the interest of continuing to attempt to shield their laborers and, thereby, to maintain domestic calm.

In the three countries covered in this book, at the start of the story the state was preeminent, prepared to rebuff external offers; indeed, it was the state that constituted the hinge on which the other parts of the triad of players in each country were balanced. Because of these states' managers' choice after 1980 in favor of the global market and the SEOs that manipulate that market, it appeared that they might have ceded not only their partnerships (if, at times, only putative ones) with the working class; they seemed in addition to have—perhaps unwittingly—abnegated their own powers to adjudicate the shape and workings of their own economies.

A quarter century on, however, this has not in fact proved to be the medium-term outcome. Whether because of long-standing loyalties to at least some of the old proletariat, fears of upheaval, a continuing clout of a portion of the working class, the specific political uses to which states put unions, or loopholes in the procedures of the SEOs—or even, in the case of France, a partial surrender on the part of the SEO it joined, the EU[13]—the state still sits in the saddle in these three nations, even if labor as a force has been irreparably weakened. But paradoxically, where unions became useless, some of the workers found ways to gain the attention of their rulers.

---

12. Murray Hiebert, "China Gets a Passing Grade from Foreign Firms," *WSJ*, November 28, 2005, A11.

13. In March 2005, the EU member states agreed to reform the body's rules, meeting German and French demands that euro nations get more flexibility to continue spending without penalty even if it meant that their budget deficits temporarily surpassed the mandatory limit of 3 percent of GDP. See "Europe Agrees to Ease Rules on Budgets," *NYT*, March 21, 2005.

Bibliography

Adams, William James. 1995. "France and Global Competition." In *Remaking the Hexagon: The New France in the New Europe*, edited by Gregory Flynn. Boulder, Colo.: Westview Press.

Amsden, Alice. 1989. *Asia's Next Giant: South Korea and Late Industrialization*. Oxford: Oxford University Press.

Andrews, Edmund L. 1997. "The Jobless Are Snared in Europe's Safety Net." News of the Week in Review. *NYT*, November 9, 6.

Audley, John, Sandra Polaski, Demetrios G. Papademetriou, and Scott Vaughan. 2004. *NAFTA's Promise and Reality: Lessons from Mexico for the Hemisphere*. Washington, D.C.: Carnegie Endowment for International Peace.

Australian Government. Department of Family and Community Services. 2000. "Changes in Social Expenditures." Policy Research Paper No. 4. http://www.facsia.gov.au/research/prp04/sec2.htm, accessed July 25, 2007.

Barbieri, Paolo, with Serge Paugam and Helen Russell. 2000. "Social Capital and Exits from Unemployment." In *Welfare Regimes and the Experience of Unemployment in Europe*, edited by Duncan Gallie and Serge Paugam, 201–11. Oxford: Oxford University Press.

Bastian, Jens. 1998. "Putting the Cart before the Horse? Labour Market Challenges Ahead of Monetary Union in Europe." In *Beyond the Market: The EU and National Social Policy*, edited by David Hine and Hussein Kassim, 91–106. London: Routledge.

Beer, Samuel H., and Adam Bruno Ulam. 1973. *Patterns of Government: The Major Political Systems of Europe*. 3d ed. New York: Random House.

Bell, D. S., and Byron Criddle. 1988. *The French Socialist Party: The Emergence of a Party of Government*. 2d ed. Oxford: Clarendon Press.

Berger, Suzanne. 1981. "Lame Ducks and National Champions: French Industrial Policy in the Fifth Republic." In *The Fifth Republic at Twenty*, edited by William Andrews and Stanley Hoffmann, 292–310. Albany: State University of New York Press.

Bermeo, Nancy. 2001. "Conclusion: Unemployment, the New Europe, and the Old Inequalities." In *Unemployment in the New Europe*, edited by Bermeo, 329–54. New York: Cambridge University Press.

Bernstein, Richard. 2003. "Europe's Lofty Vision of Unity Meets Headwinds." *NYT*, December 4.

Bhalla, A. S., and Shufang Qiu. 2004. *The Employment Impact of China's WTO Accession*. London: Routledge/Curzon.

Blecher, Marc. 2002. "Hegemony and Workers' Politics in China." *CQ* 170:283–303.

———. 2004. "The Working Class and Governance in China." In *Governance in China*, edited by Jude Howell, 193–206. Lanham, Md.: Rowman & Littlefield.

Boltho, Andrea. 1996. "Has France Converged on Germany? Policies and Institutions since 1958." In *Regional Diversity and Global Capitalism*, edited by Suzanne Berger and Ronald Dore, 89–194. Ithaca: Cornell University Press.

Bonnin, Michel. 2000. "Perspectives on Social Stability after the Fifteenth Congress." In *China under Jiang Zemin,* edited by Hung-mao Tien and Yun-han Chu, 153–61. Boulder, Colo.: Lynne Rienner.

Böröcz, József. 1999. "From Comprador State to Auctioneer State." In *States and Sovereignty in the Global Economy,* edited by David A. Smith, Dorothy J. Solinger, and Steven C. Topik, 193–209. New York: Routledge.

Boyer, Robert. 1984. "Wage Labor, Capital Accumulation, and the Crisis, 1968–82." In *The French Workers' Movement,* edited by Mark Kesselman, 17–38. London: George Allen & Unwin.

Brilliant, Myron A., and Jeremie Waterman. 2004. "China's WTO Implementation: A Three-Year Assessment." N.p.: U.S. Chamber of Commerce, September.

Burgess, Katrina. 1999. "Loyalty Dilemmas and Market Reform: Party-Union Alliances under Stress in Mexico, Spain, and Venezuela." *WP* 52, 1:105–34.

———. 2004. *Parties and Unions in the New Global Economy.* Pittsburgh: University of Pittsburgh Press.

Burgess, Katrina, and Steven Levitsky. 2003. "Explaining Populist Party Adaptation in Latin America: Environmental and Organizational Determinants of Party Change in Argentina, Mexico, Peru, and Venezuela." *Comparative Political Studies* 36, 8:881–911.

Burgoon, Brian. 2001. "Globalization and Welfare Compensation: Disentangling the Ties that Bind." *IO* 55, 3:509–551.

Cai, Yongshun. 2002. "The Resistance of Chinese Laid-Off Workers in the Reform Period." *CQ* 170:327–44.

———. 2005. *State and Laid-Off Workers in Reform China.* New York: Routledge.

Cameron, David Ross. 1995. "From Barre to Balladur: Economic Policy in the Era of the EMS." In *Remaking the Hexagon,* edited by Gregory Flynn, 117–57. Boulder, Colo.: Westview Press.

———. 2001. "Unemployment, Job Creation, and Economic and Monetary Union." In *Unemployment in the New Europe,* edited by Nancy Bermeo, 7–51. New York: Cambridge University Press.

Cameron, Maxwell A., and Brian W. Tomlin. 2000. *The Making of NAFTA: How the Deal Was Done.* Ithaca: Cornell University Press.

Camp, Roderic Ai. 1996. *Politics in Mexico.* 2d ed. New York: Oxford University Press.

———. 1999. *Politics in Mexico: The Decline of Authoritarianism.* 3d ed. Oxford: Oxford University Press.

———. 2003. *Politics in Mexico: The Democratic Transformation.* 4th ed. New York: Oxford University Press.

Carr, Barry. 1996. "Crossing Borders: Labor Internationalism in the Era of NAFTA." In *Neoliberalism Revisited: Economic Restructuring and Mexico's Future,* edited by Gerardo Otero, 209–31. Boulder, Colo.: Westview Press.

Castañeda, Jorge G. 1993. "The Clouding Political Horizon." *CH* 2:59–66.

———. 2004. "NAFTA at 10: A Plus or a Minus?" *CH* 2:51–55.

Castillo V., Gustavo del. 1996. "NAFTA and the Struggle for Neoliberalism: Mexico's Elusive Quest for First World Status." In *Neoliberalism Revisited: Economic Restructuring and Mexico's Political Future,* edited by Gerardo Otero, 27–42. Boulder, Colo.: Westview Press.

Chan, Anita. 2000. "Globalization, China's Free (Read Bonded) Labour Market, and the Chinese Trade Unions." *Asia Pacific Business Review* 6, 3–4:260–81.

Chan, Kam Wing. 1994. *Cities with Invisible Walls: Reinterpreting Urbanization in Post-1949 China*. Hong Kong: Oxford University Press.

Chang Kai. 2005. "The Legislation of Right to Strike in China." Paper presented at the conference "Globalisation, Migration and Labour Mobility in India and China." The Asian Business Economic Research Unit and the Institute for Global Movements, Monash University, Melbourne, Australia, September 29–30.

Chao, Julie. 2002. "Retiree Jailed for Trying to Organize China's Pensioners." Cox Washington Bureau, August 27.

Chen, Calvin, and Rudra Sil. 2006. "Communist Legacies, Postcommunist Transformations, and the Fate of Organized Labor in Russia and China." *Studies in Comparative International Development* 41, 2:62–87.

Chen, Feng. 2000. "Subsistence Crises, Managerial Corruption and Labour Protests in China." *CJ* 44:41–63.

——. 2003. "Between the State and Labour: The Conflict of Chinese Trade Unions' Double Identity in Market Reform." *CQ* 176:1006–28.

Chen, Jie. 2004. *Popular Political Support in Urban China*. Stanford, Calif.: Stanford University Press.

Cheng, Hang-Sheng. 1997. "A Mid-Course Assessment of China's Economic Reform." In *China's Economic Future: Challenges to U.S. Policy*, edited by Joint Economic Committee, Congress of the United States, 24–33. Armonk, N.Y.: M. E. Sharpe.

Cheng, Yuk-shing, and Dic Lo. 2002. "Research Report: Explaining the Financial Performance of China's Industrial Enterprises; Beyond the Competition-Ownership Controversy." *CQ* 170:413–440.

Chengzhen qiye xiagang zhigong zaijiuye zhuangkuang diaocha ketizu [Investigation of urban enterprises' laid-off staff and workers' reemployment situation project topic group]. 1997. "Kunjing yu chulu" [A difficult pass and the way out]. In *Shehuixue yanjiu* [Sociology Research] 6. Reprinted in *Xinhua wengao*, shehui [New China manuscript, society] 1998, 3:21–28.

Chenut, Helen Harden. 2005. *Fabric of Gender: Working-Class Culture in Third Republic France*. University Park, Pa.: Pennsylvania State University Press.

Chinesenewsnet.com. 2002. "Zhonggong zhongyang zhengzhiju changwu weiyuanhui zhaokai huiyi yanjiu jinyibu jiejue hao kunnan chunjong shengchan shenghuo wenti de gongzuo" [Chinese Communist Party Central Committee Politburo Standing Committee convenes a meeting to research work on the progressive solution to the production and livelihood problems of those in difficulty]. December 12.

Chow, Nelson W. S. 1988. *The Administration and Financing of Social Security in China*. Hong Kong: Centre of Asian Studies.

Chow, Nelson, and Xuebin Xu. 2001. *Socialist Welfare in a Market Economy: Social Security Reforms in Guangzhou, China*. Aldershot, U.K.: Ashgate.

Chu, Harry. 1999. "Chinese Rulers Fear Angry Workers May Finally Unite." *LAT*, June 4.

Clift, Ben. 2006. "The New Political Economy of Dirigisme: French Macroeconomic Policy, Unrepentant Sinning and the Stability and Growth Pact." *British Journal of Politics and International Relations* 8:1–22.

Cohen, Stephen. 1977. *Modern Capitalist Planning: The French Model*. Berkeley: University of California Press.

Cohen, Stephen, Serge Halimi, and John Zysman. 1986. "Institutions, Politics, and Industrial Policy in France." In *The Politics of Industrial Policy*, edited by

Claude E. Barfield and William A. Schambra, 106–27. Washington, D.C.: American Economic Institute.

Coleman, Kenneth M., and Charles L. Davis. 1983. "Preemptive Reform and the Mexican Working Class." *Latin American Research Review* 18, 1:3–31.

Collier, Ruth Berins. 1992. *The Contradictory Alliance: State-Labor Relations and Regime Change in Mexico.* Research Series No. 83. Berkeley: International and Area Studies, University of California.

Collier, Ruth Berins, and David Collier. 1991. *Shaping the Political Arena: Critical Junctures, the Labor Movement, and Regime Dynamics in Latin America.* Princeton, N.J.: Princeton University Press.

Comisión Económica para América Latina. 1981. *Statistical Yearbook for Latin America* ([New York]: United National Publication.

Cook, Maria Lorena. 2005. Review of *Parties and Unions in the New Global Economy,* by Katrina Burgess. *Perspectives on Politics* 3, 2:415–16.

Cook, Sarah. 2000. "Politics, Policy Processes and the Poor: Responding to Poverty in China's Cities." Report on a research project, "The Political and Social Dynamics of Poverty in China," undertaken as part of the DFID funded IDS Poverty research Programme. December.

Cortell, Andrew P. 2006. *Mediating Globalization: Domestic Institutions and Industrial Policies in the United States and Britain.* Albany: State University of New York Press.

Crepaz, Markus M. L. 2002. "Global, Constitutional and Partisan Determinants of Redistribution in Fifteen OECD Countries." *CP* 34, 2:169–88.

Croll, Elisabeth J. 1999. "Social Welfare Reform: Trends and Tensions." *CQ* 59:684–99.

Dai Lushui and Li Yan. 2001. "Qiantan jiaru WTO dui jiuye xingshi de yingxiang yu duice" [Superficially talking about the influence of entering the WTO on the situation of employment and how to handle that]. *ZGLD* 9:12–14.

Daley, Anthony. 1992. "The Steel Crisis and Labor Politics in France and the United States." In *Bargaining for Change: Union Politics in North America and Europe,* edited by Miriam Golden and Jonas Pontusson, 146–80. Ithaca: Cornell University Press.

Daley, Suzanne. 1999. "Under Attack, Premier Offers France's Left an Embrace." *NYT,* October 3.

Das, Bhagirath Lal. 1999. *The World Trade Organisation: A Guide to the Framework for International Trade.* London: Zed Books.

Davis, Deborah S. 1999. "Self-employment in Shanghai: A Research Note." *CQ* 157:22–43.

Demographia. 2001. Paris Population Analysis and Data Product. March 24. From http://www.demographia.com/db-parismet1921.htm.

Deyo, Fred C., ed. 1987. *The Political Economy of the New Asian Industrialism.* Ithaca: Cornell University Press.

Dillon, Sam. 1997a. "Workers Win Showdown with Factory in Mexico." *NYT,* December 14.

———. 1997b. "After Four Years of NAFTA, Labor Forging Cross-Border Ties." *NYT,* December 20.

Ding, X. L. 2000. "The Informal Asset Stripping of Chinese State Firms." *CJ* 43:1–28.

Dion, Michelle. 2002a. "Neoliberal Reform of Mexico's Welfare Regime, 1980s–1990s." Paper presented at the annual meeting of the American Political Science Association, Boston, August 31.

——. 2002b. "Mexico's Welfare Regime Before and After the Debt Crisis: Organized Labor and the Effects of Globalization." Paper presented at the annual meeting of the Southern Political Science Association, Savannah, Ga., November 7–9.

Dittmer, Lowell. 2003. "Leadership Change and Chinese Political Development." *CQ* 176:903–25.

Dornbusch, Rudiger. 1989. "The Latin American Debt Problem: Anatomy and Solutions." In *Debt and Democracy in Latin America,* edited by Barbara Stallings and Robert Kaufman, 7–22. Boulder, Colo.: Westview Press.

Duckett, Jane. 2003. "China's Social Security Reforms and the Comparative Politics of Market Transition." *Journal of Transition Politics and Post-Communist Studies* 19, 1:80–101.

——. 2004. "Research Report: State, Collectivism and Worker Privilege: A Study of Urban Health Insurance Reform." *CQ* 177:155–73.

Dussel Peters, Enrique. 1996. "From Export-Oriented to Import-Oriented Industrialization: Changes in Mexico's Manufacturing Sector, 1988–1994." In *Neoliberalism Revisited: Economic Restructuring and Mexico's Political Future,* edited by Gerardo Otero, 63–83. Boulder, Colo.: Westview Press.

——. 2000. *Polarizing Mexico: The Impact of Liberalization Strategy.* Boulder, Colo.: Lynne Rienner.

Eckstein, Alexander. 1977. *China's Economic Revolution.* New York: Cambridge University Press.

Economist. 1999. "France: The Grand Illusion." June 5, 17.

Ellman, Michael. 1987. "Eurosclerosis?" In *Unemployment: International Perspectives,* edited by Morley Gunderson, Noah M. Meltz, and Sylvia Ostry, 47–62. Toronto: University of Toronto Press.

Enriquez, Sam. 2006. "Candidates Pledge to Put Mexico to Work." *NYT,* June 11.

Fairclough, Gordon, and Kim Jung Min. 2003. "Labour: The Dangers of Militancy." *FEER,* November 27, 20.

Fan, Maureen. 2007. "In China, a State Job Still Brings Benefits and Bragging Rights." *Washington Post,* May 29.

Feng Lanrui and Zhao Lukuan. 1982. "Urban Unemployment in China." *Social Sciences in China* 3, 2:123–42.

Feng Lei, Bao Shenghua, and Chen Mengyang. 2002. "Liaoning shebao gaige chongguan" [Liaoning's social security reform's important period]. *Liaowang* [Outlook] 11:26–27.

Feng Tongqing. 2005. "Social Transition and Positive Adjustments in the State Enterprise-Worker Relationship." *Chinese Sociology & Anthropology* (Summer): 35–36.

Fewsmith, Joseph. 1994. *Dilemmas of Reform in China: Political Conflict and Economic Debate.* Armonk, N.Y.: M. E. Sharpe.

——. 1999a. "China in 1998: Tacking to Stay the Course." *AS* 39, 1:99–113.

——. 1999b. *The Impact of the Kosovo Conflict on China's Political Leaders and Prospects for WTO Accession.* Seattle: National Bureau of Asian Research.

——. 1999c. *China and the WTO: The Politics behind the Agreement.* Seattle: National Bureau of Asian Research.

——. 2001a. *China since Tiananmen: The Politics of Transition.* New York: Cambridge University Press.

——. 2001b. *Elite Politics in Contemporary China.* Armonk, N.Y.: M. E. Sharpe.

Fleck, Susan, and Constance Sorrentino. 1994. "Employment and Unemployment in Mexico's Labor Force." *Monthly Labor Review* 117, 11:3–31.

Forney, Matt. 1997. "We Want to Eat." *FEER,* June 26.

Frazier, Mark W. 2002. *The Making of the Chinese Industrial Workplace: State, Revolution, and Labor Management.* New York: Cambridge University Press.

Frazier, Mark W. 2004. "China's Pension Reform and Its Discontents." *CJ* 51:97–114.

———. 2006. "Welfare State Building in China in Comparative Perspective." Paper presented on the panel "Asian Welfare States," at the annual meeting of the American Political Science Association, August 31–September 3, Philadelphia.

French, Howard W. 2004. "Workers Demand Union at Wal-Mart Supplier in China." *NYT,* December 16.

Friedman, Barry L. 1996. "Employment and Social Protection Policies in China: Big Reforms and Limited Outcomes." In *Changes in China's Labor Market: Implications for the Future,* edited by Gregory K. Schoepfle, 151–66. Washington, D.C.: U.S. Department of Labor, Bureau of International Labor Affairs.

Gallagher, Mary E. 2005. *Contagious Capitalism: Globalization and Politics of Labor in China.* Princeton, N.J.: Princeton University Press.

———. 2006. "Mobilizing the Law in China: 'Informed Disenchantment' and the Development of Legal Consciousness." *Law and Society Review* 40, 4:783–816.

Garrett, Banning. 2001. "China Faces, Debates, the Contradictions of Globalization." *AS* 41, 3:409–27.

Garrett, Geoffrey. 1998a. *Partisan Politics in the Global Economy.* New York: Cambridge University Press.

———. 1998b. "Global Markets and National Politics: Collision Course or Virtuous Circle?" *IO* 52:787–824.

———. 2001. "Globalization and Government Spending around the World." *Studies in Comparative International Development* 35, 4:3–29.

Garrett, Geoffrey, and Peter Lange. 1991. "Political Responses to Interdependence: What's 'Left' for the Left?" *IO* 45, 4:539–64.

Gereffi, Gary. 1996. "Mexico's 'Old' and 'New' Maquiladora Industries: Contrasting Approaches to North American Integration." In *Neoliberalism Revisited: Economic Restructuring and Mexico's Political Future,* edited by Gerardo Otero, 85–105. Boulder, Colo.: Westview Press.

Gledhill, John. 1995. *Neoliberalism, Transnationalization and Rural Poverty: A Case Study of Michoacan, Mexico.* Boulder, Colo.: Westview Press.

Gold, Thomas B. 1986. *State and Society in the Taiwan Miracle.* Armonk, N.Y.: M. E. Sharpe.

Goldstein, Daniel. 2003. "U.S. Presses Soy Case as China Retains Ban." Bloomberg News, August 26.

Gong Li. 2000. *Kuashiji nanti: jiuye yu shehui baozhang* [A difficult issue straddling the century: Employment and social security]. Kunming: Yunnan renmin chubanshe [Yunnan People's Publishing].

Gong'anbu dixi yanjiusuo "quntixing shijian yanjiu" ketizu [Ministry of Public Security Fourth Research Institute's "mass incidents research" group]. 2001. "Woguo fasheng quntixing shijian de diaocha yu sikao" [Investigation and reflections on our country's mass incidents]. *NBCY* 31 (576), August 10.

Goodman, Peter S. 2003. "China Trade Policy's Ripple Effect: Limit on Soybean Imports Is Felt Widely around the Country." *Washington Post,* November 11.

Gordon, Philip H., and Sophie Meunier. 2001. *The French Challenge: Adapting to Globalization.* Washington, D.C.: Brookings Institution Press.

Gourevitch, Peter. 1978. "The Second Image Reversed: The International Sources of Domestic Politics." *IO* 32, 4:881–912.

Grayson, George W. 1993. *The North American Free Trade Agreement*. Headline Series 299. New York: Foreign Policy Association.

Greenhalgh, Susan. 2008. *Just One Child: Science and Policy in Deng's China*. Berkeley: University of California Press.

Greenhalgh, Susan, and Edwin A. Winckler. 2006. *Governing China's Population: From Leninist to Neoliberal Biopolitics*. Stanford: Stanford University Press.

Gruber, Lloyd. 2000. *Ruling the World: Power Politics and the Rise of Supranational Institutions*. Princeton, N.J.: Princeton University Press.

Guang, Lei. 2009. "Broadening the Debate on *Xiagang*: Ideological Change, Policy Innovation and Practices in History." In *China's Shattered Rice Bowl: Laid-off Workers in a Workers' State*, edited by Thomas B. Gold, 15–37. New York: Palgrave McMillan.

Guojia jiwei hongguan jingji yanjiuyuan ketizu [State Planning Commission, Macroeconomic Research Group]. 2000. "Jianli shehui baohu tixi shi wo guo shehui wending de guanjian" [Establishing a social protection system is the key to our country's social stability]. *NBCY* 511 (May 5): 8–14.

Guojia tongjiju chengshi shehui jingji diaocha zongdui, bian [National statistics bureau, urban society and economy investigation general team, ed.]. 2003. *Zhongguo cheng shi tongji nianjian—2002* [China city statistical yearbook—2002]. Beijing: Zhongguo tongji chubanshe [Chinese Statistics Press].

Haggard, Stephan, and Robert R. Kaufman. 1992a. "Introduction: Institutions and Economic Adjustment." In *The Politics of Economic Adjustment: International Constraints, Distributive Conflicts, and the State*, edited by Haggard and Kaufman, 3–37. Princeton, N.J.: Princeton University Press.

——. 1992b. "The Political Economy of Inflation and Stabilization in Middle-Income Countries." In *The Politics of Economic Adjustment: International Constraints, Distributive Conflicts, and the State*, edited by Haggard and Kaufman, 270–315. Princeton, N.J.: Princeton University Press.

——. 1995. *The Political Economy of Democratic Transitions*. Princeton, N.J.: Princeton University Press.

Halpern, Nina. 1985. "Economic Specialists and the Making of Chinese Economic Policy, 1955–1983." Ph.D. dissertation. University of Michigan, Ann Arbor.

Han Donglin. 2005. "Why Has China's Agriculture Survived WTO Accession?" *AS* 45, 6:931–48.

Hauser, Richard, and Brian Nolan, with Konstanze Morsforf and Wolfgang Strengmann-Kun. 2000. "Unemployment and Poverty: Change over Time." In *Welfare Regimes and the Experience of Unemployment in Europe*, edited by Duncan Gallie and Serge Paugam, 25–46. Oxford: Oxford University Press.

Heath, Jonathan. 1998. "Original Goals and Current Outcomes of Economic Reform in Mexico." In *Mexico's Private Sector: Recent History, Future Challenges*, edited by Riordan Roett, 37–62. Boulder, Colo.: Lynne Rienner.

Helleiner, Eric. 1999. "Sovereignty, Territoriality, and the Globalization of Finance." In *States and Sovereignty in the Global Economy*, edited by David A. Smith, Dorothy J. Solinger, and Steven C. Topik, 138–57. London: Routledge.

Hellman, Judith Adler. 2002. Review of *Social Movements and Economic Transition: Markets and Distributive Conflict in Mexico*, by Heather L. Williams. *American Political Science Review* 96, 2:457–58.

Hemerijck, Anton, and Martin Schludi. 2000. "Sequences of Policy Failure and Effective Policy Responses." In *Welfare and Work in the Open Economy*, vol. 1, edited by Fritz W. Scharpf and Vivien A. Schmidt, 125–228. Oxford: Oxford University Press.

Hershatter, Gail. 1986. *The Workers of Tianjin, 1900–1949*. Stanford, Calif.: Stanford University Press.

Hicks, Alexander. 1999. *Social Democracy and Welfare Capitalism: A Century of Income Security Politics*. Ithaca: Cornell University Press.

Hiebert, Murray. 2005. "China Gets a Passing Grade from Foreign Firms." *WSJ*, November 28.

Hirschman, Albert O. 1970. *Exit, Voice, and Loyalty*. Cambridge, Mass.: Harvard University Press.

Hirst, Paul, and Grahame Thompson. 1997. "Globalization in Question: International Economic Relations and Forms of Public Governance." In *Contemporary Capitalism: The Embeddedness of Institutions*, edited by J. Rogers Hollingsworth and Robert Boyer, 337–61. New York: Cambridge University Press.

Hoffman, Charles. 1967. *Work Incentive Practices and Policies in the People's Republic of China, 1953–1965*. Albany: State University of New York Press.

Hollingsworth, J. Rogers, and Robert Boyer. 1997. "Coordination of Economic Actors and Social Systems of Production." In *Contemporary Capitalism: The Embeddedness of Institutions*, edited by Hollingsworth and Boyer, 1–48. New York: Cambridge University Press.

Howard, Pat. 1991. "Rice Bowls and Job Security: The Urban Contract Labour System." *AJCA* 25:93–114.

Howell, Chris. 1992. *Regulating Labor: The State and Industrial Relations Reform in Postwar France*. Princeton, N.J.: Princeton University Press.

——. 2003. "The State and the Reconstruction of Industrial Relations Institutions after Fordism: Britain and France Compared." Paper presented at the 99th Meeting of the American Political Science Association, Philadelphia, August 28–31.

Howell, Jude. 1993. *China Opens Its Doors: The Politics of Economic Transition*. Hemel Hempstead, U.K.: Harvester Wheatsheaf.

——. 2000. "Organising around Women and Labour in China: Uneasy Shadows, Uncomfortable Alliances." *Communist and Post-Communist Studies* 33:355–77.

Hu Angang. 1998. *Employment and Development: China's Employment Problem and Employment Strategy*. National Conditions Report. Beijing: National Conditions Analysis and Study Group of the Chinese Academy of Sciences. April 30.

——. 2000. "Shishi jiuye youxian zhanlue, wei renmin tigong gengduode gongzuo gangwei" [Realize employment preference strategy, for the people supply more jobs]. Zhongguo kexueyuan, Qinghua daxue Guoqing yanjiu zongxin [Chinese Academy of Science and Tsinghua University National Conditions Research Center]. Speech outline delivered at Specialists' Forum directed by State Planning Commission Vice Chairman Wang Chunzheng, September 29.

——. 2001a. "Chuangzhaoxing de cuihui: Zhongguo di jiegou biange (1996–2000 nian)" [Creative destruction: China's structural evolution (1996–2000)]. Unpublished manuscript.

——. 2001b. "China's Present Economic Situation and Its Macro-Economic Policies." Paper presented at the RAND-China ReformForum Conference, Santa Monica, Calif., November 29–30.

Huber, Evelyne, Charles Ragin, and John D. Stephens. 1993. "Social Democracy, Christian Democracy, Constitutional Structure, and the Welfare State." *American Journal of Sociology* 99, 3:711–49.

Huber, Evelyne, and John D. Stephens. 2001. *Development and Crisis of the Welfare State: Parties and Policies in Global Markets.* Chicago: University of Chicago Press.

Hurst, William. 2003. "The Forgotten Player: Local State Strategies and the Dynamics of Chinese Laid-Off Workers' Contention." Paper presented at the conference "Reassessing Unrest in China," Washington, D.C., December.

Hurst, William, and Kevin O'Brien. 2002. "China's Contentious Pensioners." *CQ* 170:345–60.

Hussain, Athar, et al. 2002. *Urban Poverty in the PRC.* Asian Development Bank Project No. TAR: PRC 33448.

Hutsebaut, Martin. 2003. "The Future of Social Protection in Europe: A European Trade Union Perspective." http://pre20031103.stm.fi/english/tao/publicat/financing/hutsebaut.htm, accessed July 25, 2007.

Imai, Hiroshi. 2002. "Special Report: China's Growing Unemployment Problem." *Pacific Business and Industries RIM* (Tokyo) II, 6:22–40.

Information Office of the State Council of the People's Republic of China. 2001. "Labor and Social Security in China." Pamphlet. Beijing. April.

Iritani, Evelyn. 2007. "U.S. to Slap Duties on China Paper." *LAT,* March 31.

Jackman, Richard. 1998. "The Impact of the European Union on Unemployment and Unemployment Policy." In *Beyond the Market: The EU and National Social Policy,* edited by David Hine and Hussein Kassim, 60–78. London: Routledge.

Jackson, Richard, and Neil Howe. 2004. *The Graying of the Middle Kingdom: The Demographics and Economics of Retirement Policy in China.* Washington, D.C.: Center for Strategic and International Studies and the Prudential Foundation.

Jacobson, Harold K., and Michel Oksenberg. 1990. *China's Participation in the IMF, the World Bank, and GATT: Toward a Global Economic Order.* Ann Arbor: University of Michigan Press.

Jefferson, Gary H., and Thomas G. Rawski. 1992. "Unemployment, Underemployment and Employment Policy in China's Cities." *MC* 18, 1:42–71.

Jiang, Xueqin. 2001. "Fighting to Organize." *FEER,* September 6, 72–75.

Jones, Leroy, and I. Sakong. 1980. *Government, Business and Entrepreneurship in Economic Development: The Korean Case.* Cambridge, Mass.: Harvard University Press.

Judt, Tony. 1997. "The Social Question Redivivus." *Foreign Affairs* 76, 5:59–117.

Kaelberer, Matthias. 2002. "Review Article: Ideas, Interests, and Institutions—The Domestic Policies of European Monetary Cooperation." *CP* 35, 1:105–23.

Kahler, Miles. 1992. "External Influence, Conditionality, and the Politics of Adjustment." In *The Politics of Economic Adjustment: International Constraints, Distributive Conflicts, and the State,* edited by Stephan Haggard and Robert R. Kaufman, 89–136. Princeton, N.J.: Princeton University Press.

Kapstein, Ethan B. 1997. "Conclusion: Toward a Political Economy of Social Policy." In *Sustaining the Transition: The Social Safety Net in Postcommunist Europe,* edited by Ethan B. Kapstein and Michael Mandelbaum, 173–87. New York: Council on Foreign Relations.

Katzenstein, Peter J. 1978. "Conclusion: Domestic Structures and Strategies of Foreign Economic Policy." In *Between Power and Plenty: Foreign Economic Policies of*

Advanced Industrial States, edited by Katzenstein, 295–336. Madison: University of Wisconsin Press.

———. 1985. *Small States in World Markets: Industrial Policy in Europe.* Ithaca: Cornell University Press.

Kaufman, Robert R. 1986. "Democratic and Authoritarian Responses to the Debt Issue: Argentina, Brazil, Mexico." In *The Politics of International Debt,* edited by Miles Kahler, 187–217. Ithaca: Cornell University Press.

———. 1989. "Economic Orthodoxy and Political Change in Mexico: The Stabilization and the Adjustment Policies of the de la Madrid Administration." In *Debt and Democracy in Latin America,* edited by Barbara Stallings and Robert Kaufman, 109–26. Boulder, Colo.: Westview Press.

Kaufman, Robert, and Alex Segura-Ubiergo. 2001. "Globalization, Domestic Politics, and Social Spending in Latin America: A Time-Series Cross-Section Analysis, 1973–97." *WP* 53:553–87.

Kernen, Antoine. 2002. "Worker Protest in China: Toward a New Public Management of Social Conflicts." Paper presented at the annual meeting of the Association for Asian Studies, April 4–7, Washington, D.C.

Kernen, Antoine, and Jean-Louis Rocca. 1999. "The Reform of State-Owned Enterprises and Its Social Consequences in Shenyang and Liaoning." Manuscript.

———. 2000. "Social Responses to Unemployment and the 'New Urban Poor': Case Study in Shenyang City and Liaoning Province." *China Perspectives* 27:35–51.

Kesselman, Mark. 1984a. "Introduction: The French Workers' Movement." In *The French Workers' Movement: Economic Crisis and Political Change,* edited by Mark Kesselman with the assistance of Guy Groux, 1–13. London: George Allen & Unwin.

———. 1984b. Conclusion to *The French Workers' Movement: Economic Crisis and Political Change,* edited by Mark Kesselman with the assistance of Guy Groux, 311–22. London: George Allen & Unwin.

———. 1989. "The New Shape of French Labour and Industrial Relations: Ce n'est plus la même chose." In *Policy-Making in France: From de Gaulle to Mitterrand,* edited by Paul Godt, 165–75. London: Frances Pinter.

———. 1996. "Does the French Labor Movement Have a Future?" In *Chirac's Challenge: Liberalization, Europeanization, and Malaise in France,* edited by John T. S. Keeler and Martin A. Schain, 143–60. New York: St. Martin's Press.

Kesselman, Mark, Joel Krieger, Christopher S. Allen, Stephen Hellman, David Ost, and George Ross. 2002. *European Politics in Transition.* 4th ed. New York: Houghton Mifflin.

Kitschelt, Herbert, Peter Lange, Gary Marks, and John D. Stephens. 1998. Introduction to *Continuity and Change in Contemporary Capitalism,* edited by Kitschelt, Lange, Marks, and Stephens, 1–8. New York: Cambridge University Press.

Knight, K. G. 1987. *Unemployment: An Economic Analysis.* London: Croom Helm.

Kohli, Atol. 2004. *State-Directed Development: Political Power and Industrialization in the Global Periphery.* New York: Cambridge University Press.

Kokubun, Ryosei. 1986. "The Politics of Foreign Economic Policy-Making in China: The Case of Plant Cancellations with Japan." *CQ* 105:19–45.

Koo, Hagen. 2001. *Korean Workers: The Culture and Politics of Class Formation.* Ithaca: Cornell University Press.

Kornai, Janos. 1992. *The Socialist System: The Political Economy of Communism.* Princeton, N.J.: Princeton University Press.

Korpi, Walter, and Joakim Palme. 2003. "New Politics and Class Politics in the Context of Austerity and Globalization: Welfare State Regress in 18 Countries, 1975–95." *American Political Science Review* 97, 3:425–46.

Korzec, Michal. 1988. "Contract Labor, the 'Right to Work' and New Labor Laws in the People's Republic of China." *Comparative Economic Studies* 30, 2:117–49.

Krugman, Paul. 1996. "First, Do No Harm." In "Responses to Kapstein: Workers and Econo-mists; The Global Economy Has Left Keynes in Its Train." *Foreign Affairs* 75, 4:164–70.

Kurtz, Marcus J. 2002. "Understanding the Third World Welfare State after Neoliberalism." *CP* 34, 3:293–313.

Lam, Willy Wo Lap. 1994. "Dissidents Say Detentions, Sentencing Increase." *SCMP*, December 24.

———. 2003. "Beijing Faces Winter of Discontent." CNN.com, September 30.

Lampton, David M. 2001. *Same Bed, Different Dreams: Managing U.S.-China Relations, 1999–2000.* Berkeley: University of California Press.

Lardy, Nicholas. 2002a. "Adjustment of Foreign Trade Policies and Foreign Direct Investment." Comment presented at the China Development Forum, Beijing, March 24–25.

———. 2002b. *Integrating China into the Global Economy.* Washington, D.C.: Brookings Institution Press.

Lawrence, Susan V. 2000. "Risk Assessment: For Better or Worse." *FEER*, October 5.

LBT. 1999. "Zongli zai guoyou qiye xiagang zhigong jiben shenghuo baozhang he zaijiuye gongzuo huiyishang di zongjie jianghua" [Premier Zhu Rongji's summary speech in the work conference on state-owned staff and workers' basic livelihood guarantee and reemployment work]. *LBT* 3, January 13.

———. 2001. "2001 nian laodong he shehui baozhang gongzuo yaodian" [The gist of the labor and social security for the year 2001]. *LBT* 2:8–11.

Le Cacheux, Jacques E. 1995. "The Franc Fort Strategy and the EMU." In *Remaking the Hexagon: The New France in the New Europe,* edited by Gregory Flynn, 69–86. Boulder, Colo.: Westview Press.

Lee, Chae-Jin. 1984. *China and Japan: New Economic Diplomacy.* Stanford, Calif.: Hoover Institution Press.

Lee, Ching Kwan. 1998. "The Labor Politics of Market Socialism: Collective Inaction and Class Experiences among State Workers in Guangzhou." *MC* 24, 1:3–33.

———. 1999. "From Organized Dependence to Disorganized Despotism: Changing Labour Regimes in Chinese Factories." *CQ* 155:44–71.

———. 1999. "The Politics of Working-Class Transitions in China." Paper presented at the conference "Wealth and Labor in China: Cross-Cutting Approaches of Present Developments," Centre d'Études et de Recherches Internationales, Paris, December 6–7.

———. 2000. "The 'Revenge of History': Collective Memories and Labor Protests in North-eastern China." *Ethnography* 1, 2:217–37.

———. 2002a. "From the Specter of Mao to the Spirit of the Law: Labor Insurgency in China." *Theory and Society* 31:189–228.

———. 2002b. "Three Patterns of Working-Class Transitions in China." In *Politics in China: Moving Frontiers,* edited by Françoise Mengin and Jean-Louis Rocca, 62–92. New York: Palgrave.

———. 2007. *Against the Law: Labor Protests in China's Rustbelt and Sunbelt.* Berkeley: University of California Press.

Lee, Hong Yong. 1991. *From Revolutionary Cadres to Party Technocrats in Socialist China.* Berkeley: University of California Press.

———. 2000. "Xiagang, the Chinese Style of Laying Off Workers." *AS* 40, 6:914–37.

Lee, Ming-kwan. 2000. *Chinese Occupational Welfare in Market Transition.* New York: St. Martin's Press.

Lefébure, Pierre, and Eric Lagneau. 2001. "Media Construction in the Dynamics of Euro-Protest." In *Contentious Europeans: Protest and Politics in an Emerging Polity,* edited by Doug Imig and Sidney Tarrow, 187–204. Lanham, Md.: Rowman & Littlefield.

Lehoucq, Fabrice. 2007. "Structural Reform, Democratic Governance, and Institutional Design in Latin America." *CP* 39, 2:229–48.

Leung, Trini. 2002. "The Third Wave of the Chinese Labour Movement in the Post-Mao Era." *CLB,* June 5, 7.

Levy, Daniel C., and Kathleen Bruhn, with Emilio Zebadua. 2001. *Mexico: The Struggle for Democratic Development.* Berkeley: University of California Press.

———. 2006. *Mexico: The Struggle for Democratic Development.* 2d ed. Berkeley: University of California Press.

Levy, Jonah D. 2000. "France: Directing Adjustment?" In *Welfare and Work in the Open Economy: Diverse Responses to Common Challenges,* vol. 2, edited by Fritz W. Scharpf and Vivien A. Schmidt, 308–50. Oxford: Oxford University Press.

Levy, Jonah D., Mari Miura, and Gene Park. 2003. "Exiting Étatisme? New Directions in State Policy in France and Japan?" Paper presented at the workshop "The State after Statism: New State Activities in the Age of Globalization and Liberalization." University of California, Berkeley, November 1–15.

Li, Cheng. 2001a. "China in 2000: A Year of Strategic Rethinking." *AS* 41, 1:71–90.

———. 2001b. *China's Leaders: The New Generation.* Lanham, Md.: Rowman & Littlefield.

Li Peilin. 2003. "Dangqian zhongguo shehui fazhan de rogan wenti he xin qushi" [Current issues and new trends in social development]. In *Shehui lanpishu: 2003 nian; Zhongguo shehui xingshi fenxi yu yuce* [Social blue book: 2003 analysis and predictions of China's social situation], edited by Ru Xin, Lu Xueyi, and Li Peilin. Beijing: shehui kexue wenxian chubanshe [Social Science Documents Co.].

Li Shigeng and Gao Ping. 2000. "Shiye baoxian zhidu cunzai di wenti he duice" [Existing issues and how to deal with them in the unemployment insurance system]. *LBT* 6:32.

Li, Xiao-Ming. 2000. "China's Macroeconomic Stabilization Policies Following the Asian Financial Crisis: Success or Failure?" *AS* 40, 6:936–57.

Lim, Lin Lean, and Gyorgy Sziraczki. 1996. "Employment, Social Security, and Enterprise Reforms in China." In *Changes in China's Labor Market: Implications for the Future,* edited by Gregory K. Schoepfle, 45–87. Washington, D.C.: U.S. Department of Labor, Bureau of International Labor Affairs.

Lin, Yi-min, and Tian Zhu. 2001. "Ownership Restructuring in Chinese State Industry: An Analysis of Evidence on Initial Organizational Changes." *CQ* 166:305–41.

Lindbeck, Assar, and Denis Snower. 1988. *The Insider-Outsider Theory of Unemployment.* Cambridge, Mass.: MIT Press.

Lintner, Valerio. 2001. "European Monetary Union: Developments, Implications and Prospects." In *European Union: Power and Policy-Making,* 2d ed., edited by Jeremy Richardson, 321–34. London: Routledge.

Linz, Juan J. 1975. "Totalitarian and Authoritarian Regimes." In *Handbook of Political Science, Volume 3: Macropolitical Theory,* edited by Fred I. Greenstein and Nelson W. Polsby, 175–411. Reading, Mass.: Addison-Wesley.

Linz, Juan J., and Alfred Stepan. 1996. *Problems of Democratic Transition and Consolidation: Southern Europe, South America and Post-Communist Europe.* Baltimore: Johns Hopkins University Press.

Liu, Binyan. 1997. "The Working Class Speaks out." *CF,* August 1.

Lu Yu-shan. 1994. "CPC Guards against Mass Disturbances." *Tangdai* [Contemporary Times], 38 (May 15): 20–22.

Lustig, Nora. 1998. *Mexico: The Remaking of an Economy.* 2d ed. Washington, D.C.: Brookings Institution Press.

Ma, Josephine. 2002. "Campaign Aims to Pacify Poor as Anger at Wealth Gap Grows." *SCMP,* February 8.

Machin, Howard, and Vincent Wright. 1985. "Economic Policy under the Mitterrand Presidency, 1981–1984: An Introduction." In *Economic Policy and Policy-Making under the Mitterrand Presidency, 1981–1984,* edited by Machin and Wright, 1–43. London: Frances Pinter.

Maxfield, Sylvia. 1990. *Governing Capital: International Finance and Mexican Politics.* Ithaca: Cornell University Press.

Mazey, Sonia. 2001. "European Integration: Unfinished Journey or Journey without End?" In *European Union: Power and Policy-Making,* 2d ed., edited by Jeremy Richardson, 27–50. London: Routledge.

McGregor, Richard. 2006. "Data Show Social Unrest on the Rise in China." *Financial Times,* January 19.

McNamara, Kathleen R. 1998. *The Currency of Ideas: Monetary Politics in the European Union.* Ithaca: Cornell University Press.

Meng, Xin. 2000. *Labour Market Reform in China.* New York: Cambridge University Press.

Meyer, Lorenzo. 1998. "Mexico: Economic Liberalism in an Authoritarian Polity." In *Market Economics and Political Change: Comparing China and Mexico,* edited by Juan D. Lindau and Timothy Cheek, 127–57. Lanham, Md.: Rowman & Littlefield.

Middlebrook, Kevin. 1989a. "The CTM and the Future of State-Labor Relations." In *Mexico's Alternative Political Futures,* edited by Wayne Cornelius, Judith Gentleman, and Peter H. Smith, 291–305. San Diego: Center for U.S.-Mexican Studies, University of California, San Diego.

———. 1989b. "The Sounds of Silence: Organised Labour's Response to Economic Crisis in Mexico," *Journal of Latin American Studies* 21, 2:195–220.

———. 1995. *The Paradox of Revolution: Labor, the State, and Authoritarianism in Mexico.* Baltimore: Johns Hopkins University Press.

Miller, H. Lyman. 1999. "Institutions in Chinese Politics: Trends and Prospects." In *China's Future: Implications for US Interests; Conference Report,* edited by Library of Congress, 37–48. Washington, D.C.

Miller, Tom. 2005. "Up from the Abyss: Reviving the Northeast." *China Economic Quarterly* Q2:19–40.

Milner, Helen V., and Robert O. Keohane. 1996a. "Internationalization and Domestic Politics: A Conclusion." In *Internationalization and Domestic Politics,* edited by Keohane and Milner, 243–58. Cambridge: Cambridge University Press.

———. 1996b. "Internationalization and Domestic Politics: An Introduction." In *Internationalization and Domestic Politics,* edited by Keohane and Milner, 3–24. Cambridge: Cambridge University Press.

Miura, Mari, and Bruno Palier. 2003. "Veto Players and Welfare Reform: The Paradox of the French and Japanese Unions." Paper presented at the annual meeting of the American Political Science Association, Philadelphia, August 27–31.

Moore, Thomas G. 2000. "China and Globalization." In *East Asia and Globalization*, edited by Samuel S. Kim, 105–31. Lanham, Md.: Rowman & Littlefield.

Morici, Peter. 1993. "Grasping the Benefits of NAFTA." *CH* 2:49–54.

Morris, Peter. 1994. *French Politics Today*. Manchester, U.K.: Manchester University Press.

Morris, Richard. 1985. "Trade Unions in Contemporary China." *AJCA* 13:51–67.

Moss, Bernard H. 1988. "After the Auroux Laws [AL]: Employers, Industrial Relations and the Right in France." *West European Politics* 11, 1:68–80.

Muet, Pierre-Alain. 1985. "Economic Management and the International Environment, 1981–1983." In *Economic Policy and Policy-Making under the Mitterrand Presidency, 1981–1984*, edited by Howard Machin and Vincent Wright, 70–96. London: Frances Pinter.

Murillo, Maria Victoria. 2001. *Labor Unions, Partisan Coalitions, and Market Reforms in Latin America*. Cambridge: Cambridge University Press.

Murphy, David. 2002. "Labour Unrest: Nothing to Celebrate." *FEER*, April 4, 32.

Nanfang zhoumo. 2001. "New Social Security System Draws up Its Curtain in Liaoning Province." *Nanfang zhoumo* [Southern Weekend], July 26.

Naughton, Barry. 1992. "Implications of the State Monopoly over Industry and Its Relaxation." *MC* 18, 1:14–41.

———. 1995. *Growing Out of the Plan: Chinese Economic Reform, 1978–1993*. New York: Cambridge University Press.

———. 1996. "China's Emergence and Prospects as a Trading Nation." *Brookings Papers on Economic Activity* 2:273–344.

———. 1999. "The Chinese Economy through 2005: Domestic Developments and Their Implications for US Interests." In *China's Future: Implications for US Interests; Conference Report*, edited by Library of Congress, 49–66. Washington, D.C.: Library of Congress.

———. 2003. "The Chinese Economy: WTO, Trade, and U.S.-China Relations." In *U.S.-China Relations, Fifth Conference* 18, 1:39–44. Washington, D.C.: Aspen Institute.

OECD. 1991–1999. *Employment Outlook, Statistical Annex*. Various editions. Paris.

Orenstein, Mitchell A., and Lisa E. Hale. 2001. "Corporatist Renaissance in Post-communist Central Europe." In *The Politics of Labor in a Global Age: Continuity and Change in Late-Industrializing and Post-socialist Economies*, edited by Christopher Candland and Rudra Sil, 258–82. Oxford: Oxford University Press.

Oliveira, Orlandina de, and Brigida Garcia. 1997. "Socioeconomic Transformation and Labor Markets in Urban Mexico." In *Global Restructuring, Employment, and Social Inequality in Urban Latin America*, edited by Richard Tardanico and Rafael Menjivar Larin, 211–32. Coral Gables, Fla.: North-South Center Press.

Overholt, William H. 1999. "China in the Balance." Nomura Strategy Paper, Hong Kong, May 12.

Oxley, Howard, and John P. Martin. 1991. "Controlling Government Spending and Deficits: Trends for the 1980s and Prospects for the 1990s." *OECD Economic Studies* 27 (Autumn): 145–89.

Packenham, Robert A. 1998. "Market-Oriented Reforms and National Development in Latin America." In *Market Economics and Political Change: Comparing China and*

Mexico, edited by Juan D. Lindau and Timothy Cheek, 59–94. Lanham, Md.: Rowman & Littlefield.

Pan, Philip P. 2002. "'High Tide' of Labor Unrest in China: Striking Workers Risk Arrest to Protest Pay Cuts, Corruption." *Washington Post,* January 21.

Park, Albert, and Fang Cai. 2003. "How Has Economic Restructuring Affected China's Urban Workers?" Unpublished manuscript.

Parsons, Craig. 2003. *A Certain Idea of Europe.* Ithaca: Cornell University Press.

Pastor, Manuel. 1987. *The International Monetary Fund and Latin America.* Boulder, Colo.: Westview Press.

———. 1999. "Globalization, Sovereignty and Policy Choice: Lessons from the Mexican Peso Crisis." In *States and Sovereignty in the Global Economy,* edited by David A. Smith, Dorothy J. Solinger, and Steven C. Topik, 210–28. London: Routledge.

Pastor, Manuel, and Carol Wise. 1997a. "State Policy, Distribution and Neoliberal Reform in Mexico." Paper No. 229. Washington, D.C.: Latin American Program, Woodrow Wilson International Center for Scholars.

———. 1997b. "State Policy, Distribution and Neoliberal Reform in Mexico." *Journal of Latin American Studies* 29, 2:419–56.

———. 2003. "NAFTA and the WTO in the Transformation of Mexico's Economic System." In *Mexico's Politics and Society in Transition,* edited by Joseph S. Tulchin and Andrew D. Selee, 179–214. Boulder, Colo.: Lynne Rienner.

Pearson, Margaret M. 1999a. "China's Integration into the International Trade and Investment Regime." In *China Joins the World: Progress and Prospects,* edited by Elizabeth Economy and Michel Oksenberg, 161–205. New York: Council on Foreign Relations.

———. 1999b. "The Major Multilateral Economic Institutions Engage China." In *Engaging China: The Management of an Emerging Power,* edited by Alastair Iain Johnston and Robert S. Ross, 207–34. London: Routledge.

———. 2001. "The Case of China's Accession to GATT/WTO." In *The Making of Chinese Foreign and Security Policy in the Era of Reform, 1978–2000,* edited by David M. Lampton, 337–70. Stanford, Calif.: Stanford University Press.

———. 2005. "The Institutional, Political, and Global Foundations of China's Trade Liberalization." In *Japan and China in the World Political Economy,* edited by Kellee S. Tsai and Saadia M. Pekkanen. London: Routledge.

———. 2005. "The Business of Governing Business in China: Institutions and Norms of the Emerging Regulatory State." *WP 57* (January): 296–322.

Peopledaily.com. 2004. "Premier Wen delivers government work report." From http://english.peopledaily.com.cn/20040305/eng20040305_136592.s. Full text, last updated at BJ time, Tuesday, March 16, 2004. Delivered at the Second Session of the 10th National People's Congress, March 5.

Perry, Elizabeth J. 1993. *Shanghai on Strike.* Stanford, Calif.: Stanford University Press.

———. 1994. "Shanghai's Strike Wave of 1957." *CQ* 137 (1994): 1–27.

———. 1995. "Labor's Battle for Political Space." In *Urban Spaces in Contemporary China,* edited by Deborah S. Davis, Richard Kraus, Barry Naughton, and Elizabeth J. Perry, 302–25. New York: Cambridge University Press.

Perry, Elizabeth J., and Li Xun. 1997. *Proletarian Power: Shanghai in the Cultural Revolution.* Boulder, Colo.: Westview Press.

Philion, Stephen. 1998. "Chinese Welfare State Regimes." *Journal of Contemporary Asia* 28, 4:518–36.

Pierson, Paul. 1994. *Dismantling the Welfare State: Reagan, Thatcher, and the Politics of Retrenchment.* New York: Cambridge University Press.

Piven, Frances Fox, and Richard A. Cloward. 1979. *Poor People's Movements: Why They Succeed, How They Fail.* New York: Vintage Books.

Polaski, Sandra. 2004. "Jobs, Wages, and Household Income." In *NAFTA's Promise and Reality: Lessons from Mexico for the Hemisphere,* edited by John Audley, Sandra Polaski, Demetrios G. Papademetriou, and Scott Vaughan, 11–37. Washington, D.C.: Carnegie Endowment for International Peace.

Pomfret, John. 2000. "Leaders of Independent Chinese Labor Union Fear Crackdown." *Washington Post,* December 15.

Pontusson, Jonas. 1992. "Introduction: Organizational and Political-Economic Perspectives on Union Politics." In *Bargaining for Change: Union Politics in North America and Europe,* edited by Miriam Golden and Jonas Pontusson, 1–41. Ithaca: Cornell University Press.

Purcell, Susan Kaufman. 1992. "Mexico's New Economic Vitality." *CH* 2:54–58.

Putterman, Louis. 1992. "Dualism and Reform in China." *Economic Development and Cultural Change* 40:467–93.

Ramirez, Rogelio de la O. 1996. "The Mexican Peso Crisis and Recession of 1994–1995: Preventable Then, Avoidable in the Future?" In *The Mexican Peso Crisis: International Perspectives,* edited by Riordan Roett, 11–32. Boulder, Colo.: Lynne Rienner.

Rawski, Thomas G. 1999a. *China: Prospects for Full Employment.* Employment and Training Papers 47. Geneva: International Labour Office, Employment and Training Department.

——. 1999b. "Reforming China's Economy: What Have We Learned?" *CJ* 41:139–56.

——. 2002. "Recent Developments in China's Labor Economy." Unpublished manuscript. Pittsburgh.

Renmin ribao haiwaiban. 2001. "Guowuyuan bangongting fabu tongzhi: Jiaqiang chengshi jumin zuidi shenghuo baozhang gongzuo" [The State Council Office announces a circular: Strengthen urban residents' minimum livelihood guarantee work]. *Renmin ribao haiwaiban* [People's Daily Overseas Edition], November 19.

Reynolds, Clark W. 1993. "Power, Value, and Distribution in the NAFTA." In *Political and Economic Liberalization in Mexico: At a Critical Juncture?* edited by Riordan Roett, 69–92. Boulder, Colo.: Lynne Rienner.

Rhodes, Martin. 1998. "Defending the Social Contract: The EU between Global Constraints and Domestic Imperatives." In *Beyond the Market: The EU and National Social Policy,* edited by David Hine and Hussein Kassim, 36–69. London: Routledge.

Riskin, Carl. 1987. *China's Political Economy: The Quest for Development since 1949.* Oxford: Oxford University Press.

Roberts, Bryan R. 1993. "The Dynamics of Informal Employment in Mexico." In *Work without Protections: Case Studies of the Informal Sector in Developing Countries,* edited by Gregory K. Schoepfle, 101–25. Washington, D.C.: U.S. Department of Labor, Bureau of International Labor Affairs.

Roberts, Ivor, and Beverly Springer. 2001. *Social Policy in the European Union: Between Harmonization and National Autonomy.* Boulder, Colo.: Lynne Rienner.

Rocca, Jean-Louis. 1999. "Old Working Class, New Working Class: Reforms, Labour Crisis and the Two Faces of Conflicts in Chinese Urban Areas." First draft of a paper presented at the Second Annual Conference of the European Union–China Academic

Network, January 21–22, Centro de Estudios de Asia Oriental, Universidad Autónoma de Madrid, Spain.

———. 2002. "Three at Once: The Multidimensional Scope of the Labor Crisis in China." In *Politics in China: Moving Frontiers*, edited by Françoise Mengin and Jean-Louis Rocca, 3–30. New York: Palgrave.

Rochlin, James F. 1997. *Redefining Mexican "Security."* Boulder, Colo.: Lynne Rienner.

Rodrik, Dani. 1997. *Has Globalization Gone Too Far?* Washington, D.C.: Institute for International Economics.

Ros, Jaime, 1993. "Free Trade Area or Common Capital Market? Mexico-U.S. Economic Integration and NAFTA Negotiations." In *Assessments of the North American Free Trade Agreement*, edited by Ambler H. Moss Jr., 53–80. Coral Gables, Fla.: North-South Center Press.

Rosenthal, Elisabeth. 2003. "Workers' Plight Brings New Militancy in China." *NYT*, March 10.

Ross, George. 1984. "The CGT, Economic Crisis, and Political Change." In *The French Workers' Movement: Economic Crisis and Political Change*, edited by Mark Kesselman with the assistance of Guy Groux, 51–74. London: George Allen & Unwin.

Rothstein, Bo, and Sven Steinmo. 2002. "Restructuring Politics: Institutional Analysis and the Challenges of Modern Welfare States." In *Restructuring the Welfare State: Political Institutions and Policy Change*, edited by Rothstein and Steinmo, 1–19. New York: Palgrave Macmillan.

Roxborough, Ian. 1989. "Organized Labor: A Major Victim of the Debt Crisis." In *Debt and Democracy in Latin America*, edited by Barbara Stallings and Robert Kaufman, 91–108. Boulder, Colo.: Westview Press.

Ru Xin, Lu Xueyi, and Dan Tianlun, eds. 1998. *1998 nian: Zhongguo shehui xingshi fenxi yu yuce* [1998: Analysis and prediction of China's social situation]. Beijing: Shehui kexue wenxian chubanshe [Social Science Documents Publishing Co.].

Rubio, Luis. 1993. "Economic Reform and Political Change in Mexico." In *Political and Economic Liberalization in Mexico: At a Critical Juncture?* edited by Riordan Roett, 35–50. Boulder, Colo.: Lynne Rienner.

Rudra, Nita. 2002. "Globalization and the Decline of the Welfare State in Less-Developed Countries." *IO* 56, 2:411–445.

Rueschemeyer, Dietrich, Evelyne Huber Stephens, and John D. Stephens. 1992. *Capitalist Development and Democracy*. Cambridge: Polity Press.

Sage, Adam. 2005. "Day of Strikes a Test for Villepin." *Australian*, October 5.

Samstad, James G. 2002. "The Unanticipated Persistence of Labor Power in Mexico: The Transition to a More Democratic Corporatism." Paper presented at the annual meeting of the American Political Science Association, Boston, August 28–September 1.

Sancton, Thomas. 2000. "The French Connected." *Time*, June 12, 43–51.

Sandholtz, Wayne, and John Zysman. 1989. "1992: Recasting the European Bargain." *WP* 42, 1:95–128.

Schain, Martin. 1984. "Relations between the CGT and the CFDT: Politics and Mass Mobilization." In *The French Workers' Movement: Economic Crisis and Political Change*, edited by Mark Kesselman with the assistance of Guy Groux, 257–76. London: George Allen & Unwin.

Scharpf, Fritz W. 2000. "Economic Changes, Vulnerabilities, and Institutional Capabilities." In *Welfare and Work in the Open Economy: From Vulnerability to Competitive-*

ness, vol. 1, edited by Fritz W. Scharpf and Vivien A. Schmidt, 21–124. Oxford: Oxford University Press.

Schmidt, Vivien A. 1996. *From State to Market? The Transformation of French Business and Government.* New York: Cambridge University Press.

———. 1997. "Democracy at Risk? France, Great Britain, and Germany between Globalization and Europeanization." Paper presented at the conference "State and Sovereignty in the World Economy," Laguna Beach, Calif., February.

———. 1999. "Convergent Pressures, Divergent Responses: France, Great Britain, and Germany between Globalization and Europeanization." In *States and Sovereignty in the Global Economy,* edited by David A. Smith, Dorothy J. Solinger, and Steven C. Topik, 172–92. New York: Routledge.

———. 2000a. "Still Three Models of Capitalism? The Dynamics of Economic Adjustment in Britain, Germany, and France." In *Die Politische Konstitution von Maerkten,* edited by Roland Czada and Susanne Luetz. Opladen, Germany: Westdeutscher.

———. 2000b. "Values and Discourse in the Politics of Adjustment." In *Welfare and Work in the Open Economy: From Vulnerability to Competitiveness,* vol. 1, edited by Fritz W. Scharpf and Vivien A. Schmidt, 229–309. Oxford: Oxford University Press.

———. 2006. *Democracy in Europe: The EU and National Polities.* Oxford: Oxford University Press.

Schmitter, Philippe C. 1997. "The Emerging Europolity and Its Impact upon National Systems of Production." In *Contemporary Capitalism: The Embeddedness of Institutions,* edited by J. Rogers Hollingsworth and Robert Boyer, 395–430. New York: Cambridge University Press.

Schwabish, Jonathan, Timothy Smeeding, and Lars Osberg. 2004. "Income Distribution and Social Expenditures: A Crossnational Perspective." Unpublished manuscript.

Schwartz, Benjamin I. 1966. *Chinese Communism and the Rise of Mao.* Cambridge, Mass.: Harvard University Press.

Sciolino, Elaine. 2003. "France Seeks Pension Reform, Confronting Unions." *NYT,* May 9.

———. 2005. "The Continental Dream: Will the French Shatter It?" *NYT,* April 15.

———. 2006. "French Students Step up Protests against New Job Law." *NYT,* March 15.

Sewell, William H., Jr. 1980. *Work and Revolution in France.* New York: Cambridge University Press.

Sheehan, Jackie. 1998. *Chinese Workers: A New History.* London: Routledge.

Shue, Vivienne. 2004. "Legitimacy Crisis in China." In *State and Society in 21st-Century China: Crisis, Contention, and Legitimation,* edited by Peter Hays Gries and Stanley Rosen, 24–49. New York: Routledge/Curzon.

Simon, Denis Fred. 1987. "The Evolving Role of Foreign Investment and Technology Transfer in China's Modernization Program." In *China Briefing 1987,* edited by John S. Major, 41–67. Boulder, Colo.: Westview Press.

Sinclair, Peter. 1987. *Unemployment: Economic Theory and Evidence.* Oxford: Basil Blackwell.

Sisci, Francesco. 2001. "Another China." Unpublished manuscript.

Sklair, Leslie. 1989. *Assembling for Development: The Maquila Industry in Mexico and the United States.* London: Unwin Hyman.

Smith, Craig S. 1999. "Workers in China Organize to Oppose Restructurings." *WSJ,* June 7.

———. 2004. "In Setback for Chirac, French Veer Left in Regional Vote." *NYT,* March 29.

———. 2005. "Chirac Appeals for Calm as Violent Protests Shake Paris's Suburbs." *NYT,* November 3.

Smith, Timothy B. 2004. *France in Crisis: Welfare, Inequality and Globalization since 1980.* New York: Cambridge University Press.

Smith, W. Rand. 1993. "International Economy and State Strategies—Recent Work in Comparative Political Economy." *CP* 25, 3:351–72.

——. 1995. "Industrial Crisis and the Left: Adjustment Strategies in Socialist France and Spain." *CP* 32, 1:1–24.

——. 1998. *The Left's Dirty Job: The Politics of Industrial Restructuring in France and Spain.* Pittsburgh: University of Pittsburgh Press; Toronto: University of Toronto Press.

——. 2000. "Unemployment and the Left Coalition in France and Spain." In *Unemployment in Southern Europe: Coping with the Consequences,* edited by Nancy Bermeo, 111–34. London: Frank Cass.

Solinger, Dorothy J. 1984. *Chinese Business under Socialism.* Berkeley: University of California Press.

——. 1987. "The 1980 Inflation and the Politics of Price Control in the PRC." In *Policy Implementation in Post-Mao China,* edited by David M. Lampton, 81–118. Berkeley: University of California Press.

——. 1991. *From Lathes to Looms: China's Industrial Policy in Comparative Perspective.* Stanford, Calif.: Stanford University Press.

——. 1999. *Contesting Citizenship in Urban China.* Berkeley: University of California Press.

——. 2000. "The Potential for Urban Unrest." In *Is China Unstable?* edited by David Shambaugh, 79–94. Armonk, N.Y.: M. E. Sharpe.

——. 2001a. "Globalization and the Paradox of Participation: The China Case." *Global Governance* 7, 2:173–96.

——. 2001b. "Why We Cannot Count the Unemployed." *CQ* 167:671–88.

——. 2002. "Labor in Limbo: Pushed by the Plan Towards the Mirage of the Market." In *Politics of China: Moving Frontiers,* edited by Françoise Mengin and Jean-Louis Rocca, 31–61. New York: Palgrave.

——. 2004. "Policy Consistency in the Midst of Crisis: Managing the Furloughed and the Farmers in Three Cities." In *Holding China Together: Diversity and National Integration in the Post-Deng Era,* edited by Barry Naughton and Dali Yang, 149–92. New York: Cambridge University Press.

——. 2005. "Path Dependency Reexamined: Chinese Welfare Policy in the Transition to Unemployment." *CP* 38, 1:83–101.

——. Forthcoming. "*Dibaohu* in Distress: The Meager Minimum Livelihood Guarantee System in Wuhan." In *China's Social Welfare Mix,* edited by Jane Duckett and Beatriz Carrillo.

Song Xiaowu. 2001. *Zhongguo shehui baozhang zhidu gaige* [The reform of China's social security system]. Beijing: Qinghua daxue chubanshe [Qinghua University Publishing Co.].

Stallings, Barbara. 1992. "International Influence on Economic Policy: Debt, Stabilization, and Structural Reform." In *The Politics of Economic Adjustment: International Constraints, Distributive Conflicts, and the State,* edited by Stephan Haggard and Robert R. Kaufman, 41–88. Princeton, N.J.: Princeton University Press.

Stallings, Barbara, and Wilson Peres. 2000. *Growth, Employment, and Equity: The Impact of the Economic Reforms in Latin America and the Caribbean.* Washington, D.C.: Brookings Institution Press.

State Council. 2001. "Circular from the State Council General Office on Further Enhancing Work on the Minimum Livelihood Guarantee for Urban Residents." *XH,* November 17.

———. 2002. "White Paper on Employment, Social Security." *Asian Wall Street Journal*, April 29.

———. 1993. Document 110. Herald Translation Service, Chinalaw Web, from http://www. qis.net/chinalaw/prclaw66.htm.

———. Information Office. 2004. "China's Employment Situation and Policies." April 26. From http://english.peopledaily.com.cn/200404/26/eng20040426_141553.s.

Steinfeld, Edward S. 1998. *Forging Reform in China: The Fate of State-Owned Industry.* Cambridge: Cambridge University Press.

Stephens, John D., Evelyne Huber, and Leonard Ray. 1998. "The Welfare State in Hard Times." In *Continuity and Change in Contemporary Capitalism,* edited by Herbert Kitschelt, Peter Lange, Gary Marks, and John D. Stephens, 164–93. New York: Cambridge University Press.

Stevens, Anne. 2003. *Government and Politics of France.* 3d ed. New York: Palgrave.

Streeck, Wolfgang. 1995. "From Market Making to State Building? Reflections on the Political Economy of European Social Policy." In *European Social Policy: Between Fragmentation and Integration,* edited by Stephan Leibfried and Paul Pierson, 389–431. Washington, D.C.: Brookings Institution Press.

Sun, Yan. 2004. *Corruption and Market in Contemporary China.* Ithaca: Cornell University Press.

Symes, Valerie. 1995. *Unemployment in Europe: Problems and Policies.* London: Routledge.

Tagliabue, John. 2003a. "Protest Strike in France Interrupts Travel." *NYT,* April 4.

———. 2003b. "Militant Unions May Scuttle a French Pension Proposal." *NYT,* May 17.

Tang Jun. 2002. "The New Situation of Poverty and Antipoverty." In *2002 nian: Zhongguo shehui xingshi yu yuce (shehui lanpishu)* [Year 2002: Analysis and forecast of China's social situation (Blue book on Chinese society)], edited by Ru Xin, Lu Xueyi, Li Peilin et al. January 1. [FBIS Translated Text].

———. 2003. "Zhongguo chengshi jumin zuidi shenghuo baozhang zhidu de 'tiaoyueshi' fazhan" [The 'leap forward style' of development of Chinese urban residents' minimum livelihood guarantee]. In *Shehui lanpishu: 2003 nian; Zhongguo shehui xingshi fenxi yu yuce* [Social blue book: 2003 analysis and predictions of China's social situation], edited by Ru Xin, Lu Xueyi, and Li Peilin, 243–51. Beijing: Shehui kexue wenxian chubanshe [Social Science Documents Co.].

Tanner, Murray Scot. 2002. "Rethinking Law Enforcement and Society: Changing Police Analyses of Social Unrest." Draft paper for the Conference on Law and Society in Contemporary China. Berkeley, Calif., September.

———. 2004. "China Rethinks Unrest." *Washington Quarterly* 27, 3:137–56.

Tardanico, Richard. 1997. "From Crisis to Restructuring: Latin American Transformations and Urban Employment in World Perspective." In *Global Restructuring, Employment, and Social Inequality in Urban Latin America,* edited by Richard Tardanico and Rafael Menjivar Larin, 1–46. Coral Gables, Fla.: North-South Center Press.

Tardanico, Richard, and Rafael Menjivar Larin. 1997. "Restructuring, Employment, and Social Inequality: Comparative Urban Latin American Patterns." In *Global Restructuring, Employment, and Social Inequality in Urban Latin America,* edited by Tardanico and Larin, 233–80. Coral Gables, Fla.: North-South Center Press.

Tarrow, Sidney. 2004. "Center-Periphery Alignments and Political Contention in Late-Modern Europe." In *Restructuring Territoriality,* edited by Christopher K. Ansell and Giuseppe Di Palma, 45–65. New York: Cambridge University Press.

Teichman, Judith A. 1995. *Privatization and Political Change in Mexico.* Pittsburgh: University of Pittsburgh Press.

——. 2001. *The Politics of Freeing Markets in Latin America: Chile, Argentina and Mexico.* Chapel Hill: University of North Carolina Press.

Thompson, Ginger. 2001a. "Farm Unrest Roils Mexico, Challenging New Chief." *NYT,* July 22.

——. 2001b. "Mexican Labor Protest Gets Results." *NYT,* October 8.

Tian Bingnan and Yuan Jianmin. 1997. "Shanghai xiagang renyuan de diaocha yanjiu" [Investigation research on Shanghai laid-off personnel]. *Shehuixue* [Sociology] 2:7–12.

Tobin, James. 1987. "Macroeconomic Diagnosis and Prescription." In *Unemployment: International Perspectives,* edited by Morley Gunderson, Noah M. Meltz, and Sylvia Ostry, 12–40. Toronto: University of Toronto Press.

Toledo, Enrique de la Garza. 2002. "Free Trade and Labor Relations in Mexico." Paper presented at the International Labor Standards Conference, Stanford Law School, Stanford, California, May 19–21.

Tuiran, Rudolfo. n.d. "The Sociodemographic Effects of the Crisis in Mexico." http://lanic.utexas.edu/project/etext/mexico/selby/chap4.html, accessed September 15, 2005.

Turner, Lowell. 1991. *Democracy at Work: Changing World Markets and the Future of Labor Unions.* Ithaca: Cornell University Press.

United Nations Conference on Trade and Development. 2002. *Trade and Development Report, 2002.* New York: United Nations.

United Nations Development Program. 1999. *China Human Development Report—1999: Transition and the State.* New York: United Nations.

United States Trade Representative. 2002. *2002 Report to Congress on China's WTO Compliance.* Washington, D.C.

Vail, Mark I. 2003. "Institutional Legacies, Political Discontinuities, and the Dynamics of French and German Social-Protection Reform." Paper presented at the annual meeting of the American Political Science Association, Philadelphia, August 28–31.

Van de Ven, Hans J. 1991. *From Friend to Comrade: The Founding of the Chinese Communist Party, 1920–1927.* Berkeley: University of California Press.

Van Ness, Peter. 1984. "Three Lines in Chinese Foreign Relations, 1950–1983: The Development Imperative." In *Three Visions of Chinese Socialism,* edited by Dorothy J. Solinger, 113–42. Boulder, Colo.: Westview Press.

Wade, Robert C. 1990. *Governing the Economy.* Princeton, N.J.: Princeton University Press.

Walder, Andrew G. 1984. "The Remaking of the Chinese Working Class, 1949–1981." *MC* 10, 1:3–48.

——. 1986. *Communist Neo-traditionalism: Work and Authority in Chinese Industry.* Berkeley: University of California Press.

——. 1987. "Wage Reform and the Web of Factory Interests." *CQ* 109:22–41.

——. 1991. "Workers, Managers and the State: The Reform Era and the Political Crisis of 1989." *CQ* 127:467–92.

——. 1992. "Property Rights and Stratification in Socialist Redistributive Economies." *American Sociological Review* 57:524–39.

——. 2004. "The Party Elite and China's Trajectory of Change." *China: An International Journal* 2, 2:189–209.

Walder, Andrew G., and Gong Xiaoxia. 1993. "Workers in the Tiananmen Protests." *AJCA* 29:1–29.

Walters, William. 2000. *Unemployment and Government: Genealogies of the Social.* New York: Cambridge University Press.

Wang Depei. 2001. "San min yu erci gaige" [Three types of people and the second reform]. *Gaige neican* [Reform Internal Reference] 7:24–26.

Wang Dongjin. 2001. "Shehui baozhang zhidu gaige de zhongdian" [Critical points on the reform of the social security system]. *Gaige neican* [Reform internal reference] 10:2–5.

Wang Shaoguang. 2000. "The Social and Political Implications of China's WTO Membership." *Journal of Contemporary China* 9, 25:373–405.

——. 2004. "Shunying minxin de bianhua: Cong caizheng zijin liuxiang zongguo zhengfu jinqi de zhengce tiaozheng" [A change that complies with popular sentiments: A recent policy readjustment in the flow of financial funds toward the Chinese government]. Paper presented to the Center for Strategic and International Studies, Washington, D.C. Unpublished manuscript, January 16.

——. 2007. "The Great Transformation: The Emergence of Social Policies in China." Paper presented at the University of Southern California USC US-China Institute conference, "The Future of U.S.-China Relations," April 20.

Ward, Peter M. 1993. "Social Welfare Policy and Political Opening in Mexico." *Journal of Latin American Studies* 25, 3:623–24.

Weaver, Lisa Rose. 2002. "Taking on the State: China's Rustbelt Revolt." CNN, April 1.

Wedeman, Andrew. 2003. *From Mao to Market: Rent Seeking, Local Protectionism, and Marketization in China.* New York: Cambridge University Press.

Weintraub, Sidney. 1993. "The Economy on the Eve of Free Trade." *CH* 2:56–60.

West, Loraine A. 1997. "The Changing Effects of Economic Reform on Rural and Urban Employment." Draft of paper presented at the conference "Unintended Social Consequences of Chinese Economic Reform," Harvard School of Public Health and Fairbank Center for East Asian Studies, Harvard University, May 23–24.

White, Gordon. 1987. "The Changing Role of the Chinese State in Labour Allocation: Towards the Market?" *Journal of Communist Studies* 3, 2:129–50.

——. 1993. *Riding the Tiger: The Politics of Economic Reform in Post-Mao China.* Stanford, Calif.: Stanford University Press.

White, Gordon, Jude Howell, and Shang Xiaoyuan. 1996. In *Search of Civil Society: Market Reform and Social Change in Contemporary China.* Oxford: Clarendon Press.

Whiting, Susan. 2001. *Power and Wealth in Rural China: The Political Economy of Institutional Change.* New York: Cambridge University Press.

——. 2007. "Central-Local Fiscal Relations in China." China Policy Series No. 22. New York: National Committee on United States-China Relations.

Whitney, Craig R. 1997a. "Why Blair's Victory May Not Travel Well in Europe." News of the Week in Review. NYT, May 4, 3.

——. 1997b. "French Jobless Seize Unemployment Offices to Press for $500 Bonus." *NYT,* December 30.

——. 1998. "French Unemployed Turn Their Ire on Socialists." *NYT,* January 6.

Wilson, Frank. 1985. "Trade Unions and Economic Policy." In *Economic Policy and Policy-Making under the Mitterrand Presidency, 1981–1984,* edited by Howard Machin and Vincent Wright, 255–78. London: Frances Pinter.

Wonacott, Peter, and Phelim Kyne. 2003. "In Shift, U.S. Investors Intensify Criticism of China Trade Policies." *WSJ,* October 6.

Wong, Christine P. W. 1991. "Central-Local Relations in an Era of Fiscal Decline: The Paradox of Fiscal Decentralization in Post-Mao China." *CQ* 128:691–715.

——. 2005. "Can China Change Development Paradigm for the 21st Century? Fiscal Policy Options for Hu Jintao and Wen Jiabao after Two Decades of Muddling Through." Berlin, January. Unpublished manuscript.

Wong, Christine P. W., Christopher Heady, and Wing T. Woo. 1995. *Fiscal Management and Economic Reform in the People's Republic of China.* Hong Kong: Oxford University Press.

Wong, Linda. 1998. *Marginalization and Social Welfare in China.* London: Routledge.

Woodward, Susan L. 1995. *Socialist Unemployment: The Political Economy of Yugoslavia, 1945–1990.* Princeton, N.J.: Princeton University Press.

WTO. Trade Policy Review Body. 2002. WTO Trade Review, April 16.

Wu Yan. 1999. "Laid-Off Workers to Get Extra Pay." *China Daily,* August 31.

Xue Zhaoyun. 2000. "Dui xiagang zhigong zaijiuye xianzhuang di diaocha, sikao yu jianyi" [Research, reflections, and suggestions about the reemployment situation of laid-off staff and workers]. *Gonghui gongzuo tongxun* [Bulletin of Trade Union Work] 7:8–10.

Yang, Dennis Tao, and Cai Fang. 2003. "The Political Economy of China's Rural-Urban Divide." In *How Far across the River? Chinese Policy Reform at the Millennium,* edited by Nicholas C. Hope, Dennis Tao Yang, and Mu Yang Li. Stanford, Calif.: Stanford University Press.

Yang Shengwen. 2001. "Kexi de yibu: Cong beijing deng bashengshi xiagang zhigong lingqu shiye baoxianjin renshu chaoguo jin zhongxin renshu kan chu zhongxin gongcuo" [A heartening step: Look at the work of exiting the center from Beijing and eight provinces and cities' numbers of laid-off staff and workers getting unemployment insurance money has surpassed the numbers entering the center]. *LBT* 9:27–31.

Yang Shuchang. 1999. "Zaijiuye yao zou xiang shichanghua" [In reemployment we must go toward marketization]. *ZGJY* 3:19.

Yang Yiyong. 2001. "Wanshan shehui baozhang tixi shi shehui jinbu di xuyao" [Perfecting the social security system is the demand of social progress]. *NBCY* 550 (February 9): 15–19.

Yang Yiyong, et al. 1997. *Shiye chongji bo* [The shock wave of unemployment]. Beijing: Jinri zhongguo chubanshe [China Today Publishing].

Yeh, Andrew. 2007. "China Demands US Rethink on Duties." *Financial Times,* April 1.

Yu Guangyuan. 2004. *Deng Xiaoping Shakes the World.* Edited by Ezra F. Vogel and Steven I. Levine. Norwalk, Conn.: EastBridge.

Yu Wei. 1999. "Financing Unemployment and Pension Insurance." In *Dilemmas of Reform in Jiang Zemin's China,* edited by Andrew J. Nathan, Zhaohui Hong, and Steven R. Smith, 127–38. Boulder, Colo.: Lynne Rienner.

ZGJY. 1998. "Fanshiye: Faguo di xilu he cuoshi" [Combating unemployment: France's thinking and measures]. *ZGJY* 1.

——. 2000. "Faguo de peixun yu jiuye" [France's training and employment]. *ZGJY* 1:41–44.

ZGLD. 1999. "Shiye baoxian tiaoli" [Unemployment insurance regulations]. Zhonghua renmin gongheguo guowuyuan ling di 258 hao [PRC State Council Order No. 258]. *ZGLD* 3:44–45.

Zhang Zuoji. 2001. "Guanyu shehui baozhang tixi jianshe di youguan wenti" [Some relevant issues in the construction of the social insurance system]. *LBT* 7:6–11.

Zhao Zhongheng and Wei Zhikui. 2000. "Yanglao baoxian zhidu chuangxin yunxingzhong di san da nanti" [Three big difficulties in blazing a trail in running a pension insurance system]. *ZGLD* 1:12–15.

Zhonggong zhongyang zuzhibu ketizu [Chinese central organization department research group]. 2001. "2000–2001 Zhongguo diaocha baogao—xin xingshixia renmin neibu maodun yanjiu" [2000–2001 Chinese investigation report—research on internal contradictions within the people under the new situation]. Beijing: Zhongyang bianyi chubanshe [Central Compilation and Translation Press].

Zweig, David. 2002. *Internationalizing China: Domestic Interests and Global Linkages.* Ithaca: Cornell University Press.

Index